Contemporary Biographies in Healthcare

Contemporary Biographies in Healthcare

SALEM PRESS

A Division of EBSCO Information Services, Inc.

Ipswich, Massachusetts

GREY HOUSE PUBLISHING

∞ The paper used in these volumes conforms to the American National Standard for Permanence of Paper for Printed Library Materials, Z39.48-1992 (R1997).

Library of Congress Cataloging-in-Publication Data

Contemporary biographies in healthcare. -- [1st ed.].

  p. : ill. ; cm. -- (Contemporary biographies in--)
Includes bibliographical references and index.
Part of a series that is supplemental to the Salem Press series: Careers in--
Contents extracted from the monthly magazine: Current biography.
ISBN: 978-1-61925-236-3

  1. Medicine--Biography. 2. Medical personnel--Biography. 3. Allied health personnel--Biography. I. Title: Careers in-- II. Title: Current biography.

R134 .C66 2014
610.92/2

Contents

Appendixes
Historical Biographies

Publisher's Note

Contemporary Biographies in Healthcare is a collection of twenty-eight biographical sketches of "living leaders" in the fields of healthcare and allied health. All of these articles come from the pages of *Current Biography*, the monthly magazine renowned for its unfailing accuracy, insightful selection, and the wide scope of influence of its subjects. These up-to-date profiles draw from a variety of sources and are an invaluable resource for researchers, teachers, students, and librarians. Students will gain a better understanding of the educational development and career pathways of healthcare professionals to better prepare themselves for a career in health and related industries.

The geographical scope of *Contemporary Biographies in Healthcare* is broad; selections span the Eastern and Western Hemispheres, covering numerous major geographical and cultural regions. All of the figures profiled are still working at one or more of their specialties, including cardiology, fitness training, radiology, pharmaceutical, health and human services, and epidemioloy.

Articles in *Contemporary Biographies in Healthcare* range in length from 1,000 to 4,000 words and follow a standard format. All articles begin with ready-reference listings that include birth details and concise identifications. The article then generally divide into several parts, including Early Life and Education, and Life's Work, a core section that provides straightforward accounts of the periods in which the profiled subjects made their most significant contributions to the healthcare field. Often, a final section, Significance, provides an overview of the person's place in history and their contemporary importance. Essays are supplemented by bibliographies, which provide starting points for further research.

As with other Salem Press biographical reference works, these articles combine breadth of coverage with a format that offers users quick access to the particular information needed. Articles are arranged alphabetically by last name. A general bibliography offers a comprehensive list of works for students seeking out more information on a particular individual or subject, while a separate bibliography of selected works highlights the significant published works of the professionals profiled.

An appendix consisting of ten historical biographies culled from the Salem Press *Great Lives* series, introduces readers to professionals in healthcare of historical significance integral to those whose work and research revolutionized the field.

The editors of Salem Press wish to extend their appreciation to all those involved in the development and production of this work; without their expert contribution, projects of this nature would not be possible. A list of contributors appears at the beginning of this volume.

Contributor's List

Berman, Janet Ober
Burke, Alison
Cavalli, Dimitri
Curry, Jennifer
DeStephano, Mark T.
Donnelly, Sarah J.
Eniclerico, Ronald
Firrincili, Dan
Hagan, Molly
Hartig, Seth
Kim, David J.
Kiper, Dmitry
Liebman, Roy
Luna, Christopher
Moldawer, David
Muteba, Bertha
Paradowski, Robert
Roush, Margaret E.
Rolls, Albert
Segura, Liliana
Shin, Ji-Hye
Tarullo, Hope
Thomas, Cullen F.
Woodbury, Mary

Contemporary Biographies in Healthcare

Agatston, Arthur

Cardiologist, writer, nutritionist, researcher

Born: 1947, New York, New York, United States

"If a patient of mine has a heart attack, I ask myself: 'What have I done wrong?,'" the cardiologist, nutrition researcher, and writer Arthur Agatston said to John Tanasychuk of the Fort Lauderdale, Florida, *Sun-Sentinel* (April 11, 2004). For the past decade, the Miami Beach, Florida-based Agatston has been widely known as the "South Beach Diet doctor," referring to the eating regimen he created with the help of the dietitian and nutritionist Marie Almon, a colleague of his at Miami's Mount Sinai Medical Center. The label also links him with his books, all of which contain the words *South Beach Diet* in their titles. He wrote them, as he has often said, not to enable people to look good in bathing suits or drop a clothing size or two in a few weeks but to help them avoid getting heart disease or having strokes.

The first of Agatston's books, *The South Beach Diet: The Delicious, Doctor-Designed, Foolproof Plan for Fast and Healthy Weight Loss* (2003), has sold more than nine million copies and has been translated into some three dozen languages. Among his other books are cookbooks (one of which landed on Amazon.com's top-five sellers before its publication date), a manual for maintaining a healthy heart, and a guide to "good" fats and "good" carbohydrates (carbs, as they are called colloquially), which rank low on the so-called glycemic index. (The index is a scale devised by a Canadian scientist that measures blood-sugar levels after a given food is eaten; Agatston used it in developing the South Beach diet.) "It has been a great revelation to me that weight loss is not about low carbs or low fat, but the right carbs and the right fats," Agatston has said, as quoted by *Market Wire* (April 25, 2005). "I am seeing a growing consensus among nutrition experts about the importance of the right carbs like whole grains, fruits and vegetables in the diet, as well as including unsaturated fats like olive and canola oils—all consistent with the South Beach Diet."

In 2004 Agatston used part of his earnings from *The South Beach Diet* to set up the Agatston Research Foundation, in Miami, "for the purpose of conducting and funding original research on diet, cardiac, and disease prevention" (www.agatstonresearchfoundation.org). In 2005 he signed a contract with Kraft Foods, which launched a line of South Beach Diet prepared meals and other items. He also maintains the South Beach Diet website, which, as of 2013, had more than half a million subscribers. For a fee of $4 per week ($16 per month), subscribers have access to recipes, meal-planning tools, a weight-loss tracker, a daily newsletter, and "private discussions" with online nutritionists.

Agatston's approach to healthful eating is not without critics. "What it comes down to," Marion Nestle, a professor of nutrition, food studies, and public health at New York University, said to Abby Goodnough of the *New York Times* (October 7, 2003), "is that this is a standard 1,200- to 1,400-calorie-a-day diet, so of course people are going to lose weight. I do think there's something to the glycemic index, but I just don't think it's the be-all and end-all, and that it's the root of obesity." In a conversation with Alex Witchel for the *New York Times* (April 14, 2004), Nestle said that the South Beach diet does not address the fundamental issue of overeating. "I don't understand why it's gotten the attention it has," she said. "For the first two weeks it's a standard low-carbohydrate diet. It's very hard to argue with restricting bread, white rice, pasta, soft drinks, all great ideas when trying to lose weight. But the hype is [Agatston] never talks about quantity. It's calories that make a difference in losing weight or not." Robert Eckel, the president of the American Heart Association, told reporters for *People* (April 16, 2004) that Agatston is "respected in cardiology," but he voiced concern that Agatston was "playing into the carbohydrate message." "Obesity is calories—there is nothing magic about carbs versus fat," Eckel added. In response to such criticism, Agatston told Witchel, "When choosing the right fats and the right carbohydrates, in general, the quantity takes care of itself." Thus, he explained, weighing one's foods, as people following certain diets must do, is unnecessary. "Also," he said, "I'm not claiming any unique vision; I've learned a lot from other people. The diet is a consensus of current opinion." He repeated that point in his conversation with Tanasychuk, saying, "The country was ready for [the South Beach diet]. Because a lot of what we have in the book has been percolating through doctors and the public. … Everything in there was kind of obvious. If you've really been on top of nutrition, there's nothing in there that's really controversial. There's no substance to the criticism as far as I'm concerned."

Education and Early Career

Arthur Stephen Agatston was born on January 22, 1947, in New York City, to Howard James Agatston and Adell (Paymer) Agatston. He has two sisters and one brother. His paternal grandfather, Sigmund Agatston, had the surname "Agatstein" when he immigrated to the United States from Poland; fearing anti-Semitic prejudice, he changed his name when he applied to medical school. Sigmund Agatston graduated from Columbia Presbyterian Medical School in 1903 and became an ophthalmologist; his innovative technique for early detection of eye disease became a standard in the field. Arthur Agatston's father, Howard James Agatston, also was an ophthalmologist; he practiced in Roslyn, New York, on Long Island, where Agatston grew up. "I knew since I was in elementary school that I wanted to be a doctor," Agatston said to Marie Guma-Diaz for the *Miami* (Florida) *Herald* (December 10, 2005). "I watched my dad's work in the community, and learned to like the doctor-patient relationship. The love for the academic studies came later."

Agatston earned a B.A. degree from the University of Wisconsin at Madison in 1969 and an M.D. degree in 1973 from the New York University (NYU) School of Medicine, in New York City. He completed his internship and residency in internal medicine at the Montefiore Medical Center, which is affiliated with the Albert Einstein College of Medicine, in the New York City borough of the Bronx. From 1977 to 1979 he was a cardiology fellow at NYU Medical Center. The next year he joined the staff of the Mount Sinai Medical Center, in Miami, which is associated with the University of Miami's Miller School of Medicine.

Later Career

In 1988, with his colleague Warren Janowitz, a radiologist, Agatston began working on a way to determine the amount of calcium present in people's coronary arteries. Excessive levels of calcium often lead to arteriosclerosis, a chronic disease that impairs blood circulation and places people at risk for heart attacks or strokes. Agatston and Janowitz were later members of a team that developed electron beam tomography (EBT), a fast, noninvasive technique for scanning every part of the body; with EBT, doctors can detect and quantify even small calcium deposits in the arteries that carry oxygenated blood to the heart. The so-called Agatston score is a measure of the amount of calcium in the coronary arteries. In a conversation with Soriya Daniels for the *Cleveland* (Ohio) *Jewish News* (February 13, 2004), Agatston said that the widespread adoption of EBT was his "most rewarding experience."

Beginning in about the late 1980s, Agatston noticed that among his patients who suffered from hypertension and other heart-related ailments, a majority were gaining weight and were developing abnormal blood chemistries. He, too, had become a little fatter around his midsection, and in the United States as a whole, obesity was becoming increasingly common. Agatston thought that the problem might be related to the growing popularity of low-fat, high-carbohydrate diets, such as the one that the American Heart Association had been recommending. "If it was low-fat, [we thought] you could eat with impunity, and I did, as did the country in general," Agatston told an interviewer for *People* (April 26, 2004). Agatston feared that U.S. food companies, reacting to the advice of the American Heart Association and others, were selling too many items containing processed carbohydrates. Foods of that kind contain large amounts of flour, sugar, and high-fructose corn syrup. "Nobody in the history of man ever ate complex carbohydrates like we have," Agatston said to Abby Goodnough for the *New York Times* (October 7, 2003).

> **"After dietary intervention, children's weight, blood pressure, and academic test scores improved compared to children without the HOPS [Healthier Options for Public Schoolchildren] process."**

Agatston began investigating how the body processes carbohydrates. "My concern was not with my patients' appearances," he told Soriya Daniels. "I wanted to find a diet that would help prevent or reverse the myriad of heart and vascular problems that stem from obesity." During his research he learned about the glycemic index (GI), developed in the late 1970s by David J. A. Jenkins, a specialist in the nutritional sciences at the University of Toronto, Canada. The glycemic index ranks foods, on a scale of zero to 100, according to how much the quantity of glucose in an individual's blood increases within two to three hours of eating those foods. Foods with a high GI score include baked potatoes, white bread, and most pastas; those with low scores include foods rich in fiber, such as whole- and multigrain bread, lean meat, and most vegetables. Foods with high scores (over 55) are digested more quickly than those with low scores, and people often feel hungry much sooner after eating the former than after consuming the latter. Using that information Agatston drew up what he called the "modified carbohydrate diet"—the precursor to the South Beach Diet. He and a select group of his private patients who tested the diet began to lose weight.

In about 1996 Agatston, in collaboration with Marie Almon, the chief clinical dietitian at Mount Sinai, worked out a more detailed diet, one that did not need to be supplemented with exercise. They printed instructions for following the diet and distributed them to a greater number of people than had tested the diet earlier. Along with their weight, cholesterol levels decreased in most of the people in the new sample group. Agatston presented his findings at national meetings of the American College of Cardiology and the American Heart Association. Meanwhile word of the diet had spread in the Miami area and reached the media, which dubbed it the "South Beach diet," referring to an upscale section of Miami Beach. Several Miami eateries changed their menus to appeal to diners on the diet. What had "started as research … got the glitz added to it by the local media," Agatston commented to Howard Cohen for the *Miami Herald* (May 1, 2003).

In April 2003 the health-and-fitness publishing house Rodale, based in Emmaus, Pennsylvania, published Agatston's first book, *The South Beach Diet: The Delicious, Doctor-Designed, Foolproof Plan for Fast and*

Healthy Weight Loss. The book remained on the *New York Times* best-seller list for 38 consecutive weeks. Among Agatston's other books are *The South Beach Diet Cookbook: More than 200 Delicious Recipes that Fit the Nation's Top Diet* (2004), which had a first-run printing of 1.5 million copies—a record for a cook-book; *The South Beach Diet Good Fats/Good Carbs Guide: The Complete and Easy Reference for All Your Favorite Foods* (2004), which was *Publishers Weekly*'s number-one best-seller for 18 weeks; *The South Beach Diet Dining Guide* (2005); and *The South Beach Heart Program: The 4-Step Plan that Can Save Your Life* (2006). Newer titles include *The South Beach Diet: Super Charged* (2009) and *The South Beach Diet Wake-Up Call: Why America is Getting Fatter and Sicker* (2012).

The South Beach diet is divided into three stages. In phase one, which lasts two weeks, no foods rich in carbohydrates—pasta, potatoes, fruit, bread, cereal, and rice—are permitted; alcoholic beverages are also off-limits. Meals consist of "normal-size portions of lean meat, fish, eggs, reduced-fat cheese, nonfat yogurt, nuts, and plenty of vegetables." According to Agatston, dieters can lose as many as 13 pounds in those first two weeks. (The website factsaboutfitness.com reported that in one study of the diet, the results of which were published in the *Archives of Internal Medicine,* the "average weight loss among the subjects was 13.6 pounds in 12 weeks, … not the first two weeks.") In phase two, dieters may eat certain fruits and carbohydrate-laden foods having low GI scores (whole-grain items, for example); they are advised to remain in that stage until they reach their desired weights. Alex Witchel characterized the final stage of the diet, meant to be adopted permanently, as "a more lenient version" of the second phase.

The South Beach Diet has often been compared with another popular regimen, introduced in 1972 in the book *Dr. Atkins' Diet Revolution,* by Robert Atkins, who maintained that the harmful effects of saturated fats had been highly exaggerated and that high-carbohydrate diets were far more harmful than diets consisting mostly of proteins and fats. People who maintain the Atkins diet avoid refined sugar, milk, white rice, white potatoes, or white flour (found in white bread; most cakes, cookies, and pastries; and most pasta). They may eat virtually unlimited amounts of meat, poultry, fish, eggs, cheese, and cream, and, after the first two weeks on the diet, limited amounts of fruits, vegetables, and whole-grain foods. One major difference between the Atkins Diet and the South Beach Diet, according to experts, is that Atkins' practitioners enter a metabolic state known as ketosis, in which the body, lacking sufficient carbohydrates, converts stores of fat into energy. Agatston has said that when he designed his diet, he consciously tried to avoid triggering ketosis in his patients, because, in hypertensives, it can cause serious adverse effects.

The popularity of the South Beach Diet led to Agatston's alliance with Kraft Foods, one of the world's largest food and beverage companies. In 2004 Kraft began placing the South Beach Diet trademark on some of its products. The next year the company introduced a line of South Beach Diet products, among them frozen entrees and snacks. "Things can be nutritious and come from a package," Agatston's collaborator Marie Almon said to Lisa Belkin of the *New York Times Magazine* (August 20, 2006). "It depends what's in the package, not the fact that there is a package." Some of Kraft's South Beach items came under attack because of their high levels of sodium; daily ingestion of sodium in greater than moderate amounts has been linked with hypertension. Speaking with Howard Cohen and Kathy Martin of the *Miami Herald* (May 5, 2005), Agatston acknowledged that he would not recommend some of the new Kraft products to patients suffering from heart disease or high blood pressure, but he defended the South Beach Diet's overriding principle. "America is overfed," he said. "If you lose weight and reverse the metabolic syndrome, blood pressure comes down."

In his recent book *The South Beach Diet Wake-Up Call: Why America Is Still Getting Fatter and Sicker* (2012), Agatston warns that "we're raising a generation that could be the first in modern history with shorter life spans than their parents … I predict that our current population of adults between ages 30 and 45 could have the dubious distinction of being remembered as the 'sickest generation,' or 'Generation S'" (www.prevention.com/print/26211, October, 2013). Agatston told Brenda Medina of the *Miami Herald* (February 23, 2013) that this generation "grew up on junk food and led more sedentary lives. … That lifestyle can lead to heart diseases." The strategies in his book, he said, focus on "eating healthy, getting rid of unhealthy foods, cooking more at home, shopping for healthy foods, and incorporation a meatless meal or two into your weekly menu planning." Agatston also places emphasis on the importance of physical activity: "We need to start taking the stairs, mowing our lawns, walking a little more. We need to get moving."

Thanks to his books, Agatston told Lisa Belkin, he gained "a bully pulpit and an opportunity to change the way Americans eat. One of the obvious places to start is with children. And that means schools." In July 2004 Agatston, as the head of the Agatston Research Foundation, signed a contract with the Osceola County (Florida) School District that allowed him to take control of the meals supplied by cafeterias in four elementary schools, all in Kissimmee, a city whose population is about 50,000. Starting in the fall of 2004, he began testing a program called HOPS—Healthier Options for Public Schoolchildren—in which more nutritious and fewer high-fat foods were on the schools' menus, and some items (among them white bread, turkey or pork with gravy, sweetened breakfast cereals, and Tater Tots are banned. Currently, the HOPS program reaches 13,500 students in the Miami-Dade County School District (the fourth-largest school district in the United States) and 50,000 students nationwide. According to the Baptist Health Medical Group Web page profiling Agatston, the HOPS program "showed that after dietary intervention, children's weight, blood pressure, and academic test scores improved compared to children without the HOPS process.

Since May 2012 Agatston has been the medical director of Wellness and Prevention for Baptist Health South Florida. In addition to his duties at the University of Miami School of Medicine, where he serves as an associate professor of medicine, Agatston is a clinical professor of medicine at Florida International University Herbert Wertheim College of Medicine. He has maintained a private practice as a partner with South Florida Cardiology Associates, in Miami, now a Baptist Health Medical Group facility. . He lectures on nutrition nationally and internationally, serves as a consultant for the Clinical Trials Committee of the National Institutes of Health, and co-directs the Symposium on Prevention of Cardiovascular Disease, which meets annually. Agatston has served on committees of the American Society of Echocardiography and the American College of Cardiology. He serves on the board of directors for the Society of Atherosclerosis Imaging and the American Dietetic Association Foundation. Agatston has written more than 100 articles and abstracts for journals, including the *Journal of the American College of Cardiology*, the *Annals of Internal Medicine*, and the *American Journal of Cardiology.*

Agatston and his wife, Sari Agatston, a lawyer, married in 1983. Sari Agatston has assisted her husband with all his books, which is why he often uses the first-person plural when talking about them, and she handles the financial and other aspects of his businesses. The Agatstons are the parents of sons Adam and Evan and live in Sunset Island, a section of Miami Beach. Interviewers have described Agatston as approachable, self-effacing, and friendly and as trim but not buff. In his leisure time Agatston enjoys reading books about history and politics and playing golf.

Further Reading:

Agatston Research Foundation Web site

Baptist Health Medical Group Web site

Boston Globe pB7 Sep. 22, 2003

Cleveland Jewish News p40 Feb. 13, 2004

Journal of Health Care for the Poor and Underserved Vol. 21, no. 2 (May 2010, Supplement): p93+

Miami Herald Living pE1 May 1, 2003, pA1+ May 5, 2005, p13 Dec. 10, 2005, Feb. 23, 2013

New York Times pF1+ Oct. 7, 2003, pF1+ Apr. 14, 2004

New York Times Magazine p30+ Aug. 20, 2006

People p65 Apr. 26, 2004

South Beach Diet Web site; (Fort Lauderdale, Florida)

Sun-Sentinel pD1+ Apr. 11, 2004

WebMD Web site

Selected Books:

The South Beach Diet: The Delicious, Doctor-Designed, Foolproof Plan for Fast and Healthy Weight Loss, 2003

The South Beach Diet Cookbook: More Than 200 Delicious Recipes That Fit the Nation's Top Diet, 2004

The South Beach Diet Good Fats/Good Carbs Guide: The Complete and Easy Reference for All Your Favorite Foods, 2004

The South Beach Diet Dining Guide, 2005

The South Beach Diet Quick and Easy Cookbook: 200 Delicious Recipes Ready in 30 Minutes or Less, 2005

The South Beach Diet Parties & Holidays Cookbook: Healthy Recipes for Entertaining Family and Friends, 2006

The South Beach Diet Heart Program: The 4-Step Plan That Can Save Your Life, 2007

The South Beach Diet Taste of Summer Cookbook, 2007

The South Beach Diet: Super Charged (2009), *The South Beach Diet: Super Quick Cookbook* (2010)

The South Beach Diet Wake-Up Call: Why America is Getting Fatter and Sicker (2012)

The South Beach Diet Gluten Solution Cookbook: 175 Delicious, Slimming, Gluten-Free Recipes (November, 2013)

Antinori, Severino

Italian gynecologist and fertility researcher

Born: 1945, Abruzzo, Italy

Dr. Severino Antinori, who has declared his intention to clone a human being, regularly faces condemnation from colleagues, the media, and the Catholic Church. (Though the church vehemently condemns his work in advanced fertility techniques and human cloning, Antinori remains a Roman Catholic.) Antinori appears to enjoy the controversy surrounding his work and even the personal risk he faces in pursuing it. He remarked to Tim Adams of the *Observer* (December 2, 2001), "I have three bodyguards. Not one. Three! And a car with dark screens. It's like a president! Three bodyguards!" Antinori's critics have called him bombastic, irresponsible, and self-promoting, and his fervent public announcements have earned him the nickname "Dr. Volcano" in Italy.

Antinori prefers the term "genetic reprogramming" to describe the technique of cloning. "There are 100 million men who don't produce any sperm, and genetic reprogramming is the sole solution. Genetic reprogramming! Not cloning," he told Sergio Pistoi for *Scientific American* (April 2002). "Cloning is a Hollywood-style term." Clones are created when the genetic material from one human cell is injected into an egg cell that has had its genes removed. The fertilized egg cell is then implanted into the female's womb, who will then eventually give birth to a genetically identical twin of the donor. "Cloning creates ordinary children," Antinori has said, as quoted by Graham Jones for CNN.com (August 7, 2001). "They will be unique individuals, not photocopies of individuals."

Education and Early Career

Severino Antinori was born in 1945 in Abruzzo, in southern Italy. His interest in science began at a young age when he assisted his uncle, a veterinarian, with his rural practice. Antinori's family later moved to Rome, where he enrolled in university and began his studies in medicine. After graduating from the University of Rome La Sapienza in 1972, Antinori focused first on gastroenterology and then later in gynecology before eventually obtaining a position with the Instituto Materno Regina Elena, a public fertility hospital in Rome. He received further training in Sweden, Germany, the United States, and Great Britain. After clashing with colleagues at Regina Elena, Antinori resigned from his post. With his wife, also a physician, he founded the Associated Researchers for Human Reproduction (RAPRUI) clinic in 1985. The clinic, which has successfully treated infertile couples, is located in the same section of Rome as the Vatican, the home of the Catholic Church.

In the 1970s Antinori attended a lecture in Rome in which the British physician Patrick Steptoe spoke on human fertilization. (Steptoe and his colleague Robert Edwards made history in 1978 after their pioneering technique of in-vitro fertilization, or IVF, produced the first successful "test tube baby," Louise Brown.) The experience of attending Steptoe's lecture was life-changing for Antinori, who immediately decided to retrain as an embryologist. In interviews given in later years, Antinori has referred to Steptoe as a personal hero. "People said Steptoe was crazy, that it would never work," he told Tim Adams. "But I knew straight away it would work. Knew that he would not create a monster! I could see he was a pioneer. Like the Wright Brothers! Like Galileo! And now we have a million test tube babies. Who is calling Steptoe and Edwards Frankenstein now?" Steptoe, who was so vilified for his work in the 1970s, died in 1988, one week before he was to be knighted by the Queen of England.

In the late 1980s Antinori pioneered a technique called subzonal insemination (SUZI), in which the donor sperm is positioned below the barrier around the egg (oocyte). "You know what the [Catholic Church's] cardinals said when I invented SUZI?" he remarked to Sergio Pistoi. "That I was violating the barrier that God had put up to protect life." SUZI was later superseded by another technique, intracytoplasmic sperm injection (ICSI), in which a single sperm is injected directly into the nucleus of an egg. (While Antinori claims to have pioneered ICSI, Dr. Andre van Steirteghem and his colleagues at the Center for Reproductive Medicine at University Hospital in Brussels, Belgium, are officially credited with developing the technique.) ICSI represented a breakthrough in the treatment of male infertility, particularly for men with extremely low sperm counts, and it is now a viable procedure for couples using IVF. (According to Pistoi most fertility clinics in the United States offer ICSI.)

"Cloning creates ordinary children. … They will be unique individuals, not photocopies of individuals."

In 1989 Antinori caused a stir after he helped a 47-year-old menopausal woman become pregnant and deliver a baby with a donated egg implant. In 1994 he helped Rosanna Della Corte, then in her 60s, get pregnant via IVF with a donated egg and her husband's sperm. Della Corte had lost her 17-year old son, Ricardo, in a 1991 motorcycle accident. When she successfully gave birth (thus setting the record for the oldest women ever to bear a child), she named her new son Ricardo as well. The Vatican labeled the procedure "horrible and grotesque," according to Margaret Mallon of the *Herald* (HeraldScotland, August 8, 2001). In 1996 Antinori oversaw the fertility treatment of a 59-year-old unmarried British woman who eventually gave birth to twins.

Antinori has expressed the view that cloning, or "genetic reprogramming," holds promise for the treatment of infertility in cases for which IVF and ICSI would be ineffective. In particular, genetic reprogramming would make conception possible for men who do not produce sperm. Antinori has said that his efforts to clone a human being are motivated by a desire to help such men and their partners. "My only aim is to give infertile couples the gift of happiness in the form of children. Cloning is the next step, that's all," he told Margaret Mallon. Antinori believes that in the future, cloning will be as commonplace a treatment for infertility as IVF is today. "In a year or so the world will accept cloning," he told Margaret Mallon. "After the first one is born, it will be beautiful. There will be a million in the world before long."

In the meantime, however, efforts to promote cloning have encountered stiff opposition. In July 2001 the U.S. House of Representatives voted to ban human cloning. President George W. Bush expressed support for the ban, calling it a "strong ethical statement," as quoted by Graham Jones for CNN.com (August 7, 2001). Antinori told Margaret Mallon that, in his view, the ban represented a "return to the Dark Ages." In his interview with Tim Adams, Antinori compared the leaders of the United States and Great Britain to religious fundamentalists. "Let me tell you something. That George Bush is the same as bin Laden! He is a fundamentalist! The Taliban say, 'Allah-akhbar.' Bush says, 'God Bless America!' And your Mr. Blair," he continued, addressing the British reporter, "Pah! … They want to stop me! Stop science! The French would have me in prison for 20 years." In March 2009 President Barack Obama reiterated the position of the United States. "The government will never open the door for human cloning," he said. Obama nevertheless signed an order to lift restrictions on federal funding for embryonic stem cell research, in the hope that stem cell research would "unlock the potential for scientists to find better treatments for ailments ranging from diabetes to Parkinson's disease to cancer."

Later Career

In August 2001 Panayiotis Zavos, a retired professor of reproductive physiology at the University of Kentucky, in Lexington, teamed up with Antinori; together they announced their intention to begin human cloning trials on a group of volunteers. Antinori and Zavos defended their plans before an international committee at the National Academy of Sciences in Washington, D.C. Due to increasingly strict regulations on cloning in many countries, they stated that they were considering performing the trials in a remote country or on a boat in international waters. Soon after the announcement, Antinoti was expelled from the International Association of Private Assisted Reproductive Technology clinics and laboratories (A PART)—even though he had once been the organization's vice president. According to the A PART website (www.a-part. at), the consortium, founded in 1998, "has taken no position on [human cloning] and will not do so in the future." The group nevertheless felt that Antinori had become too controversial. Sarah-Kate Templeton, writing for the *Glasgow Sunday Herald* (October 21, 2001), quoted the president of A PART, Professor Wilfried Feichtinger, as noting Antinori's "disreputable conduct in recent months related to the topic of human reproductive cloning, which has injured the reputation of A Part."

Antinori's statements also reportedly influenced the British government's decision to change its laws regarding cloning. As explained by the BBC News (February 27, 2002), therapeutic cloning in the United Kingdom is governed by the Human Fertilisation and Embryology Act 1990, which erected barriers against human cloning. This act was amended by Parliament in January 2001 to permit therapeutic cloning research using embryonic tissues, that is, research on embryonic tissue cloning as a technique to regenerate tissues but not for reproductive purposes. In November 2001 England's High Court granted a judicial review of that amendment, thus effectively suspending it and leaving human cloning (for either therapeutic and reproductive purposes) unregulated and thus legal. After that decision led Antinori to proclaim Great Britain the future site of his cloning experiments, however, lawmakers swiftly passed the Human Reproductive Cloning Act of 2001 (given royal assent in December 2001), which made human cloning for reproductive purposes a "specific criminal offense," according to the *London Sunday Times* (April 7, 2002). (The Court of Appeals later reversed the November 2001 decision, whereupon the plaintiffs turned to the House of Lords. But as the BBC News reported on March 13, 2003, the House of Lords rejected the legal challenge to the January 2001 law, leaving strictly regulated therapeutic cloning legal while retaining the December 2001 ban on cloning for reproductive purposes.)

In April 2002 Antinori reported that a woman taking part in his program was eight weeks pregnant with a cloned embryo. He divulged the information during a question-and-answer period at a lecture at the Zayed Center for Follow-up and Coordination in Abu Dhabi, United Arab Emirates. "Our project is at a very advanced stage," he stated, as quoted by Sarah-Kate Templeton for the *Glasgow Sunday Herald* (April 7, 2002). "One woman among thousands of infertile couples in the program is eight weeks pregnant. We have nearly 5,000 couples in this project now." The story, initially reported by the English-language newspaper *Gulf News*, was picked up by newspapers around the world; when questioned further by the media in Europe and the United States, however, Antinori refused to elaborate upon his statements. The announcement sent shockwaves through the scientific community, and Antinori's unwillingness to substantiate his claim infuriated Zavos and other (unnamed) scientists in the consortium, prompting them to sever ties with the Italian doctor. An anonymous source told Templeton, "We have severed links with Severino. In this case we really do not know what Severino is talking about. Severino has made several statements in the past that are untrue and that is why we decided that we and Severino are no longer in harmony. No one from the original team works with him anymore. No one trusts Severino, and no one can make science with him."

Many scientists have voiced concern that cloning procedures pose significant safety risks. According to Amanda Onion, reporting for ABCNews.com (August 7, 2001), some research estimates show that almost 98 percent of cloning attempts on animals do not succeed. Creators of Dolly, a cloned sheep, made more than 225 attempts before they were successful. Research by biologist Rudolph Jaenisch of the Whitehead Institute at the Massachusetts Institute of Technology suggested that cloned animals that reach adulthood face a host of abnormalities later in life, such as obesity and organ failure, according to Onion. Dolly, for example, suffered from obesity, premature aging, and arthritis. (Dolly died in February 2003, at about half the life expectancy for a sheep of her breed.) Arthur Caplan, director of the Center for Bioethics at the University of Pennsylvania questioned the morality of cloning at a time when the technology has yet to be perfected, as he explained to Margaret Mallon: "When Dolly was made, ten sheep were born dead, five were born deformed. … We might accept those odds if we were talking about sheep cloning, but what person in their right mind would accept those odds today in making a baby? It's clearly immoral within the next year or two to be doing anything like human cloning if you stand ten times the chance of making a dead or deformed human being as you do of making a clone." Antinori, however, believes that fertilization and cloning procedures are safer in human beings than in animals, as he explained to Sergio Pistoi: "Maybe they are culturing the animal embryos in an inappropriate way. We have the expertise to do all that properly," in humans.

Among his colleagues working in the field of infertility, Antinori is an unpopular figure. Lord Robert Winston, director of the infertility clinic at Hammersmith Hospital in London, criticized Antinori and expressed doubts regarding his professionalism. "Antinori is a bombast, he's a maverick, he's an empty vessel. He does not have the credentials to be able to do what he claims he will do," Winston told Tim Adams. Antinori "is nowhere near being in the position he says he is of being able successfully to produce a healthy human clone," Winston continued. "It is extraordinarily dangerous, fantastically risky." Yet, while many of Antinori's colleagues have called him irresponsible for attempting to clone a human being at such an early stage in the development of the technique, at least one expert expressed cautious support for the Italian doctor's work: "He's very serious," Dr. W. Paul Dmowski, a professor of obstetrics and gynecology at Rush Medical College in Chicago, told John Crewdson of the *Chicago Tribune* (June 23, 2002), "and I can tell you that I have seen some of the data that he produced. He's concerned about his patients, he's concerned about not doing something that can be harmful." In 2002 Antinori founded the World Association of Reproductive Medicine (WARM) in Rome, with the "goal of creating international collaboration between scientists studying reproductive health."

In May 2006 it was announced that a 62-year-old child psychiatrist, Patricia Rashbrook from East Sussex, England, was pregnant after being treated by Dr. Antinori, who stated that ages 62 or 63 was the upper limit for IVF in health women. He also remarked that "he would only consider couples with at least 20 years' life expectancy left for fertility treatment." In 2009 when Antinori was informed that a 66-year old woman, Elizabeth Munro, was pregnant, he criticized her decision, saying that "he felt she was too old and may not live long enough to raise her child." In a comment to John Follain and Daniel Foggo of the London *Sunday Times,* he stated, "I am shocked by the idea of a 66-year-old woman giving birth … I respect the choice medically, but I think anything over 63 is risky because you cannot guarantee the child will have a loving mother or family. It is possible to give a child to the mother up to the age of 83 but it is medically criminal to do this because the likelihood is that after a year or two the child will lose his mum and suffer from psychological problems."

Although Antinori has held professorships of human reproduction at the University of Rome, and has published dozens of articles in medical journals, he has been shunned from professional societies for his flamboyant statements. Antinori and his wife, Caterina, have two daughters: Monica, a gynecologist and embryologist, and Stella, a biology student. The family has three homes in Italy—one in the city, one in the mountains, and one at the beach. Antinori is an enthusiastic fan of Italy's Lazio Football Club and once attempted to purchase the team; in his free time, he plays soccer for a local amateur team. In 2002 Antinori unsuccessfully campaigned in regional elections as a Right-to-Life candidate. He has never refrained from making grandiose statements, and on at least one occasion has compared himself to the 17th-century astronomer Galileo, who also was lambasted by the Catholic Church. He insists that his motivations are noble, telling Tim Adams: "If you remember nothing else, remember this! I am for life! Life is wonderful! I am a force of life!"

Further Reading:

Chicago Tribune C1 Jun. 23, 2002

CNN.com Aug. 7, 2001

The Herald (Scotland) p12 Aug. 8, 2001

The Observer Dec. 2, 2001

Scientific American p38+ Apr. 2002

(Glasgow) *Sunday Herald* Oct. 21, 2001, Nov. 4, 2001

Sunday Herald Sun p4 Apr. 7, 2002

(London) *Sunday Times* Apr. 7, 2002, May 17, 2009

Ayala, Francisco

Evolutionary biologist

Born: 1934, Madrid, Spain

Francisco J. Ayala is regarded as one the world's foremost authorities in the field of evolutionary biology. He pioneered the use of molecular biology techniques to study the process of evolution. "Before Ayala," Andrei Tatarenkov, a former researcher in Ayala's lab, told Gordy Slack for *UC Irvine Today* (August 29, 2002), "theories about the origin of the species were mostly based on mathematical models. The early work of Ayala and [his mentor] Dobzhansky was really the first experimental work." Ayala's research with *Drosophila* (a fruit fly genus that he used as a model organism) has provided insight into not only the lineage of species but also into the prevalence of genetic variation, the hierarchical population structure, and evolutionary rates. In recent years Ayala has dedicated himself to the research of protozoan parasites, namely those responsible for Chagas disease and malaria, in an effort to find a cure for various tropical diseases. Ayala, a former priest, has also garnered attention in scientific circles for being opposed to the encroachment of religion into science—a stance that is reflected in his books *Darwin and Intelligent Design* (2006), *Darwin's Gift to Science and Religion* (2007), and *Am I a Monkey? Six Questions about Evolution* (2010).

Education and Early Career

Francisco José Ayala Pereda was born in Madrid, Spain, on March 12, 1934. He was the fourth of the six children of Soledad Pereda Ayala and Francisco Ayala. His mother was a homemaker; his father worked as a businessman. The younger Ayala grew up in the shadow of the Spanish Civil War, a failed military uprising against the country's republican government that escalated into a violent, protracted conflict. After a three-year struggle (1936–39), the government was overthrown by the rebels, whose leader, Francisco Franco, ruled Spain with an iron fist for four decades.

Francisco Ayala developed an early interest in science while attending a private Catholic school in Madrid. In 1951, on completing his secondary education at Colegio de San Fernando, Ayala enrolled at the University of Madrid, where he majored in physics. After receiving his B.S. degree in 1955, he spent the next five years at the Pontifical Faculty of San Esteban, in Salamanca, studying theology and preparing for the priesthood. At San Esteban, Ayala became fascinated with genetics. "I had studied science as an undergraduate at the University of Madrid, and I continued to be interested in it," he recalled to Rachel Saslow for the *Washington Post* (April 27, 2010). "When I was studying theology, I started to read much more about human evolution and genetics."

After his ordination as a Dominican priest in 1960, Ayala decided to leave the priesthood. In 1961 he traveled to New York City, and with the help of renowned evolutionary biologist Theodosius Dobzhansky, who would become his mentor, Ayala entered the graduate program in evolutionary biology and genetics at Columbia University. Ayala first became aware of the ongoing debate between science and religion while studying at Columbia. "It was an unexpected turn of events for me, coming from conservative Spain, to discover that there was in the United States a strong creationist current that saw [Charles] Darwin and the theory of evolution as contrary to religious beliefs,"

Ayala wrote in his 2007 book *Darwin's Gift to Science and Religion*. "In Salamanca, in my theological studies, evolution had been perceived as a friend, not an enemy, of the Christian faith." Under Dobzhansky's guidance, Ayala performed genetic experiments on fruit flies (*Drosophila*) and observed the process by which new biological species are formed (also known as speciation).

In 1964, a year after earning his M.A. degree in genetics, Ayala was awarded a Ph.D. in genetics. It was while conducting research for his thesis, however, that he discovered new ways of calculating population fitness (the capacity of an organism to survive and reproduce successfully). Additionally, Ayala was able to show that the evolutionary rate (how quickly a new species evolves) of a species is dependent on its degree of genetic variation, which is critical to its ability to adapt to changes in the environment.

Following his time at Columbia University, Ayala underwent a year of postdoctoral training at Rockefeller University, also in New York City. In 1965 he joined the faculty at Rhode Island's Providence College as an assistant professor of biology. He returned to Rockefeller University in 1967, accepting a similar position there. During his four years or so at Rockefeller, Ayala observed several closely related *Drosophila* species in an effort to find a link between the amount of genetic polymorphism (DNA sequence variations among populations) and the rate at which a new species evolves. One area of investigation focused on rainforest *Drosophila* species (*D. birchii* and *D. serrata*) and the effects of radiation-induced genetic mutations on the ability of those populations to quickly adapt to a changing environment. Ayala discovered that the adaptation rate of the populations exposed to radiation was significantly greater than those of the nonirradiated populations. He concluded that natural selection plays a larger role in populations that have a greater variety of genotypes available for selection.

In 1971, the same year he became a naturalized citizen, Ayala was appointed assistant professor of genetics at the University of California (UC) at Davis, where Dobzhansky joined him. Three years later Ayala was promoted to full professor, a post he held until 1987. From 1977 to 1981 he served as the school's associate dean for environmental studies, director of the Institute of Ecology, and chair of the division of environmental studies.

While teaching at UC Davis, Ayala employed revolutionary molecular genetic techniques, including electrophoresis (an innovative method that sorts and measures DNA strands to analyze genetic variation) and gene cloning (manipulating DNA to create multiple copies of a single gene), to observe the amount and pattern of genetic differences among several groups of species across a broad geographic distribution. The adaptive importance of genetic variation was another focus of Ayala's research. He examined the effect of environmental factors—such as population density (the average number of individuals living in a unit of area), food supply, and temperature—on the selection of genetic variants, or *alleles* (different version of the same genes). His findings supported the view that natural selection is the driving force affecting genetic polymorphism.

Ayala also teamed up with noted paleontologist James W. Valentine to examine the fossil record (fossilized plant and animal remains) in an attempt to gain awareness regarding which components contribute to the increasing diversification as well as to understand the sudden decline of many species. Ayala collaborated with other colleagues on a series of experiments comparing the genetic differences between living species found in habitats that are stable and replete with natural resources, like coral reefs, and those found in similarly homogeneous environments with fewer resources. The diverse organisms collected from both the resource-rich and the resource-poor areas displayed high levels of genetic diversity, confirming that stable environments maintain genetic variation. This is attributed to the fact that these species become better adapted to the various environmental factors and resources; as a result there may be little natural selection among the well-adapted organisms. In 1980 Ayala was invited to join the National Academy of Sciences (NAS) for his pioneering work on population genetics.

In 1981 Ayala testified as an expert witness for the defense in *McLean v. Arkansas Board of Education*, a federal court case that contested Arkansas's Act 590, which dictated that both evolution and creationism be taught in public-school science classrooms. "Frank Press, the newly elected president of the National Academy of Sciences, asked me whether I thought the academy should get involved," Ayala told Slack. "I said it should. What was at stake was not a particular branch of science, but the survival of rationality in this country. If we allowed the Book of Genesis to be taught as science, that would be as bad for science as it would be for religion." The judge agreed; he overturned Act 590 on the basis that it was unconstitutional. Ayala was the principal author of the National Academy of Sciences's publication *Science, Evolution, and Creationism* (1984), which substantively became the NAS's amicus brief in *Edwards v. Aguillard,* brought before the U.S. Supreme Court in 1987. (The law was ruled unconstitutional.) In 1984 the American Association for the Advancement of Science conferred on Ayala its Scientific Freedom and Responsibility Award.

In addition to his studies with *Drosophila* fruit flies, Ayala conducted joint research with French doctor Michel Tibayrenc on *Trypanosoma cruzi*, the protozoan parasite that is responsible for Chagas disease, an incurable, potentially deadly disease that is native to Latin America and affects nearly 20 million people worldwide. Tibayrenc thought that *T. cruzi* might actually be more than one species. In January 1985, after receiving a government fellowship, Tibayrenc traveled with his family from France to California, where he collaborated with Ayala. Over the next 20 months, they employed molecular genetic methods to study the genetic diversity of natural populations of *T. cruzi* and made several important findings. Although Tibayrenc's initial theory about *T. cruzi* was incorrect, the team found that the parasite reproduces primarily by cloning itself. They also discovered that other disease-causing protozoa, including those that cause sleeping sickness and malaria, also reproduce by cloning.

Later Career

In 1987 Ayala accepted the position of distinguished professor of biological sciences at the University of California, Irvine, and two years later he became the Donald Bren Professor of Biological Sciences and founding director of the Bren Fellows Program while also teaching philosophy. In 1990 Ayala and Tibayrenc's findings were published in the scientific journal *Proceedings of the National Academy of Sciences of the United States of America* (*PNAS*), in an article entitled "A Clonal Theory of Parasitic Protozoa."

During his time as a member of the National Advisory Council for the Human Genome Project (1990–93), Ayala recommended that a portion of the budget (between three percent and five percent) should be allocated toward figuring out the ethical, legal, and social ramifications of the project's outcome. In 1994 President Bill Clinton named Ayala to the U.S. President's Committee of Advisors on Science and Technology, a post Ayala held until 2001.

In the early 1990s Ayala also turned his attention to *Plasmodium falciparum*, a protozoan parasite commonly found in Africa that is responsible for the most virulent, or infective, form of human malaria. At the time, the disease afflicted between three hundred million and five hundred million people around the world each year, resulting in more than a million deaths annually, chiefly among African children. With the help of colleagues, Ayala observed the genetic diversity among several *Plasmodium* species and determined that *P.*

falciparum was more closely related to *P. reichenowi*, a parasite commonly found in chimpanzees, than to other *Plasmodium* species that infect humans (*P. vivax, P. malariae*) or birds (*P. gallinaceum, P. lophurae*).

In 1998 Ayala teamed up with Stephen Rich, a former UC Irvine graduate student, to examine the amount of genetic variation that existed among DNA from diverse strains of *P. falciparum*. They analyzed the DNA arrangement of ten genes in 30 strains of *P. falciparum*, relying mainly on published data. After discovering only slight variation, Ayala and Rich reasoned that all 30 strains had descended from the same ancestral strain (a "malarial Eve") within the last 57,500 years. The finding contradicted earlier investigations by others who had observed noticeable differences among the genes for antigenic proteins (those foreign proteins that are targeted by the human immune system). To explain this inconsistency, Ayala and his colleagues determined that these mutations had occurred in response to the human immune system. Ayala and Rich also concluded that the spread of *P. falciparum* from its origins in Africa to tropical and subtropical regions around the world had occurred within the last five thousand years and coincided with the evolution of farming in Africa.

"If we allowed the Book of Genesis to be taught as science, that would be as bad for science as it would be for religion."

Since 2000 Ayala has been a professor of logic and the philosophy of science at UC Irvine. In 2003 he was named a University Professor in the University of California system—a distinguished title he still holds. From 2004 to 2006 Ayala served as president of the nonprofit scientific society Sigma Xi.

In 2009 Ayala and his colleagues garnered attention with a paper that was published in the September issue of *PNAS*. The article traced the origin of *Plasmodium falciparum* to a closely related species, *P. reichenowi*, which infects chimpanzees. This time the team was able to study not just one isolate of the chimpanzee parasite, but eight other isolates from chimps born in the wild. The team concluded that *P. falciparum* came from a single branch of *P. reichenowi*, probably via a single chimp-mosquito-human transmission. Ayala also made headlines the following January, for another paper that appeared in *PNAS*. In this article he wrote that strains of the human parasite *P. falciparum* had recently been found in apes, suggesting that even if malaria were stamped out, the human population could still be at risk via contagion from gorillas or chimpanzees.

In 2010 Ayala was awarded the Templeton Prize (2010), which honors a "living person who has made an exceptional contribution to affirming life's spiritual dimension, whether through insight, discovery, or practical works." Ayala's many other accolades include the Medal of the College of France (1979); the W. E. Key Award from the American Genetics Association (1985); the Scientific Freedom and Responsibility Award of the American Association for the Advancement of Science (1987); the Gold Medal of the Italian National Academy of Sciences (1998); the William Procter Prize for Scientific Achievement (2000), from Sigma Xi; the National Medal of Science (2001); and the American Institute of Biological Sciences (AIBS) Distinguished Scientist Award (2007).

Ayala spent three years (1993–96) as president and board chairman of the American Academy of Arts and Sciences (AAAS). In addition to his memberships in the AAAS and the National Academy of Sciences, Ayala has been elected a foreign member of the Royal Academy of Sciences of Spain; the Russian Academy of Sciences; the Russian Academy of Natural Sciences; and the Serbian Academy of Sciences and Arts. Ayala has more than seven hundred publications to his name. Since 2007, with John Avise and others, Ayala has edited the *In Light of Evolution* series, the proceedings of Arthur M. Sackler colloquia sponsored by the National Academy of Sciences (six volumes through 2012).

In April 2010, UC Irvine announced that it would rename its science library the Francisco J. Ayala Science Library. In October 2011 Ayala presented a $10 million endowment—$1 million each year for the next decade—to UC Irvine's School of Biological Sciences; it is the largest endowment to date by a faculty member. The donation was amassed from the proceeds of his two-thousand-acre vineyard, located in northern San Joaquin and Sacramento counties. Ayala grows grapes for his own private label and for other wineries.

Since 1985, Ayala has been married to his second wife, Dr. Hana (Lostakova) Ayala, an ecologist. They live in Irvine. Ayala has two sons, Francisco José and Carlos Alberto, from his first marriage, to Mary Henderson.

Further Reading:

(London) *Guardian* May 5, 2010, Aug. 14, 2012

New York Times Apr. 29, 2008, Jul. 31, 2012

Los Angeles Times Sep. 4, 1999, Aug.14, 2012

Washington Post Apr. 26, 2010, Jul. 31, 2012

UC Irvine Today (later, *Today @ UCI*) Aug. 29, 2002, Aug. 12, 2012

Selected Books:

Ayala, Francisco, ed., *Molecular Evolution* (1976)

Dobzhansky, Theodosius, and Francisco J. Ayala, eds., *Studies in the Philosophy of Biology* (1977)Ayala, Francisco J., and James W. Valentine, *Evolving: The Theory and Processes of Organic Evolution* (1979)

Ayala, Francisco J., and John A. Kiger Jr., *Modern Genetics* (1980; second edition, 1984)

Ayala, Francisco J., *Population and Evolutionary Genetics: A Primer* (1982)

Robert John Russell, Francisco J. Ayala, and William R. Stoeger, eds., *Evolutionary Molecular Biology: Scientific Perspectives on Divine Actions* (1999)

Wuketits, F. M., and Francisco J. Ayala, eds., *Handbook of Evolution: The Evolution of Living Systems (Including Hominids),* two volumes (2005)

Ayala, Francisco J., *Darwin and Intelligent Design* (2006)

Ayala, Francisco J., *Darwin's Gift to Science and Religion* (2007)

Ayala, Francisco J., and Camilo J. Cela-Conde, *Human Evolution: Trails from the Past* (2007)

Ayala, Francisco J., *Am I a Monkey? Six Big Questions about Evolution* (2010)

Ayala, Francisco J., and Robert Arp, eds., *Contemporary Debates in Philosophy of Biology* (2010)

Ayala, Francisco J., *Evolution* (2012)

Bang, Abhay

Born: 1950, Nagpur, India

Bang, Rani Chari

Born: 1951, Nagpur, India

Indian community health physicians

According to the Web site of the John D. and Catherine T. MacArthur Foundation, "In India, more than 100,000 women die each year due to complications of pregnancy and childbirth, most within 24 hours of delivery—nearly 20 percent of the global maternal death toll. And for every maternal death in India, there are 10 newborn deaths—a total of 1.1 million, or one-quarter of all newborn deaths worldwide." The doctors Abhay Bang and Rani Chari Bang have been working to solve this problem for more than 20 years: In the mid-1980s the husband-and-wife team founded the Society for Education, Action and Research in Community Health (SEARCH), which, as the MacArthur Foundation notes, "did what many considered impossible—dramatically reduced newborn deaths and improved women's health in one of India's most impoverished regions. [The pair] demonstrated how in a region where 95 percent of all births take place at home, often hundreds of miles from a hospital, it was possible to reduce newborn death by 70 percent, complications from pregnancy and delivery by nearly 75 percent, and the need for emergency obstetric care by more than 30 percent."

Abhay Bang explained to a MacArthur Foundation interviewer, "The standard recommendation to a woman who needs medial attention is, 'Go to the hospital'—but in rural parts of India there are so few doctors that this is like telling her, 'Do nothing.' We decided to follow [the activist Mohandas] Gandhi's message to go to the villages. Instead of waiting for people to come to us, we found a way to take the care to the people." The Bangs achieved their impressive results by seemingly simple means: one of their major strategies is to train teams of women in rural villages (many of whom had had no previous formal education) to provide home-based care—from basic hygiene to treatment of common ailments—in the poorest villages in India. According to Priya Shetty in the *Lancet* (January 15, 2011), they "began childhood pneumonia management in 1988 and then the home-based neonatal programme in 1995." In honoring SEARCH with a 2006 MacArthur Award for Creative and Effective Institutions, Jonathan Fanton, the head of the MacArthur Foundation, stated, "Working in remote villages, the Society for Education, Action and Research in Community Health has put the well-being of women and infants on the global agenda. Your path-breaking research has been a potent catalyst for change, first by uncovering shocking statistics, and then by proving with sound evidence that local solutions work. Your method is as powerful as it is modest: by listening to patients, simple strategies are discovered to save the lives of newborns and protect the health of mothers. Your program is a model of community healthcare that is influencing the government of India and the international development community."

According to Anusha Subramanian, writing in *Business Today* (August 19, 2012), SEARCH attracts "doctors and interns from all over the world, who come for research and training in community health." In mid-2012, Subramanian noted, SEARCH employed just nine doctors (five of whom had had training in the United States), paying them a small fraction of what they could have earned in an urban hospital. Psychologist Venkatesh Aiyyar (who quit his job of ten years at the Institute for Psychological Health, near Mumbai, to work at SEARCH) told Subramanian: "What's interesting here is that you are constantly in touch with the people you are treating." Subramanian noted that SEARCH "relies on numerous sources for its funding: "Ten per cent of its funds come in through its affordable hospital for local tribals. Another 20 per cent comes from training activities, and 30 per cent from research. Donations and awards account for the remaining 40 per cent." The SEARCH Web site prominently features a quotation from Gandhi: "I shall give you a talisman. When faced with a dilemma as to what your next step should be, remember the most wretched and vulnerable human being you ever saw. The step you contemplate should help him."

Education and Early Career

Abhay Bang was born in 1950 in Nagpur, India, to parents who abided by the Gandhian welfare movement known as Sarvodaya. "I spent my early childhood in Gandhi's Sevagram ashram, in the company of luminaries like Acharya Vinoba Bhave," he noted to Jeetha D'Silva of *Mint* (October 3, 2007). (Bhave is considered Gandhi's spiritual successor.) Bang added, "These influences have shaped me to a large extent." During his youth, he had a brief but life-altering conversation with his elder brother Ashok, in which the brothers concluded that they would devote their lives to helping improve food supplies and access to health care, what they considered to be India's two greatest challenges. While Ashok went on to study agricultural sciences, Abhay pursued the field of medicine. Upon graduating from Nagpur University, he enrolled at the Postgraduate Institute of Medical Education and Research (PGIMER), located in Chandigarh, India, to obtain his medical degree. While there, Singh recounts, he became distraught over the government's willingness to spend liberally on the training of doctors who usually ended up leaving the country to practice in the United States. For this reason, Abhay left the institute to start an organization called Medico Friend Circle, which asked medical professionals to remain in India to treat poor rural Indians. When he returned to Nagpur University to complete postgraduate studies, Bang met Rani Chari, his future wife.

The youngest of five children, Rani Chari, also from Nagpur, grew up in a wealthy Iyengar family. (Iyengar is a Brahmin caste subscribing to the Visishtadvaita philosophy codified by Ramanuja). An article by Alex Perry for *Time* (November 7, 2005) lists Rani Chari's age as 54, making it evident that she was born in about 1951. Her father, a general practitioner, wanted her to follow in his footsteps. She, on the other hand, had dreams of working with the poor. She recalled to D'Silva, "My family initially resisted the idea. My father wanted me to go abroad and study and probably look at practicing in a big city." Then, while studying medicine at Nagpur University, she met Abhay Bang. The two married in 1977 after she completed her training as a gynecologist. Not long afterwards, the Bangs moved to Wardha, Maharashtra, to join Chetna Vikas, a nonprofit organization started by Abhay's family; the couple worked in impoverished villages in the Wardha district. In order to accomplish their long-term goals, they left India to study public health at Johns Hopkins University in Baltimore, Maryland. "To develop sustainable solutions, we had to adopt a community-based approach. This necessitated conducting research, based on which we could develop new knowledge and practical, replicable public health models," Abhay explained to D'Silva.

Later Career

After obtaining master's degrees in public health, the Bangs returned to India and established SEARCH in December 1985 (some sources say 1986). The duo set up a laboratory in an old warehouse and began surveying the villagers of Gadchiroli, a heavily forested and hilly district in northeastern Maharashtra State. Gadchiroli's economic situation is summed up on the region's official government Web site: "There [is] no large scale industry in the entire district except the paper mill at Ashti in Chamorshi Taluka and [the] paper pulp factory at Desaiganj. Due to this, the district is economically backward. There are many rice mills in the district as the paddy is the main agriculture [feature] here." Conventional wisdom held that population control was India's number-one medical priority and that rural medical personnel should focus on family planning; the Bangs found, however, that contraception was only one of many needs. More than 90 percent of their patients had gynecological diseases of various sorts, for example. (Despite this staggering figure, fewer than one in 10 of the women had ever been examined by a gynecologist.) In 1989 they published their findings in the medical journal the *Lancet.* "Within a year or two, there was an entirely new approach to women's health worldwide," Abhay Bang told Perry. "The global population policy changed from looking at mere reproduction to the whole issue of women's reproductive health. That was our first experience of how powerful this approach could be."

"Bit by bit, it seems, we are closer to our youthful dream of a health-care revolution that would be Arogya-Swaraj—people's health in people's empowered hands."

As in much of rural India, the infant-mortality rate in Gadchiroli was high, and the Bangs set out to research the most common causes of neonatal deaths (defined as deaths within the first four weeks after birth). They found, according to Alex Perry, "no problems that couldn't be treated by a health worker with rudimentary skills, some infant sleeping bags [to provide warmth] and an abacus." (Priya Shetty explains in the January 15, 2011, *Lancet* that Abhay Bang designed an abacus system to help his health workers to count breaths and diagnose pneumonia.) The Bangs began approaching village *dais,* traditional birth attendants, many of whom were illiterate. They offered to provide the *dais* with basic equipment and train them to use it in order to fight sepsis (infection), hypothermia, and pneumonia—the leading causes of infant death. Next, the Bangs trained partners to work with the *dais.* These new health workers (called *arogya doots,* or "health messengers") were typically married women with at least a few years of formal schooling and children of their own. Because they were literate, they could keep records and carry out more complex medical interventions. The teams of health workers visited women during their pregnancies and were present at deliveries. "With two attendants at the delivery there is a kind of semi-skilled division of labor—the village version of what you might find in a hospital in the city," Abhay Bang told the MacArthur Foundation interviewer. The health workers, who were paid somewhat more than they could have earned as agricultural workers, also made several visits after the childbirth—to give breastfeeding advice, check for any complications, and help with the care of the newborn. The health workers carried with them scales (to help identify babies whose low birth weights put them at risk), thermometers, sleeping bags, or "warm bags" (made by local seamstresses to ward off hypothermia), abacuses crafted by local carpenters, and drugs for such common illnesses as diarrhea and malaria. Elizabeth Day, writing in the *Observer* (March 19, 2011) quoted Anjana Uikey (who was one of the first *arogya doots* to be trained) as saying that the "experience has been one of enormous personal growth. I'm being useful to the village and on a daily basis I have people who are grateful to me. Now I get a lot of respect. Earlier, I was nobody and today the whole village knows my name.

In late 1999 the Bangs published an article in the *Lancet* entitled "The Effect of Home-Based Neonatal Care and Management of Sepsis on Neonatal Mortality: Field Trial in Rural India." Although they had originally hypothesized that their form of home-based care would reduce the neonatal mortality rate by about 25 percent over the course of three years, they found instead that the rate had been lowered by almost 62 percent—at a cost, as recounted an editorial in the *Winnipeg Free Press* (September 27, 2010), among other sources, of about $7 per baby. The editorial continues, "'Empowering people to take care of their own health and solve their own problems,' Dr. Bang suggests, is an important step to solving the larger problems that the whole world shares. Massive international programs are needed, but we should never forget that individual initiatives can also work miracles."

The Bangs have criticized Indian government officials for underreporting infant deaths nationwide; Abhay Bang told interviewer Lyla Bavadam of *Frontline* (a publication of the *Hindu,* September 10–23, 2005), "We found that the government functionaries try to solve the problem by not counting it. The higher officers accept such false reports because these paint a rosy picture. ... Without true figures neither the severity of the problem can be realised, nor any accountability can be sought from anybody. The situation is tragic as well as absurd." He explained why he feels too little attention has been paid to the issue of infant mortality: "The picture of a hungry, wasted, miserable child moves you. Media can highlight it. The child is malnourished, but still alive, hence it can be visited, photographed, seen; whereas a dead child has vanished. ... So, for the media, leaders and the public, child mortality is [only] notional."

In spite of SEARCH's positive statistical results, the Bangs have been criticized for allowing women with little education to administer complex drugs to villagers. Dr. Abhay Bang's response to those critics is firm and unequivocal: "Our workers have given 15,000 injections. The rate of complication has been zero," he told Elizabeth Day, who noted that the "insistence that patients must be treated in 'techno-centric' hospitals by western-trained physicians is, to [Abhay Bang's] mind, simply not viable in rural India, where lack of transport and an inability to pay for treatment often mean that sick people stay away." Further, as Abhay Bang explained to the *Lancet*'s Priya Shetty, "The community health workers are meticulously trained and go through regular checks to ensure that their actions are exactly by the book. If they are even slightly in doubt, they consult one of the doctors who work with the programme. The case fatality is equal to or lower than in small and medium size hospitals."

In 2006 the Bangs started an initiative called NIRMAN, for identifying and nurturing young social change–makers in Maharashtra. According to the NIRMAN Web site, "NIRMAN educational philosophy finds its roots in the Nayee Talim principle proposed by Mahatma Gandhi and Vinoba Bhave. As against the conventional education system which compartmentalizes formal education and real life, NIRMAN aims to bridge this gap and achieve education through real problem solving," advocating problem-based learning instead of classroom-based learning. SEARCH collaborates on NIRMAN with MKCL (Maharashtra Knowledge Corporation Limited). The program (it is not a membership youth organization and has no political, religious, or commercial purpose) consists of a series of three residential camps that take place at SEARCH's Shodhgram medical facility over the course of one year. In evaluating applicants, SEARCH seeks out participants of various regional, economic and academic backgrounds in order to "add depth and breadth" to the program, which includes "study visits, educative sessions, reading assignments, internships, fellowships, individual mentoring, group actions and various other activities."

Besides their recognition by the MacArthur Foundation in 2006, the Bangs have received numerous awards during the course of their careers. These include, among many others, a state award from the Government of Maharashtra for their work in tribal areas (1987); the Mahatma Gandhi Award (1994); the Natu Foundation Award (1996); the Dr. Sheshadri Gold Medal for their contributions to community medicine, awarded by the Indian Council of Medical Research (1996); the Yashwantrao Chavan Pratisthan Award for outstanding contribution to rural development in Maharashtra (2000); the Satpal Mittal Award from the Indian Association of Parliamentarians (2002); the Ramshastri Prabhune Puraskar for social justice (2002); the Rajiv Gandhi Award (2003); the Maharashtra Bhushan Award, one of the highest honors given by the government of Maharashtra (2003); the Diwaliben Mohanlal Mehta Award (2004); the Spirit of Mastek Award from the Mastek Foundation (2005), the Stree Shakti Puruskar National award (2005); the Jamanalal Bajaj Award from the Jamanalal Bajaj Foundation in Mumbai (2006); and the Dory Storms' Child Survival Recognition Award from the CORE Group Washington (2010) . In 2005 the Bangs, who have written four books and numerous journal articles for medical publications (including the *Lancet, Bulletin of WHO*, *Journal of Perinatology,* and *Indiana Paediatrics*, were named Global Health Heroes by the editors of *Time*.

Dr. Rani Bang also conducts sessions on sex education for adolescents and teenagers In 2010 she wrote *Putting Women First: Women and Health in a Rural Community.* The Bangs' eldest son, Anand, works with SEARCH. The Bangs have two younger sons, Amrut and Sarvesh.

Writing in the *Lancet,* Priya Shetty explained that in 2010, "WHO and UNICEF endorsed [the Bangs'] approach to treating newborn babies at home. The clutch of interventions is being rolled out across India, and policy makers from Bangladesh, Nepal, and many African countries have visited Gadchiroli to study the pioneering work of the two doctors in newborn care. 'Bit by bit, it seems' says Abhay Bang, 'we are closer to our youthful dream of a health-care revolution that would be Arogya-Swaraj—people's health in people's empowered hands.'" Writing in *Forbes India* (June 4, 2010), Bang asserted, "Research with the People will be characterised by five features: 1) People should need it, 2) people should do it, 3) people should understand it, 4) people should use it, and 5) people should own it."

The Bangs' Shodhagram ("research village") medical complex contains a lab, pharmacy, surgical suite, library, wards, and—at the suggestion of the forest-dwelling Gond tribe, whose members are served by the facility—a shrine to the goddess Danteshwari.

Further Reading:

(India) *Business Today* Aug. 19, 2012

CityBlogPune Web site Dec. 1, 2009

Forbes India Jun. 4, 2010

Frontline (a publication of the *Hindu)* Vol. 22, no. 19 (Sep. 10–23, 2005)

Indian Express May 18, 2003, Dec. 10, 2005

Lancet, Vol.354, no. 9194 (Dec. 4, 1999): 1955–1961, Vol. 377, no. 9761 (Jan. 15, 2011): 199 MacArthur Foundation Web site, Aug. 24, 2006

Mint Oct. 3, 2007
Observer Mar. 19, 2011
SEARCH Web site
Time magazine Nov. 7, 2005
Times of India Jun. 14, 2011

Blanks, Billy

American fitness guru and trainer

Born: 1955, Erie, Pennsylvania, United States

Billy Blanks's sudden ascent to stardom as a fitness guru in the late 1990s had all the hallmarks of a true American success story. Born poor, dyslexic, and physically impaired by an abnormal hip joint, he overcame these obstacles to become a seven-time world karate champion, a small-budget action-movie star, and the inventor of Tae-Bo. Tae-Bo is an exercise routine that combines hip-hop dancing with ballet, karate, tae kwon do, and boxing. Blanks first conceived of the idea in the late 1980s, when he was pondering how to encourage more women to take up martial arts. To make the workout more palatable, he removed much of the ceremony surrounding the more traditional martial arts and replaced it with such activities as dancing and weight training.

Although Blanks's following was small at first, word soon spread to the Hollywood elite about the effectiveness of Blanks's exercise regimen. People flooded his gym in Sherman Oaks, California, and Blanks moved to a larger gym to accommodate his growing class size. Then, recognizing the impact of Tae-Bo, he released his first Tae-Bo exercise video in August 1998. In addition to the release of new workout videos, Blanks signed a book deal with Bantam Books for an estimated $1.5 million dollars (*The Tae-Bo Way*, 1999). Over 500 million videos, including *Tae-Bo II: Get Ripped Advanced Workout* (2001) *and Billy Blanks: Tae Bo Cardio Explosion* (2011), have been sold over the last two decades. Blanks's brand continues to pioneer new ground, while remaining a leader in the fitness industry.

Education and Early Career

Born in Erie, Pennsylvania, in 1955, Billy Blanks was the fourth child of Isaac and Mabeline Blanks's 15 children. (They had ten sons and five daughters.) Isaac, a foundry worker, and Mabeline, a homemaker, struggled to make ends meet and to keep their children safe in the tough neighborhood in which they lived. Both parents were strict, but they kept their children out of trouble. "My father taught me that to get something out of life, you have to work for it," Blanks remarked in an interview with Dan Jewel and Karen Brailsford of *People* (December 15, 1997). Despite trying to follow such a philosophy, Billy had a difficult time in school. Diagnosed with dyslexia, he spent most of his youth struggling with his school work. In addition, the abnormality in his hip joints, combined with his clumsiness, made him an object of ridicule among his siblings and school friends.

As a preteen Blanks became fascinated with the character Kato, played by Bruce Lee, on the television program *The Green Hornet*, and through Kato, he grew interested in karate. Nearly evicted from his first karate class because of his hip trouble, he determinedly practiced before a mirror to learn the moves and to compensate for his disability. The hard work paid off. As he remarked in his interview with Dan Jewel and Karen Brailsford of *People*, "I was supposed to be the black sheep. Karate gave me confidence." Starting in his childhood, Blanks competed for karate titles on a local level and eventually worked his way up to state and national competitions. In 1975 he became the first Amateur Athletic Union champion, a title he would go on to win four more times. About a year later he married his high-school friend Gayle Godfrey, who was then 17 and the mother of a two-year-old daughter, Shellie, from a previous relationship. "It's an astonishing thing," Gayle told Jewel and Brailsford. "A lot of men don't take care of their own children, let alone someone else's." In addition to Shellie, who works as a trainer in Blanks's gym and is an accomplished martial artist, the couple also had a son, Billy Jr., who became a dancer, singer, and fitness instructor.

While Blanks supported his family by working a number of odd jobs, he slowly built a reputation as a martial-arts star. His victories at a number of state and national championships bolstered his rising status, and he earned a seventh-degree black belt in tae kwon do, the chief Korean form of karate. He also won black belts in five other forms of karate. His greatest karate achievement came in 1980, when he was named the captain of the first U.S. Olympic karate team. His hopes of Olympic competition were dashed, however, when President Jimmy Carter stopped American participation in the 1980 Moscow Olympic games to protest the Soviet invasion of Afghanistan. Blanks nevertheless continued to compete on an international level. During the 1980s he won the Karate World Championship for seven consecutive years. He also captained the American karate team that went on to win 36 gold medals in a variety of international competitions. Blanks earned admission to the Karate Hall of Fame in 1982 and also, according to his Web site, became the 1984 Massachusetts Golden Gloves Champion and the Tri-State Golden Gloves Champion of Champions.

Later Career

In 1988, determined to follow the path to film stardom that his idol Bruce Lee had taken, Blanks moved his family to Los Angeles, California. His competitive career was winding down, and he began to put his martial arts training to use by working as a bodyguard for celebrities. While guarding Catherine Bach (of *Dukes of Hazzard* fame) on location in the Philippines, he landed a part in *Bloodfist* (1989). Afterward he appeared in a number of action films, including *Driving Force* (1989), *Lionheart* (1990), *The King of the China Kickboxers* (1991), *Talons of the Eagle* (1992), *Timebomb* (1992), *TC 2000* (1993), *Showdown* (1994), *Expect No Mercy* (1995), and *Balance of Power* (1996). He also played small parts in such high-profile films as *The Last Boy Scout* (1991), *Kiss the Girls* (1997*), Dance Club: The Movie* (2007*), American Grandmaster: The Life and Death of Mr. Parker* (2008), and *Jack and Jill* (2011).

Blanks didn't abandon his martial arts workouts, though. He set up a studio in his garage to lead classes, and word of mouth about his bold new fitness program—which he called Tae-Bo—quickly spread. According to his Web site, *Tae* is a Korean word meaning "foot or leg" and stands for the emphasis of lower body movements; *Bo* is short for bo(xing), which alludes to upper body striking and defense. All the individual letters of *Tae-Bo* have an important meaning: *T = Total*; *A = Awareness*; *E = Excellent*; *B = Body*; and *O = Obedience*. Blanks's Web site also gives information on certification as a Tae-Bo trainer, how to become a Tae-Bo instructor, and where to find a Tae-Bo class.

After he retired from karate competition in 1991, Blanks devoted more of his time to developing Tae-Bo. As the buzz on the benefits of his intense training program traveled farther afield, it eventually reached the ears of show-business celebrities. First, one of Jane Fonda's workout instructors went to a class; she was so impressed by Blanks's program that she began bringing friends to see him. When the singer and dancer Paula Abdul started attending classes and praising his workout sessions, his business really began to take off. Soon, Blanks says, such celebrities as Cuba Gooding Jr., Valerie Bertinelli, Brooke Shields, Lisa Rinna, Carmen Electra, Neve Campbell, Queen Latifah, Viveca Fox, Sinbad, and Shannon Tweed pushed through his front door to experience the benefits of Tae-Bo. Blanks claims he is as tough on his famous students as he is on everyone else. "If I think you're out of shape, I'm going to tell you," Blanks told Dan Jewel and Karen Brailsford. "I'm not going to lie to you just because of who you are."

Soon Tae-Bo became one of the hottest exercise routines in southern California. At $9 per class, the gym was getting so crowded that a fire marshal had to designate a maximum occupancy. In 1995 Blanks moved from his small gym to a larger one in Sherman Oaks. Two years later, he trained the actress Ashley Judd for her fight scenes in the film *Kiss the Girls*, in which Blanks had a small part as an instructor. From 1998 to the present, he has made television appearances on the *Oprah Winfrey Show, ER, Melrose Place, The Martin Short Show,* the *Wayne Brady Show, Ellen*, and the *Wendy Williams Show*.

"If I think you're out of shape, I'm going to tell you. I'm not going to lie to you just because of who you are."

In August 1998 Blanks released the first of his Tae-Bo workout videos. By the middle of March 1999 the videos had grossed more than $75 million. Within six months Blanks became the most widely recognized fitness trainer in the country. "The only difference between me and Michael Jordan," he told Dan Snierson of *Entertainment Weekly* (April 2, 1999), "is Michael had TV coverage. But now I'm on TV and people are getting a chance to see what Billy Blanks is all about." Blanks is also a well-known face in TV commercials and advertisements. He did a commercial for Subway fast foods in 2000 and has appeared (with co-hosts) in various infomercials: with Kelly Packard, for "Billy's Boot Camp" fitness exercises (2004); Charlotte Ross, for "Boot Camp Elite" fitness exercises (2006); and Stacy Keibler, for "Billy Blanks's PT 24/7" workout system.

When he is not filming new workout DVDs or movies, Blanks continues to teach daily Tae-Bo classes in his gym. In his spare time, he mixes music for his clients. He also likes to build classic cars and is particularly proud of a 1969 Roadrunner he constructed. Though his fame grows almost daily, he remains a devoted family man, humble in his belief that faith has kept him strong. "When I get up at 5:30 A.M.," he remarked in *Vibe* (May 1999), "the first thing I do is praise the Lord for giving me another day."

Billy and Gayle Blanks were divorced in 2008, after 33 years of marriage. In November 2008 Blanks again became a father, to a new daughter named Angelika. The mother was his Japanese interpreter Tomoko Sato, whom he later married, in 2009. He has also adopted his wife's two daughters, Marriett and Erika Peterson.

In addition to his fitness training activities, in 1999 Blanks, with Gayle Blanks, established the Billy Blanks Foundation, which is "dedicated to equipping high-risk individuals with life skills that allow them to achieve their full potential." He has also done notable work with the military. He often travels with Tae-Bo instructors, including his daughter Shellie, to "integrate cross-gender, generational, and racial messages into their appearances at training camps and hotspots worldwide." His training work with the U.S. Armed Forces has included trips to Iraq, Bosnia, Kosovo, Sarajevo, Greece, African nations, Germany, and Italy.

Further Reading:

Billy Blanks personal Web site

Entertainment Tonight Apr. 30, 1999

Entertainment Weekly p99 Apr. 2, 1999

IMDb Web site

People p81+ Oct. 16, 1995, p79+ Dec. 15, 1997

Time magazine p77 Mar. 15, 1999; *Vibe* p128 May 1999

Selected Films:

Driving Force, 1989

Lionheart, 1990

King of the Kickboxers, 1991

China O'Brien II, 1991

The Last Boy Scout, 1991

Talons of the Eagle, 1992

Timebomb, 1992; *TC 2000,* 1993

Showdown, 1994

Back in Action, 1994

Tough and Deadly, 1995

Expect No Mercy, 1995

Balance of Power, 1996

Kiss the Girls, 1997

Assault on Devil's Island, 1997

Dance Club: The Movie, 2007

American Grandmaster: The Life and Death of Mr. Parker, 2008

Jack and Jill, 2011

Selected DVDs:

Billy Blanks' Tae-Bo: Instructional Workout, Basic, Advanced, 8-Minute Workout, 1999

Tae-Bo Extreme! Billy Blanks, Tae-Bo, Push Your Limits, 2002

Billy Blanks' Tae-Bo: Fat Blasting Cardio & Total Body Fat Blaster, 2005

Billy Blanks' Tae-Bo: T3 Total Transformation Training, 2008

Billy Blanks: Tae-Bo Ripped Extreme, 2011

Chan, Margaret

Chinese physician, international health organization official

Born: 1947, Hong Kong

On November 9, 2006, Margaret Chan was elected director-general of the World Health Organization (WHO), and in May 2012 she was re-elected for a second term. Chan is the first person from China to head the U.N. agency, which was founded in 1948 with the goal of helping people around the globe achieve the highest possible level of physical, mental, and social well-being. Among its many tasks, the WHO works with governments to strengthen national health programs, conducts research into numerous health-related topics, combats the spread of infectious diseases, and mounts educational campaigns about such topics as the dangers of smoking and the importance of eating a balanced diet.

Prior to joining the WHO, Chan had worked for more than two decades for the Hong Kong department of health, serving as its director from 1994 until 2003. During her eventful tenure as director, she dealt with deadly outbreaks of the H5N1 virus (better known as avian, or bird, flu), in 1997, and severe acute respiratory syndrome (SARS), in 2003. While she was lauded in some quarters for her handling of those crises, other observers questioned the speed and efficiency of her response. Even her detractors agree, however, that Chan was a credible choice to be the public face of the WHO. "She's smart, popular and … considerably more personable than the average WHO administrator," Bryan Walsh wrote for *Time* (July 25, 2006).

Education and Early Career

Margaret Fung Fu-chun was born in 1947 in Hong Kong. She initially intended to be a teacher, and between 1966 and 1969 she attended the Northcote College of Education, now part of the Hong Kong Institute of Education. Upon her graduation, she taught various subjects—including geography, math, and home economics—for a year at a high school in Hong Kong. She then moved to Canada because her husband-to-be, David Chan, had decided to study medicine at the University of Western Ontario. She enrolled at Brescia University College, the affiliated women's school, and earned a bachelor's degree, in 1973. Margaret Chan then embarked on her own medical studies at the University of Western Ontario. At the time preference was being given to applicants with liberal arts rather than science backgrounds, and some journalists have therefore characterized her admission to the school as particularly noteworthy. In 1977 she earned an M.D., and the following year, after completing an internship at Victoria Hospital in London, Ontario, she returned with her husband to Hong Kong. According to Lawrence K. Altman, M.D., in a "Doctor's World" column in the *New York Times* (August 9, 2005), Chan felt she had to return to Hong Kong when her mother-in-law fell ill. She told Altman, "'As a traditional Asian woman, I followed my husband." As a graduate of a foreign medical school, however, she found no opportunities available to her to pursue pediatrics, her primary interest. She therefore joined the department of health in Hong Kong as a medical officer in a division devoted to maternal and child health.

In 1985 Chan earned a master's degree in health administration at Singapore National University and received a promotion, to the rank of senior medical officer. In 1989 she became an assistant director of the department of health, and in 1994 she became the department's first female director. Chan, who was sent by the department to complete a management program at Harvard University in 1991, "also successfully demonstrated her managerial skills in both financial and human resource management," according to her official curriculum vitae, "running a complex organisation which consisted of 7,000 staff with a diverse cultural and professional background and a budget of nearly half a billion U.S. dollars a year."

Later Career

In May 1997 a three-year-old Chinese boy died after experiencing flu-like symptoms, and after local authorities could not identify the strain of virus that caused his illness, Chan was called in. "Every year the WHO will tell us what the circulating strains are. So when we get specimens from hospitals and clinics, we test them against our panels of reference," Chan explained to Ruth Mathewson of the *South China Morning Post* (August 22, 1997). "But in this case, we tested, we tested and we tested and we couldn't get any result. It was an atypical A virus and we couldn't type it. According to WHO protocol ... we referred it to [government laboratories in] the United Kingdom, Atlanta, and [the Netherlands]." Chan continued, "They tested it again, again, and again. It was very difficult—because they'd been testing it against human standards." Finally, scientists at the Centers for Disease Control, in Atlanta, Georgia, began comparing the sample to viruses known to infect pigs, birds, and horses. They made a chilling discovery: the boy had been infected with a form of a virus previously found only in birds. The deadly mutated virus was dubbed H5N1, but in the media it was more widely called avian flu or bird flu. Several more cases of the flu emerged by the end of the year, and Chan tried to calm—some say mislead—the public. In what has been widely called a serious blunder, she announced, according to the Singapore *Straits Times* (November 11, 2006), "I eat chicken every day, so do not worry."

The disease continued to spread, ultimately causing six human deaths by the end of the year. In December Chan ordered the slaughter of some 1.5 million chickens and ducks—all of the poultry on the island of Hong Kong—to prevent the further spread of the disease. "This is probably the single most difficult task I've ever had," Chan told the *London* (Ontario) *Free Press* (June 8, 1999). "We realized from the outset what impact a new influenza virus could have. The global community could have been very helpless."

In 2003 China again came to the attention of the world's health authorities when the origins of SARS were traced to a specific floor in a Kowloon hotel. Between January and April of that year, the illness—which typically involves a high fever, difficulty breathing, and a dry cough—killed more than 120 people. Although the Chinese government initially denied the severity of the problem, Chan was soon forced to call for the quarantine of infected patients in the earliest stages of the disease. She further warned that many people who appeared to recover were merely experiencing a delay of the virus's most dangerous stages and cautioned great care when releasing patients. As the crisis developed, Chan held daily press briefings presenting updates on SARS and the efforts to contain it, winning praise from journalists for her friendly demeanor and accessibility. By June 2003 the virus was said to be contained, and both the WHO and the U.S. government lifted the travel advisories they had placed on Hong Kong.

In addition to its human toll, however, the virus had forced the Hong Kong economy into a recession, and Chinese government officials were heavily criticized in the wake of the incident. Chan, despite her ability to charm reporters, was not exempt from the criticism. According to an article by Chris Yeung in the *South China Morning Post* (June 27, 2003), Chan had told a radio station in February that there was no need for alarm—after government authorities had already internally confirmed that 305 people, five of whom died, had been stricken with a rare illness. Chan later admitted during a government investigation that her department had been slow in dealing with SARS and that the outbreak might have been avoided had the first patient diagnosed with the illness not been allowed to leave the hospital prematurely; she broke down in tears several times during the hearings. The council ultimately voted to officially censure her. She told Lawrence K. Altman of the *New York Times* (May 18, 2003), "We had no idea what we were dealing with and we did not even know it was a virus." She told Altman that in dealing with SARS, the Chinese government had learned not to "be afraid to say you don't know what you are dealing with. SARS is too big for any country to handle single-handedly."

In July 2003 Chan announced she was resigning from the Hong Kong department of health to join the WHO. Chan had previously served on various WHO committees: organizer, forty-third session of the Regional Committee for the Western Pacific (1992); chairperson, forty-ninth session; moderator, Western Pacific Region Ministerial Roundtable on Social Safety Net (1999); vice chairperson, Working Group on Framework Convention on Tobacco Control (1999–2000); chairperson, Guidelines on Methodologies for Research & Evaluation of Traditional Medicine (2000); and chairperson, International Conference for Drug Regulatory Authorities 2001 Planning Committee (2000–2002). At the WHO Chan became director of the Department for Protection of Human Environment, a position with responsibilities in the areas of food safety, noise pollution, sanitation, and water quality, as well as Representative of the Director-General for Pandemic Influenza (a newly created position). In September 2005 Chan was named Assistant Director-General for Communicable Diseases—a crucial job that placed her in charge of quelling epidemics in their early stages. "We have to get every epidemiological signal," she told Mary Ann Benitez of the *South China Morning Post* (June 28, 2005). "If there are birds dying, what is causing that? If people come down with the flu, is it the usual influenza or some other type of flu?"

In 2005 the H5N1 virus returned to Southeast Asia and spread into Russia and Kazakhstan, inciting fears of a possible pandemic. Chan sprang into action, touring countries that had experienced the outbreak and negotiating with Roche Pharmaceuticals—the company that produces Tamiflu, an effective treatment for the illness—to provide the WHO with large quantities of the drug in the event they were needed. In hearings before the U.S. Congress, Chan told the House's International Relations Committee (December 7, 2005), "Conditions favoring the start of a pandemic are certain to persist, because the virus has become endemic in large parts of several Asian countries. The risk of more human cases will persist, and every single human case gives the virus a chance to undergo the changes it needs to ignite a pandemic." Chan told the committee, "We need a much better capacity to detect, to confirm and to report human cases in affected countries." In an interview published in the *Bulletin of the World Health Organization* (January 2006), Chan reiterated the bitter lesson of the 2003 SARS outbreak: "SARS was an excellent example in demonstrating to countries that because infectious diseases do not respect borders, there is no such thing as a localized outbreak. An outbreak in one country one day can very rapidly become a problem for countries on the other side of the world." By March 2006 more than 160 million birds had been killed—either by the virus or by health officials attempting to stop its spread to humans. Chan estimated that the virus had cost about $10 billion in damage and affected some 300 million farmers. Years later, in a May 2013 address to the World Health Assembly, Chan (by then in her second term as the WHO's director-general) recalled that, "Experiences during the SARS outbreak sparked extensive revisions of the International Health Regulations. These revisions gave the world a greatly strengthened legal instrument for detecting and responding to public health emergencies, including those caused by a new disease."

In May 2006 Lee Jong-wook of South Korea, the director-general of the WHO, died suddenly. The Chinese government nominated Chan as its choice for his successor, marking the first time China had nominated someone to head a U.N. agency. Past accusations resurfaced that during Chan's tenure with the Hong Kong department of health, the government had mishandled the early stages of the SARS outbreak. Chan told William Forman for the *Associated Press Worldstream* (August 5, 2006) that SARS had provided China with a "wake-up call" and that the country was ready to be a more open and responsible member of the global community. Responding to accusations that if elected head of the WHO, she would be prejudiced in favor of China, Chan told the *Japan Economic Newswire* (August 2, 2006), "If elected, I am not serving Hong Kong's or China's interests, but the world's interests. As an international civil servant, I [would] serve the interests of [all the] member states."

On November 9, 2006, the executive board of the WHO selected Chan to be the organization's next director-general. In her acceptance speech, Chan laid out her vision of the WHO's global health mandate, reiterating that "All regions, all countries, all people are equally important. [The WHO] is a health organization for the whole world. Our work must touch on the lives of everyone, everywhere, but we must focus our attention on the people in greatest need." She expressed particular concern for the health of those in poverty-stricken regions of Africa. Though some in Hong Kong protested the appointment (particularly those with loved ones affected by SARS), Lau Nai-Keung wrote for the South *China Morning Post* (November 17, 2006), "The WHO did not give Dr. Chan the job for political reasons: the only considerations were professional ones. This shows the vast difference in perception of the same incident [the SARS outbreak], between impartial and professional international observers, and some locals incited by populist sentiment." An editorial in the respected medical journal the *Lancet* (November 18–24, 2006) stated: "Chan's election is a great victory for China. Importantly, it brings 1.3 billion people directly into the global health system. This welcome transformation in China's engagement will require unprecedented levels of transparency, from sharing information to upholding human rights. Chan will be the leader of this new era of Chinese openness and accountability in health. The quality she will now need above all is imagination. We wish her every success."

When a swine flu (H1N1) virus that previously had infected pigs but only very rarely humans emerged in a new and much more virulent and contagious form in 2009, causing widespread alarm, Malcolm Moore commented in the London *Telegraph* (May 1, 2009) that, "Dr Chan has been holed up in a WHO 'war room' at its Geneva headquarters, which is running around the clock to co-ordinate an action plan against the virus." Moore quoted the manager of WHO's Strategic Health Operations center as saying that Chan was "very much driving the process" of responding to a possible pandemic. Moore recalled that Chan's media performance during the 2003 SARS outbreak had been "dazzling."

The global pandemic that had been feared did not materialize. In the aftermath the WHO, which had been criticized at first as being too slow to respond, was instead accused of over-reacting, and it was alleged that—as James LeFanu of the London *Telegraph* (November 17, 2013) wrote, citing an investigation by the *British Medical Journal*—"key scientists advising the World Health Organisation on planning for an pandemic" had too close ties to the pharmaceutical industry. Chan announced that the WHO would establish "stricter rules of engagement with industry" but denied that commercial interests had influenced her decision-making. Other observers focused on a broader concern. Writing in the *New York Times* (January 29, 2010), Thomas Abraham asserted that, "The non-debate over whether there is a new type of flu sweeping the world has detracted from a real issue: The world's poorest countries have yet to receive the vaccine they were promised, while many of the world's rich countries are wondering what to do with vaccine supplies their citizens do not want," thus "exposing the fault lines that divide the haves from the have nots in today's globalized world." Abraham noted that Chan, along with U.N. secretary general Ban Ki-moon, was attempting to bring more fairness to vaccine distribution.

Reflecting on the course of the 2009 swine flu scare, Gardiner Harris and Lawrence K. Altman noted in the *New York Times* (May 9, 2009) that in 2005, "rules adopted by the W.H.O. gave the director general complete authority to change the global pandemic alert level," and they quoted Dr. David L. Heymann, who had recently left the WHO to become chairman of the United Kingdom's Health Protection Agency, as saying that Chan was "the first director general who has been able to wield these new powers. ... She has the most powerful mandate ever.'"

"If we let down our guard, slacken our efforts, problems that are so close to being brought under control will come roaring back."

In July 2011, as a candidate for reappointment, Chan had issued a statement entitled "Dr. Chan's Vision on WHO Priorities and Strategies," Chan vowed to give special attention to the following six issues: health systems and capacity building; control of chronic noncommunicable diseases at both the population-wide and individual levels; health security (achieving collective security against the spread of infectious diseases and other threats that can cause public health emergencies of international concern); health development for poverty reduction, especially to improve women's and children's health; access to medical products, with special attention to quality and cost; and priority work for vulnerable groups, including women and the people of Africa. Chan wrote that a "major achievement for WHO occurred with the May 2011 adoption of a framework of action supporting pandemic influenza preparedness through better surveillance and risk assessment and more equitable distribution of the benefits of vaccines, antiviral medicines and diagnostic tests. The need now is to ensure that recommended actions are fully implemented."

Chan's first term as director-general ended on June 2012. Marking its conclusion, she released *Keeping Promises; Accountability of Dr Margaret Chan during Her First Term as WHO Director-General,* in which she assessed her own performance and that of the WHO against the agenda of six personal commitments she had set in 2006, as a candidate for the position. As she noted, these were "not always formal WHO priorities, which are established by Member States." The report documented remarkable progress in some areas while not glossing over shortcomings; of the goal of complete polio eradication, for example, Chan wrote, "This commitment has not been met," and then discussed the formidable obstacles remaining and plans to address them. At the end of the report, Chan discussed organizational initiatives, noting that she had "established a Global Policy Group, which gives all Regional Directors a formal platform for jointly shaping WHO policies, solving problems, and promoting greater coherence throughout the Organization," and that she had instituted "managerial safeguards" and "budgetary discipline" even while expanding the WHO's work with a "growing number of intergovernmental negotiating bodies."

The World Health Assembly appointed Chan for a second five-year term on May 23, 2012. Her new term began on July 1, 2012, and will continue until June 30, 2017. In her acceptance speech Chan pledged to "improve the health of the most vulnerable." She remarked, "In my view, universal coverage is the single most powerful concept that public health has to offer. It is a powerful equalizer. It is the best way to cement the gains made during the past decade." She added that the "biggest challenge over the next five years will be to lead WHO in ways that will help maintain the unprecedented momentum for better health that marked the start of this century. The future of funding for international health development is uncertain. If we let down our guard, slacken our efforts, problems that are so close to being brought under control will come roaring back."

Margaret Chan was made an officer of the Order of the British Empire by Queen Elizabeth II, in 1997, the same year in which she was named a fellow of public health medicine at Britain's Royal College of Physicians. In 1999 King Bhumibol Adulyadej of Thailand awarded Chan the Prince Mahidol Award in the field of public health, for her leadership in the control of the outbreak of avian influenza in Hong Kong. An honorary degree of Doctor of Science was conferred on Chan by her alma mater, the University of Western Ontario, in the same year, for her contribution to public health.

In his August 9, 2005, profile of Margaret Chan in the *New York Times*, Lawrence K. Altman reported that she and David Chan had married before entering medical school. The Chans have a son, Anthony, who practices law. David Chan, an ophthalmologist, became the chief executive of the Hong Kong Eye Hospital in Yaumatei.

Further Reading

Associated Press Aug. 5, 2006, Nov. 8, 2006

Bulletin of the World Health Organization Vol. 84, no. 1 (January 2006)

Japan Economic Newswire Aug. 2, 2006

Lancet p1, Vol. 368, no. 9549 (Nov. 18–24, 2006): p1743

London (Ontario) *Free Press* Jun. 8, 1999

New York Times p15 May 18, 2003, Aug. 9, 2005, May 9, 2009, pA1, Jan. 29, 2010

South China Morning Post p17 Aug. 22, 1997, p4 Jan. 1, 1998, p5 Aug. 31, 1998, p16 Feb. 5, 2001, p4 Jul. 20, 2003, p16 Aug. 22, 2003, p3 Jun. 28, 2005, Aug. 8, 2006, p18 Nov. 17, 2006

(Singapore) *Straits Times* Nov. 11, 2006

(London) *Telegraph* May 1, 2009, Nov. 17, 2013; *Time* magazine Jul. 25, 2006

Desmond-Hellmann, Susan

Oncologist, translational scientist, foundation CEO, university chancellor, biotech executive

---

Born: 1957, Napa, California, United States

On December 17, 2013, Dr. Susan Desmond-Hellmann was named chief executive officer of the Bill and Melinda Gates Foundation, effective May 1, 2014. At the time of her appointment, Desmond-Hellmann was serving as the chancellor of the University of California at San Francisco (UCSF); she was the first woman to hold that position, which she assumed on August 3, 2009. The University of California at San Francisco is among the top healthcare training facilities in the United States, and Desmond-Hellmann is an alumna of the residency program there. In her announcement of Desmond-Hellmann's resignation as chancellor, University of California President Janet Napolitano specified that Desmond-Hellmann—the Arthur and Toni Rembe Rock Distinguished Professor as well as chancellor at UCSF — would retain her faculty appointment and remain an active member of the UCSF community.

Desmond-Hellmann had returned to UCSF to train a new generation of oncologists (as well as other physicians, researchers, and pharmacists) after presiding over product development at the drug developer Genentech. There she oversaw the production of several of the most effective cancer-fighting drugs on the market. As Julian Guthrie wrote for the *San Francisco Chronicle* (April 11, 2010), Desmond-Hellmann's successes at Genentech had "made her a millionaire hundreds of times over"; she could have retired, but instead she was drawn by UCSF's potential to foster important and life-saving research. A similar motivation, "to contribute to creating a more equitable world," led her to become the third chief executive officer of the Bill and Melinda Gates Foundation, and the first to come to that position from outside Microsoft. According to Danielle Ivory, writing in the *New York Times* (December 17, 2013), as CEO of the Gates Foundation, Desmond-Hellmann "will oversee a $40 billion endowment that tackles major global issues like public health, poverty and education."

Advancements in technology have led to better drugs for cancer patients, but the cost of research—among a host of other factors—has driven up prices on the most effective drugs, which has adversely affected patient treatment. "We need to make drug development faster, cheaper, and more predictable," Desmond-Hellmann told Guthrie. "We need to get to the point where when a patient hears the words, 'You have cancer,' the patient also hears, 'And here is what we have for you.'"

Desmond-Hellmann, who spent two years in the late 1980s conducting AIDS research in Uganda with her husband, has been the recipient of a number of awards and honors. When she was with Genentech, *Fortune* magazine listed her among the "Top 50 Most Powerful Women in Business" in 2001 and from 2003 to 2008. In 2005 and again in 2006, the *Wall Street Journal* selected Desmond-Hellmann for its annual "50 Women to Watch" list. In 2007 she was inducted into the Biotech Hall of Fame, and in 2009 she was awarded the Edison Achievement Award for leadership in innovation. In 2010 Desmond-Hellmann was inducted into the American Academy of Arts and Sciences and elected to the Institute of Medicine.

Education and Early Career

The second of seven children, Susan Desmond was born in 1957 in Napa, California, and was raised in Reno, Nevada. Her father, Frank Desmond, a retail pharmacist, ran a Keystone Owl Rexall Drugstore when Desmond-Hellmann was growing up. Her mother, Jennie Desmond, a former English teacher, is a breast cancer survivor (as is Desmond-Hellmann's elder sister).

Susan Desmond worked as a bookkeeper in her father's pharmacy. She enjoyed watching him interact with customers, but the example of the family physician, Dr. Noah Smirnoff, especially inspired her. Before high school, she knew that she wanted to be a doctor. It was a career path that fit Desmond-Hellmann's self-described "nerdy" nature, which she felt was embraced and encouraged by her family. "There was a lot of emphasis on being a good student, on studying, and discussion about science and about medicine," she told Joanna Breitstein for the website PharmExec (April 1, 2006). "When I was growing up, I was very much the nerdy student. I admired people who were smart."

After graduating as valedictorian from her high school, Desmond enrolled in the University of Nevada, Reno, so that she could live at home and save money. She finished her undergraduate premedical degree in three years and stayed in Reno to earn her medical degree beginning in 1978. She planned to pursue sports medicine, but a month-long rotation with oncologist Dr. Stephen Hall at the Veterans Administration Hospital in Reno changed her mind. Desmond shifted her focus to internal medicine and then oncology.

When it came time to apply for an internship and a residency, UCSF was Desmond's first choice. Despite her stellar grades, winning a spot at UCSF was a long shot—most of the students in the applicant pool came from Ivy League schools. Lloyd "Holly" Smith, the former chair of the UCSF Department of Medicine, recalled Desmond's application to Guthrie: "Sue came from the University of Nevada, an institution we hadn't had any experience with. We took a chance on her because the university had written these letters filled with superlative descriptions. They said they had not seen a student like her."

Despite the support, Desmond felt like an underdog because of her background and gravitated toward another state-school student, Nicholas Hellmann from the University of Kentucky, who would later, in 1987, become her husband. Desmond distinguished herself by becoming board-certified in both internal medicine and oncology and serving as an assistant professor of hematology-oncology at UCSF. Like her husband—an infectious disease specialist—and a number of other researchers in San Francisco during the 1980s, Desmond-Hellmann was concerned about the deadly AIDS epidemic. In particular, her concern focused on Kaposi's sarcoma, a viral cancer common in patients with AIDS. To educate herself about the epidemic and help fight it, in 1988 she sought and earned a master's degree in public health, focusing on epidemiology and biostatistics, from the University of California, Berkeley.

In 1989 Desmond-Hellmann and her husband received an offer from the Rockefeller Foundation, one of the oldest foundations devoted to public health, to study the heterosexual transmission of HIV/AIDS in Uganda. For two years, Desmond-Hellmann and her husband lived in Uganda, where they conducted research at the Uganda Cancer Institute at Makerere University in Kampala, where they were also visiting faculty members. "It completely changed what I expected of myself," she told Carolyn Johnson of the experience in an interview for ABC 7 News, KGO-TV San Francisco (April 5, 2012). "I felt like I was so privileged and was incredibly fortunate compared to everyone I met in Uganda so I raised the personal bar of what I expected of myself in a powerful way." The couple returned to the United States in 1991, and Desmond-Hellmann opened up a private oncology practice in Nick Hellmann's home state of Kentucky. But Desmond-Hellmann was unsatisfied, particularly with the treatment options available to her patients. "We needed better weapons against cancer," she told a reporter for the journal *Nature Reviews: Drug Discovery* (July 2005), "and I wanted to be a part of that."

On returning to the United States, Nick Hellmann was offered a job with the biopharmaceutical company Bristol-Myers Squibb, in Connecticut. In 1993 Desmond-Hellmann began to work for the company as well. As associate director of clinical cancer research, she helped to develop the breast cancer drug Taxol (the same drug her mother would later use after being diagnosed with breast cancer). Taxol, officially approved by the Food and Drug Administration (FDA) to treat early-stage breast cancer in 1998, was a breakthrough in what is known as "targeted drug" therapy, which "aimed at destroying tumors without the side effects of traditional chemotherapy," Alex Berenson reported for the *New York Times* (July 12, 2005). Government officials and patients were outraged by the cost of Taxol, which in 1992 was $4,000 a year. (Drug prices, particularly prices for anticancer drugs, have risen significantly since Taxol; as Berenson pointed out, in 2002 Bristol-Myers Squibb and ImClone Systems charged as much as $100,000 a year for the advanced-stage colon-cancer drug Erbitux.) Still, Desmond-Hellmann was exhilarated by the difficult work, and in 1995, she was recruited by the biotechnology corporation Genentech in San Francisco.

Desmond-Hellmann began her career with Genentech as a clinical scientist, where she applied the work of doctors Frederic de Sauvage, now vice president of molecular oncology at Genentech, and Dan Eaton, now senior director of protein chemistry, to clinical study. De Sauvage and Eaton identified the hormone thrombopoietin as a key regulator of blood platelets. The resulting drug was unsuccessful, but Desmond-Hellmann quickly distinguished herself among her colleagues. Within a year of her hiring, she was put in charge of all clinical trials. After that, Arthur D. Levinson, the former CEO of Genentech and current chair of the board at Apple, told Guthrie: "Every six to twelve months, I was promoting her. Her instincts were excellent."

In 1999 Desmond-Hellmann became executive vice president of development and product operations; in March 2004, she became president of product development. During her time at Genentech, the company became the number-one producer of anticancer drug treatments in the United States, largely thanks to her work and willingness to approach cancer treatments in a new way. Interviewed for *Nature Reviews: Drug Discovery*, Desmond-Hellmann herself ascribed her success at Genentech to her "try anything" attitude. Genentech, considered by many to be an upstart in the pharmaceutical industry, became the steward of a new era in cancer treatment. Of the early research that she saw to fruition, Desmond-Hellmann told Guthrie, "The period from 1997 to 2001 was an amazing time in oncology. It was a special time because there was such an unmet need." Among the drugs that Desmond-Hellmann and Genentech developed were the breast cancer drug Herceptin, which many consider to be her crowning achievement, and Avastin, which was originally developed to treat colon cancer. Other drugs that received FDA approval during Desmond-Hellmann's time with Genentech include Lucentis, which treats the "wet" form of macular degeneration; Tarceva, for advanced nonsmall-cell lung cancer; Rituxan, for certain types of non-Hodgkin's lymphoma; and Xolair, to treat allergy-related asthma.

The development of Herceptin was revolutionary because it was the first drug to target a particular mutation, associated with a specific type of breast cancer, in which cells overproduce a protein called HER2. Before the drug, the same treatments were applied to all patients with breast cancer, though researchers and doctors now understand that there are several distinct forms of the disease that require different, personalized therapies. HER2-positive breast cancer was considered to be one of the most deadly forms, but with Herceptin, it has become one of the most treatable. According to a number of sources, Desmond-Hellmann's father shares a story in which he and his wife, who was receiving chemotherapy at the time, overheard a doctor talking to another patient whose tumor had recurred. The doctor comforted the woman with "good news"; he was prescribing her an "incredible new drug called Herceptin." Pointing to Jennie Desmond, the doctor added, "You can thank the daughter of this lady for bringing it to you." The drug, like other anticancer medications, is expensive, however. Herceptin cost patients $20,000 per year in 1998, and by 2012 it cost some $70,000 per year, according to the Intenet publisher Medical News Today (MNT).

Avastin was the first drug to work by effectively blocking the blood cells that feed cancerous tumors. This restricts the tumor's growth and reduces the cancer's ability to spread to other areas of the body. Avastin, approved by the FDA to treat colon and lung cancer in 2006, was also approved through an accelerated approval process to treat metastatic breast cancer in 2008. The FDA revoked the latter decision in 2011, citing potentially life-threatening risks that might outweigh the drug's benefits. Doctors and patients can, however, still choose to use the drug to treat certain cancers. As Medical News Today reported on January 25, 2013, Avastin—the only medicine with FDA approval to treat patients with metastatic colorectal cancer combined with intravenous 5FU-based chemotherapy as first treatment, as well as treatment for people whose cancer has intensified after chemotherapy by itself—has also been approved by the FDA as a treatment for people whose cancer has intensified after an Avastin-based regimen.

Later Career

Genentech merged with the Swiss pharmaceutical giant Roche in March 2009. Desmond-Hellmann resigned her position with the company in April, though Roche executives reportedly asked her to stay. Later that year, on August 3, 2009, Desmond-Hellmann became the ninth chancellor of UCSF. During her tenure, Desmond-Hellmann looked for ways to combat the school's increasing financial troubles with budget cuts while maintaining the funding necessary to run a research-based institution. Given the lack of funding for UCSF within the University of California (UC) system—only 5 percent of UCSF's budget comes from state funds —Desmond-Hellmann took steps to make the school more autonomous by securing funding from a variety of new sources. She even began the fundraising initiative by donating $1 million of her own money. Unlike its sister schools under the UC umbrella, UCSF does not have an undergraduate program, and tuition accounts for only 1 percent of the school's annual budget. (Most schools raise tuition or increase enrollment in the face of financial woes.) UCSF derives most of its revenues from its patient-care institutions, such as medical centers, its new children's hospital, and a number of clinics owned and operated by the school. Desmond-Hellmann promoted an even stronger focus on those efforts. Denise Grady, writing in the *New York Times* (October 10, 2011), indicated that UCSF's new Mission Bay campus, devoted to medical and biotech research, figured prominently in Desmond-Hellmann's strategy to "supplement the usual sources of income like patient fees, grants and tuition by increasing collaborations between the university and the biotech companies that have sprung up in the Bay Area — many of them spinoffs from research that began at the university."

Desmond-Hellmann has expressed an interest in partnering research facilities with pharmaceutical companies, and encouraging students to begin their own start-ups. "Increasingly, big biotech and big pharma are coming straight to academia for innovation. We're testing this," she told Kerry Dolan for *Forbes* (30 Apr. 2012). Desmond-Hellmann added that the school had already partnered with Pfizer. In addition to working directly with UCSF scientists, Pfizer provides funds for research projects. The program has been an experiment, Desmond-Hellmann noted. "I don't know if this will work," she told Dolan, "but we're going to test it and we're going to measure outcomes and I'm very convinced that Pfizer and others will come back for more if it is successful." Noteworthy among UCSF's private fundraising efforts is a $60 million–dollar endowment for the Discovery Fellows Program, funded by Sequoia Capital chairman Michael Moritz and his wife, Harriet Heyman, together with UCSF; the Discovery Fellows Program is the largest endowed program for Ph.D. students in the history of the University of California.

In 2011 the school received $532.8 million from the U.S. National Institutes of Health, making UCSF the recipient of the largest grant among public institutions, second overall to the private Johns Hopkins University in Baltimore. UCSF's Clinical and Translational Science Institute (CTSI), established in 2006 with a $108 million grant from the NIH, received a second five-year award of $112 million in 2011. (Translational research turns basic-science discoveries into treatments for patients.) UCSF was also one of the leading institutional recipients of science-based stimulus funds under the American Recovery and Reinvestment Act. Nevertheless, in a January 2012 presentation to the University of California's Board of Regents, Desmond-Hellmann projected that as currently structured in relation to the rest of the UC system, UCSF would be losing money by 2015—the same year the school is scheduled to open a brand new medical center at Mission Bay. "What we have here," she said in reference to UCSF's current relationship to UC, as quoted by Nanette Asimov for the *San Francisco Chronicle* (January 20, 2012), "is not sustainable." According to Asimov, Desmond-Hellmann further pointed out that UCSF devotes the most money to the UC system, yet sees the least in return. She also proposed her solution: a system in which UCSF maintains a more flexible relationship with UC, without seceding or becoming a private institution but having its own board of directors.

"We need to get to the point where when a patient hears the words, 'You have cancer,' the patient also hears, 'And here is what we have for you.'"

Among Desmond-Hellmann's signature contributions as chancellor was establishing precision medicine as a goal for UCSF. Precision medicine—based on collection and analysis of massive amounts of data (genomic, molecular, environmental and clinical)—seeks to identify the root causes of diseases and to develop targeted therapies to treat them. In May 2013 Desmond-Hellmann convened a "summit" conference, Precision Medicine: A Revolution in Health, bringing together the world's leaders in precision medicine to spur the application of tremendous recent advances in technology, genetics and biomedical research to the acute needs of patients. In a news release about the conference, Kristen Boles quoted Desmond-Hellmann as saying, "So much of that knowledge is available right now in our health records and genetic data. Now we need the tools to access it, so we can make sense of that data and truly provide personal, predictive, precise care to our patients."

Accepting the CEO position at the Gates Foundation, Desmond-Hellmann was poised to take on global challenges in public health, poverty and education. The foundation works in more than a hundred countries, including the United States. Danielle Ivory noted that in 2012 the foundation had awarded more than $3 billion in grants to hundreds of groups, including a 1.5 billion grant to the GAVI Alliance (formerly known as the Global Alliance for Vaccines and Immunisation) to expand children's access to immunization in poor countries. The foundation has sponsored large-scale programs to combat malaria and polio. According to Ivory, the foundation had recently announced plans to contribute to a $17 million pool of grants for National Public Radio to increase coverage of education and global health and development issues. In other educational initiatives, the foundation generously supports a United Negro College Fund scholarship program

($1.37 billion, according to the foundation's Web site) and effective teaching development programs in Tampa, Memphis, and Pittsburgh, among others. "Sue's background in public health policy, research and development, and higher education, make her an exceptional fit for this role. She impressed us as an innovator and an outstanding leader and manager," said Bill Gates, co-chair of the foundation.

At the Biotechnology Industry Organization, Desmond-Hellmann served on the executive committee of the board of directors from 2001 until 2009. From 2004 to 2009, she served on the corporate board of the Santa Clara–based biotech company Affymetrix. Desmond-Hellmann served a three-year term (2005–2008) as a member of the American Association for Cancer Research board of directors. She was appointed to the California Academy of Sciences board of trustees in 2008, and in 2009, she joined the Federal Reserve Bank of San Francisco's Economic Advisory Council for a three-year term. In December 2010 Desmond-Hellmann was appointed to the board of directors of Procter & Gamble (P&G), and she was elected a Trustee of the Howard Hughes Medical Institute in November 2012. She joined the board of directors at Facebook in March 2013. She also serves on the California Academy of Sciences board of trustees and the Albert and Mary Lasker Foundation's board of directors. In June 2011, Princeton University awarded her an honorary Doctor of Science degree.

Nicholas Hellmann is currently the executive vice president of medical and scientific affairs at the Elizabeth Glaser Pediatric AIDS Foundation. Susan Desmond-Hellmann is a sports enthusiast; she skies, mountain bikes, and wakes up before five in the morning on weekdays to run.

Further Reading:

Bill and Melinda Gates Foundation Web site Dec. 17, 2013

Forbes Apr. 30, 2012

KGO-TV San Francisco Apr.5, 2012

Medical News Today Oct. 1, 2012

Nature Reviews: Drug Discovery Vol. 4, no.7 (July 2005): p532, Vol.10, no. 3 (March 2011): p170

New York Times Jul. 12, 2005, Oct. 10, 2011, Apr. 12, 2013, Dec. 17, 2013

Pharmaceutical Executive, Apr. 1, 2006

San Francisco Chronicle Apr. 11, 2010, Jan. 20, 2012

Greenfield, Susan

British neuroscientist, lecturer, writer, broadcaster

Born: 1950, London, United Kingdom

"I wish there were more dialogue between [philosophers] and neuroscientists," the British neuroscientist Susan Greenfield told Aisling Irwin for the *Times Higher Education Supplement* (December 16, 1994). "The philosophers ask big questions such as 'what is consciousness?' The scientists still find this really embarrassing. They know so much about the brain that they are daunted by the big questions."

As one of the most visible proponents of "consciousness studies," a field of study which seeks to establish a relationship between subjective consciousness and the brain's neurochemistry, Greenfield has spent much of her career promoting such dialogue. Her studies of enzymes in the brain have contributed significantly to the understanding of both Parkinson's and Alzheimer's disease. Greenfield is familiar to the British public from her numerous lectures, television series, books, and newspaper articles. In early 2000 Greenfield was named a Commander of the Order of the British Empire (CBE) by the British government, and in April 2001 she accepted an appointment as life peer in Britain's House of Lords. She is currently a Professor of Pharmacology at Oxford University.

Education and Early Career

Susan Adele Greenfield was born in London, England, on October 1, 1950, and she grew up in Chiswick, a neighborhood in West London. Her father, Reginald Myer Greenfield, was an electrician. Her paternal grandfather had come to England from Poland; for a time, before falling into financial ruin, he managed a London chocolate factory. Susan Greenfield's mother, Doris Margaret Winifred Greenfield, was a dancer and a chorus girl who belonged to the Entertainments National Service Association (ENSA), a troupe that presented shows to British troops during World War II. Doris Greenfield eventually left ENSA to raise her daughter. (More than a decade later, the Greenfields also had a son.) Susan Greenfield has repeatedly expressed gratitude towards her parents in interviews; she told Christian Tyler of the *Financial Times* (August 2, 1997) that hers was "an unconventional, carpe diem, noisy, fun-loving sort of family; a lovely atmosphere of everything being possible, and being a hoot anyway." Although her father was consistently employed, she recalled to Robert Crampton for the London *Times* (May 2, 2001) that "we were always broke, it was always 'if only we had more money, we could do this or this.'"

Greenfield's mother had broken off a privileged education in order to pursue a career in entertainment, and she instilled in her daughter a love of learning. In fact, Greenfield has credited a remark by her mother—who once observed that neither of them knew what the other saw when looking at the color red—with piquing her initial interest in consciousness studies. Greenfield won a grant to the private Godolphin and Latymer School for Girls in West London (her mother had attended the school as well), where she received high grades in Greek, Latin, ancient history, and mathematics. Learning Greek, she has said, provided her with a solid foundation for her later study of neuroscience: "If you can do Greek grammar, you can do anything," she explained to Andrew Cohen for *Worldlink* (March 1, 2001). "There is beauty and symmetry and order to it."

Greenfield's accomplishments at Godolphin and Latymer subsequently earned her a scholarship to study classics at Oxford University's St. Hilda's College. She was the first in her family to go to college. Before leaving for Oxford, in 1970, Greenfield spent six months on a kibbutz in Israel. (Her father was Jewish; her mother was Christian.) It was the first time she had been out of England.

While she matriculated at Oxford as a classics major, Greenfield initially intended to study philosophy. Her interest in philosophy soon yielded to one in psychology, which she studied for a year. Finally, after being inspired by a science class dissection of a brain, she began to pursue neuroscience. "I got very interested in the physiological aspects of the brain," she told Aisling Irwin. "I didn't know so much was known." Two professors in the school's pharmacology department, David Smith and William Paton, advised her closely, and at the end of her first year studying science, Greenfield won a scholarship to study at another Oxford college, St. Hugh's. At St. Hugh's she researched acetylcholinesterase, an enzyme that Dr. Smith had found in cerebrospinal fluid (found only in the brain and the spinal cord). Greenfield confirmed Smith's hypothesis that the enzyme was emanating from the brain; she also discovered that it affected communication between cells in the brain and that it was missing from the cerebrospinal fluid of those suffering from Parkinson's disease. In 1977 Greenfield completed a doctorate in brain chemistry.

For the next seven years, Greenfield worked at Oxford as a fellow, and in 1985 she was named university lecturer in synaptic pharmacology and fellow and tutor in medicine at Lincoln College, Oxford. In 1993 Greenfield played a leading role in a movement to gain more full professorships for women. (At the time less than five percent of full professors at Oxford were women.) She also worked as a sexual harassment officer at Lincoln College.

Later Career

In 1994 Greenfield became the first woman to give the Royal Institution's annual Christmas Lectures, which present advances in science to the public. The Christmas Lectures were first held in 1825; the chosen lecturers have included such prominent scientists as the physicist Michael Faraday, the astronomer Carl Sagan, and the evolutionary biologist Richard Dawkins. "I'd like to be judged on my own worth but it would be stupid to say that I want the fact that I am female to be ignored," she told Aisling Irwin. "I am very excited but I am conscious of what it means. Another bastion has fallen." The lectures, which focused on different methods of studying the brain, how it works, how it develops, and how it remembers, were broadcast on BBC2, a television channel, for five days, beginning on December 28. They showcased Greenfield's knack for explaining "heavy science" in accessible terms.

Following the lecture series, Greenfield appeared in a spate of television series and radio spots and began contributing articles to newspapers. (She credits her study of the classics for her ability to write better than many of her contemporaries.) In 1995 she published *Journey to the Centres of the Mind*, an analysis of consciousness based on recent discoveries about the communication between neurons. In *Journey* Greenfield presented her theory of consciousness, a central tenet of which states that clusters of neurons create emotions that compete against each other within the brain.

When she wasn't explaining her ideas to the public, Greenfield headed a research group dedicated to extending her discoveries about Parkinson's disease. Her research continued to focus on the enzyme she had studied as a student, acetylcholinesterase. She also surmised that the field of consciousness studies, because it focuses on the connection between subjective consciousness and the physical brain, held the key to understanding Parkinson's disease. Greenfield also found similarities between the degeneration of brain cells in patients with Parkinson's and those with Alzheimer's disease. The research group Greenfield headed included psychologists, pharmacologists, and cell biologists, and had equal numbers of men and women. "There's a cross-fertilisation of ideas," she told Aisling Irwin. "It's much richer." At Oxford Greenfield remained a synaptic pharmacology lecturer until 1996, when she was promoted to the post of professor of pharmacology.

In spite of her serious research, several of Greenfield's scientist peers felt that she was spending too much time on popular radio or television shows. "Some of them grumble about pop science," she explained to Geraldine Murray for *Scotland on Sunday* (August 17, 1997), "but I just want people to know that science is exciting and that not everything is known yet. I also think it's important that people—especially young women—realise you don't have to be a grey-suited man to be a scientist." In response to charges that she was "dumbing down" difficult concepts to make them more palatable to the populace, she told Decca Aitkenhead of the London *Guardian* (June 8, 1998): "This concept of dumbing down … it makes me so angry. All you are doing is reaching out. It's not cheapening or trivialising the work. How can people be so lofty? If you are helping some housewife on a housing estate to understand what Prozac is doing to her brain, what's wrong with that?" In early 1997 Greenfield appeared on the popular television show *Desert Island Discs* in which participants are asked to select the eight songs they would bring with them if marooned on a desert island. "The pinnacle of my career was being asked to do *Desert Island Discs*," she told Aitkenhead. Among the songs she chose were Beethoven's Ninth Symphony (a frequent selection on the show) and the Rolling Stones' song "Brown Sugar."

In 1995 Greenfield was elected to the Gresham Chair of Physic in London, a position that entailed giving six public lectures a year for the City of London. She served in the position until 1999. From late 1997 until early 2000, she wrote a fortnightly column for one of London's main Sunday newspapers, the *Independent*. Greenfield has used her popular platform to address issues pertaining to youth culture and its effects on the next generation of scientists. In her view many young people opt for instant gratification over intellectual pursuits, thus allowing a barrage of popular images to replace their own creativity. In 2008 her interest in how young people think and feel was further discussed in her book, *ID: The Quest for Identity in the 21ˢᵗ Century*. Greenfield has frequently decried the use of illegal drugs because of their harmful effects on the brain, and has been outspoken in opposing the decriminalization of marijuana; in interviews she has recommended sex or laughter as alternative means of recreation. In May 1999 she was a presenter on a radio program entitled *Turn On, Turn Off,* about the brain and how it is affected by drug use.

While Greenfield has had extensive contact with young people entering the scientific professions, she thinks that many lack the thirst for innovation: "We are indeed producing scientists; but I would call them technologists, people who can press buttons, interact with machines," she told Christian Tyler. In 1997 she was listed as one of the "50 most powerful women in Britain" by the London *Guardian* (May 27, 1997).

Three years after delivering the Christmas Lectures at the Royal Institution, Greenfield published a companion book, *The Human Brain: A Guided Tour* (1997). A paperback edition was published in 1998, and the book has since been translated into 14 languages. Both the paperback and the hardcover edition made England's best-seller list. "*The Human Brain: A Guided Tour* will appeal as a Baedeker to the brain, even to the non-scientist," Roger Bannister wrote in his review of the book for the London *Times* (July 10, 1997).

In 1997 Greenfield and a colleague, Dr. David Vaux, co-founded a company called Synaptica to fund their research into Parkinson's and Alzheimer's without applying for grant money, an oftentimes arduous process. In founding Synaptica Greenfield and Vaux received financial backing from Oxford University, as well as funds from venture capitalists. Synaptica patented several of the discoveries Greenfield's research group had made. (In 2000 Synaptica patented a brain molecule that researchers thought might prove helpful in finding treatments for the diseases.)

In June 1998 Greenfield was appointed director of the Royal Institution; she was the first female director in the organization's history. As part of her compensation, she was given an apartment in the Institution building, located in London's luxurious Mayfair neighborhood. As director Greenfield established a Science Media Centre and a Young Scientist's Centre; inaugurated a sister organization in Adelaide (RiAus) to serve the whole of Australia; expanded the public events schedule from the occasional public lecture several times a year to, often, three events a week; and assisted with a major refurbishment and expansion of the Royal Institution's building (including nanotechnology labs, web-streaming facilities, restaurants, and interactive exhibition spaces). According to Matthew Bell of the *Independent* (June 30, 2013), Greenfield's tenure at the Royal Institution "ended abruptly in [January] 2010, when she was dismissed because of mounting debts. She had overseen a major refurbishment, and sued for sexual discrimination, but settled out of court."

Greenfield saw her prestige increase significantly in 2000, beginning with her CBE honor. That summer she published *The Private Life of the Brain*, a book that, like *Journey to the Centres of the Mind*, analyzes consciousness as a patchwork of neural networks competing against each other for dominance. *The Private Life of the Brain* was praised for its simple and direct language, and for its skill in presenting complex and abstract ideas to a lay audience. "I expect many people will not only buy this book, but will read it too," David Papineau wrote for the London *Independent* (June 10, 2000). "If so, they will find much to enjoy in Greenfield's expertise about the chemical workings of the brain." Papineau nevertheless faulted Greenfield for failing to explain adequately how subjective thoughts and feelings arise from neural networks. Also in 2000, Greenfield hosted *Brain Story*, a critically acclaimed six-episode television series on BBC2. She followed the television series with a book of the same title. "*Brain Story* is delightfully written, lavishly illustrated and is targeted at anyone with even a casual interest in the workings of the brain," Keith Sutherland wrote for the *Times Higher Education Supplement* (October 13, 2000). In late 2000 Greenfield was named "Woman of the Year" in a London *Observer* readers' poll.

In April 2001 the House of Lords Appointments Commission named Greenfield a life peer, one of 15 people ennobled into the House of Lords, the United Kingdom's upper chamber of Parliament, that year. Members of the House of Lords—which is much less powerful than the House of Commons and which serves chiefly as a forum for public debate—are appointed rather than elected. Greenfield, who claims to have voted at various times for both the Labour and the Conservative party, applied for the position on the advice of friends after she became tired of "waving my arms about in lectures and newspaper columns about science funding and nothing ever happening," as she explained to Robert Crampton. Among her more notable gestures since joining the House of Lords was her decision to reject a call for a European cultural and scientific boycott of Israel in protest of the Israeli government's policies towards the Palestinians. "The idea of an academic boycott on Israel is deplorable and reflects British academia in a very bad light because the reasons for it are wrong and groundless," Greenfield said, as quoted by Sharon Sadeh for *Haaretz* (October 12, 2002). Also during 2001 Greenfield served as president of the Association for Science Education.

In September 2003 Greenfield published *Tomorrow's People: How Technology is Changing the Way We Think and Feel*, predicting that people in the future could lose their individuality, be completely dependent on computers, no longer read and write, and rearrange their lives around new technological developments. The book received mixed reviews. Bryan Appleyard harshly criticized the book, which, he believed, had a thesis similar to that of his 1992 work *Understanding the Present*: "that developments in science and technology may have negative effects on human life, either reducing us to passive consumers or providing us with the means of destroying ourselves," as he wrote for the *New Statesman* (October 6, 2003). Moreover, Appleyard considered Greenfield's book to be riddled with poor writing and confusing arguments. "The problem is that in her own field, the brain, Greenfield is on firm ground. But, in areas such as politics, sociology and history, she is pure dinner party." John Cornwell, however, reviewing *Tomorrow's People* for the Sunday *Times* (September 21, 2003), deemed the book important. "Greenfield has maddening gaps in her grasp of intellectual history, not least her apparent ignorance of classic commentaries on post-Enlightenment individualism, and of the postmodern predicament under the influences of the [Information Technology] revolution. This gives her text and bibliography the impression of a holey Swiss cheese. All the same, this is a brave and stimulating book by somebody who has thought long and seriously about the implications of cognitive science for our everyday lives."

"What we really should be doing is thinking proactively about how, for the first time, can we shape an environment that stretches individuals to their true potential."

Greenfield's ideas about the unprecedented effects of technology were expanded in her later book, *ID: The Quest for Identity in the 21st Century* (2009), in writing which, she wrote in the book's introduction, she wanted "to see if neuroscience can make an important contribution to helping us with the truly big questions, and even offer new insights on the eternal problems that have been with us humans for hundreds of thousands of years." Greenfield continued to explore the theme of technologically driven changes in contemporary human cognition—"arguably comparable in its significance to Climate Change," she asserts at her Web site—in *You and Me* (2011) and *Mind Change: How 21st Century Technology Is Changing the Way We Think and Feel* (2013). In the preface to *Tomorrow's People,* Greenfield spoke of her experience of the "thwarted glamour of writing a novel" after that book, at first intended to be fiction, instead evolved as a nonfiction study; ten years later she published her first novel, *2121: A Tale from the Next Century* (2013), imagining the implications of human brain's vulnerability to technological change. Asked by Serge Schmemann, who was moderating a panel discussion published in the *International Herald Tribune* (Nov. 30, 2012), if she thought the dangers she perceived in omnipresent media technology ought to be met with a regulatory response from government or other institutions, Greenfield responded that her "emphasis would be away from regulation, to education. You can regulate 'til you're blue in the face; it doesn't make it any better. … what we really should be doing is thinking proactively about how, for the first time, can we shape an environment that stretches individuals to their true potential."

In the course of her career, Greenfield has published more than 200 articles in science journals, been awarded 30 honorary degrees, obtained a number of patents, and received more than 40 grants. Greenfield also founded or cofounded and currently serves as director of the companies Enkephala Ltd. (2005), Greenfield PPS Ltd. (2007), and Mind Change (2011). In addition she has been an invited speaker at more than 100 international conferences. In 1998 Greenfield received the Michael Faraday medal from the Royal Society, for her contribution to the public understanding of science. She was elected in 2002 to an honorary fellowship of the Royal College of Physicians and in 2007 to an honorary fellowship of the Royal Society of Edinburgh and also to the Australian Davos Connection. She was appointed chancellor of Edinburgh-based Heriot Watt University in 2005 and held that position until 2012. Her work was further recognized with the award of the Legion of Honor by the government of France as well as the American Academy of Achievement's Golden Plate award, both received in 2003. In 2010 Greenfield was awarded the Australian Medical Research Society Medal.

She joined the advisory boards of the Kusuma School of Biological Sciences at the Indian Institute for Technology and the Dementia Foundation for Spark of Life in 2011 and of Israel Brain Technologies, Young Scientists, and the Save the Childhood Movement in 2012. In 2012 Greenfield was made an honorary fellow of the Institute of Risk Management and also became vice patron of POWER International. In that year she also became a governor of the Florey Institute for Neuroscience and Mental Health.

To her friends Greenfield is known as Springy (short for "Spring-Greens"), a nickname acquired when she was one of four Susans in a class. She lives in London. When asked what she did to "calm down," she told Christian Tyler: "I'm not calm. People often say to me: 'You realise you wear people out, don't you?' When other people do gardening or photography or listen to music, that's when I do these things on consciousness. Actually my hobbies are shopping and eating. I really do love shopping—clothes-shopping, bubble-bath shopping." She also enjoys exercise and travel, although she is prone to bring her laptop with her on vacation so she can continue her work. "As long as you're stretching yourself and know more than you knew last week throughout your whole life, then that's great," she told Geraldine Murray.

In 1991 Greenfield married Dr. Peter Atkins, a physical chemist and author of a best-selling chemistry textbook, whom she met while working at Lincoln College. Atkins had one daughter from a previous marriage, but the couple, who separated in the spring of 2003, had no children together. Greenfield and Atkins divorced in 2005. In an interview with Cole Moreton of the *Independent* she discussed her single status and hope for the future: "You can be lonely when you're with someone … as much as when you're by yourself. … There's no point in living life if it's not fun. Let's see, what am I doing next?"

Further Reading:

British Medical Journal p78 Jul. 10, 1999

Financial Times p3 Aug. 2, 1997

(London) *Guardian* p4 Jun. 8, 1998

(Glasgow) *Herald* p14 Apr. 28, 2001

(London) *Independent* Jun. 30, 2013

International Herald Tribune Nov. 30, 2012

(London) *Observer* p29 Jul. 9, 2000; *Scotland on Sunday* p4 Aug. 17, 1997

Susan Greenfield personal Web site

(London) *Times* Dec. 26, 1994, May 2, 2001

Times Higher Education Supplement p17 Dec. 16, 1994

Selected Books:

Fiction:

2121: A Story for the 22nd Century (2012)

Nonfiction:

Blakemore, Colin, and Susan Greenfield, eds., *MindWaves: Thoughts on Intelligence, Identity, and Consciousness,* 1987

Journey to the Centres of the Mind: Toward a Science of Consciousness, 1995

Greenfield, Susan, ed., *The Human Mind Explained,* 1996

The Human Brain: A Guided Tour, 1997

Greenfield, Susan, ed., *Brainpower: Working Out the Human Mind,* 1999

Brain Story, 2000

Private Life of the Brain, 2000

Tomorrow's People: How 21st Century Techology Is Changing the Way We Think and Feel, 2003

ID: The Quest for Meaning in the 21st Century, 2008

You and Me: The Neuroscience of Identity (2011)

Heymann, David L.

American epidemiologist, international health advocate, educator

---

Born: 1946, Pennsylvania, United States

Unlike many other epidemiologists, who specialize in one or two diseases, David L. Heymann is an expert in many. Indeed, he is a world leader in epidemiology, the branch of medical science that deals with the incidence, distribution, and control of diseases in populations. In July 1998 Heymann was appointed the executive director of the communicable diseases program of the World Health Organization (WHO), a specialized agency of the United Nations (U.N.) that is headquartered in Geneva, Switzerland. In 2003 the WHO's new director-general, Lee Jong-wook, named him the organization's Assistant Director-General for Health Security and Environment and Representative of the Director-General for Polio Eradication. Referring to the importance of Heymann's work, Lee told Altman, "No job today, including the director-general's job in WHO, is more important than leading this polio campaign." Lee stated that Heymann is not only the "most important communicable disease control expert in WHO, but truly in the world."

As an employee of the U.S. Centers for Disease Control and Prevention (CDC) beginning in the late 1970s, Heymann spent a dozen years working as an epidemiologist in sub-Saharan Africa. During that time he investigated the first outbreak of Ebola hemorrhagic fever (so-called because its symptoms include internal and external bleeding); among the deadliest viral diseases known to humankind, Ebola causes death in 50- to 90 percent of cases. In 2003 Heymann was instrumental in the international effort to stop the SARS epidemic, which affected thousands of people and killed hundreds. "David L. Heymann has had an extraordinary career," the physician Lawrence K. Altman wrote in the *New York Times* (August 12, 2003). "The epidemiologist has helped discover two new diseases (Ebola and Legionnaire's), rid the world of an old one (smallpox) and stop [the] spread of the newest"—SARS, that is, "severe acute respiratory syndrome." "The tools used to control one disease often can be used to control another," Heymann told Altman. "What makes epidemiology such an important and useful science is that it can be applied to any disease anywhere."

Heymann left the WHO in April 2009, when he accepted the position of chairman of the United Kingdom's Health Protection Agency, and in that year he also took up an appointment as chair of the Centre on Global Health Security at Chatham House, London. When Public Health England was formed in 2012 after a restructuring of the National Health Service, Heymann became its chair, heading up its governing advisory board.

Heymann has been engaged in work that has saved the lives of countless people and may save or improve the lives of millions—and, in years to come, even billions more. That work includes the surveillance and control of tropical, emerging, and communicable diseases, among them measles; German measles; malaria, which many estimate has killed more people than all wars combined; tuberculosis, which kills about 2 million people every year; HIV/AIDS, from which about 3 million people die every year; leprosy; polio; and onchocerciasis, or river blindness, which is caused by a parasitic worm spread by the black fly and affects at least 18 million people in Africa and Central and South America. Since it was established, in 1988, the WHO's polio-eradication program has made great strides toward eliminating the disease, which affects the body's central nervous system and can lead to paralysis and death. While polio has become extremely rare in the United States, it remains common in India, Nigeria, and Pakistan and, to a lesser extent, in Egypt, Afghanistan, Niger, and Somalia. Infectious diseases such as polio, malaria, tuberculosis, and HIV/AIDS are the world's leading killers of children and young adults, accounting for more than 13 million deaths a year, according to the U.N. Integrated Regional Networks Information Web site. "This suffering—and its social consequences—should not be happening," Heymann said, as quoted at the U.N. Web site. "We are the first generation ever to have the means of protecting the world from the most deadly and common infectious diseases. Today, we possess the knowledge and the drugs, vaccines and commodities to prevent or cure tuberculosis, malaria, HIV, diarrhoeal diseases, pneumonia, and measles practically anywhere on our planet."

Education and Early Career

David L. Heymann was born in Pennsylvania in 1946. He earned a B.A. degree in science from Pennsylvania State University in 1966 and a medical degree from Wake Forest University School of Medicine (then the Bowman Gray School of Medicine of Wake Forest University) in 1970. Heymann's interest in public health began when he worked for Project HOPE in Tunisia, in 1969, during his years at Wake Forest. Project HOPE ("HOPE" is an acronym for "Health Opportunities for People Everywhere") is a medical philanthropic organization founded by William B. Walsh in Washington, D.C., in 1958. Since its establishment more than five thousand health-care volunteers have worked with the project's staff to conduct programs in more than 120 countries, bringing medical aid to millions of people. On the mission to the port city of Tunis, the capital of Tunisia, Heymann worked aboard the *USS HOPE*, the organization's 15,000-ton ship, which contains three operating rooms, a pharmacy, an isolation ward, a radiology department, and closed-circuit television, which enabled local doctors and students who visited the docked ship to observe operations. After he returned from Tunisia, Heymann began an internship at Washington Hospital Center. In the early 1970s, when young Americans were being drafted to serve in the Vietnam War, he fulfilled part of his military duty as a doctor on a Coast Guard icebreaker in the Antarctic.

In considering his options for a career in medicine, Heymann concluded that he could do greater good as a public-health specialist than as a practicing physician working for a hospital or in private practice. With that in mind, he enrolled at the London School of Hygiene and Tropical Medicine, in England, where he earned a diploma in tropical medicine and hygiene in 1974.

Heymann spent the next two years in India (1974–76) as a medical officer with WHO's Smallpox Eradication Programme, a highly successful venture that later, in 1980, achieved its goal of ridding the world of smallpox. An estimated two million people died from smallpox annually in the decades preceding its eradication, which marked the first time a naturally occurring disease had been completely wiped out. Continuing his far-flung travels as a doctor, Heymann then ministered to workers constructing the oil pipeline on the North Slope of Alaska. After that he joined the Epidemic Intelligence Service, the epidemiology program office of the U.S. Centers for Disease Control and Prevention, in Atlanta, Georgia. Later, through the CDC, he completed his epidemiology training.

In 1976, in his first assignment with the CDC, Heymann investigated what was then a mysterious respiratory illness that had afflicted members of the American Legion who had attended a state convention in Philadelphia, Pennsylvania. Heymann and his fellow investigators were the first to study the new illness, which became known as Legionnaire's disease. (It is caused by the *Legionella* bacterium, which can spread through air-conditioning systems.) Heymann then spent 13 years, from 1976 to 1989, on assignment with the CDC in sub-Saharan Africa, specifically in Cameroon, the Ivory Coast, Malawi, and Zaire (which is now the Democratic Republic of the Congo and borders the far smaller Republic of the Congo). At the beginning of that stint, Heymann traveled to Yambuku, in Zaire, to participate in the investigation of the outbreak of a hemorrhagic fever. The fever was later traced to a previously unknown virus dubbed Ebola. Heymann collected blood samples from local residents so as to conduct laboratory tests to determine how many people had been infected with the disease. He later helped to investigate the second Ebola outbreak, in Tandala, also in Zaire, in 1977. Nearly two decades later, in 1995, Heymann faced the disease again, when he directed the concerted international response to the Ebola outbreak in Kikwit, in the same nation. Due to the unknown nature of the Ebola virus, news of its appearance initially created considerable fear and concern. The work of Heymann and his colleagues indicated that Ebola occurred sporadically but was not likely to become epidemic. (The largest number of people known to have died in a single outbreak—425—succumbed in Uganda in 2000–01.)

From 1977 to 1980, Heymann also investigated a number of diseases in Cameroon, where indigenous forest peoples ("Pygmies") had been infected with a disease related to that caused by the Ebola virus. Heymann also conducted surveys in Cameroon on the paralysis caused by the polio virus, in order to determine the effectiveness of polio immunization programs. In Malawi Heymann studied cases of drug-resistant malaria, a disease caused by a parasite that is spread among humans through the bites of infected mosquitoes. His team's investigative method—inspired by one used by car manufacturers that check production quality by testing samples from various lots or batches—was very effective in helping to guide subsequent treatment programs. Whereas most previous tests of the drug-resistant strains of malaria had been conducted in laboratories, Heymann had his team perform clinical tests in the field, on patients infected with the disease. For example, he and his fellow epidemiologists would test a select group of several dozen malaria patients, collecting their blood to determine the disease's resistance to drugs that the patients had been given earlier. If all of the selected patients had responded to the antimalarial drugs, Heymann's team concluded that the strain's level of resistance was less than 1 percent. If one or more of the patients had not responded to the drugs, the team would select and conduct blood tests on a new group of malaria patients to try to determine the level of resistance. The WHO still uses this method of malaria testing.

Later Career

In 1988 Heymann joined the WHO as chief of research activities for the U.N.'s Global Programme on AIDS, which also encompasses other sexually transmitted diseases. He worked in Geneva, the site of the WHO's headquarters. In 1995 Heymann was named director of the WHO's Programme on Emerging and Other Communicable Diseases, and in 1998 he became executive director of the Communicable Diseases program. From early 2003 until 2009, Heymann directed the WHO's program to eliminate polio, serving as Assistant Director-General for Health Security, Environment, and World Representative of the Director-General for Polio Eradication. Since its founding, in 1988, the WHO's polio program—which to date has cost over $5 billion—has reduced the incidence of paralysis caused by the disease by more than 90 percent. According to the WHO Web site, in 1988 more than 350,000 children in 125 countries were newly afflicted with paralytic polio; by 2003 fewer than 2,000 cases in seven countries were recorded. At the end of 2012, the Global Polio Eradication Initiative—identified at its Web site as a "public-private partnership led by national governments and spearheaded by the World Health Organization (WHO), Rotary International, the US Centers for Disease Control and Prevention (CDC), and the United Nations Children's Fund (UNI-

CEF)"—reported that "polio was at the lowest levels ever—with fewer cases in fewer districts of fewer countries than ever before." Yet although the WHO has gone a long way toward achieving its goal, a single case of polio can lead to its spreading to thousands of other individuals, and as a result of a person coming into the country carrying the disease, the disease has re-emerged in a few countries where it had been eradicated. The WHO had initially set 2000 as the year by which it hoped to have completely eliminated the scourge of polio, but civil strife in many countries where the disease is prevalent, as well as logistical and cultural obstacles, put that goal beyond reach. Later attempts also fell short. (Currently the Global Polio Eradication Initiative has instituted a strategic plan to end all polio disease—entailing both wild poliovirus eradication and the elimination of what are called circulating vaccine-derived polioviruses (cVDPVs), which derive from a certain type of oral vaccine—by 2018.)

"If you lose your optimism, you can't do your job. Someone once told me that when you start in public health, there's a whole series of candles that are lit. Those who succeed in public health continue to let at least some of those candles remain lit."

On March 15, 2003, before he assumed his position as WHO's representative for polio eradication, Heymann announced the first global-health-emergency warning in the 55-year history of the U.N. agency. He announced the appearance of a new, fatal kind of pneumonia, known as SARS (severe acute respiratory syndrome), which is caused by an airborne virus—one that spreads through an infected person's coughing or sneezing, for example, and infects an individual's lungs. The virus had killed people in East Asia and had been carried unwittingly by infected individuals to dozens of countries, among them Canada and the United States. As the epidemic neared its end, Rob Stein reported in the *Washington Post* (June 7, 2003) that more than 8,000 SARS cases had been recorded in 30 countries and that more than 700 victims had died. The failure of the government of mainland China, where the outbreak of the disease apparently began, to acknowledge publicly the reality of the SARS epidemic for several months after its appearance prevented the WHO or any other organization from taking steps immediately to prevent the further spread of the disease.

After alerting the world to the SARS crisis, Heymann and other WHO workers scrambled to coordinate, with local health providers in areas with infected residents, the critical process of identifying and isolating individuals infected with the disease. By April 2003, through the work of its network of 12 international laboratories, the WHO had determined with 99 percent certainty the cause of SARS, as Heymann told Lawrence Altman of the *New York Times* (April 16, 2003). By conducting experiments with monkeys—which was necessary, as Altman explained, because "the lack of an effective treatment for SARS and the relatively high death rate make it unethical to conduct such experiments on humans"—WHO scientists had identified as the cause of the disease, a previously unknown coronavirus that infected the lungs. That discovery made possible the first step in halting the spread of the virus: namely, the development of a reliable diagnostic test to determine who was infected. By the summer of 2003, Heymann and his colleagues, along with the many health-care workers around the world who had treated those infected, had effectively contained SARS. According to WHO statistics, 8,098 people worldwide contracted SARS, and of this number 774 died.

In arresting the spread of the disease, Heymann and his WHO team combined traditional methods of epidemiology with use of the Internet. Referring to such innovations, the doctor told Altman, "It was a new way of thinking about monitoring emerging diseases, and we realized the fruits of that vision in stopping SARS." Some ten years later, in an article in the *New York Times* (March 14, 2013) about the arrest of SARS, Heymann elaborated on the advances the Internet made possible: "The information technology at our disposal allowed us to instantaneously adapt our response as the outbreak unfolded. Virus experts from around the world worked together virtually—by phone, videoconference and through the Web—to share information and report progress. Within a month, they identified the virus responsible for SARS. … Doctors shared their knowledge about what treatments worked and what did not. The media provided clear information that captured the world's attention."

In late 2003 and early 2004, an upsurge of polio cases in western and central Africa, beginning in Nigeria, prompted the WHO to intensify its efforts to immunize children against the disease. The new, $4.6 billion initiative, which included sending WHO representatives door-to-door to immunize newborns and infants, was at first met with apprehension by some Nigerian political and religious leaders, who believed that the vaccine would render girls infertile. Although the Nigerian government eventually agreed to allow the WHO to proceed with its anti-polio campaign, by June 2004 the polio virus had spread from Nigeria to ten other African countries, including three that had previously become entirely polio-free. In the *International Herald Tribune* (October 28, 2004), in an article co-authored by Julie Louise Gerberding (the head of the CDC), Carol Bellamy (the executive director of UNICEF), and Glenn Estess Sr. (president of Rotary International), Heymann expressed both optimism and apprehension about the future of polio-eradication efforts: "We are within sight of a milestone in human history. But these final steps are the toughest and require the greatest commitment—at the country level, to immunize the poorest and hardest to reach children, and from the global community, to fast-track funding to this initiative and safeguard the enormous investments that have been made over the past 15 years."

Asked what he has learned about epidemics through all his experiences, Heymann told Madeline Drexler of the journal *Biosecurity and Bioterrorism: Biodefense Strategy, Practice, and Science* (2003), "What's become clear to me is that there's always a reason why an infectious disease amplifies or spreads. These organisms, these infectious diseases, can find weak points wherever they are and amplify. AIDS found sexual behavior and amplified after it got into urban areas. Ebola finds improper hospital practices and spreads to health workers and then to their families. SARS found health practices that permitted it to spread into hospitals and then out into the community through health workers. … Microbes are always outsmarting humans."

The WHO's limited ability to pressure countries to cooperate with its investigations and to warn nations of possible epidemics (by issuing travel alerts, for example, as it did regarding SARS—an unprecedented action) compounded the difficulties of combating the spread of SARS. During the SARS crisis, Heymann and his WHO colleagues fought for, and won, from the World Health Assembly (the WHO's governing body), the power to investigate health crises even in countries whose governments have not admitted the existence of such problems. The WHO's new powers led to the establishment of the first global emergency communications hotline, to enable WHO to coordinate its international efforts more effectively and receive health information as fast as possible, which is vital when dealing with infectious diseases.

Heymann and his colleagues staunchly advocated various changes to the International Health Regulations, the only treaty-based international law governing what a country or agency can or cannot do to protect populations from disease while at the same time respecting the national sovereignty of foreign nations and their determination to protect their economic interests. The process of revising the International Health Regulations has been ongoing since the 1990s. The SARS outbreak and the WHO's role in combating it brought the issues at stake into greater focus. "I'm optimistic that a solution can be found to everything," Heymann told Madeline Drexler. "If you lose your optimism, you can't do your job. Someone once told me that when you start in public health, there's a whole series of candles that are lit. Those who succeed in public health continue to let at least some of those candles remain lit."

Heymann remained with the WHO until April 2009, when he was named chairman of the board of the UK Health Protection Agency (HPA). In 2009 he was appointed senior fellow and head of the Centre on Global Health Security at Chatham House, London. A year later he also became Professor of Infectious Disease Epidemiology at the London School of Hygiene and Tropical Medicine. In July 2012 Heymann became acting chair of Public Health England—a new government agency formed in a reorganization of the National Health Service as a result of the Health and Social Care Act 2012—and he was confirmed as chair in November 2012. (The Health Protection Agency became part of Public Health England in April 2013.) In that role Heymann is to "support and advise the chief executive officer," Duncan Selbie. According to the press release announcing Heymann's appointment, the "Chair and Board are also responsible for reviewing strategy for the agency, and for supervising how the agency is organised and maintained." In announcing PHE's "Priorities for 2013/2014," Selbie and Heymann declared that they sought a "transformational change in our nation's approach to health": "The truth is that for years we have all focused more on treatment and illness than on prevention and resilience. … We need to focus much more on prevention and early intervention, helping people to help themselves and their communities to be as healthy as they can be and for as long as possible, and intervening before conditions become unmanageable."

Heymann has published more than 145 scientific articles on infectious diseases and related issues in peer-reviewed medical and scientific journals, such as *American Journal of Preventive Medicine, Emerging Infectious Diseases,* and *JAMA, Journal of the American Medical Association* His contributions to edited volumes include "Evolving Infectious Disease Threats to National and Global Security" in *Global Health Challenges for Human Security* (2003) and "Emerging and Re-emerging Infections," *Oxford Textbook of Public Health,* fifth edition (2009). Heymann was the editor of the eighteenth (2004) and nineteenth (2008) editions of *Control of Communicable Diseases Manual* and of the WHO's *World Health Report 2007: A Safer Future* (2007). With Guénaël Rodier, he prepared *Global Surveillance of Communicable Diseases*, a special issue of the National Center for Infectious Disease's journal *Emerging Infectious* Diseases (vol. 4, no. 3, July–September 1998). He is member of the Institute of Medicine of the U.S. National Academies and the Academy of Medical Sciences (United Kingdom). Heyman chairs the Strategic Advisory Group of Hilleman Laboratories, a joint venture of MSD (Merck Sharp & Dohme Corp.) and the Wellcome Trust. He is also a member of the Board of Advisors of Claremont Graduate University's School of Community and Global Health.

Honors accorded Heymann include the Award for Excellence of the American Public Health Association (2004), the Donald Mackay Award of the American Society for Tropical Medicine and Hygiene (2005), and the Heinz Award on the Human Condition (2007). In 2009 he was appointed Commander of the Most Excellent Order of the British Empire (CBE) for services to global public health. Heymann was named to a Welling Professorship at George Washington University School of Public Health in 2005, and in 2007 he served as a consulting professor at Stanford University's Center for International Security and Cooperation. According to the 2007 Heinz Award citation, Heymann is "widely considered to be the most accomplished

American physician working in the field of international public health. … The efforts he has led, and will continue to lead, to anticipate and to prevent and treat communicable diseases, provide better and longer lives to people around the world."

David L. Heymann is married and lives in London; he has three children.

Further Reading:

Biosecurity and Bioterrorism: Biodefense Strategy, Practice, and Science Vol. 1, no. 4 (Dec. 2003): p233+

Centers for Disease Control and Prevention Web site

Chatham House Web site

JAMA Feb. 25, 1998

London School of Hygiene and Tropical Medicine Web site

New York Times pA6 Apr. 16, 2003, with photo, pF7 Aug. 12, 2003, with photos, Mar. 14, 2013, Jul. 29, 2003

Project HOPE Web site

Scientific American Vol. 290 (Mar. 2004): p. 48+

Washington Post pA10 May 18, 2003, pA27 Jun. 15, 2003

World Health Organization Web site

Books:

Garrett, Laurie, *The Coming Plague* (New York: Farrar, Straus and Giroux, 1994).

Jalal, Massouda

Afghan physician, political activist

Born: 1962, Gulbahar, Afghanistan

Massouda Jalal is the first woman in the history of Afghanistan to seek the office of president; she is also one of only a handful of women to sit on the *loya jirga*, Afghanistan's "grand council"—a historic feat in and of itself. After almost a quarter century of armed conflict, Afghan women outnumber men by a ratio of two to one. Yet of the 1,500 delegates who participated in the loya jirga convened on June 10, 2002, for the purpose of appointing a transitional government until elections were held in 2004, fewer than 200 were women. After five years of Taliban rule, though, even that figure represented a sea change in the country's social configuration. The Taliban's mistreatment of women in the name of Islam has been widely reported. The group, which controlled the country from 1996 to November 2001, stripped the country's female population of its freedoms and imposed on Afghanistan a literal-minded, heavy-handed interpretation of Islamic law, or *Shari'ah*. Women were ousted from public life; studying and holding jobs that required social contact with men were also prohibited. Women who ventured outside the domestic realm were required to shroud themselves in burqas, billowing head-to-toe cloaks with screened slits for the eyes, and to be es-corted by male relatives. Those who disobeyed risked drawing the attention of the baton-wielding religious police, which sometimes resulted in physical abuse.

The Taliban no longer has a stranglehold on the country, but many women, especially those in urban centers, are wary of coming out from the protection of invisibility the burqa affords them. But after the Taliban was forced out, the female population began to re-enter society with a mix of wariness and excitement. When Kabul University reopened (after effectively being closed down in 1996 by the Taliban), the response from the female population was overwhelming: so many female applicants turned up for the entrance exam that the university's administrators were forced to extend the testing period by a day. Despite threats and intimidation, women registered to vote in elections in larger numbers than predicted, although many were prevented by male relatives from actually voting.

Education and Early Career

Massouda Jalal was born in Gulbahar (Kapisa province), in about 1967. One of seven children, she moved to Kabul to attend high school. She is a member of the predominantly Sunni Muslim Tajik ethnic group, also referred to as the Farsiwan, because the group's language is Farsi. There are approximately 3.5 million ethnic Tajiks in Afghanistan, making them the country's second largest ethnic group, following the Pashtuns. The Tajiks constitute the bulk of Afghanistan's educated elite; they also dominated the ethnic makeup of the Northern Alliance, officially known as the United Islamic Front for the Salvation of Afghanistan, which claimed power after driving out the largely Pashtun Taliban.

Jalal began her life as a physician after graduating from medical school in Kabul in 1988. In the early 1990s, be-fore Taliban rule, Jalal worked in Mazar-i-Sharif, in northern Afghanistan, with Doctors without Borders (Medecins sans Frontières), an international humanitarian aid organization that provides medical relief in countries in which the healthcare infrastructure is either insufficient or nonexistent. She also took a teaching position at the medical school of Kabul University. (Women were first admitted Kabul University in 1959. By 1990 women constituted approximately 70 percent of the student body; currently some 38 percent are female.) Jalal was forced to quit her clinical job and give up her teaching position when the Taliban came into power. "It was just announced," she told Stephen Pincock of the *Lancet* (October 9, 2004). "We had no choice."

During the five years of Taliban rule, Jalal spent time working for the United Nations. First she worked for the U.N. High Commissioner for Refugees (UNHCR), the U.N. refugee agency, and then went on to covertly organize women's bakeries for the U.N.'s World Food Programme (WFP)—an activity that Taliban authorities considered a threat to society, since it brought women together and provided them with independent income. Called "widows' bakeries," the collectives provided a rare opportunity for Afghan women, many of whose husbands had been killed in war, to work outside the home. The bakery groups also organized lectures on gender and health issues. While working for the WFP, Jalal, like the rest of her female colleagues, was not allowed to associate with her male co-workers or visit the WFP head office. At first she and her female colleagues tried to meet face-to-face with the men they worked with in order to conduct meetings and discuss business, but the fear of getting caught held them back; eventually the women were forced to rely on middlemen to deliver messages and conduct meetings on their behalf.

Though eager to organize a new women's group in the wake of the Taliban's demise, Jalal has said she had a hard time persuading other women to join her. In explaining this reluctance, Jalal pointed out that five years of tyranny had wreaked psychological havoc on the women of Afghanistan; the fear of entering the public domain, even among educated women, remained (and remains) great. "A lot of women in Kabul are educated but have no experience, and after five years of staying home under the Taliban, they lack confidence and courage," she told Pamela Constable of the *Washington Post* (December 9, 2001). "We have more legal ease now, but that still doesn't mean women are the same as men."

Later Career

The first post-Taliban assembly of the loya jirga took place on June 10, 2002, in a large tent erected on the sports field of Kabul Polytechnic University. The loya jirga is traditionally composed of regional delegates and tribal elders. The 2002 assembly included women as well as representatives from refugee and nomadic groups. (Women also participated in loya jirgas convened in 1964 and 1977). Approximately 160 seats in the loya jirga were reserved for women's groups. Women were allowed to share the debate floor with men, but they were assigned to separate dormitories, dining halls, and rest areas.

At the loya jirga, Jalal nominated herself for president, hoping to begin a "new page in Afghanistan's political history," as a correspondent wrote for Agence France Presse (June 12, 2002). In her speech before the council, Jalal stated, "I'm working in an aid agency in Kabul helping thousands of my countrymen, and I hope that the women delegates will help me because this is the first time that an Afghan woman has stood for such a post." She characterized herself to the delegates as "an independent person," and added, "I am free in my mind, I have never been in any party," as quoted by a correspondent for Radio Singapore International (May 28, 2002).

Jalal's husband Faizullah, a Kabul University professor of international relations, supported his wife's quest for the presidency, though he acknowledged that she stood little chance of actually winning. Dr. Jalal told Stephen Pincock of the *Lancet,* "I am confident I can win," but she, too, viewed her candidacy as a symbolic gesture. "The world will now know that Afghan women have the capacity [to run for president]," she said, as quoted by Mohammad Bashir for Agence France Presse (June 14, 2002). "It enhances the position of Afghan women. After this people will take us more seriously."

Shortly after Jalal's self-nomination, Muhammad Fahim, the defense minister under Hamid Karzai (then the U.S.-supported interim leader of Afghanistan), pressured Faizullah Jalal to withdraw his wife's candidacy, claiming that it violated Islamic law. Fahim offered Massouda Jalal a seat in Karzai's government in exchange for stepping down before the vote. The Jalals rejected the offer. Faizullah, who also serves as his wife's spokesman, told reporters, as quoted by Philip Smucker for the *Christian Science Monitor* (June 21, 2002), that her candidacy is "good for democracy. Let's see what's going to happen and what's going to be the outcome." Faizullah Jalal was subsequently denounced in public by Fahim. According to Smucker, Fahim told Jalal, "You are not a man, that is why you put your wife up to this. How dare you oppose the program!"

"Respect for human rights is a requirement for enduring peace. Let no country stand alone in protecting the human rights of its people."

According to press reports, a majority of the loya jirga's male delegates felt that women should not even have been present at the grand council meeting. The imam [Islamic cleric] Qari Abdurrahman Qarizada expressed similar sentiments, arguing that the teachings of Islam proved that women were too intellectually and physically inferior to hold positions of responsibility, much less be president. Even Hamid Karzai expressed antipathy toward Massouda Jalal's candidacy. According to Harry McGee in the Sydney *Sunday Tribune* (June 16, 2002), when Jalal stood up in front of the assembly to speak, Karzai asked the delegates whether they wanted to hear him "or the woman." Jalal was undaunted. In her speech she told the assembly, "I am a Muslim woman and I have rights. … For over two centuries there has been a cruel betrayal of women. This is a golden time for the people of Afghanistan. Now is the time to forget the clashes and conflicts of the past." Her speech also addressed the country's need for a strong central government, police force, and national army, and emphasized that the chosen government must actively improve education and promote adult literacy in Afghanistan. She further declared in her speech, as reported by Mohammad Bashir, "I would put at the top of my agenda my Islamic obligations, observance of equal rights for men and women, and I would continually struggle for the reconstruction of Afghanistan."

Several addresses by women delegates at the loya jirga were aired on national television. After the assembly had concluded, Dr. Nazdama, a female delegate who goes by one name, discussed the impact of the female delegates with a female reporter. "The last nine or ten days have changed things a lot in the whole of Afghanistan," she remarked, as quoted by Carlotta Gall of the *New York Times* (June 25, 2002). "Six months ago you would have not been able to stand here and talk, nor could I have done so."

The votes for president were taken by secret ballot rather than by a traditional show of hands, so that the delegates would be free to vote as they saw fit. Both Jalal and Karzai—as well as foreign minister Abdullah Abdullah and finance minister Hedayat Arsala—supported the secret ballot. "The basis of democracy is the closed ballot," Abdullah said, as quoted by a reporter for the *Deutsche Presse-Agentur* (June 13, 2002). When the votes were tallied, Jalal came in second place, with 171 votes. That result put her far behind Karzai, who garnered 1,295 of the 1,500 votes cast, but ahead of Dr. Medai, who received 85 votes. After the count Jalal told reporters she had succeeded in altering the way Afghan women are perceived. "I think it has changed the mentality of people, for women not to be so weak, or like second-class citizens," she said, as quoted by Gall.

Meanwhile, in December 2001, the WFP bakeries had reopened. Jalal expressed hope that they would provide desperately needed jobs for Afghan women. "I don't see very many employment opportunities for women," she said, as quoted by Laura King for the Associated Press (December 20, 2001). "But we hope this will change, especially if we show what women can do."

After the conclusion of the loya jirga, Jalal returned to her job as national program officer of the WFP for the regions of Paktia, Khost, and Logar in eastern Afghanistan, and she taught pedeatric medicine at Kabul University. In 2004 she again announced her intention of running for president, but she dropped out before the votes were counted. She was asked to serve in President Hamid Karzai's cabinet as Minister of Women's Affairs. Jalal accepted and held that post from 2004 to 2006. In 2009 the initial field of some 44 candidates (later winnowed significantly) included two women—a doctor who was the widow of a murdered aviation minister in the Karzai government and a member of parliament—but not Jalal. Together they received a smaller percentage of the vote than Jalal had received in 2004.

In 2007 Jalal established the Jalal Foundation, a nonprofit organization that brings together 50 women's councils and organizations. She founded the organization "to continue to better the lives of women in Afghanistan," according to the foundation website, seeking to provide training and refer women to capacity-building opportunities; to pioneer services, such as protection centers for women in the provinces; to advocate for mainstreaming women into government programs, services, and budgets; to initiate or support initiatives that foster women's leadership and political participation, particularly for young women; and to generate in the international community sustained attention to the plight of women in Afghanistan.

In remarks she planned to deliver at the March 2013 United Nations Commission on the Status of Women conference in New York, Jalal asserted that in anticipation of the scheduled withdrawal of U.S. troops from Afghanistan by the end of 2014, Karzai's government was in the process of "blindly pursuing a peace and reconciliation process with the Taliban in a way that gives political concession to high officials and extending economic assistance to combatants so that they may return to the fold of mainstream life. ...Putting criminals back to the community without making them pay for their human rights offences is like tinkering with a time bomb." "To the minds of many people," she continued, "the return of the Taliban signals an 'open season' once more to extreme forms of women's rights violations." Jalal calls on all democratic governments to "join us in strengthening [the] human rights watch in our country. ... Respect for human rights is a requirement for enduring peace. And lasting peace is a requirement to the long term enjoyment of human rights and justice. Let no country stand alone in protecting the human rights of its people. Human rights are not bounded by territory." (Sponsorship for Jalal's trip to New York was cancelled shortly before the conference; her prepared address was published at the openDemocracy Web site, dated March 6, 2013, along with another address she had planned to give at the conference.)

Dr. Jalal and her husband have three children. She currently resides in the Badakshan province in northeast Afghanistan. In May 2010, Jalal was awarded UN Watch's Morris B. Abram Human Rights Award.

Further Reading:

Agence France Presse Jun. 12, 2002, Jun. 13, 2002, Jun. 14, 2002

Associated Press Dec. 20, 2001

Christian Science Monitor p7 Jun. 21, 2002

Deutsche Presse-Agentur Jun. 13, 2002

(London) *Guardian* Jul. 15, 2004, Oct. 12, 2004

Human Rights Watch Web site

Jalal Foundation Web site

Lancet Oct. 9, 2004

New York Times pA11 Jun. 25, 2002, with photos

Radio Singapore International May 28, 2002

(Sydney) *Sunday Tribune* p19 Jun. 16, 2002

Washington Post pA28 Dec. 9, 2001

Books:

Skaine, Rosemarie, *Women of Afghanistan in the Post-Taliban Era* (Jefferson, N.C.: McFarland, 2008).

Kaleeba, Noerine

Ugandan AIDS activist and educator

Born: 1951, Mukono, Uganda

In 1987 Noerine Kaleeba founded The AIDS Support Organization (generally known by the acronym TASO) to help educate the Ugandan public about acquired immunodeficiency syndrome (AIDS) and the human immunodeficiency virus (HIV) that causes it. TASO provides medical and emotional support services to those suffering from the disease, and it seeks to lessen the stigma associated with contracting AIDS. In the 25 years since it was founded, TASO has cared for more than 300,000 individuals and reached out to more than a million of their household members with services such as HIV counseling and testing. Kaleeba told an interviewer for the television program *Frontline* (May 5, 2005), "Initially what we set out to do was primarily for ourselves—to find support; to find the answers to questions that come to you when you or your loved one is diagnosed; to find another person who has a similar story to yours. But we soon found that unless we make a difference in the levels of basic information about this disease among health care workers and within the community, that the compassion that we were seeking so much was not going to be possible."

Education and Early Career

Noerine Kaleeba was born on December 25, 1951 in Mukono, Uganda, into a polygamous family; her father had four wives, and she had, in total, 28 siblings. Little else about her early life has been published; most media accounts of her life begin in 1986, when she was taking care of four young daughters—Elizabeth, Marion, Fiona, and Kristen—and working as a physiotherapist at Mulago Hospital, in Kampala, Uganda. She specialized in orthopedics, physiotherapy, and community rehabilitation. Her husband, Christopher, was living in England, studying at the University of Hull for a master's degree in sociology and political science. In June 1986 Kaleeba received a telegram from the British Consulate in Uganda informing her that Christopher had become extremely ill. Several days later British doctors told Kaleeba over the phone that her husband had been diagnosed with AIDS and was not expected to live long. "My initial reaction was absolute denial, that they must have made a mistake, because how can my husband, who wasn't white, who wasn't homosexual, who wasn't gay, how could he have AIDS?," Kaleeba told the *Frontline* interviewer, "The early information that was becoming available was in relation to white gay men in San Francisco, so I said, 'They must have made a mistake.'" She continued, "My husband was infected through a blood transfusion. We didn't know it at the time, but looking back, we came to the conclusion that this must have been the source of his infection. He was run over by a bus in 1983 and bled profusely, and he was taken to the hospital, but at the time there was a war raging, and there was no blood within the blood bank, so relatives were invited to donate blood. One of those people who donated blood was his own brother, who later turned out to have been HIV positive."

Kaleeba traveled to Hull, in northeastern England, to be with her husband, who was being treated at the Castle Hill Hospital there. She found Christopher in grave condition; barely able to move, he had lost 80 pounds. "We were the only black couple in a 600-bed hospital," Kaleeba told Curtis Abraham of the *New Scientist* (March 8, 2003).

"We were also the first heterosexual AIDS case they had seen. Despite this, the nurses went out of their way to the extent that Christopher, who was in so much pain, could be made to smile." After three months of treatment, however, he insisted they return to Uganda. Although the country had a much lower standard of healthcare than that available in England, Christopher wanted to spend his remaining time with his children.

While the couple was in England, the Ugandan government had launched an AIDS awareness campaign, and on their return to their native country, they immediately became the focus of intense public scrutiny. Kaleeba, who has said that the campaign sowed more fear than understanding, told *Frontline*, "There were so many people who turned up at the airport to actually see what an AIDS patient looks like. I was very angry because many of the people who turned out [were strangers]. I was aware that they had turned out at the airport out of curiosity, not out of compassion, because they didn't touch my husband; they didn't come to shake hands. … It was, I suppose, my first glimpse at stigma." The staff at Mulago Hospital, in Kampala, where Christopher was taken, also refused to touch him, erroneously believing that AIDS could be spread through casual contact. Kaleeba, her mother-in-law, and a close family friend became his primary caretakers.

Kaleeba began roaming the hospital, looking for others who were infected and inviting them back to Christopher's room for informal support sessions, during which the couple shared what they had learned about the disease in England and discussed the impact AIDS was having on their country. Christopher died on January 23, 1987, surrounded by his family. In July 1987 Kaleeba sought a meeting with Ugandan president Yoweri Museveni. "I actually bulldozed myself into a team that was going to see him," she told *Frontline*. "After all the officials had spoken, I said, 'Mr. President, my husband has just died of AIDS … and I want to do something about this disease, so I want to work with these government officials.' He looked at me and said, 'Oh, your husband has died of AIDS?' I said, 'Yes.' And he said 'What about you?' I said: 'Mr. President, I don't know. But all I know is that if I have AIDS, I would like to do something about it before it kills me.' So he turned around to Sam Okware [the commissioner of health services] and said: 'Put that Noerine Kaleeba on the committee.'"

Later Career

Later that year, Kaleeba and 15 other Ugandans whose lives had been affected in some way by AIDS founded TASO—an extension of the informal group that had begun meeting in Christopher's hospital room. The organization first aimed to initiate a conversation about AIDS and change its status as a taboo subject. "This disease thrives on secrecy, and unless we, the people who have been affected by this pandemic, stick our necks out and address it, then the stigma won't go away," Kaleeba told Curtis Abraham. "So our initial efforts were met with a lot of suspicion. People would come and peep and then go away. But as they began to see the solidarity of people coming together, eating together and hugging each other, then people started tentatively coming. Within six months we were totally overwhelmed." According to Agnes K. Namaganda of the Kampala, Uganda, *Daily Monitor* (March 24, 2012), Kaleeba also thought she was "infected by default. With this sense of urgency that she, too, would succumb to the disease anytime, she threw herself behind this voluntary work to the point of resigning from her paid job as the Principal of Mulago's School of Physiotherapy in 1990, much as she had four young daughters to look after and see through school." Kaleeba served as TASO's director until 1995.

TASO also promoted sexual education in Uganda; Kaleeba advocated what has become known as the ABC method of fighting the spread of AIDS, which involves abstinence, being faithful, and using condoms.

Kaleeba told interviewer Margot Adler on the PBS radio show *Fresh Air* (April 22, 2002). "We have to agree that abstinence is possible." Yet, she continued, "if you are not abstaining from sexual intercourse, then be faithful to the sexual partner that you have. ... But we also know that being faithful is a situation that is not necessarily possible for everybody all the time. This is where the C comes in, and that is consistent condom use." Kaleeba acknowledges that certain aspects of Ugandan culture have contributed to the spread of AIDS. She asked Moyiga Nduru of Inter Press Service (December 6, 2004), "How can you abstain when you are coerced to have sex? How can you remain faithful when you are married at the age of 16?" She told *Frontline*, "I think AIDS is now teaching us to recognize that as long as women are not educated, [they are vulnerable]. Keeping a young girl in school as long as possible is a protective factor, because we know that she can make better choices with regard to sex." TASO also aimed educational efforts at lowering the number of infected women who give birth. Kaleeba told Jane Perlez of the *New York Times* (October 28, 1990), "Among rural women, many say 'People are dying. We should have more children.' Even among my clients, people still have babies even though they are HIV positive because it is very important for an African woman to have a baby. The clients feel they must leave more children behind. They say: 'I will take the chance. If the child is positive he will die, if not he will live.'"

In addition to its educational component, TASO runs medical clinics several times per week to supplement the care patients are receiving from their own physicians and to treat the opportunistic conditions—such as herpes and tuberculosis—that often plague those with AIDS. The group also provides antiretroviral therapy (ART), which slows the spread of HIV. (Thanks to efforts by the global community, antiretroviral drugs are less expensive than they originally were; they are still, however, prohibitively costly for patients in the developing world. The Ugandan government, funded in part by the World Bank, agreed to begin providing ART at no cost to as many of its affected citizens as possible.) Within Kaleeba's own family, by 2002, four siblings and their spouses, along with eight nieces and nephews, had tested positive for HIV, which at times placed her in the difficult position of determining which family members would receive subsidized therapy. "Francis, one of my brothers, is now on antiretroviral therapy," she told Adler. "But what about the rest of the family members? What about Andrew? What about George? What about Josephine, his wife? What about Rebecca, the youngest in my family, who has HIV [and] is three and a half years [old]. And every time I look into the eyes of that child, I say, 'How can this child continue to suffer?'" (In a June 12, 2006, article for *New York Newsday,* Rachel Scheier wrote that by then four of Kaleeba's siblings had died, and an additional three had been diagnosed as HIV-positive. "There have been so many funerals for nieces, cousins, and in-laws," Scheier wrote, "that it's hard to keep count.")

Kaleeba feels that the emotional support TASO provides to AIDS patients is as important as the medical support. She told Abraham, "A major part of the inspiration behind the organization was Christopher himself. I used to ask him when he was ill: As you are lying there, what is the most precious thing? What do you think is most important? And he would say: Just touching me, holding my hand, just being there. And you don't have to be a doctor to do that." She is one of the few surviving founding members of TASO, 12 of whom have died of AIDS-related complications. Kaleeba herself tested negative for the disease, yet according to Agnes Namaganda, she nevertheless was convinced for years that she in fact had contracted AIDS. Only in 2006, after she again tested negative, did she gain confidence in the negative finding.

In the years after TASO's founding, Uganda became a rare success story in the fight against AIDS in Africa. According to the Web site of the AIDS group AVERT, the prevalence of HIV in Uganda's population declined significantly throughout the 1990s; an estimated 15 percent of the population was infected in 1990, but by 1999 that figure had been reduced to 9 percent. (TASO's campaigns to spread AIDS awareness have been widely credited for the decrease, and the Ugandan government's support of such programs has succeeded in winning significant amounts of funding from industrialized nations such as the United States and Britain.) But in a recent article in the *New York Times* (August 2, 2012) Josh Kron reported that the Uganda AIDS Indicator Survey stated that Uganda and Chad are two African countries where "AIDS rates are on the rise again. Billions of dollars were spent on AIDS in Uganda and the reversal is disappointing. HIV infection rates have increased to 7.3 percent from 6.4 percent in 2005." In the same article, Dr. Christina Ondoa, Uganda's Minister of Health, stated that AIDS "remains a significant problem" and "presents the government with an opportunity to recommit ourselves."

"We soon found that unless we make a difference in the levels of basic information about this disease among health care workers and within the community, that the compassion that we were seeking so much was not going to be possible."

At present, TASO has an established infrastructure network of 11 service centers, 4 regional offices, a training center, and a capacity-building project covering all 4 regions and major towns of Uganda. TASO operates 22 outreach clinic sites in public health facilities where clients receive a comprehensive package of care and support services. TASO also has, according to its Web site, "supported over 30,000 orphans and vulnerable children with therapeutic feeding, food, and nutrition security intervention, scholastic materials, formal and apprenticeship training, seed grants, farm inputs, health, sanitation and hygiene care, psychosocial and children protection support."

After eight years as TASO's executive director, Kaleeba was recruited by the Joint United Nations Programme on HIV/AIDS (UNAIDS) to serve as community mobilization adviser in Sub-Saharan Africa, a position she took up in January 1996. From her post in Geneva, Switzerland, she coordinated TASO's efforts with those of the United Nations AIDS program until retiring in 2006. She then worked for a consortium of four UK-based foundations—the Diana Fund, Comic Relief, the Elton John AIDS Foundation, and the Children Investments Fund Foundation—to develop a holistic program for children orphaned or made vulnerable by HIV/AIDS. In 2007 she moved back to Mukono, Uganda, where she is an independent consultant, supports TASO as its patron and founder. In 2008 she cofounded the Komo Learning Centres, a nonprofit organization to provide educational solutions to help AIDS orphans, children with disabilities or health problems, and those too poor to pay school fees or who simply have no school in their vicinity.

Kaleeba continues to work to combat AIDS by educating people about the disease. She thinks it must be discussed openly, and that government leaders should be pressed to commit to further research and education: "There has to be a high degree of political openness arising from the political leaders, the heads of state. You should also have openness at the community level, in households. You need to get traditional leaders, people living with HIV, or families affected by HIV/AIDS to begin articulating their own issues and how AIDS has impacted them. And lastly, you also need to get international solidarity. Uganda would not have been able to do what it did without international solidarity. It's not just about money, but it's also about starting scientific studies that educate us. All of that leads to reduced stigma and learning more about the path of this virus."

In 1995 Kaleeba was awarded the Belgium government's Royal Development Prize. In 2009 she was knighted by the Republic of Italy. Three honorary degrees have been conferred on her, from Nkumba University in Uganda, Dundee University in Scotland, and Geneva School of Diplomacy and International Relations in Switzerland. She has served with several international bodies, including the World Health Organization Global Commission on HIV/AIDS, the Global AIDS Policy Coalition, and the Uganda AIDS Commission. Kaleeba has also been a trustee of international boards such as Maristopes International, Noahí Ark (Sweden), and ActionAid UK.

Kaleeba has written or contributed to numerous publications on HIV/AIDS, including *Open Secret: People Facing Up to HIV and AIDS in Uganda* (2000) and *A Broken Landscape: HIV & AIDS in Africa* (2003). Her autobiography is entitled *We Miss You All: AIDS in the Family* (2005).

Further Reading:

AVERT Web site

(Kampala, Uganda) *Daily Monitor* Mar. 24, 2012

Fresh Air Apr. 22, 2002

Frontline May 5, 2005

Komo Learning Centres Web site

New Scientist p50 Mar. 8, 2003

New York Newsday pC8 July 11, 2000, pA5 Jun. 12, 2006

New York Times pA16 Oct. 28, 1990, Aug. 12, 2012

TASO Web site

Selected Books:

Open Secret: People Facing Up to HIV and AIDS in Uganda (2000)

A Broken Landscape: HIV & AIDS in Africa (2003)

We Miss You All: AIDS in the Family (2005)

Kuipers, André

Dutch physician, astronaut

Born: 1958, Amsterdam, the Netherlands

André Kuipers became the second Dutch person to fly into space when he participated in a mission to the International Space Station (ISS) that launched on April 19, 2004. Kuipers traveled as a member of the European Space Agency (ESA), an organization of European countries (currently there are 20 member states), which contracts with American and Russian space missions to send up its astronauts. A trained medical doctor and an expert on the effects of weightlessness on the human body, Kuipers performed an array of experiments on that mission during his 11-day journey into space. In 2011 Kuipers was chosen for another mission to the ISS. He returned to Earth in July 2012, having spent 192 days in space—and a total of 204 days in space in all, according to Denise Chow of SPACE.com (July 1, 2012).

While efforts toward manned space flight suffered a enormous setback when the *Columbia* space shuttle disintegrated while re-entering the Earth's atmosphere on February 1, 2003—taking the lives of the seven astronauts aboard—Kuipers has enthusiastically continued to advocate the benefits of manned journeys. One of the goals that the Dutch government held for Kuipers's flight was to inspire the nation's schoolchildren; although the Netherlands claims a sizable technology industry, the country suffers from a dearth of graduates with degrees in science, engineering, or technology. "With this mission, we show people that science and technology is not something boring but is very exciting and interesting," Kuipers told John Kelly and Chris Kridler of *Florida Today* (April 18, 2004). In a NASA preflight interview conducted in November 2011, Kuipers made it clear that his feelings about space flight had not changed: "I like the expression from, that we're standing with our toes in an ocean that's still to be discovered. We're only with our toes in the water at the moment and there's so much to discover and it will continue in ways that, that we cannot ever imagine now."

Education and Early Career

André Kuipers was born in Amsterdam on October 5, 1958, the son of Bram and Rie Kuipers. He first became interested in space travel when he was 12 years old, inspired by science-fiction books. By his early teens, he had made up his mind to become an astronaut. "I thought, I have to go to space," he told Liesbeth de Bakker in an interview for the Radio Nederland Web site (April 15, 2004). In the Dutch school system, he entered the "Atheneum-B" program at the Van der Waals Lyceum (later called the Amstel Lyceum), which prepares students for university study with an emphasis on mathematics and science. (The Atheneum B program is roughly the equivalent of a series of advanced placement courses in U.S. high schools.) After graduating, in 1977, Kuipers attended the University of Amsterdam, earning his medical doctorate in 1987. At the university Kuipers studied in the Vestibular Department of the university's medical center (vestibular research focuses on human balance); there, he researched the human equilibrium system—the mechanisms that control spatial orientation.

Kuipers worked in the Royal Netherlands Air Force Medical Corps in 1987 and 1988. There he learned to fly and continued his research on spatial orientation, specifically as it related to accidents and near-accidents of pilots in high-powered aircraft. Leaving the Air Force, he spent 1989 and 1990 at the research-and-development department of the Netherlands Aerospace Medical Centre, in Soesterberg, where he studied Space Adaptation Syndrome (SAS), also called space motion sickness. Similar to motion sickness as it is experienced on Earth, SAS manifests symptoms that vary from stomachaches and lethargy to vomiting and nausea, but its exact causes remain unknown. (Several scientists suspect its main cause to be the sudden juxtaposition of different kinds of input received by differing human senses, which disrupts the equilibrium system.) At the Medical Centre, Kuipers also did research on contact lenses for pilots, vestibular systems, and blood pressure and cerebral blood flow under high-acceleration and microgravity conditions. In addition, he performed medical examinations of pilots and delivered lectures on the physiological aspects of flying.

Later Career

Kuipers started working with the European Space Agency in 1991, mostly on experiments that tested the physiological effects of weightlessness on astronauts. The Anthrorack (a device he worked on that performs various tests on the impact of low gravity on the human body) was sent as one of the European-funded projects on the *Columbia* space shuttle in a flight in April 1993. He also worked on two other systems, designed to study lung and bone physiology, that were used in a 1995 ESA mission to the *Mir* space station. Another project that Kuipers worked on, the Torque Velocity Dynamometer, used for musculoskeletal experiments, was sent on a subsequent *Columbia* mission, in 1996. Also with the ESA, Kuipers worked on two projects—the Muscle Atrophy Research and Exercise System and the Percutaneous Electrical Muscle Stimulator—that were installed on board the U.S. laboratory module *Destiny,* which was brought to the ISS by the space shuttle *Atlantis* in early 2001. In addition to designing experiments for space, beginning in 1991 Kuipers also worked on ESA's parabolic-flight campaigns, in which specially designed airplanes follow a parabolic flight path to create a brief state of freefall, in order to mimic the zero-gravity environment of space. Kuipers participated in such campaigns as an experimenter, test subject, and flight surgeon.

In October 1998 the ESA and the Dutch government jointly announced that Kuipers was going to join the European Astronaut Corps. He began training as an astronaut in July 1999 while continuing to research the effects of reduced gravity and weightlessness on astronauts at the European Space Research and Technology Centre (ESTEC), in Noordwijk, the Netherlands. In 2002 Kuipers finished the ESA basic training for astronauts, which includes systems training for the ISS and science- and technology education. In December 2002 he was assigned the position of flight engineer for the April 2004 Russian mission to the ISS.

One of the experiments Kuipers helped research for the ESA, the Advanced Respiratory Monitoring System, flew on the space shuttle *Columbia* on its final mission, in January 2003. Even though the *Columbia* disintegrated during its return to Earth, the data from the experiment had already been collected and was available for study. After the *Columbia* disaster, all American manned missions into space were suspended, forcing NASA to rely on the Soyuz spaceships of the Russian Aviation and Space Agency (Rosaviakosmos) to replace astronauts serving months-long stints aboard the ISS. In the two Soyuz missions after the *Columbia* disaster, in April 2003 and October 2003, Kuipers worked on the ground control for the Soyuz crews. In the latter mission, Kuipers was recruited as the backup for the Spanish astronaut Pedro Duque.

For Kuipers's place aboard the April 2004 Soyuz mission, the Dutch government paid about $15 million to the Russian government, through the ESA. They also engaged in a publicity campaign to stir the interest of Dutch schoolchildren, turning Kuipers into something of a national celebrity. The Dutch government christened Kuipers's mission "DELTA"—both an acronym for "Dutch expedition for life science, technology, and atmospheric research" and a reference to the Delta Works, a system of dykes and dams that protects Zeeland, a Dutch province, from flooding. One of the experiments Kuipers conducted on the mission, "Seeds in Space," was designed specifically to appeal to schoolchildren: in order to deduce whether the direction in which plants grow is determined by light or gravity, 70,000 schoolchildren grew lettuce from seeds in two chambers—one with light and one without—while Kuipers did the same in space. (The experiment revealed that on Earth, plants without light will still grow up, whereas in space, plants with light but no gravity will grow towards the light, while those with neither light nor gravity will grow in all directions.)

"We're standing with our toes in an ocean that's still to be discovered. We're only with our toes in the water at the moment and there's so much to discover and it will continue in ways that, that we cannot ever imagine now."

Kuipers conducted 21 experiments in all over his 11-day mission. Many of the experiments had few immediately obvious goals other than furthering research into manned space flight, although the practice of manned space flight faced heavy criticism after the *Columbia* accident. One of the experiments Kuipers conducted tested the effects of weightlessness and space radiation on three million *Caenorhabditis elegans* worms, which have many genes in common with humans. "If the worm spends 10 days exposed to cosmic radiation and weightlessness, it will be the equivalent of 10 years in space for a human," Nathaniel Szewczyk, a NASA researcher working on the worms project, explained to Delphine Thouvenot of the Agence France Presse (April 19, 2004). Defending such research, Kuipers told a correspondent for *TNO Magazine* (April 2004), "It's as useful as any other scientific research: it enables us to gather knowledge. In that respect, scientists who carry out research into space flight are just the same as scientists who work in more ordinary laboratories. What space-flight scientists particularly want is to disengage the weight factor for longer." Kuipers added, "You can never say exactly what the benefit of a particular piece of scientific research is. … The researchers who first worked on light with one wavelength—that is, laser—didn't know what applications it had. Now you can use laser light to measure the distance to the moon, carry out an eye operation, and play CDs." Other experiments, however, had overtly practical purposes. One experiment focused on low-energy lamps, which Dutch researchers contended could help in lighting stadiums and highways as well as in heating large rooms. Additional experiments involved a special vest containing vibrating cells similar to those used in mobile phones; the vest was designed to help astronauts orient themselves in space but may also prove useful for firefighters and the disabled.

Kuipers's copilots on the Soyuz, Michael Fincke of NASA and Gennady Padalka of Rosaviakosmos, spent 183 days on the space station, replacing the American Michael Foale and the Russian Aleksandr Kaleri, both of whom had lived in the ISS since the October 2003 Soyuz mission. Kuipers, Padalka, and Fincke finished preparations for their mission near the end of March. "We've worked hard, I haven't even had time to phone my friends," Kuipers told a reporter from the Agence France Presse (March 31, 2004). "Now we can rest a bit." In interviews before the flight, he told reporters that he was not nervous about the launch or possible malfunctions, just worried that he would not sufficiently complete his experiments. "As far as this aspect is concerned, astronauts are under too much pressure," he told the *TNO* correspondent. "Every minute is taken up. You have hardly any margin [for error]. As soon as an experiment takes longer than planned or you have to repair something, you've got a time problem. And for the scientists on the ground, who've done years of preparation, it's a real disaster if something goes wrong."

The launch from Kazakhstan's Baikonur Cosmodrome, on April 19, 2004 (Moscow time), was successful. Kuipers became the fifth ESA astronaut, as well as the first Dutch astronaut to enter space since Wubbo Ockels flew on the U.S. space shuttle *Challenger*, in 1985. Among those watching the takeoff at Baikonur were members of Kuipers's family, Dutch prince Johan Friso, representatives of the Dutch government, and the ESA Director of Human Spaceflight, Jörg Feustel-Büechl. "The current space mission is one more very important landmark in our cooperation with Russia," Feustel-Büechl told reporters, as quoted by Nikolai Teterin for the Telegraph Agency of the Soviet Union (April 19, 2004). "It is particularly notable since we have recently marked the fifteenth anniversary of our cooperation with Rosaviakosmos. There are many remarkable events during the past few years, including successful experiments and launchings. The flight of Dutch astronaut André Kuipers is one more fantastic landmark in our joint work with Russia." On the flight Kuipers brought some Dutch cheese, a science-fiction comic book, and a photograph of the seven astronauts who died in the *Columbia* disaster. The Soyuz rocket successfully entered orbit minutes after the launch, and two days later it docked with the space station. Kuipers entered the station first, followed by Fincke and Padalka. "It was a real pleasure to get on board, and I'm very tempted to stay," Kuipers later quipped, as quoted by John Kelly and Chris Kridler of *Florida Today* (April 24, 2004).

Kuipers returned to Earth with Michael Foale and Aleksandr Kaleri on April 30, 2004 (coinciding with the national Dutch holiday Queen's Day), landing near the town of Arkalyk, Kazakhstan. The returning crew's descent took only three and a half hours, and the landing went exactly as planned. "[The touchdown] was heavier, or more violent, than I thought," Kuipers told Bahila Bukharbayeva of the Associated Press (April 30, 2004). "I braced myself but nevertheless my head went forward—but no wounds. But it is a nice feeling if the parachute goes open and, yes, it was a beautiful ride. Everything works fine. It's great!" Shortly after Kuipers landed, Jörg Feustel-Büechl told the press that 19 of Kuipers's 21 experiments had been successful. According to the Expatica Web site (May 17, 2004), Kuipers "carried out an extensive experiment programme in the fields of human physiology, biology, microbiology, physical science, earth observation, education and technology." Kuipers spent two weeks in quarantine in Star City, the Russian cosmonaut center, located near Moscow; during that time his body re-adapted to Earth's gravity. "After you return you have less resistance," he told reporters, as quoted on the Expatica Web site. "In the beginning I was very tired and had trouble from muscle pain, back pain and dizziness. But I have quickly recovered."

Assigned as a backup crew member for the first Canadian International Space Station increment in 2005, Kuipers was trained on the U.S. and Russian station modules and had training for spacewalks as well as robotics operation. From 2007 he served as the backup for ESA astronaut Frank De Winne, of Belgium, in preparation for Europe's second long-duration spaceflight to the ISS. Kuipers trained intensively on all station modules and on Europe's Automated Transfer Vehicle, and he became familiar with the experiments conducted in ESA's Columbus Space Laboratory, a module first attached to the ISS in 2008. In May 2009 Kuipers was assigned to Eurocom duties at the Columbus Control Centre, at the German Space Operations Centre of the German Space Agency (DLR), near Munich, and European Astronaut Centre (EAC), near Cologne, in support of De Winne's six-month mission.

In August 2009 Kuipers was assigned to Expedition 30/31, a long-duration mission to the ISS, for which he trained in the United States, Japan, Russia, and Germany. Together with cosmonaut Oleg Kononenko, the mission commander, and NASA astronaut Don Pettit, Kuipers was launched in a Soyuz TMA-03M space capsule on December 21, 2011, from Baikonur Cosmodrome. During this mission, which lasted 192 days, he conducted or assisted in some 50 experiments. Kuipers was the prime crew member for the rendezvous and docking of ESA's third Automated Transfer Vehicle. During the mission, "Pettit and Kuipers shared with the public stunning photos of Earth from space, through Twitter and the Flickr photo-sharing site," wrote Denise Chow at SPACE.com. During the mission, Kuipers also wrote a children's book, *André the Astronaut* (published October 2012), in which a child named André flies to the moon accompanied by his "inseparable friend," a mouse.

On this mission Kuipers was also involved in berthing SpaceX's *Dragon* ferry, in what proved to be a very successful first demonstration flight for NASA's commercial cargo transportation program. The unmanned *Dragon* capsule was launched to the ISS, according to Denise Chow, "on a test flight to demonstrate the spacecraft's ability to carry cargo to and from low-Earth orbit. As *Dragon* approached the station," she explained, "Pettit and Kuipers used the outpost's robotic arm to pluck it from space and manually park it to the complex. The successful test flight lays the groundwork for NASA to use commercial spaceships to ferry cargo, and one day astronauts, to the space station."

Kuipers was granted the title Knight of the Order of Orange-Nassau in 2004 and Knight of the Order of the Netherlands Lion in 2012. The Russian Federation conferred on Kuipers its Order of Friendship in November 2013. In that year he also was awarded an honorary doctorate from the University of Amsterdam. He is a member of the Aerospace Medical Association, the Dutch Aviation Medicine Society, and the Dutch Association for Spaceflight. Kuipers was appointed an ambassador for the World Wildlife Fund in June 2004. In that year he also became special professor of space and medicine at the Free University of Amsterdam.

Kuipers is married to Helen Conijn, a journalist. He has four children: two, Robin and Megan, from his first marriage, to Anne Sofie Simonsson, and two, Sterre and Stijn, with Helen Conijn. In his free time Kuipers enjoys flying, scuba-diving, cross-country skiing, swimming, hiking, history, and traveling.

Further Reading:

Associated Press Apr. 18, 2004

European Space Agency Web site;

Florida Today p3 Apr. 14, 2004, with photo

NASA International Space Station Web site

SPACE.com Web site

Spaceflight Now Web site

Spaceflight 101 Web site

TNO Magazine Apr. 2004

Universe Today Nov. 9, 2003, with photo

Volkskrant Web site, Jun. 30, 2012

Books:

Hall, Rex D., David J. Shayler, and Bert Vis, *Russia's Cosmonauts: Inside the Yuri Gagarin Training Center* (Berlin: Praxis Publishing, 2005)

Llinás, Rodolfo

Colombian-born neurophysicist, educator, writer

Born: 1934, Bogotá, Colombia

"Groups of neurons, millions strong, act like little hearts beating all on their own. It's like a 'Riverdance' performance." That description of neurons came from Rodolfo Llinás, then the chairman of the Department of Neuroscience and Physiology at the New York University (NYU) School of Medicine, during an interview with Sandra Blakeslee of the *New York Times* (December 2, 2008). Also called nerve cells, neurons are cells in the brain, spinal cord, and other parts of a vertebrate's nervous system; they process and transmit information by electrochemical signaling, in a manner that Llinás, in that interview, was likening to Irish step dancing. Elaborating on that analogy, he said, "Some cells are tapping in harmony and some are silent, creating myriads of patterns that represent the properties of the external world. Cells with the same rhythm form circuits to bind information in time. Such coherent activity allows you to see and hear, to be alert and able to think."

Known as the "founding father of brain science," Llinás is an expert on the electrophysiology of the brain—the way the brain carries out its jobs by means of electrochemical activity. At the beginning of his career, in the early 1960s, he worked at the Australian National University with the Nobel Prize–winning neuroscientist John C. Eccles and other members of the first team to construct a physiological chart of an entire region of the brain—the outer layer of the cerebellum, known as the cerebellar cortex. Later, successively, from 1965 until 1976, Llinás joined the faculties of the University of Minnesota; the American Medical Association Institute of Biomedical Research; Northwestern University; Wayne State University; the University of Illinois; the University of Iowa; and New York University, where from 1976 until the end of 2011, he was the chairman of the Department of Neuroscience and Physiology (until 1995, the Department of Physiology and Biophysics). He then was named University Professor—marking, according to the department's Web site, the first time such an honor was bestowed on a medical center faculty member—and he remains the Thomas and Suzanne Murphy Professor of Neuroscience.

The brain is the most complex organ in the human body and the most "expensive" in terms of energy. At about three pounds, it constitutes about one-fiftieth of body mass but consumes 25 percent of the energy resources. The brain is divided into sections according to function. The cerebral cortex, as part of the thalamocortical loop, is the central processor and is responsible for consciousness, memory, language, and reasoning. The brainstem consists of the hindbrain and the midbrain and acts as a relay center for such involuntary activities as the beating of the heart and breathing. The cerebellum (Latin for "little brain") plays a major role in the integration of sensory perception and motor control. It receives information, in the form of electrochemical signals, from other parts of the brain, through input fibers. The different parts of the brain communicate with one another by firing electrochemical signals from one neuron to another in neural chains. A neuron's action is either excitatory, meaning that it passes a signal to the next neuron, or inhibitory, meaning that it stops a signal. Each signal begins with an electrical event, when ions (charged molecules) generate a so-called action potential that triggers chemical events involving synapses, the gaps that exist between neurons. The job of the cerebellar cortex, the outer layer of the cerebellum, is to modulate the information it receives from clusters of neurons within the cerebellum, known as deep nucleii, and transmit the information to other parts of the brain, by way of climbing fibers. Those fibers wrap around Purkinje neurons in the cerebellum, causing them to fire. Other structures involved in the process of sensory integration include the inferior olivary bodies, or olives, and the thalamus. The two olives (often referred to in singular form, as the IO), located in the brain stem, also transmit information to the cerebellum through mossy and climbing fibers. The thalamus, located just above the brainstem, relays information from the cerebellum to the cerebral cortex.

Llinás's research has helped to elucidate the electrophysiological activities that link the cerebellum to other parts of the brain. One of his most controversial findings threw into question the generally accepted notion that neurons do not act independently but only react to stimuli. Also a matter of dispute is his theory that the IO and the thalamus are constantly communicating with other parts the brain via oscillations. Llinás has found evidence suggesting that, when those oscillations occur at high or regular frequencies, a person's motor and cognitive skills indicate that he or she is fully awake and functioning at a high level. The thalamus enters into low-frequency oscillation after a person has been awake and active for many hours, and he or she falls asleep. Llinás believes that when abnormal rhythms—called thalamocortical dysrhythmias—link certain parts of the brain, a variety of maladies may result: Parkinson's disease, epilepsy, depression, chronic pain, tinnitus, obsessive-compulsive disorders, and some symptoms of schizophrenia. Llinás has suggested treating those disorders with deep brain stimulation (DBS), in which pinpointed parts of the brain are stimulated with a few volts of electricity through implanted electrodes. Deep brain stimulation has been used with notable success with some victims of Parkinson's disease; it has also been used successfully to treat some victims of movement disorders or intractable depression. Among his other achievements, Llinás discovered in mammalian neurons what are called dendrite calcium spikes ("spikes" in the sense of a sudden burst of activity) and dendritic inhibition, and he has shown the existence of presynaptic calcium current in squids. An essay by Llinás about his life and work is included in the series *History of Neuroscience in Autobiography* (Volume 5, 2006).

In his autobiographical essay, Llinás makes it clear that his life's work has been guided by the conviction that, "we can understand the nature of brain activity, or more fundamentally, the nature of what we are. … Deep in the recesses of my being, I have always felt that our nature is no more mysterious than the rest of the physical world. The biggest impediment to our true understanding seems to lie with us; by wanting to be angels we deny our nature. I remember writing, some years back, that we may ultimately prove to be simpler than our intellect feared or our vanity hoped."

Education and Early Career

Rodolfo Riascos Llinás was born to Jorge Enrique Llinás and Bertha Riascos Llinás on December 16, 1934, in Bogotá, Colombia. His father, a thoracic surgeon; his paternal grandfather, a psychiatrist; and an uncle were all professors at the National University School of Medicine in Bogotá. "From very early on," Llinás told Philip J. Hilts of the *New York Times* (May 27, 1997), "I was thinking and talking about the mind, because that is what the subject was in our house." For a year, when he was four, Llinás lived with his grandfather. One day Llinás witnessed the collapse of one of his grandfather's clients in an epileptic seizure in the waiting room; later, he asked his grandfather why a person would behave like that. His grandfather explained that the man did not want to flail about; rather, his brain was controlling his actions. "He doesn't want to," Llinás thought, as he recalled to Hilts. "How can he do something he doesn't want to? Such an incredible event!" Llinás told Hilts, "I began to wonder, when I move, how do I know whether I want to or not?" When he posed such questions to his grandfather, the older man acknowledged that he could not explain how the brain worked. Back at his parents' home, Llinás began to conduct experiments in the basement; for example, he would attach electrodes to mice and rats and observe what happened. "My mother kept after me, to make sure I was not unkind," he told Hilts, "but there it is, I was already started."

In 1952 Llinás earned a B.S. degree in general studies (equivalent to a high-school diploma in the United States) from Gimnasio Moderno, a private school in Bogotá where, he wrote in his autobiographical essay, he learned "intellectual rigor." At age 17 he enrolled in a combined undergraduate/graduate medical program at the Pontificia Universidad Javeriana, in Bogotá. As he had planned to do for years, he focused on nervous-system physiology.

During his undergraduate years Llinás met the neurosurgeon Walter R. Hess, a pioneer in hypothalamic electrical stimulation—the use of electrodes to stimulate the hypothalamus, the part of the brain that, among other functions, regulates the automatic nervous system. During visits to Hess's laboratory in Switzerland in 1954 and 1956, Llinás assisted in experiments that showed that electrical stimulation of specific areas of cats' brains could induce behavior typical of that species. An electrical signal imparted to a cat at rest, for example, could cause the animal to leap up with an arched back and erect fur, as if it had been threatened. Back in Bogotá he was unable to replicate such experiments for his thesis because he lacked the proper equipment and set-up—and even Bogotá's stray cats, he has recalled, proved to be uncooperative. Instead he earned a doctoral degree with a dissertation about circuit analysis of the visual system, a more theoretical subject. He was awarded an M.D. degree in 1959.

Llinás then traveled to the United States to study neurosurgery. He took courses at the Massachusetts Institute of Technology (MIT), in Cambridge, and conducted research at Massachusetts General Hospital (MGH), in Boston. He was disappointed to discover that "for the most part, and rightly so," the MGH neurosurgeons "were more interested in saving lives than in figuring out how the brain works," as he wrote in his autobiographical essay. After a year and a half at MIT, he left for the University of Minnesota, supported by a grant from the National Institutes of Health (NIH). In Minnesota, under the supervision of the electrophysiologist Carlo Terzuolo, he studied the electrical properties of motor neurons (or motoneurons), which originate in the spinal column and affect the movement of muscles. "I was basically left on my own," he wrote in his essay. "I would report to [Terzuolo] once a week. I cannot overstate the importance of having had Carlo be as tough as nails concerning science and as hands-off as he was during this time." Within about a year and a half, Llinás and Terzuolo had made several significant discoveries concerning inhibitory responses in the brain. One was that an inhibitory response could take place at either the level of the cell body or on a dendrite. The finding regarding dendritic inhibition was particularly controversial, because it countered the assumption that motoneuron electrical activity was driven exclusively by synaptic input directly into the soma. In general scientists had dismissed the notion that synapses could occur by way of a dendrite. Llinás and Terzuolo presented their findings about dendritic inhibition at the 1962 International Physiological Conference, in Amsterdam, the Netherlands.

Following the presentation Llinás was approached by the renowned neuroscientist John C. Eccles, who told him that he and Terzuolo were "clearly wrong," as Llinás wrote; nevertheless, Eccles invited him to work in his laboratory in Canberra, Australia. Llinás spent the next two years in Canberra, collaborating with Eccles and another researcher, Kazuo Sasaki, in an investigation of the physiology of the cerebellar cortex. Shortly after Llinás began his research there, in 1963, Eccles was awarded the Nobel Prize for Physiology or Medicine, in conjunction with Andrew Huxley and Alan Hodgkin, for his work on synapses. Eccles's team of researchers spent years mapping the synaptic interactions that occurred in the cerebellar cortex and characterizing them as either excitatory or inhibitory. Among their most surprising findings was that the climbing fibers elicited huge synaptic electrical potentials that were activated by a single input fiber, rather than the summation of many fibers acting in unison, which was formerly thought to be the case. By 1966 Llinás and his colleagues had completely mapped the cerebellar cortex, making it the first region of the brain to be physiologically charted. The group's findings were published in several papers in the *Journal of Physiology* and the *Journal of Experimental Brain Research,* as well as in two articles for *Nature*. They were also presented at the International Physiological Congress in Tokyo, Japan. Llinás completed a second dissertation on the functioning of the cerebellar cortex and earned a second Ph.D., in 1966, from the Australian National University.

Meanwhile, around that time Llinás had met Gillian Kimber, who was finishing her Ph.D. on the philosophy of mind at the university and shared his ideas about the mind. Llinás and Kimber married in December 1965 and then moved to Minneapolis, Minnesota, where Llinás became an associate professor of physiology at the University of Minnesota.

Later Career

In 1966, under the auspices of the American Medical Association Education and Research Foundation (AMA/ERF), Llinás joined Eccles at the newly established Institute for Biomedical Research (IBR) at the University of Chicago. There, until 1970, Llinás and a team of postdoctoral fellows investigated the physiology and anatomy of the cerebellum in various species. Llinás and his colleagues studied the cerebellums of vertebrates, including frogs, fish, reptiles, birds, and mammals. Among Llinás 's conclusions was that although the cerebellum is more complex in higher animals, it nonetheless has evolved to function in a similar way in many vertebrates.

In 1968 Eccles left the AMA/ERF, and Llinás became the IBR's director of neurobiology. About a year and a half after that, to the great outrage of the scientific community, the AMA decided to close down the institute. Shortly before the closing, Llinás hosted an international symposium on the evolution and development of the cerebellum; the significant findings presented there were published in 1969 in a book that he edited. In 1970 Llinás and his research group, with whom he had worked for five years, relocated to the University of Iowa, in Iowa City. In an effort to stay connected to two Chicago institutions—the University of Illinois and Northwestern University, with which he had become affiliated—Llinás and two of his research partners obtained pilot's licenses and bought a small plane; they sometimes flew to Chicago from Iowa.

Continuing their research on comparative cerebellar physiology, Llinás and his co-workers focused on the IO, which share information with the cerebellum and help control voluntary body movements. Over the next ten years, Llinás conducted research and wrote papers on neuronal networks and their relationships to the IO. Challenging the accepted dogma that dendritic spikes—the rapid firing of electrical current in dendrites—could be triggered only by sodium currents, Llinás proved that spikes in Purkinje cell dendrites were calcium-current dependent. Llinás recalled in his autobiographical essay that when he presented that unexpected finding at a conference, a onetime friend of his, Rafael Lorente de Nó, declared in front of the large audience, "Do you really believe that those are calcium spikes? Well, you are wrong." Lorente de Nó later declared to Llinás in a letter: "You have either lost your mind or your honesty." As many studies by other scientists as well as Llinás have since shown, it was Lorente de Nó who was in the wrong.

In 1976 Llinás accepted a position as the chairman of the Department of Physiology and Biophysics at the New York University School of Medicine. His continuing research found that IO neurons were electrically coupled. Some years later, in collaboration with Yosef Yarom, he discovered slow, self-generated si-nusoidal voltage changes in IO neurons—dubbed "subthreshold oscillation." That finding was so surprising that, again, some of Llinás's peers suggested that there was a flaw in his research. In his studies Llinás used harmaline, a hallucinogenic drug known to cause tremors and impaired coordination in humans and other animals. Working with brain slices, he introduced harmaline to the IO and observed an increase in currents sent to the thalamus. Then Eric J. Lang, one of Llinás's doctoral students, discovered that damage to cer-ebellar nuclei generated an increase in the coupling of the IO neurons, as Llinás had theorized in the 1970s. That finding was in complete disagreement with the accepted theory—that the cerebellum was the center for motor learning—and emphasized motor timing as the main role of the cerebellum.

"The biggest impediment to our true understanding seems to lie with us; by wanting to be angels we deny our nature. ... We may ultimately prove to be simpler than our intellect feared or our vanity hoped."

In the 1980s Llinás began to suspect that the relationship between the IO and the thalamus might be one of the most important in the brain. He discovered that the neurons from both the thalamus, the major entry point into the cerebral cortex, and the IO exhibited low-threshold spikes. When the thalamus's neurons were hyperpolarized—or separated—they, like the IO, entered a state of subthreshold oscillation. Further research suggested that high-frequency activity, called gamma, in both the cerebral cortex and the thalamus corresponded with high-level cognitive functioning, and that low-frequency activity in those regions cor-responded with states of sleep or motor malfunction. In the conviction that thalamocortical oscillations were responsible for sleep/wake cycles, the dream state, and humans' moment-to-moment internal perception of the world, Llinás began to test his theories on the human brain by means of magnetoencephalography (MEG), a then-new imaging technique used to measure magnetic fields produced by electrical activity in the brain. His studies supported his earlier findings of a correlation between cognition and the brain's electrical activity, suggesting that "different cognitive events can be related to specific electrical events at brain level," as Llinás wrote in his autobiographical essay.

In the 1990s Llinás began working with Daniel Jeanmonod, professor of neurosurgery at the University of Zürich, in Switzerland, who had come to the same conclusions he himself had regarding low-threshold thalamic oscillation. Both concluded that the symptoms of Parkinson's disease—including impaired motor skills and speech—were likely related to low-frequency oscillation of the thalamus. In studies of patients with various brain diseases, Llinás and his colleagues noticed that specific regions of their thalamus were disconnected from parts of the cerebral cortex, resulting in abnormally low oscillations, as if those regions of the brain were asleep. Llinás and Jeanmonod came up with the hypothesis that many neurological and psychiatric diseases originate when different parts of the thalamus or the cortex begin to exhibit abnormally low frequency of oscillation. They theorized that, in addition to Parkinson's disease, disorders including petit-mal epilepsy, seemingly irreversible depression, phantom-limb disorders (in which people with am-putated limbs, hands, or feet experience pain where those parts of their bodies used to be), chronic pain, tinnitus, obsessive-compulsive disorders, and some aspects of schizophrenia are caused by a disconnection between parts of the thalamus and the cortex that leads to a long-term state of thalamocortical dysrhythmia.

Llinás also speculated that the disorders might be treated by implanting electrodes into the thalamus to break the abnormal oscillation patterns. (For some years electrodes have been used to treat Parkinson's-disease victims who have not responded to drug therapy.)

In 1999 Llinás and Jeanmonod and three other scientists presented their hypothesis in a paper, "Thalamocortical Dysrhythmia: A Neurological and Neuropsychiatric Syndrome Characterized by Magnetoencephalography," published in the *Proceedings of the National Academy of Sciences* (Volume 96, Number 26, 1999). "This work is very important," Edward Jones, the president of the Society for Neuroscience and the director of the Center for Neuroscience at the University of California, told Sandra Blakeslee for the *New York Times* (October 26, 1999). "What makes it so compelling is that it doesn't come completely out of left field. It builds on a body of work that's been growing for some time. Everyone will say wow, yes!" Since then many neurosurgeons have successfully treated other neurologic and psychiatric disorders by implanting electrodes into the cortex or thalamus and stimulating carefully located parts of them. As of December 2008, some 40,000 people around the world had been treated, mostly for movement disorders. The treatment is currently being applied to patients with schizophrenia, epilepsy, Tourette's syndrome, dystonia, chronic pain, depression, phantom pain, and traumatic brain injuries. Llinás has noted that even if the treatments alleviate the symptoms of those disorders, they should not be regarded as cures; moreover, they sometimes produce unwanted side effects (which subside when the electrodes are removed). In *Science* (March 20, 2009) Miguel A. L. Nicolelis, a neuroscientist at Duke University, presented the results of a study showing that stimulating the spinal cords of rodents suffering from Parkinson's disease with a mild electrical charge reduced the severity of the their worst symptoms. Nicolelis suggested that the therapy could present a safer alternative to deep-brain stimulation for treating humans suffering from Parkinson's disease. Llinás, who was not involved in the study, told Sandra Blakeslee for the *New York Times* (March 19, 2009) that the treatment "makes good sense." He added, "How successfully it will translate to humans is an important issue. The human spinal cord is much more complex than the rodent counterpart, and long-term stimulation might result in nasty secondary effects."

On another front, with the goal of understanding the biophysics and molecular biology of synaptic transmission, Llinás has spent summers since 1962 at the Marine Biological Laboratory (MBL) at Woods Hole, Massachusetts, studying transmissions in the giant-squid synapse. That species is particularly useful because its axons and synapses are far larger than those of humans and have been the focus of many successful studies concerning the mechanisms by which nerve cells communicate with each other. Llinás's book *The Squid Giant Synapse: A Model for Chemical Transmission* was published in 1999. Llinás is the author of numerous other books, including *I of the Vortex: From Neurons to Self* (2002). He has also published more than 500 articles in professional journals, including *Neuroscience, Cerebellum,* the *European Journal of Neuroscience, Psychopharmacology,* and the *Journal of Physiology*, and he has contributed chapters to books in medicine and science. Llinás served as chief editor of *Neuroscience*; he was a member of the editorial board of the *Journal of Neurobiology* and the *Journal of Theoretical Neurobiology*; field editor of *Pflügers Archiv*; and senior editor of *Thalamus and Related Systems.*

Llinás is the recipient of numerous awards, including the John C. Krantz award, University of Maryland School of Medicine (1976); Luigi Galvani Award, Georgetown University, 1988; F. O. Schmitt Award in Neuroscience, Rockefeller University, 1989; UNESCO Albert Einstein Gold Medal Award in Science, 1991; Signoret Award in Cognition, La Salpêtrière (Paris), 1994; Robert S. Dow Neuroscience Award, University of Portland, Oregon, 1999; Breinin Lecture and Award, Emory University, 2003; Morris Lecture and Award, Wright State University (Dayton, Ohio), 2003; Santiago Grisolía Award and Medal, Valencia (Spain), 2004; Koetser Memorial Lecture and Prize, Zürich University (Switzerland), 2004; Gold Medal of the Spanish National Research Council (2012); and the Pierre Gloor Award, American Clinical Neurophysiology Society, 2013.

In the 1980s Llinás, the physiologist and biologist Frank M. Sulzman, and the neurophysiologist James Wallace Wolfe proposed to NASA that a shuttle flight be devoted to the study of the nervous system in microgravity. The result was the NeuroLab, a 16-day mission, completed in April and May 1998, in which seven astronauts studied the effects of weightlessness on the nervous system and sleep and breathing in rats, fish, snails, and crickets as well as in themselves. Llinás became the chairman of NASA/Neurolab Science Working Group in 1991.

Over his career Llinás has been invited to deliver numerous prestigious lectures at institutions all over the world. He was named Bowditch lecturer, American Physiological Society, 1973; Professorial lecturer, Collège de France, 1979; Lang lecturer, Marine Biological Laboratory, Woods Hole, Massachusetts, 1982; McDowall lecturer in Physiology, King's College, London, 1984; Ralph Gerard lecturer, University of California, Irvine, 1987; Ulf von Euler lecturer, Karolinska Institutet, Stockholm, 1987; Professorial lecturer, Collège de France, Paris, 1987; Craythorne lecturer, University of Miami School of Medicine, 1988; Earl H. Morris lecturer, 2004;Van Wagenen lecturer, American Association Neurological Surgeons, 2008; Distinguished Scientist Seminar lecturer, University of Pittsburgh, 2011; Distinguished public lecturer, University of Toronto Collaborative Program in Neuroscience, 2012; Distinguished public lecturer, University of Texas at San Antonio, 2012; and Ragnar Granit lecturer, Karolinska Institutet, Stockholm 2013.

Llinás is a member of the U.S. National Academy of Sciences, American Academy of Arts and Sciences, American Philosophical Society, Real Academia Nacional de Medicina (Madrid), the French National Academy of Science, and the Spanish Royal Academy of Medicine. He has been granted honorary degrees by the University of Salamanca (Spain), Autonomous University of Barcelona (Spain), National University of Colombia; Complutense University (Spain); Toyama University (Japan); and University of Pavia (Italy).

Llinás's favorite writers include Fyodor Dostoyevsky, Guy de Maupassant, and Gabriel García Márquez, a friend of his and a fellow Colombian. Llinás and his wife live in New York City. They have two sons: Rafael, a neurologist, and Alexander, an ophthalmologist.

Further Reading:

New York Times May 27, 1997, Oct. 26, 1999, pD2 Dec. 2, 2008, Mar. 19, 2009

U.S. News & World Report p68+ Jan. 3–10, 2000

Books:

Margulis, Lynn, and Eduardo Punset, eds*., Mind, Life, and Universe: Conversations with Great Scientists of Our Time* (White River Junction, VT: Chelsea Green Pub., 2007)

Squire, Larry R., *The History of Neuroscience in Autobiography,* vol. 5 (Burlington, MA: Elsevier Academic Press, 2006).

Selected Books:

Llinás, Rodolfo, ed., *Neurobiology of Cerebellar Evolution and Development: Proceedings of the First International Symposium of the Institute for Biomedical Research,* 1969

Llinás, Rodolfo, ed., *The Biology of the Brain: From Neurons to Networks; Readings from* Scientific American *Magazine,* 1989

Steriade, Mircea, Edward Jones, and Rodolfo Llinás, *Thalamic Oscillations and Signaling,* 1990

Llinás, Rodolfo, ed., *The Workings of the Brain: Development, Memory, and Perception; Readings from* Scientific American *Magazine,* 1990

Llinás, Rodolfo, and Constantino Sotelo, eds., *The Cerebellum Revisited,* 1992

Llinás, Rodolfo, and Patricia S. Churchland, eds., *The Mind-Brain Continuum: Sensory Processes,* 1996

Von Euler, Curt, Ingvar Lundberg, and Rodolfo Llinás, *Basic Mechanisms in Cognition and Language,* 1998

Llinás, Rodolfo, *The Squid Giant Synapse: A Model for Chemical Transmission,* 1999

Llinás, Rodolfo, *I of the Vortex: From Neurons to Self,* 2001

Maung, Cynthia

Burmese physician and humanitarian

Born: 1959, Rangoon, Burma

The Burmese doctor and humanitarian Cynthia Maung is often compared to her countrywoman Aung San Suu Kyi, the Nobel Peace laureate and leader of the nonviolent pro-democracy movement in Burma (Myanmar). Since 1989 Maung has run the Mae Tao Clinic in Thailand near its border with Burma, providing free medical care to migrant workers and refugees fleeing Burma's repressive military regime. Today the clinic, which began as a makeshift operation in a refugee camp, has a staff of about 600 providing comprehensive health services, education, and child-protection services. The clinic's caseload is approximately 150,000 cases annually; it serves 300- to 400 people per day. Each year, more than 2,500 babies are delivered at the clinic. In addition to providing medical care, the clinic also works to educate refugee children and to inform the Burmese refugee community about such issues as family planning and human rights. Maung has received numerous humanitarian awards in recognition of her work, including the Ramon Magsaysay Award, Asia's equivalent of the Nobel Peace Prize, in 2002, and the Sydney Peace Prize, in 2013.

Education and Early Career

Cynthia Maung was born in Rangoon (Yangon) on December 6, 1959, the fourth of eight children in a family belonging to the Karen ethnic group. The Karen people represent about 7 percent of the Burmese population; most are Buddhist, but some 25 percent are Christian. Maung's family was Baptist. She grew up in the rural outskirts of the southeastern city of Moulmein (Mawlamyine). From an early age, she was conscious of the importance of proper medical care; the first child born to her parents, a boy, died from an infection contracted after the midwife who delivered him cut his umbilical cord with a bamboo sliver. (Maung's mother gave birth to all of her subsequent children in a hospital.) Maung's father worked as a health assistant and often delivered medicine to rural villages.

At an early age Maung also became aware of the different attitudes of society toward men and women. As young girls, she and her sisters were not permitted to go to certain public places, such as the cinema, unless accompanied by either their father or their older brother. Maung developed a strong relationship with her sisters, with whom she spent a relatively carefree (if not exactly easy) childhood. She recalled for Paula Bock of the *Seattle Times* (September 28, 1997) that (in Bock's words), "after school, she and her sisters would fritter away time carrying water from the deep brick well and splashing each other at the cistern and rereading old magazines until the kerosene burned low and they were too sleepy to study." Although not always a stellar student, Maung was academically gifted. "I not much study and could still get high marks," she told Paula Bock. Upon finishing high school she scored among the top 500 students on a nationwide exam with a passing rate of only 20 percent, thus securing a place at the University of Rangoon medical school. There, Maung encountered for the first time Burma's fledgling pro-democracy movement, which was becoming increasingly outspoken in its criticism of General Ne Win's socialist government. Paula Bock characterized the atmosphere: "On campus there were whispers about corruption and change," Bock wrote. "A few professors urged students to examine their patients' lives, the suffering of the people, and ask themselves, 'Why?'"

At first Maung didn't pay a great deal of attention to political developments, largely because the connection between government policies and poverty wasn't clear to her. "The pervasive poverty was always apparent," she told a correspondent for the *Irrawaddy* (June 1999). "I saw the daily struggles of Burma's ordinary citizens but I didn't fully understand the politics in Rangoon." That began to change, however, after she completed her education and began practicing medicine in Eain Du Village in Karen State. There, she saw firsthand how people were abused and brutalized by government troops waging war against ethnic insurgents. "I began to smell the workings of politics through the astonishing number of villagers that were forced to serve as porters and forced laborers for the military," she recalled for the *Irrawaddy* in 1999. "There, the poverty was compounded by the civil war." Dr. Maung was keenly aware that, as the history of her clinic presented at the Mae Tao Clinic Web site explains, "living for all of these people was difficult and they all struggled to survive on a daily basis. [She] realized how poor the people were, how little they had and [she] watched as they were forced into working for the military as soldiers and porters. Many village children were not able to attend school and from necessity helped the military in order to make a small amount of money so that they could survive. Taxation was high and diseases such as TB widespread."

In 1988 public dissatisfaction with the Burmese government came to a head as student demonstrators in Rangoon began openly calling for a change in regime. Violent crackdowns by the government only resulted in increased popular support for the demonstrators, and by late summer large swaths of the general public—including Maung—had joined the student protesters. "The students began speaking about people's basic rights," she told the *Irrawaddy*. For a brief moment, it appeared as if the pro-democracy movement would prevail: on September 10, 1988, the leadership of the ruling Burma Socialist Program Party approved a resolution calling for a multiparty general election. Eight days later, however, the military seized power, abolished the constitution, and established a new ruling junta called the State Law and Order Restoration Council (SLORC). In the violent repression that followed, thousands were killed; many more were forced to flee the country.

Maung headed for the Thai border with 14 colleagues in September 1988, traveling at night and sleeping in fields during the day to escape the junta's crackdown. Upon finally reaching Thailand, after a journey of seven days, she found herself surrounded by thousands of people in need of medical care—people who were refugees like herself but who had contracted illnesses and sustained crippling injuries during their harrowing escape from Burma. Speaking specifically of the student activists who fled Burma at the time, Maung recalled for Robert Horn of the Associated Press (June 3, 1995) that, "There were many malaria cases in those early days. More than 100 students died from it that first year." In a dilapidated hut at the Mae La refugee camp, with practically no tools at her disposal, Maung sterilized a handful of medical instruments in a rice cooker and then set about treating patients for malaria and diarrhea, as well as tending to wounds inflicted by bullets, shrapnel, and land mines.

Later Career

As more and more refugees poured in over the border, the demand for medical attention grew, and in 1989 Maung established the Mae Tao Clinic in Mae Sot, in a donated barn with dirt floors and a thatched roof located a few kilometers from the Burmese border. "I was [in Mae Sot] when you could see refugees coming into Thailand all along the border," an Australian human rights worker recalled for the *Irrawaddy*. "I met Dr. Cynthia in 1989. … She sat there with 200 newly arrived refugees and spoke with them one by one."

Refugees' accounts of their escape to Thailand offer a glimpse of the brutal repression that followed the junta's rise to power. Many villagers were seriously injured or killed as soldiers moved into remote rural areas, pillaging houses and destroying cattle along the way. Some reports spoke of public executions in which men were murdered in front of their families; other reports described women who were raped while holding babies in their arms. Many of those who survived were forced to serve as slave laborers for the Burmese military, often as porters or "human minesweepers." In this environment access to health care—Burma already was ranked among the worst in Asia for health care access before the junta seized power—was further curtailed. Women and children found it especially difficult to receive basic medical treatment.

Meanwhile, as Maung's work gained attention in the international media, advocacy and human rights groups from countries such as Australia, the United States, Canada, France, Germany, the United Kingdom, Slovenia, and Thailand began providing financial and logistical support to the Mae Tao clinic. Such support made it possible for the clinic to expand its reproductive health unit and to operate mobile field clinics across the Burmese border, in areas where ethnic insurgents continued to battle government troops. Two satellite clinics Maung had established in Karen-controlled areas in the later 1990s were destroyed by forces allied to the junta; thereafter, she resorted to "backpack medics" and their mobile clinics to bring medical care to people who could not come to Mae Tao.

The Mae Tao Clinic provides inpatient and outpatient medical care for adults, children, reproductive health clients, and surgical service patients. Other services include eye care, dental care, laboratory and blood bank services, prosthetics and rehabilitation, voluntary counseling and testing for HIV and counseling services. Severe cases (less than 1 percent) are referred to Mae Sot Hospital.

Maung put the education of refugee children at the center of the clinic's mission. "We cannot expect these children to go back [to Burma] soon, so we need to give them an education," she told Sanitsuda Ekachai of the *Bangkok Post* (August 7, 2003). Sharon Bradley, in an article published in the *Sydney Morning Herald* (August 17, 2013), among other sources, writes that the "Mae Tao Clinic has become a village. In 2008, with the blessing of the Thai government, Maung built a school, called the Children's Development Centre. … Almost 1000 children, the offspring of migrant Burmese workers, arrive every day in pristine blue and white uniforms to attend lessons from kindergarten level to grade 12."

The facility also seeks to educate adults on human rights issues. According to the profile of Maung at the GO Campaign Web site, as her clinic grew, Maung "realized that in order to care for her patients, especially the children, she needed to ensure they received more than just adequate medical care—they needed rights. In 2002, Maung formed the Committee for Protection and Promotion of Child Rights (CPPCR) to combat the issues of statelessness, promote child rights, and provide protection, education, and healthcare to children of displaced, migrant Burmese living in Tak province and the Internally Displaced Persons (IDP) living in Eastern Burma." By 2014, the GO Campaign Web site noted, "CPPCR has completed birth registration forms for 21,749 children. These birth certificates provide children with the right to study in Thai schools or migrant schools in the Mae Sot area."

Maung was one of the lead authors of *Diagnosis: Critical Health and Human Rights in Eastern Burma*, a report issued in October 2010 that supported calls for a U.N. Commission of Inquiry into conditions in eastern Burma. As reported in the *Irrawaddy* (October 19, 2010), the document claimed that "abuses perpetrated by the state have contributed to a health crisis in the region." Specifically, "abuses such as forced labour and displacement affected one-third of those surveyed, and 'serve as major drivers of the health crisis as children in displaced families were three times more likely to suffer from acute malnutrition and 60 percent more likely of suffering from diarrhea.' In another startling finding, the report says that the odds of children dying before age one were doubled in households forced to provide labour during the preceding year."

Maung has received a number of humanitarian honors in recognition of her work. In 1999 she became the first recipient of the Jonathan Mann Award for health and human rights, given by the U.S.-based Global Health Council. The award was presented by former U.S. president Jimmy Carter via satellite link; Maung participated from Bangkok. Carter called Maung a "global hero" and praised her for "successfully combining public health work with a commitment to human rights," as quoted by the *Irrawaddy*. That same year Maung also received the John Humphrey Freedom Award from the International Centre for Human Rights and Democratic Development, a human rights organization established by the Canadian Parliament in 1988. Nobel laureate Aung San Suu Kyi, the leader of the nonviolent movement for democracy in Burma, presented the award, pointing out that Maung provides services so essential that many Burmese risk their lives crossing the border to seek help. In acknowledgment of her work on behalf of women refugees, Maung received the 2000 President's Recognition Award from the American Medical Women's Association, as well as the Foundation for Human Rights in Asia's 2001 Female Human Rights Special Award. Also in 2001 she received the Van Hueven Goedhart award, from the Netherlands Refugee Foundation.

"It's only through civil society engagement and participation that communities will start to heal after decades of conflict and oppression."

In 2002 Maung won the prestigious Ramon Magsaysay Award for community leadership. She was unable to attend the awards ceremony, however. While sources cited a variety of reasons for her absence, an editorial in the *Manila Times* (September 6, 2002) alleged that Maung, who is officially stateless, chose not to travel to Manila for fear that she might encounter difficulties returning to Thailand. The Thai government, in an effort to normalize relations with its northwestern neighbor, appeared to have launched a crackdown on Burmese pro-democracy activists living in Thailand. Despite a raid at the clinic in September 2003, during which Maung and her colleagues were told to prepare for deportation, they were not deported. According to Sharon Bradley, writing some ten years later in the *Sydney Morning Herald*, Burmese military intelligence continually engages in surveillance of Mae Tao.

Additional awards conferred on Maung include the Asia Hero Award from *Time* Magazine, in 2003; the Eighth Global Concern for Human Life Award from the Chou-Ta Kuan Foundation (Taiwan), 2005; Asia Democracy and Human Rights Award, from the Taiwan Foundation for Democracy, 2007; the World's Children Prize for the Rights of the Child Honorary Award (Sweden), 2007; the Catalonia International Prize (Spain); the Alumni Association Humanitarian Award, University of California-Davis (USA), in 2009; the National Endowment for Democracy's Democracy Award, in 2012; and the Sydney (Australia) Peace Prize, in 2013. The Sydney Peace Prize jury's citation states that the award was made for Dr. Maung's "dedication to multi-ethnic democracy, human rights and the dignity of the poor and dispossessed, and for establishing health services for victims of conflict." Dr. Maung responded to this honor: "The prize is a way of bringing international attention to the plight of Burma. It highlights that the peace process needs to be monitored by the international community." In December 2013 Maung received an honorary doctorate in medicine from Ubon Ratchathani University.

The Mae Tao Clinic currently faces major challenges partially connected with its location but more particularly with its funding stream. The clinic's main facilities are located on rented land; the rent has become expensive, and the area is occasionally subject to flooding. In July 2013, for the first time in its history, the clinic had to be evacuated because of flooding. Given these drawbacks, plans have been under way for some time to construct a new facility. Meanwhile, however, the clinic's funding has dropped precipitously. The clinic has always had to cope with fluctuations in funding, especially owing to changes in administration and other factors affecting the governments that eventually came to contribute substantially to its support. Shortly before Maung was awarded the Sydney Peace Prize, she learned that Australia's new government planned to eliminate its contribution toward the clinic's funding. According to the *Karen News* (January 2, 2014), Australia's contribution previously amounted to 20 percent of the clinic's budget. Moreover, since 2011, when a quasi-civilian government was installed in Burma, some of its aid partners have refocused their donations away from Thai-Burmese border NGOs such as the Mae Tao Clinic in favor of aid to Burma's centrally administered programs.

In an interview (August 29, 2013) with Eliza Villarino of Devex, a membership organization for aid donors, Maung discussed the future of her clinic in the context of the formidable obstacles to bringing peace, stability, and human rights to Burma. Despite political overtures to the rest of the world, she said, "We have seen growing displacement in Burma as a result of land confiscation and development projects. More exploitation and rights abuses will push more people to the border. There is also significant economic development on the border, which will attract laborers, many of whom are likely to be undocumented. Our workload will therefore grow." To be effective, she continued, "[Foreign aid] donors must empower local civil society organizations, not sideline them. It's only through civil society engagement and participation that communities will start to heal after decades of conflict and oppression. Donors can support civil society by empowering [local organizations] to report human rights abuses and to help them cope with trauma. … We hope to see stronger partnerships between Yangon-based groups and border-based groups, working toward a common goal."

Maung lives in Mae Sot with her husband, Kyaw Hein, who manages the Mae Tao clinic's laboratory Peace and Crystal, the couple's two biological children; three children who became part of the family after being abandoned at the clinic; and a widow to whom Cynthia Maung offered a home after meeting her at a refugee camp when Crystal was an infant. "When I first arrived in Thailand I thought I'd be here for only three months or so," she told Andrew Marshall for *Time* Asia (April 28, 2003). "Then I thought I would go back in three years. Then five years. I always thought the political situation in Burma would improve." Given her international recognition, it would not be difficult for Maung to leave Thailand and seek asylum elsewhere, as many Burmese with means have done over the years. But this is not part of her plan. "If you go and you leave," she explained to Paula Bock, "you cannot work for your people."

Further Reading:

Bangkok Post Aug. 7, 2003, Nov. 24, 2013, Dec. 19, 2013

Devex Web site

GO Campaign Web site

Irrawaddy News Magazine Vol. 7, no. 5 (Jun. 1999), Oct. 17, 2010, Jun. 26, 2012, Jul. 8, 2013, Nov. 9, 2013

Karen News Jan. 2, 2014

Mae Tao Clinic Web site

New York Times Oct. 25, 2007

Seattle Times Sep. 28, 1997, with photo

Sydney Morning Herald (Aug. 17, 2013)

Sydney Peace Foundation Web site

Time magazine (Asia edition) Apr. 28, 2003, with photo; Oct. 31, 2005

Washington Post pA51 Feb. 16, 1992, with photos

Olopade, Olufunmilayo

Nigerian-born oncologist and geneticist

Born: 1957, Ire Ekite, Nigeria

Assessing the groundbreaking research of the Nigerian-born geneticist and oncologist Olufunmilayo Olopade, James Madara, dean of the Pritzker School of Medicine at the University of Chicago, told a writer for the Healthy Life for All Foundation Web site, "Big thinking is what translates into big discovery. Dr. Olopade's thinking has been precisely on this scale: a world- and genome-wide view of connections between African descent and one of the most common cancers in women." Over the last two decades Olopade's ability to think in big and small ways as a researcher and physician—bridging intellectual zeal with patient advocacy, scientific inquiry with cultural empathy, medical ethics with social justice—has established her as a leading voice in the international medical community.

In the 1990s Olopade launched a series of landmark cross-cultural studies to identify the nature of gene mutations in breast cancer, particularly in the cases of women of African descent. With support from the National Institutes of Health and the Breast Cancer Research Foundation, Olopade compared the genetic profiles of several hundred women across Africa, North America, and Europe. Her research revealed that women of African descent expressed different gene mutations than their Caucasian counterparts and stood at higher risk for more aggressive forms of breast cancer at younger ages. She also found that the gene mutations expressed in African women resisted the conventional therapies prescribed to patients of European descent. Motivated by the cultural and environmental facets of her research, in 1992 Olopade established the Cancer Risk Clinic within the Center for Clinical Cancer Genetics and Global Health at the University of Chicago Medical Center to translate her findings into effective clinical practice, addressing the cases of African women whose genetics made them particularly susceptible to disease. Currently Olopade is the Walter L. Palmer Distinguished Service Professor of Medicine & Human Genetics; Associate Dean for Global Health; and Director, Center for Clinical Cancer Genetics, all at the University of Chicago's Pritzker School of Medicine.

In 2005 Olopade received a $500,000 John D. and Catherine T. MacArthur Foundation fellowship—often called the "genius grant"—for her pioneering research into the molecular genetics of breast cancer. The MacArthur award underscored the importance of Olopade's cross-continental, interdisciplinary approach to the prevention, detection, and treatment of breast cancer. It also served as an acknowledgment of Olopade's efforts to apply scientific inquiry to social activism. Years later Olopade, reflecting on the importance of the MacArthur in her career, told Megan Scudellari of the *Scientist* (August 1, 2013) that the "MacArthur gives you the ability to attract more funding. It allowed me to really be a physician-scientist. Physician-scientists are a dying breed, and I was being compelled to choose one or the other." Soon after receiving the award, Olopade commented to Charles Storch of the *Chicago Tribune* (September 20, 2005), that "People in Africa have been understudied, and even African-Americans in this country have been understudied." She would, she added, "continue … advocating for the vulnerable."

Education and Early Career

The fifth of six children, Olufunmilayo Falusi was born on April 29, 1957, in Ire Ekite, in what is now Ekiti State, Nigeria, to the Rev. John Falusi and Dorcas Falusi. (She is known to friends and colleagues as Funmi, pronounced FOON-me.) Her early interest in medicine was sparked by her parents' concern over the dearth of trained physicians in their village. Olopade remarked to Megan Scudellari that, "My father really wanted to have scientists and doctors in the family. My siblings before me were in engineering and science—none of them chose to be in medicine—so I was his second-to-last hope. However, at that time, I was fascinated by physics. I didn't care much for biology, but in Nigeria the option available to me was to be a doctor. I didn't have any theoretical-physicist role models. So I passed a qualifying exam and went to medical school."

In her late teens, Falusi enrolled in medical school at the University of Ibadan's College of Medicine, Nigeria's oldest and most prestigious institution of higher learning. As a student she showed exceptional promise, garnering departmental honors in pediatrics, surgery, and the clinical sciences. In 1980 she received her M.D. degree and was awarded, among other distinctions, the University of Ibadan College of Medicine's Faculty Prize and the Nigerian Medical Association Award for excellence in medicine. After graduation she participated in the National Youth Service Corps—a Nigerian government-sponsored mandatory program for university graduates—serving as a medical officer at the Nigerian Navy Hospital, in Lagos. After working for a year in that program, Falusi relocated to the United States to serve an internship and residency in internal medicine at Cook County Hospital, in Chicago, Illinois. A year after her arrival, a military coup took place in Nigeria, which led to her decision to settle in the United States. She married Christopher Olopade, whom she had met as a medical student in Nigeria, in 1983. In 1986 she was promoted to chief resident at the hospital.

In 1987 Olufunmilayo Olopade accepted a postdoctoral fellowship in hematology and oncology at the University of Chicago. Mentored by Janet Rowley, Blum-Riese Distinguished Professor of Medicine, she researched the molecular genetics of cancer, examining the specific link between genetic mutation and susceptibility to the disease. She completed her fellowship in 1991 and accepted a faculty appointment as assistant professor of hematology and oncology at the University of Chicago. At about the same time, she combined her interests in cancer genetics, prediction, and prevention to establish the Cancer Risk Clinic, an affiliate of the University of Chicago Hospitals; the clinic integrated cutting-edge scientific research with clinical care. "All of my medical training had always emphasized that prevention is better than cure," she recalled for Scudellari, "and while we were making major discoveries in genetics, it wasn't really getting translated into prevention." At the Cancer Risk Clinic she tested for cancer-susceptibility genes. "At the time, it was unheard of, Olopade told Scudellari. "We had a huge debate between geneticists and oncologists about whether this was a good thing to do or not." In an interview (undated) for the Web site of the Breast Cancer Research Foundation, Olopade described her clinic's objectives as being to "coordinate preventive care and testing for healthy patients and their families who because of genetics or family history are at increased risk for cancer" and to focus "on quality-of-life issues for young breast cancer patients, including concerns related to pregnancy, fertility, and employment." The Cancer Risk Clinic's own Web site summed up its mission as threefold—patient care, clinical research, and education (for medical students).

Later Career

In the mid-1990s Olopade focused her scientific and clinical research on the area of breast cancer—the leading cause of death among American women ages 40 to 55—and its prevalence among young nonwhite women, particularly those of African descent. (A cousin of Olopade's had succumbed to the disease at age 32.) Her efforts were motivated in part by a widely celebrated breakthrough in the greater scientific community regarding the identification of BRCA1, a gene "believed to cause about half of all inherited cases of breast cancer," as reported by Thomas H. Maugh III for the *Los Angeles Times* (September 15, 1994). Originally pinpointed in 1990 by the geneticist Mary-Claire King of the University of California at Berkeley, BRCA1 was found to be a tumor-suppressor gene that, when healthy, prevents the aberrant replication of cells; when dysfunctional it "can certainly cause cancers," as Jon Turney remarked in the London *Independent* (June 6, 1994). Citing a study published in the *Lancet*, Turney further noted, "A woman carrying the altered form of the gene has an 80 percent chance of contracting breast cancer before she reaches 70." He qualified that statement, however, by adding that "only around 5 per cent of all breast cancer cases are linked to mutations inherited from the patient's parents, and only around half of these are due to BRCA1. … Most cancer researchers think that the inheritance of a BRCA1 mutation represents one stage of a multistep process which is seen in every case of breast cancer." That qualification aside, medical professionals received news of BRCA1's discovery with great optimism. In 1995 BRCA2, a second gene linked to breast cancer susceptibility, was identified. The discovery of BRCA1 confirmed prior studies that linked heredity to cancer susceptibility and strengthened the case for genetic testing as a viable detection measure.

An early and passionate advocate of genetic testing, Olopade explained in the portion of the article she wrote for the *Chronicle of Higher Education* (July 3, 1998), "It is now widely accepted that cancer is a genetic disease, and that an accumulation of genetic defects can cause normal cells to become cancerous. … The most effective approach to preventing, diagnosing, and treating cancer is to identify individuals who are at risk. Genetic testing for cancer susceptibility can identify these individuals and provide unique opportunities to develop new strategies for early detection and prevention."

The BRCA1 discovery introduced a host of ethical and socioeconomic questions and implications for clinical practice. With regard to genetic testing, which had become the preferred method for amassing statistics on breast-cancer susceptibility, for instance, why did the findings not reflect a more diverse sampling of patients? Olopade addressed that question in an editorial column in the *New England Journal of Medicine* (November 7, 1996): "At present, the only women at high risk who are not being tested are those who are economically disadvantaged or uninformed. The situation is clearly unfair. How should physicians responsibly address this latest challenge when there are no prospective, randomized clinical trials on which to base decisions?" In particular, Olopade cited the disparities between breast-cancer victims of African heritage and those of European ancestry, which she had observed in part through years of treating and observing patients at the Cancer Risk Clinic. While visiting Nigeria for a niece's wedding in 1997, Olopade spent time at a breast-cancer clinic and was struck by how young the patients there were, in comparison with white breast-cancer patients. From the well-documented research performed by the scientific community throughout the 1990s, Olopade noted that while African American women experienced a lower incidence of breast cancer than Caucasian women, they had developed its more virulent forms at younger ages, contributing to higher mortality rates from the disease among black women. Determined to unravel the medical mystery presented by that finding, Olopade launched a cross-continental research project that sought to collect and analyze the genetic profiles of more than 100,000 breast-cancer patients under the age of 45 in the United States, Africa, and the Caribbean; with the resulting data she hoped to identify the environmental, social, and nutritional factors that increased a woman's susceptibility to breast cancer.

Olopade presented some of her findings in 2004 at a landmark conference she helped organize: the First International Workshop on New Trends in the Management of Breast and Cervical Cancers, held in Lagos. Drawing experts from the University of Chicago, the University of Ibadan, and the Medical Women's Association of Nigeria, the symposium addressed the issues of cancer awareness, detection, and prevention in African nations, including Nigeria, where breast-cancer patients' rate of surviving for five years stood at 10 percent. (By contrast, five-year survival rates for breast-cancer patients in the United States exceeded 85 percent.) As quoted in a news release from the University of Chicago Hospitals (May 14, 2004), Olopade assessed the state of Nigeria's medical practices in stark terms: "Cancer awareness, even among physicians, and much more so among women at risk, needs an enormous boost in Nigeria. … We were trying to follow about 500 young Nigerian women who had been diagnosed with breast cancer, but in a very short time, without access to optimal treatment, almost all of them had either died or been lost to follow-up." Cancer, Olopade observed, remained a leading cause of death for Africans, despite the overshadowing urgency of the continent's AIDS pandemic.

In 2005, more than a decade after the identification of BRCA1, Olopade and other researchers from the University of Chicago produced evidence that suggested unique gene expressions in the breast cancers of African women. Through an ongoing study funded by the Breast Cancer Research Foundation and the National Women's Cancer Research Alliance, Olopade compared cancer tissue from 378 women in Nigeria and Senegal with tissue samples from 930 women in Canada, deriving a number of significant conclusions in the process. Olopade determined that breast cancers in African women, for instance, originated from basal-like cells rather than the milk-secreting luminal cells of their white American and European counterparts (tumors caused by basal-like cells are more dangerous). She further observed that most African breast cancers lacked the estrogen receptors found in 80 percent of Caucasian breast cancers. Cancer tumors in African women, as a result, were largely unaffected by hormonal stimulus, and the tumors neutralized the power of such conventional estrogen-blocking drugs as Tamoxifen. On the positive side, Olopade found that African cancers were less likely to express HER2 (or human epidermal growth factor receptor), a protein that, when mutated, stimulates aggressive cancer-cell growth. Only 19 percent of Africans expressed that cell, compared with 23 percent of Caucasians. Those statistics have implications for black American women, 40 percent of whom "have a lineage that can be traced back to historical Nigeria," as Lovell A. Jones, a researcher at the University of Texas, told Cynthia Daniels of *Newsday* (December 30, 2005). As quoted in a University of Chicago Hospitals news release (April 18, 2005), Olopade concluded that while breast cancer struck fewer women in Africa than in the Americas, it "hits earlier and harder." She hoped that her findings would initiate new testing measures for breast-cancer patients of varying ethnicities. "We need to reconsider how to screen for a disease that is less common but starts sooner and moves faster," she said. "Obviously, an annual mammogram beginning at 50 is not the best route to early detection in African women, who get the disease and die from it in their 40s, and it also needs to be adjusted in African Americans and high-risk women of all racial/ethnic groups."

For her pioneering research in the molecular genetics of breast cancer and for the development of genetic testing measures for women of African heritage, Olopade was awarded the MacArthur Foundation grant in September 2005. At its Web site the foundation stated, "In bridging continents with her innovative research and service models, Olopade is increasing the probability of improved outcomes for millions of women of African heritage at risk for cancer here and abroad."

Olopade continues to refine predictive models for cancer risk that incorporate patients' genetics, ancestry, and ethnicity. "Breast cancer isn't one single disease," she told Kimberly L. Allers of *Essence* (January 2006). "It affects women of different populations in different ways." In April 2006 Olopade was awarded the inaugural Minorities in Cancer Research Jane Cook Wright Lectureship by the American Association for Cancer Research (AACR), in recognition of her contributions as a minority physician and scientist to cancer research. At the AACR annual meeting in Washington, D.C., Olopade delivered a lecture entitled "Nature or Nurture in Breast Cancer Causation." According to Sola Ogundipe, writing for *Vanguard* (April 18, 2006), the lectureship honored Olopade's recent discovery of a so-called putative suppressor gene "that is involved in several other solid breast cancer tumors," a finding that "eventually led to the identification of the gene tagged p16INK4." In April 2006 Olopade traveled to China Medical University, in Shenyang, for a two-week visiting professorship, during which she presented her groundbreaking research on cancer genetics and women of color. Regarding her decision to lecture in China, Olopade told Bennie M. Currie of *Crisis* (May/June 2006), "Our work on women of color has impact for other minority women, too. … Breast cancer is a disease that globally affects more than a million women."

"I think we can democratize how we prevent and treat cancer, so people on the periphery can take advantage of the research going on in the center. With health information tools, we can actually do that."

From 2007 until 2010, Olopade helped oversee a trial run with 16 Nigerian patients for Capecitabine, a pill form of chemotherapy aimed at African women with advanced stages of breast cancer (*Breast Journal*, September 19, 2013). They concluded that "Capecitabine monotherapy showed good overall response rates with minimal toxicity and further studies are warranted." With additional funding from the Breast Cancer Research Foundation, she is also examining the destructive interactions between Fanconi anemia-associated genes and BRCA1. (Fanconi [or Fanconi's] anemia is a rare genetic disease that is marked by congenital abnormalities and bone-marrow failure. Victims of the disorder have a significantly higher-than-average chance of getting cancer or other diseases.)

In 2008, with Sarah Gehlert, the Helen Ross Professor in the School of Social Service Administration at the University of Chicago, Olopade received a $9.7 million grant from the National Institutes of Health (NIH) to study "the possible connections between living in disadvantaged neighborhoods and the development of early onset breast cancer," according to a University of Chicago press release (March 20, 2008). Along with researchers Dana Sohmer, Tina Sacks, and Charles Mininger, Gehlert and Olopade studied 230 black women with newly diagnosed breast cancer living in "predominantly black Chicago neighborhoods to learn about environmental factors, such as neighborhood features that might lead to social isolation." Gehlert stated that "these women experience stress from dealing with situations they cannot control, from seeing crime in their neighborhood, from being afraid to go out, and not being able to form casual relationships with their neighbors that might make them feel safe."

Olopade received a Doris Duke Distinguished Clinical Scientist Award, a five-year grant from the Doris Duke Charitable Foundation, in 2000; she was given a continuation grant in 2006 and a clinical research mentorship grant in 2013. Olopade received the American Association for Cancer Research–Minorities in

Cancer Research Jane Cooke Wright Memorial Lectureship Award in 2006, the American Cancer Society Award and Lecture Award in 2009, and the National Honor Award, Officer of the Order of the Niger, in 2012. In 2011 she was appointed by President Barack Obama to the National Cancer Advisory Board. The board "advises the administration with respect to the activities of the National Cancer Institute, including reviewing and recommending for support grants and cooperative agreements, following technical and scientific peer review," according to an article by John Easton for the University of Chicago News Web site (March 11, 2011). Easton noted that Olopade continues to "work with doctors in her native Nigeria, and with government officials and drug companies across Africa, to improve education and treatment."

Olopade serves on the board of trustees of the Healthy Life for All Foundation, an advocacy group that promotes the advancement of medical technology in Nigeria. She also serves on the board of directors of the American Board of Internal Medicine, Susan G. Komen (formerly Susan G. Komen for the Cure), and the Lyric Opera of Chicago, and she is senior medical adviser for Cancer IQ (of which her daughter Feyi serves as chief executive officer). Olufunmilayo Olopade is a member of a number of professional organizations, including the American Association for Cancer Research, American Association for the Advancement of Science, American Society of Breast Disease, American Philosophical Society, American Society for Clinical Investigation, Association of American Professors, Nigerian Medical Association, American Society of Preventative Oncology, American Society of Hematology, Institute of Medicine, American Academy of Arts and Sciences, and American College of Physicians, and of Women in Cancer Research. She has been awarded honorary degrees by North Central University, Dominican University, Bowdoin College, and Princeton University.

Olopade continues to study the population genetics of breast cancer. To Megan Scudellari, she commented, "I truly believe that once you understand the genetic basis (of cancer in a population), then you can look at pathways to disrupt, and get better drugs and better prevention. … My main project now continues to be to understand how to use genomics to improve global health and global cancer research. I'm building a big database of cancer patients I can use to inform the treatment of any patient, no matter where they are in the world. I think we can democratize how we prevent and treat cancer, so people on the periphery can take advantage of the research going on in the center. With health information tools, we can actually do that."

Olufunmilayo Olopade and Christopher Olopade, a pulmonologist who is currently Professor of Family Medicine and Medicine Clinical Director of the Global Health Initiative at the University of Illinois at Chicago, have three grown children, Feyi, Dayo, and Tobi. Olopade and her husband live in the Kenwood area of Chicago.

Further Reading:

American Association for Cancer Research Web site

Breast Cancer Research Foundation Web site

Breast Journal, Sep. 19, 2013

Cancer Risk Clinic Web site

Chicago Tribune Sep. 20, 2005, Oct. 4, 2009

Chronicle of Higher Education Jul. 3, 1998

Crisis Vol. 113, no. 3 (May/Jun. 2006): p35

Essence Jan. 2006; Healthy Life for All Foundation Web site

(London) *Independent* Jun. 6, 1994

Los Angeles Times pA1 Sep. 15, 1994

New England Journal of Medicine p1455 Nov. 7, 1996

New York Times pA16 June 7, 2006; *Scientist* Aug. 1, 2013

University of Chicago Hospitals Web site

University of Chicago News Web site

Selected Books:

Williams, Christopher Kwesi O., Olufunmilayo I. Olopade, and Carla I. Falkson, eds., *Breast Cancer in Women of African Descent* (Dordrecht: Springer, 2006)

Omichinski, Linda

Canadian dietician and health advocate

Born: 1955, Montreal, Canada

"People need to learn to stop dieting and start living," Linda Omichinski, a Canadian health activist, told Jamie Baxter for the *Vancouver Sun* (April 17, 1995). "They need to relearn the skills they knew as children before they got caught up in diets—to listen to their bodies." The freedom from dieting in favor of an all-around healthy attitude toward food and exercise is one of the central tenets of HUGS, the Canadian-based advocacy organization founded by Omichinski in 1987. (The HUGS program, as noted on its Web site, is "Health focused, centered on Understanding lifestyle behaviours, Group supported, and Self-esteem building.")

Omichinski began her career as a dietician equating body weight with health. "For awhile I had listened uncritically to my clients as they told me how happy they were with the individualized diets I designed for them," she recalls on the HUGS Web site. "'I never feel deprived,' they would claim. Or they'd tell me: 'I'm really losing weight on this plan.' But then, one day, it hit me: sooner or later I'd lose contact with them for awhile, only to run into them in the local grocery store—where they were invariably embarrassed because they'd gained the weight back." Omichinski realized that dieting failed to meet the needs of her patients, forcing them to adhere to unnatural patterns of restriction and indulgence. "Diets don't work," she told Johanna Burkhard for the *Montreal Gazette* (March 24, 1993), "and over 95 percent of all dieters regain the weight they have lost and even more within a two- to five-year period." Omichinski believed that the key to breaking this cycle was to promote physical and emotional health rather than weight loss; this became the foundation of HUGS International.

Omichinski's health workshops dispelled health and diet myths and encouraged members to change their lifestyles and attitudes about food and weight loss. "In this culture, we're trained to think that we have to be thin to be healthy, happy, attractive, and worthwhile," Omichinski explains on the HUGS Web site. "We need to realize that there is no 'one' right shape, size or weight. We are trained to think we have to be thin to be healthy, happy, attractive, and worthwhile. We're trained to believe that success and value are determined by the number on the bathroom scale. But we all have different body shapes, metabolisms, and activity levels." At first, people were unsure about her message. "I think that dieticians felt particularly threatened by HUGS at first," she told Ann Douglas for *Radiance* magazine (Spring 1998). "After all, diets are what dieticians are trained in and what they know best. … It was a hard message to sell." As the no-diet movement gained momentum, however, HUGS tapped into the frustration of lifelong dieters, and Omichinski was able to expand the programs and products offered by HUGS through the use of trained "facilitators" who work elsewhere in Canada and in the United States, England, South Africa, and New Zealand. She modified and expanded HUGS's message to reach teenagers and people living with diabetes. HUGS met with moderate success despite limited resources to compete with such diet programs as Weight Watchers or Jenny Craig. "We simply don't have the finances to run the commercials required to combat those diet messages," Omichinski explained to Douglas, "even though we do have visions of what those commercials will look like!"

Education and Early Career

The daughter of Romanian immigrants, Linda was born on April 8, 1955, in Montreal, Canada. Her father, Steve, worked for the Canadian Pacific Railway, and her mother, Catherine, was a homemaker. An only child, she credits her parents with raising her in an atmosphere that nurtured her health and self-esteem. "What was so beautiful was growing up in a supportive environment," she explained in an interview with *Current Biography International*. "I was never made to feel inadequate." She grew up free from any pressure to strive for perfection, whether in school or in terms of her appearance. As a child, however, she did observe the frustrations of her mother in trying to lose weight at the urging of her doctor. "Not that she was as obsessed as people are today," Omichinski told *Current Biography International*, but she added that her mother was an "avid Weight Watchers follower." While her mother struggled with dieting, Linda never had any weight or food-related problems. "I went to Europe with my grandparents when I was 18," she recalled for *Current Biography International*, "and I came back having gained some weight—it was maybe five pounds—but my clothes didn't fit." Instead of telling her daughter she should lose the weight, Omichinski's mother helped her alter her clothing. As a result of this upbringing, Omichinski maintains, her self-esteem and body image never hinged on her weight; food was something to be enjoyed without guilt. "The focus wasn't on food or the numbers on the scale," she explained to *Current Biography International*. "Fun and dancing" were the focal points of family gatherings, not food. In addition to dance, she also enjoyed playing tennis, but she never tied her exercise to weight loss.

After high school Omichinski spent a brief stint as a chemistry major but eventually decided to pursue nutrition at Ryerson University, in Toronto. She spent two years in the Food and Nutrition Program before transferring to McGill University, in Montreal, where she earned a bachelor's degree in Food Sciences in 1979. She then completed her training as a dietician at the Health Sciences Centre, in Winnipeg, in 1983. On being certified, Omichinski began working as a consulting dietician for the Carman Memorial Hospital and Hearth Health Education Centre in Carman, Manitoba. From 1985 until 1989, she was also a consulting diabetes educator for the Carman Education Center. Her work was originally traditional: she tailored diets for people's weight-loss goals.

Later Career

After a few years of telling people how and what to eat, however, Omichinski began to feel that there was something lacking in her work and in the training she'd received. "Something was wrong," she told Ann Douglas. "It didn't feel right. I began searching and listening [to clients] some more. … It took a few years of inner searching and talking to more and more people before I realized that the focus on weight needed to be removed all together. I think the turning point for me came when a client said to me, 'Linda, I am no longer starving and bingeing. I am eating more regularly. I am beginning to enjoy healthier foods and feel the energy those foods bring me. I am enjoying walking for the fun of it. But I am not losing weight. What am I doing wrong?' That hit me like a ton of bricks. I said, 'You aren't doing anything wrong. You may be at the weight your body was meant to be.'" Omichinski's epiphany became a new mission, and she decided to work to dispel the myth that weight was a reliable measure for health.

The HUGS International Web site states its "vision" as the following: "To challenge the myths of the diet industry by shifting the attitudes and beliefs of the public consciousness from the preoccupation with weight and size to an acceptance and appreciation of healthier living." Its "mission" is "to deliver the freedom message of the nondiet model for healthy living by establishing a worldwide network of facilitators to offer our program and products." At its inception in 1987, HUGS was a ten-week program with the rationale that it would be the last program clients would ever need in pursuing their health goals. It began as a series of classes taught by Omichinski in the town of Portage la Prairie, Manitoba. In a group counseling setting, discussions about body image and health and weight myths led to examinations of the reasons people diet in the first place. As the realization sunk in that dieting was not only ineffective, but ultimately counterproductive—dieters who lose weight initially tend to regain the weight, and more, over time—Omichinski was able to attract more clients who were fed up with the demoralizing pattern of dieting to lose weight.

Over time, the HUGS classes grew, and Omichinski began receiving positive feedback as well as requests for supplementary material to the workshops. In response Omichinski wrote *You Count, Calories Don't*, a book that outlined the philosophy and goals promoted by HUGS; it was published in May of 1992. It began by introducing the reader to the idea that diets don't work and that "deprogramming a person from the diet mentality is the key to regaining control." "HUGS," Omichinski wrote, "counters the pervasive culture of slimness in our society. It helps you recognize that the desirability of a perfectly proportioned, ultra-slim body is an unnatural goal that has been forced on all of us by multimedia advertising. We are conditioned to believe that we must conform and that the illusionary perfection of slimness can be ours if we follow the perfect diet, eat the right way, and allow the pursuit of this false ideal to overtake and control our daily lives. The HUGS program helps people realize that individual differences are important. HUGS will show you how to be the best that you can be, physically and emotionally." *You Count, Calories Don't* was well received. In a review for the *Journal of Nutrition Education* (May/June 1994), Dr. Ellen Parham noted its accessibility and praised its attempt to unveil the falsehoods promoted by the diet industry. "The honesty about the failures of dieting are so important and the suggested alternatives so valuable that the book should be read by nutrition educators and recommended to their clients and students." Writing for the *Canadian Home Economics Journal* (Winter 1994), Margie Keys opined, "The information is excellent and the author's approach is sensible and realistic. A must for anyone concerned about his or her health and leading a healthy lifestyle." By February 1993, *You Count, Calories Don't* had sold 1,500 copies; a national book tour that year helped the book become a Canadian best-seller, according to her Web site. In an article entitled "More of Me to Love," Jacqui Gingras noted that as of 2013, more than 20,000 copies of Omichinski's book had been sold in Canada.

As the HUGS message was being spread in Canada, Omichinski started to develop a network of contacts to act as HUGS "facilitators" across North America, and eventually, abroad. Coupled with the success of *You Count, Calories Don't*, HUGS's expanding reach attracted media attention. But the enthusiasm generated by the book tour and newspaper articles was difficult to maintain. Recalling the "hard times" early on, Omichinski told Ann Douglas, "since the message was still very much ahead of its time, participants didn't spread the word about HUGS." Moreover, participants found—and continue to find—that while HUGS helped them reject dieting and focus on their self-esteem and overall health, maintaining that mindset posed a daily challenge, especially at first. "People come away [from HUGS] confident, but society is very much still in the diet culture," Omichinski told *Current Biography International*. To support people trying to stick with what they learned in HUGS, Omichinksi developed the idea of having a "buddy": someone to provide positive reinforcement and encouragement in the face of doubt and the enormous media pressure to be thin. In addition to having a "buddy" to help stave off self-doubt, HUGS also has a bulletin board on its Web site where clients can communicate with and encourage each other. Another key aspect to HUGS, Omichinski explained to *Current Biography International*, is recognition that success is a process. "It's not going to happen overnight."

During the 1990s HUGS continued to grow and Omichinski worked to spread the non-diet message. She spoke out against diet programs that just try to hook people by "repackaging" the diet myth, promoting regimented, restrictive eating as part of a healthy lifestyle and casting exercise as primarily a weight-loss tool. (HUGS promotes exercise for fun and energy.) She also continued to stress the fact that diets are ultimately ineffective. "If diets worked, diet companies would have gone out of business a long time ago," she told Jamie Baxter. "Instead, it's a billion-dollar industry." An invitation to speak at a conference in New Zealand sponsored by Agencies for Nutrition Action in 1997 resulted in further international exposure; in addition to being one of the keynote speakers, Omichinski was interviewed by various media outlets and the conference and subsequent contacts brought more facilitators on board. Also in 1997 Omichinski published the book *Tailoring Your Tastes*, a cookbook that helped readers choose healthier foods, alter recipes, combine foods for energy and nutrition at meals and snacks, ensure permanent changes to their tastes, and accommodate meals for a family's individuality. Two years later a new edition of *You Count, Calories Don't* was released; it included a new chapter titled "Midlife—A Time for Empowerment." In 2000 Omichinski published *Staying Off the Diet Roller Coaster*, a book geared toward people who have chosen to remain out of the diet cycle and need support sticking to their decision. It included testimonials and stories from people who were successfully managing to live a diet-free life.

The HUGS mission faced daunting opposition owing to the popularity of diets such as the Atkins Diet, which cuts carbohydrates from one's meals, prompting the body to burn fat for energy. The diet was effective for rapid weight-loss and became hugely influential (although controversial for its liberal allowance of fatty foods and red meat), and many food companies—ranging from fast-food restaurant chains to makers of bread and pasta—bowed to the success of the Atkins plan by offering low-carb options. This served to reinforce the already pervasive (and false, according to Omichinski) message that diets can both make people lose weight and make them happier. Omichinski points to the Internet as simultaneously a great place to build support networks and a major purveyor of negative messages liable to derail the work involved in remaining diet-free. "Because we now have the Internet, when a new diet comes out, it doesn't just make a little dent," Omichinski told *Current Biography International*. "It definitely affects our business. It affects people who are on a no-diet approach." Instead of dieters attempting to find the core reason they wish to lose weight, they will join the newest fad. As Omichinski told *Current Biography International*, "[technological] forwardness in our world is not necessary forwardness in other crucial areas."

Because Omichinski believes that young people are particularly vulnerable to society's emphasis on thinness and dieting, HUGS developed a set of programs called "Teens & Diets: No Weigh," which are geared toward teenagers. Designed to be fun, interactive, and educational, the programs include activities to be taught in health classes at schools. Schools, according to Omichinski, are the ideal setting for the programs. "It's harder to market the teen program," she told *Current Biography International*. "Teens are so busy … it's also harder to get them to take a program. But in school, the teacher would be capable of teaching [the HUGS program]." Despite the fact that integrating HUGS into schools proved challenging, Omichinski says that working with adolescents is important and rewarding because it's an opportunity to reach young people before they start dieting. She told *Current Biography International*, "We are preventing them from getting on the diet roller coaster for the rest of their lives. The sad part is that [teens] are very entrenched in how they look." In the program "Weight Management for Teens," Omichinski provided time-tested and proven strategies for counseling teens on weight management and building a healthy body through proper nutrition. Some course objectives of the program are as follows: contrasting mind and body hunger, naming and refuting three myths about the nutritional needs of teenage athletes, and explaining the forces that influence how teenagers feel about themselves.

In 2010 Omichinski developed a continuing education course (and book) for adults entitled *Nondiet Weight Management: A Lifestyle Approach to Health & Fitness.* This course "provides practical strategies and techniques for breaking the diet failure cycle and achieving lasting fitness and health." The course offers practitioners a "way to help clients develop nourishing eating and activity patterns, rather than focusing on weight or appearance."

"What ends up happening when people focus on dieting is that they put their lives on hold. ... When they are freed, they end up being able to fulfill their potential."

Today there are more than 75 HUGS facilitators in multiple cities across Canada and nearly as many in the United States; HUGS also has outposts in New Zealand, England, and South Africa. For people who want to complete a HUGS program but do not have facilitators nearby, there are versions that are offered on line, through the HUGS Web site. "We have grown slowly," Omichinski told Ann Douglas, "and use the same philosophy in business as what we do with lifestyle: One step at a time, recognize and appreciate the mini-successes, and don't judge success simply by external terms (i.e. weight loss when referring to lifestyle or income when referring to business success). Internal gratification is important, too."

In addition to her work with HUGS, Omichinski is a member of the advisory board of the Body Positive Institute in Canada. This nonprofit organization is "committed to providing resources and support for healthcare professionals who work in the areas of disordered eating, eating disorders, and the promotion of healthy self-esteem and positive body image," as enunciated at its Web site. Founded by Deb Burgard and Connie Sobczak, Body Positive "furthers the Health At Every Size (HAES) paradigm by ensuring healthcare professionals are supported with the most current educational resources and products, advocating services for patients, and researching innovative and adjunctive therapies."

Among the people who have aided and encouraged her work, Omichiski feels particularly indebted to her friend and fellow nondiet crusader, Francie Berg, of the Healthy Weight Network in North Dakota, who is also known for having founded the *Healthy Weight Journal.* "Francie's work has been very influential in the sense that it consists more of 'why' we need to work on a no-diet approach," Omichinski told *Current Biography International.* "[HUGS] is more the 'how-to.'" In her free time, Omichinski enjoys various types of dance, as well as tennis in the summer and cross-country skiing in the winter. "It's interesting," she observed to *Current Biography International,* "coming full circle to the loves you had when you were younger. ... I'm definitely more physical now than I was before." She continued, "What ends up happening when people focus on dieting is that they put their lives on hold. ... When they are freed, they end up being able to fulfill their potential. A lot of creativity comes out, because they're not as scared so they can be expressive. And that is a huge outcome that goes beyond food."

Omichinski lives in near Portage la Prairie, Manitoba, with her husband, Mitchell, a mechanical engineer. In 2011, according to Ted Meseyton at the Web site Grainews, Mitchell began a sizable local maple syrup business "relying solely on Manitoba maple and silver maple trees."

Further Reading:

Body Positive Web site

HUGS Web site

Radiance Spring 1998

Toronto Star May 11, 1993

Vancouver Sun pC6 Apr. 17, 1995

Selected Books:

Omichinski, Linda, *You Count, Calories Don't,* 1992

Omichinski, Linda, and Heather Wiebe Hildebrand, *Tailoring Your Tastes,* 1997

Omichinski, Linda, *Staying Off the Diet Rollercoaster,* 2000

Omichinski, Linda, *Nondiet Weight Management: A Lifestyle Approach to Health & Fitness,* 2010

Pitanguy, Ivo

Brazilian plastic surgeon, philanthropist

Born: 1926, Belo Horizonte, Minas Gerais, Brazil

The Brazilian physician Ivo Pitanguy is the world's most famous plastic surgeon, known for technical mastery and artistic finesse in refurbishing the bodies of state and Hollywood royalty, whose members regularly fly to his clinic in Rio de Janeiro. He has pioneered numerous plastic surgery techniques in his 60 years of practice, specializing in breast operations and buttock lifts, and has trained a generation of plastic surgeons from all over the world. Often called, according to Richard Lapper and Amy Stillman, writing in the *Financial Times* (February 22, 2013), the "pope of plastic surgery," Pitanguy was the first plastic surgeon to be admitted to Brazil's National Academy of Medicine and is often credited for lending medical legitimacy to the field. "His contributions are legendary," Alan Matarasso, a New York-based plastic surgeon, told Laurie Goering of the *Chicago Tribune* (May 23, 1995). "He elevated a specialty to a science and has brought a real academic bent to plastic surgery." Pitanguy's highly publicized philosophy is that everyone has the right to be beautiful. For thousands with firmer stomachs, perkier breasts, and rounder bottoms thanks to Pitanguy and his plastic surgery innovations, "the Professor," as he likes to be called—he prefers the title *Professor* to *Doctor*—is nothing short of a miracle worker. In Brazil he is a celebrity of such iconic stature that at the country's famous carnival, a tribute to Pitanguy was among the floats assembled in 1999. A samba was written about him—"perhaps the greatest compliment by local criteria," Warren Hoge noted in the *New York Times* (June 8, 1980), adding that "his every move, short of his pulse beat, is recorded in Rio's gossip columns."

Perhaps only Brazil could have produced such a celebrity. The country is the world's number-two leader in plastic surgery procedures (the United States is number one). According to a survey on aesthetic and cosmetic procedures performed in 2011 by the International Society of Aesthetic Plastic Surgery, some 1,447,000 were done in Brazil, where "80 percent of all plastic surgery is cosmetic." According to a study conducted by the International Society of Aesthetic Plastic Surgeons, in 2013 the United States had the highest number of plastic surgeons (5,950), followed by Brazil (5,024), then China (2,000). Writing in the *Canadian National Post* (July 27, 2002), Isabel Vincent described plastic surgery as "something of a national obsession in Brazil," calling the city of Rio de Janeiro the nation's plastic surgery capital. "In that city—which elevated leg waxing to an art-form, inspired the 'Brazilian wax' and gave birth to the world's smallest swimsuit, known as the 'dental floss bikini'—monthly magazines devoted to plastic-surgery techniques are sold on street corner newsstands."

Pitanguy is a firm believer that plastic surgery is not only a luxury for the rich and famous. On his clinic's website he states, "The desire for plastic surgery emanates from a transcendental desire. It's an attempt made to harmonize body and spirit and emotion and rationale, seeking to establish equilibrium that allows an individual to feel at peace with his own image and with the surrounding universe." Seeing physical beauty as something of a basic human right, he devotes a portion of his time and skills at a free clinic, the Santa Casa de Misericórdia in downtown Rio, that treats poor Brazilians who do not have the money for basic medical care, let alone plastic surgery. He performs reconstructive surgery for people who have suffered disfiguring accidents, but he also performs tummy tucks for women who can barely afford to feed themselves or their children. "Plastic surgery can be important for self esteem for anyone and should be available," Pitanguy told Vincent. "This is true democracy at work."

Education and Early Career

Ivo Hélcio Jardim de Campos Pitanguy was born in 1926 in Belo Horizonte, in the state of Minas Gerais. His father, Antônio de Campos Pitanguy, was a general surgeon; the family of his mother, Maria Staël Jardim, was in the diamond business. As a child Pitanguy was athletic and competitive, excelling in swimming and winning trophies in state tennis tournaments. Driven and ambitious, he was initially uninterested in pursuing surgery, thinking he might study biology or art instead. Eventually, however, his father convinced him to study medicine, and Pitanguy lied about his age—claiming he was 20 instead of only 16—in order to apply to medical school. He was admitted to the Federal University of Minas Gerais and finished medical school at the University of Brazil (now known as the Federal University of Rio de Janeiro). Pitanguy became devoted to plastic surgery after serving his internship at a local hospital, where he attended to emergency room patients with external and superficial injuries. "We would go in the ambulances into some of the worst areas of the city," he told Warren Hoge. He also practiced his medical training on Brazilian soldiers returning from Europe during World War II. "I saw soldiers in horrible physical conditions, but I also saw the emotional scars of their wounds" he recalled to Anthony Faiola of the *Washington Post* (November 15, 1997). "Restoration of the body became important to me there."

In the late 1940s Pitanguy traveled to the United States and to Europe as a visiting surgeon. As Alexander Edmonds recounted in the *New York Times* (August 13, 2011), "Starting in the 1940s Pitanguy trained with leading plastic surgeons in Europe and the United States. One of his mentors in Britain was Sir Harold Gillies, who pioneered techniques in modern plastic surgery while operating on mutilated World War I veterans. [Pitanguy's] long career thus spans the 20th-century transformation of the specialty from primarily reconstructive techniques to primarily cosmetic improvements." Pitanguy became proficient in various languages (he speaks English, Spanish, French, German, and Italian) and refined his techniques at such institutions as Bethesda Hospital, in Cincinnati, Ohio; the Mayo Clinic, in Rochester, Minnesota; the plastic surgery division of New York University's medical school; and clinics in Paris; Suresnes, France; London; and Derbyshire, England.

On returning to Brazil in the early 1950s, Pitanguy founded Brazil's first clinic specializing in hand surgery at the Santa Casa de Misericórdia General Hospital, in Rio. Soon thereafter he founded the hospital's plastic-surgery department, which he continues to head. At the same time he acted as the head of the Souza Aguiar Hospital's burn unit and reconstructive surgery service. It was during this time that he tested new techniques, developing procedures such as tummy tucks and buttock lifts that were among the first ones ever performed. Unlike many surgeons at the forefront of the plastic surgery movement, Pitanguy was notable early on for sharing his developments and techniques with his colleagues. Many of his early innovations have become standard procedures in such areas as liposuction and breast reduction, and although he is most famous for operating on the rich and famous, he opened a clinic for the poor in 1960. The following year the Gran Circo Norte Americano, a circus, burned to the ground in the city of Niterói, in a devastating accident that left more than 300 people dead and hundreds with serious burns. Pitanguy treated many of the victims, which led to the founding of the burn unit of the Hospital Universitário Antônio Pedro in Niterói. In 1963 he opened the Ivo Pitanguy Clinic for Plastic and Reconstructive Surgery in a Rio neighborhood.

Later Career

Pitanguy's reputation for pioneering work soon made him sought-after by Brazil's wealthier citizens as well as by global celebrities. In 1974 the American saxophone player Stan Getz had work done at Pitanguy's clinic. Two years later Pitanguy operated on the Formula One racecar driver Niki Lauda, whose face required a complete reconstruction following an accident. Over the next several years, Pitanguy's patients included Sophia Loren and Jordan's King Hussein. By the late 1970s, Pitanguy was as famous for his lavish socializing and jet-set lifestyle as he was for his surgery. He spent weekends on his own island south of Rio—flying there in his private jet—and entertaining A-list celebrities from all over the world. "If Hugh Hefner created the magazine for macho fantasy," Warren Hoge wrote in 1980, "Pitanguy has written the book." Much of his socializing included nights out with glamorous women who were also his patients, and in the early 1980s his carousing caused his dismissal from the American Society of Plastic and Reconstructive Surgeons. While the society charged Pitanguy with violating its marketing and advertising rules of conduct, some colleagues said his removal was nothing more than professional sour grapes. A medical practitioner who recalled the episode for Isabel Vincent noted plastic surgeons' reputation for having "strong egos" and described the society's claims as "couched in jealousy." (Pitanguy was readmitted to the organization in 1990.)

"To me, beauty is well-being. Today we are more focused on the superficial. ... It's a great mistake not to cultivate the brain and the spirit."

During his decades in practice, Pitanguy has seen changing trends in plastic surgery. In the beginning, men accounted for only a tiny fraction of his patients, but during the 1970s this began to change. "In the past decade, masculine preening has lost much of the onus it once carried," Warren Hoge noted, "and many men in their late 40s and 50s are now getting their eyes tucked to keep them looking as young as the upcoming executive-suite competition." During the 1980s men made up roughly 6 percent of Pitanguy's patients; by 2003, the figure had risen to about 20 percent, and newspapers widely reported the 1998 eye tuck of Fernando Henrique Cardozo, then Brazil's president.

Although women have always represented the majority of Pitanguy's patients, their demands have changed over the years as well. Until the late 1990s Brazilian women who went to Pitanguy for breast operations largely wanted breast reductions—not enlargements—as idealized beauty in Brazil prized small chests and round buttocks. (In 1997, 40 percent of plastic surgery operations done in Brazil were breast reductions, compared with 3 percent in the United States.) But the popularity of buxom American celebrities have made larger breasts more desirable among Brazilians, prompting more breast augmentations. (The silicone industry has found a booming market in Rio, thanks in part to Pitanguy.) The costs for plastic surgery have risen as well. In 1980 Pitanguy charged $10,000 for a facelift (including eye tucks); in 2004 the cost of a Pitanguy facelift, which included a two-night stay at his clinic, began around $14,000.

While Pitanguy is the first to say that there is no shame in wishing to look one's best—the press has often called him "Dr. Vanity"—he has long stressed the importance of distinguishing between a desire to look beautiful and the hope to find solutions to life's problems that cannot be fixed through plastic surgery. Writing for the London *Guardian* (March 15, 1996), John Ryle recalled how, in the years he got to know Pitanguy, "a fair bit of his working time was spent explaining to prospective patients that it would be better if they didn't have surgery. These were people convinced that cosmetic surgery would change their lives, people addicted to the knife. Dr. Pitanguy employed a psychologist, Dr. Claudia, to deal with such patients. Her job was to persuade them that he was not the answer to their problems." Pitanguy's daughter, Dr. Gisela Pitanguy, a psychotherapist, has "implemented a preoperative and postoperative support service for patients. She screens potential clients, and the clinic frequently turns away those deemed to have unrealistic expectations. "Sometimes a plastic surgeon just has to say no because he cannot perform magic," Pitanguy explained to Laurie Goering. "What I do is not just skin deep. You have to have a good sense of internal balance before you can undergo any kind of cosmetic surgery."

Patients who have passed the psychological screening receive general medical examinations and pose for a "before" picture. ("After" pictures are taken after the bandages are removed.) The patient spends the night on the clinic grounds and has surgery the next day. "Pitanguy's operations are veritable performances," Warren Hoge wrote of Pitanguy in his prime. "Fresh from an early-morning swim, tennis game or karate session, [the doctor] sweeps through the swinging doors into his clinic's three-room operating theater, where a trio of patients have been prepared for his body tailoring. A nurse helps him on with his green smock, mask, and cap. He enters the first room, followed by a number of interns and visiting doctors. The mood is cheerful, the banter lively as he greets the members of his team, positioned around the prone patient. But as Pitanguy puts on gold-rimmed reading glasses to scrutinize the five black and white photos of the patient mounted on a stand, the room becomes quiet. After studying the photographs for a few minutes, he turns and directs an associate to trace with blue tincture on the patient's body the lines of the upcoming incision." Hoge described the subsequent operation as fast and bloody, but accompanied by soothing classical music. When patients return to have their bandages removed, "they can become teary and incoherent when trying to express their thanks. … They treat [Pitanguy] as if he were someone with elemental power, a kind of creator."

Pitanguy's schedule is filled with teaching, training new surgeons, and speaking engagements. In January 1997, along with other leading surgeons across the globe, he helped found the first international school for genital and transsexual surgery, in Belgrade, Serbia. He also co-wrote a book, *Welcome to Your Facelift: What to Expect Before, During, and After Plastic Surgery* (1997), with Helen Bransford.

Pitanguy continues his work with indigent patients at the Santa Casa de Misericórdia Hospital. "It's not about fashion," Pitanguy told Alex Bellos of the *New Zealand Herald* (November 28, 2000). "It is deeper than the skin. We are improving people's self esteem." The craze over plastic surgery in Brazil, however, has given him pause. "My great fight is for these things to be done as normally as possible," he told Bellos. "We are not doing something extraordinary. The important thing is to be natural."

Pitanguy has written more than 900 medical papers on the subject of plastic surgery and is the author several books, including a 1993 memoir, *Aprendendo com a rida* ("Learning about Life"). His groundbreaking 1981 textbook, *Aesthetic Surgery of the Head and Body*, continues to be influential; it was named Best Scientific Book at that year's Frankfurt Book Fair, according to the profile of Pitanguy at the Brazilian Association of Psychiatry Web site. Pitanguy's contributions to other books include chapters on his personal techniques and surgical experience. Pitanguy is editor in chief of the bimonthly *Bulletin of Plastic Surgery of the Ivo Pitanguy Clinic*, which serves as the official journal of the Pontifical Catholic University's Plastic Surgery department and of the Carlos Chagas Institute of Post Graduate Medical Studies. The Ivo Pitanguy Study Center, part of the Ivo Pitanguy Clinic, trains plastic surgeons studying at both institutions, as well as visiting surgeons from all over the world.

Pitanguy is a founding member of the American Trauma Society and the Brazilian Hand Society. His other professional affiliations include the Brazilian National Academy of Medicine, Brazilian College of Surgeons, International College of Surgeons, American College of Surgeons, American Society of Plastic Surgeons, International Plastic and Reconstructive Aesthetic Surgery, and the British Association of Plastic Surgeons. He has been awarded honorary degrees from the University of Tel Aviv and the Universidade de Santos in São Paulo, an honorary chancellorship from the University of Paris, and an honorary membership in the Medical Society of Bologne, Italy. He has won numerous Brazilian and international prizes, including the Mérito Tamandaré medal, the Alfred Jurzykowski prize of the National Academy of Medicine, and the Medalha do Mérito Médico from the Brazilian Ministry of Health. There is also a surgical instrument named for him; Laurie Goering described the "Pitanguy Flap Demarcator" as a "sort of combination scissor and clamp."

In addition to his professional work, Pitanguy spent ten years as president of Rio's Museum of Modern Art and is a curator-member of the city's botanical gardens. His island home, Ilha dos Porcos Grande, or Big Pigs' Island, which he purchased in 1973, is located in a wildlife conservation zone and is an ecological sanctuary boasting many varieties of plants and wildlife. There, according to James Reginato, writing in *W* magazine, Pitanguy "assembled a collection of rare animals and exotic birds—saffron finches, rufous-bellied thrushes, green-winged saltators, capuchin monkeys, and numerous other species—most of which wander free." (According to *Private Islands* magazine, however, as of early 2014, the island was up for sale.)

James Reginato noted that "the 87-year-old professor is sympathetic to others who are unhappy about aging: 'I believe that you should correct the [aging] process with elegance and distinction. You should not overdo, because if you overdo, you are only creating a mask without expression, a mask of death. That should be avoided.'" Pitanguy told Reginato that he has never had cosmetic surgery: "I have a tolerant ego. … As long as you can tolerate yourself, you don't need a surgeon." "To me," Pitanguy continued, "beauty is well-being. Today we are more focused on the superficial, and when people who just live for looks lose them, they will be unhappy. It's a great mistake not to cultivate the brain and the spirit."

Pitanguy lives in Rio and Ilha dos Porcos Grande with his wife, Marilu Nascimento; they married in 1955. They have four children: Ivo, Gisela, Helcius, and Bernardo. Gisela Pitanguy is the director of the Ivo Pitanguy Clinic.

Further Reading:

Brasilian Academy of Letters

Brazilian Association of Psychiatry Web site

Canadian National Post Jul. 27, 2002

Chicago Tribune p1 May 23, 1995

Financial Times Feb. 22, 2013

International Society of Aesthetic Plastic Surgeons Web site

Ivo Pitanguy Clinic Web site

New York Times p44 Jun. 8, 1980

New Zealand Herald Nov. 28, 2000

W magazine Jul. 2008

Washington Post pA1 Nov, 10, 1997

Books:

Edmonds, Alexander, *Pretty Modern: Beauty, Sex and Plastic Surgery in Brazil* (Durham, N.C.: Duke University Press, 2010)

Gilman, Sander L., *Making the Body Beautiful* (Princeton: Princeton University Press, 1999).

Rogge, Jacques

Belgian athlete, orthopedic surgeon, international Olympics administrator

---

Born: 1942, Ghent, Belgium

On July 16, 2001, members of the International Olympic Committee (IOC), the administrative body that governs the Olympic Games, elected Jacques Rogge, an orthopedic surgeon from Belgium and former three-time Olympian yachtsman, as its new president. Among his top priorities were reducing the size of the Olympic Games, which had become expensive and more difficult to organize; cracking down on "doping" or the use of performance-enhancing drugs by Olympic athletes; and restoring the good name of the IOC, which had been tarnished in several scandals involving bribery and kickbacks. "If we want [the Olympics] to remain an important social force, sport must be credible for public opinion and for society," Rogge told Stephen Wilson of the Associated Press, (June 24, 2001). "That means we have to do more in terms of doping, we have to clean up sport from every source of corruption, and we have to give a more human face to sport than it has today. We need a great emphasis on the defense of the values." Re-elected to a second term as president of the IOC in 2009—his first term was eight years, and his second term was four years—Rogge presided over the organization until 2013. "He was absolutely the right person at the right time," noted senior Norwegian IOC member Gerhard Heiberg, as quoted by Wilson of the Associated Press (September 3, 2013). "He has brought stability to the organization."

Education and Early Career

Jacques Rogge was born on May 2, 1942 in Ghent, Belgium. Rogge came from an athletic background. "My grandfather was a professional cyclist at the turn of [the twentieth] century," Rogge told Wilson. "My father was a track and field athlete and a rower." Jacques picked up a love of sailing from his parents, who began taking him out on the North Sea when he was three years old. As a child he attended boarding school in England, where he began playing rugby.

Rogge watched the Olympics on television for the first time in 1960, when the Summer Games were held in Rome, Italy. He was thrilled as he saw Herb Elliott of the United States win the gold medal in the 1,500-meter dash. "I was shocked in the best sense watching Elliott fly away from the rest of the field," he told Sebastian Coe for the London *Daily Telegraph* (November 11, 2001). "He did it with such style. Almost as though he was in his own world, it was surreal." Rogge began his career as an athlete during the 1960s, sailing and playing rugby professionally. "I was better in sailing," he told Wilson in 2001, "but preferred rugby." He played rugby as a member of the Belgian national team for ten years, winning one championship. As a professional yachtsman, Rogge was the Belgian champion 16 times, and, in international competition, the world champion once and the runner-up twice. Rogge competed in the Summer Olympics as a yachtsman three times, in Mexico City, Mexico, in 1968; Munich, West Germany, in 1972; and Montreal, Canada, in 1976. (His best finish was fourteenth, in the 1972 Games.)

The 1972 Olympic Games in Munich were marred by tragedy when, on September 5, members of Black September, a radical Palestinian terrorist group, infiltrated the Olympic Village. The terrorists killed an Israeli athlete and a coach and kidnapped nine other Israeli athletes. The terrorists demanded that Israel release two hundred imprisoned Palestinian guerillas. Black September had planned to fly the athletes to Egypt, but the German police attempted to free them at the Munich airport. The shoot-out between the police and the terrorists left the nine athletes, one policeman, and five terrorists dead. After a one-day pause, the competition resumed. "At that time, I was really wondering if I would continue, was it worthwhile, had the games any sense?" Rogge recalled for Wilson. "For two days, I said, 'Going home or staying?' Ultimately I stayed, but I was not proud of staying, and for the rest of the games I had no fun, no joy. Later on, with maturity, I think it was right to stay, otherwise the terrorists would have won their case, and the games would have been destroyed."

Rogge retired from professional sports in 1977, when he turned 35. "In many ways I died when I … retired from competition," he told Jim White of the London *Guardian* (November 10, 2001), "[N]othing compares to playing sport. I would do anything to be young again and competing. That is what the Olympics is about." All during his years of competition, as recounted by Jacquelin Magnay in the *Telegraph* (July 15, 2011), Rogge "had continued with his medical studies at the State University of Ghent, where his specialisation was knee surgery. 'I just liked the challenge: the knee is the most difficult joint to work on, to get good results.' He ended up running sports medicine centres in Deinze and Ghent, conducting about 400 operations every year." Of his medical practice, Rogge commented, "From surgery I have got a much-needed sense of humility, of the uncertainty of life, of the frailty of every ambition. … And surgery teaches you to be systematic. It is like being a pilot, a profession full of checklists. Also, you have to be able to make tough decisions." Rogge also joined the faculties of the University of Ghent and the Université Libre (Free University) in Brussels, as a lecturer in sports medicine.

Later Career

In addition to his medical practice and teaching, Rogge became increasingly involved in the administrative end of the Olympics, joining the Belgian Olympic Committee as an athlete's representative. In 1976 he headed the Belgian Olympic delegation to the Winter Games in Innsbruck, Austria. Four years later Rogge headed the Belgian delegation to the Summer Games in Moscow. That year, President Jimmy Carter announced that the United States would not send a team to compete in the Moscow Games, in order to protest the Soviet Union's invasion of Afghanistan in December 1979. Carter urged other nations to boycott the Moscow Games as well. Belgium considered boycotting the Olympics, but Rogge insisted that Belgian athletes should be allowed to compete, because he believed that politics and the Olympics should be kept separate. "This was a milestone in my life," Rogge said, as quoted by Jeré Longman of the *New York Times* (July 17, 2001). "We thought it was our duty to participate in the Olympic Games. I still feel sorry for those athletes who were denied the Games they deserved. It gave me the resolve that, while we have to work closely with governments to develop sport, we have to preserve our independence." Rogge also headed the Belgian delegation to the Summer Games in Los Angeles, California, in 1984; the Winter Games in Calgary, Canada, in 1988; and the Summer Games in Seoul, South Korea, in 1988.

In 1989 Rogge was elected president of the European Olympic Committee (EOC). Two years later, he became a member of the International Olympic Committee (IOC). In that capacity Rogge received international attention when he warned that certain sports, such as beach volleyball and golf, had to prove their international popularity if they wished to remain part of the Olympics. The press interpreted his comments as a sign that certain sports would be eliminated from the Olympics. During the 1990s Rogge assumed more responsibilities within the IOC and served on several important committees. From 1992 to 1994, he sat on the Olympic Program Commission. In 1992 he joined the IOC's Medical Commission and was elected its vice president in 1994. In this post Rogge became a vocal opponent of doping by Olympic athletes. He was named president of the Coordination Commission for the 2000 Summer Olympic Games in Sydney, Australia. The Games that year were largely considered a success, and Rogge's leadership was widely hailed; he received ample public praise from the IOC president Juan Antonio Samaranch. In 1998 Rogge was named to the IOC's executive board.

In December 1998 the IOC was rocked by a bribery scandal. High-ranking officials of the Salt Lake Organizing Committee (SLOC) were accused of buying votes from IOC members with money, lavish gifts, and offers of free medical care and scholarships for their relatives, in an effort to win the 2002 Winter Games for Salt Lake City. (In 2000 a federal grand jury indicted Thomas Welch, the former president of the SLOC, and David Johnson, the former vice president, on 15 counts involving conspiracy, mail fraud, wire fraud, and interstate travel in the aid of racketeering; in 2001, however, Judge David Sam of the U.S. District Court in Salt Lake City dismissed all of the charges against them.) Samaranch named Rogge to a six-member panel that investigated the allegations of bribery and wrong-doing against as many as 25 members of the IOC. As quoted by Ray Moseley of the *Chicago Tribune* (January 24, 1999), Rogge called those involved guilty of "unacceptable, brutal corruption." In March 1999 the IOC expelled six members. Four other members had already resigned from the IOC, and several others were reprimanded. A number of critics called on Samaranch to resign as president, citing his extravagant habits of flying first-class and staying in luxury hotels. The IOC, however, gave Samaranch an overwhelming vote of confidence. Rogge publicly defended the IOC president, saying that Samaranch "is not a corrupt man, absolutely not," as quoted by John Powers in the *Boston Globe* (January 14, 1999). "Why should someone resign at a moment of crisis? We need leadership. We do not need resignations. It would be ridiculous." In response to widespread criticism from the media, politicians, and sponsors, Samaranch called for reforming the IOC and adopting measures to root out and deter corruption. In a formal vote in December 1999, the IOC approved 50 different reform measures, most notably banning all-expenses-paid visits by its members to cities bidding for the Olympic Games.

In 1997 the IOC awarded the 2004 Summer Games to Athens, Greece. Disagreements among officials in the Greek government and the local organizers of the Games, however, resulted in numerous delays in preparing the city to host the Olympics. Preparations were to include building an Olympic Village to house more than 16,000 athletes, sports facilities for the events, a new airport, and better roads to ease traffic. By 2000 the IOC was concerned that Athens would not be ready to host the Olympics in 2004, and Samaranch instructed Rogge to oversee the preparations in Athens and ensure that the city would be ready for the Games. Rogge publicly called on government officials and organizers in Greece to stop bickering. "I would call for a four-year truce," he said, as quoted by a writer for the London *Times* (October 11, 2000). "They cannot afford to quarrel. They have to unite. Now is the time to pull all the ranks together and work in a united way." In November 2000 Rogge led an IOC delegation to inspect the preparations in Athens and found that significant progress had been made.

After serving as the IOC's president since 1980, Samaranch decided to step down when his term expired in July 2001. Rogge declared himself a candidate for the position, joining a crowded field that included four other IOC members: Kim Un-Yong of South Korea, Richard Pound of Canada, Anita Defrantz of the United States, and Pál Schmitt of Hungary. As an orthopedic surgeon and former Olympian, Rogge, who is fluent in five languages and well known for his diplomatic skills, was widely seen as a formidable candidate. He had ten years of experience as a member of the IOC, including three years on its executive board, yet he was also untouched by the Salt Lake City bribery scandal. (In fact, Rogge boasted that he never visited any of the cities bidding for the Games.) Rogge campaigned on the platform of honesty, pledging to take tough stands against corruption in the IOC and against doping by Olympians. He expressed concern about the exorbitant costs of hosting the Olympic Games. On July 16, 2001, the 127-member IOC elected Rogge as its eighth president. He was the second Belgian to lead the organization. (Henri de Baillet-Latour of Belgium served as president from 1925 until 1942.) Rogge's election as president of the IOC required him to retire, after more than 25 years, from his medical practice in Belgium and to assume his new duties at the IOC's headquarters in Lausanne, Switzerland.

Rogge told the press that his top priority as the IOC president was "defending the credibility of sport, which is under attack from doping, corruption, and violence," as quoted by Dick Leonard in *Europe* (November 2001). "If, tomorrow, the mothers of young children do not want to send them to sports clubs because they could receive drugs, that will be the end of sport," he reiterated, as quoted by Oliver Holt in the London *Times* (July 17, 2001). "We need to keep sport clean and credible, otherwise its popularity will decline. We will never catch every cheat but we can keep cheating to an absolute minimum." Rogge also pledged to reduce the size of the Olympics. "The games have reached the limits of what an organizing committee can deliver," he told a reporter for *Sport Express*, as quoted by Fred Weir of the *Christian Science Monitor* (July 17, 2001). "We have to consider if we should reduce the program, the venue capacity, the growing dependence on and cost of technology and the number of press accreditations."

In his first official act as the IOC president, Rogge awarded the Olympic Order, the IOC's highest honor, to Samaranch, in honor of his predecessor's contributions to sports and his commitment to the Olympics' values. Rogge was also kept busy defending the IOC's controversial decision to award the 2008 Summer Games to Beijing, which was made a short time before his election. Many human-rights activists objected to giving the Games to China, citing its repressive policies and persecution of political dissidents and religious groups. Several critics suggested that China's Communist regime would exploit the Games for propaganda purposes, as the Nazis did when the Games were held in Berlin, in 1936. In late August 2001, Rogge visited Beijing, China, to meet with members of the Chinese Olympic Committee and Jiang Zemin, China's president. "Of course we are concerned with human rights, but, again, the IOC [is] not a political organisation," Rogge said during his visit, as quoted by Mark Hodgkinson of the London *Daily Telegraph* (August 28, 2001). "The Games will have a big impact on China. They will develop the economic side, they are going to make changes to the social environment—that, of course, includes human rights, and they will also encourage sport." Several human rights activists, however, accused the IOC of hypocrisy, recalling that it had previously barred South Africa from the Olympics because of the nation's racist apartheid policies.

The terrorist attacks of September 11, 2001, in New York City and Washington, D.C., raised questions about security at the upcoming Winter Games in Salt Lake City, slated for February 2002. The IOC gave Rogge the authority to cancel the Games, but he pledged that they would go on as scheduled. In an interview with Alan Abrahamson of the *Los Angeles Times* (October 8, 2001), Rogge said that security would be the top priority at the Olympics and that "everything humanly possible will be done" to ensure the safety of the athletes and spectators. He added that although the security would be extensive, it would remain discrete in order to avoid being, as he told Abrahamson, "as stringent as one soldier standing with a rifle behind every athlete."

In November 2001, one month after the United States began its "war on terror," Rogge formally requested that President George W. Bush temporarily suspend hostilities during the Olympics. The IOC president cited an ancient Greek tradition in which all warring parties agreed to a truce during the Games. Bush denied Rogge's request, but he agreed to submit a resolution to the United Nations that called for the safe passage of all athletes during the Olympics. Although he was disappointed, Rogge said that he understood Bush's decision. "We have to be realistic," Rogge told Alan Abrahamson of the *Los Angeles Times* (December 9, 2001). "The IOC will never bring peace to the world. The IOC can only express a symbolic appeal. How can the IOC bring peace to the world when the governments or religions do not achieve this?"

The Olympic Winter Games began as scheduled in Salt Lake City on February 8, 2002. Several days earlier the IOC had denied a request from the United States Olympic Committee that American athletes be allowed to carry a tattered American flag that was recovered from the ruins of the World Trade Center into the Rice-Eccles Olympic Stadium during the opening ceremony, on the grounds that numerous countries had suffered losses during the attacks and that it would be unfair to single one out. After a widespread public outcry, Rogge overruled the IOC, and the display of the flag moved spectators and audiences around the world. In another move that won him accolades, instead of staying at a luxury hotel, Rogge opted for modest accommodations with the athletes in the Olympic Village.

The 2002 Games thrilled fans with many memorable athletic feats, but the Games also saw controversy. Two cross-country skiers, Larissa Lazutina of Russia and Johann Muehlegg of Spain, had their gold medals taken away by the IOC after they tested positive for darbepoetin, a banned substance. The most controversial event involved the pairs figuring-skating competition on February 11. A team of nine judges voted 5–4 to award gold medals to the Russian skaters Elena Berezhnaya and Anton Sikharulisze instead of to Jamie Salé and David Pelletier of Canada. The decision shocked many people, who thought that Sale and Pelletier delivered a performance far superior to that of Berezhnaya and Sikharulisze, who made noticeable mistakes during their routine. Many observers alleged that the judging was rigged in favor of the Russians. The IOC investigated the controversy and learned that Marie-Reine Le Gougne, the French judge, had been pressured to vote for the Russian pair. On February 16 Rogge announced that the IOC executive board, after consulting with the International Skating Union (ISU), had voted to award gold medals to Salé and Pelletier as well. (Berezhnaya and Sikharulisze were allowed to keep their gold medals.) Rogge earned widespread praise in the media for his handling of "Skategate." Despite the controversy, the 2002 Games were widely considered a success, and the NBC television network, which broadcast them, reported impressive ratings. After the 2002 Games, Rogge devoted his attention to administrative matters, including monitoring the preparations for the 2004 Summer Games in Athens. He also moved forward with his proposals to scale back the Games, and the IOC continued to explore the question of which events might be eliminated from future Olympics.

Despite cost overruns and building delays, the Summer Olympics proceeded smoothly in Athens in 2004, and afterward Rogge praised the Games's "state-of-the-art venues" and "flawless" security precautions. "These Games were held in peace and brotherhood," he said. As the 2008 Summer Games approached, Rogge and the IOC were criticized for not pressing China harder on human rights issues. Rogge countered that the IOC was not a political or governmental organization, and he and other IOC officials pointed to positive developments on human rights in China and elsewhere connected with the IOC's standards for the Games. In advance of the Games, however, as reported by Andrew Jacob of the New York Times, Rogge "called on the authorities in Beijing to respect their 'moral engagement' to improve human rights in the months leading up to the Games and to provide the news media with greater access to the country." Tensions over Internet censorship and restrictions on journalists nevertheless remained an undercurrent to the Games. In the end, however, China was praised by the BBC (August 24, 2008), among other news organizations, for "hosting one of the best organised Games in history and staging some of the most memorable opening and closing ceremonies ever seen." The opening ceremonies of the 2010 Winter Olympics in Vancouver were overshadowed by the death earlier in the day of Georgian luger Nodar Kumaritashvili, who crashed on a training run. Speaking with Stephen Wilson, Rogge later singled out this event as unquestionably the low point of his IOC presidency.

In 2012 the Summer Games returned to London. Writing in the *Guardian* (August 12, 2012), Richard Williams reported that at the opening ceremony Rogge "paid tribute to Britain's role in inventing and codifying so many modern sports, and in providing the ethical framework that inspired Pierre de Coubertin to revive the Games." "So much about the reality of London 2012 seemed surprising, even unprecedented," Williams said, describing an "event that began with an explosion of goodwill and never lost its capacity to charm and to amaze."

The London Games were produced on time and on budget, but the costs of hosting the Games, Winter or Summer, have become staggering—a problem that concerned Rogge well before his election as president of the IOC. "On one hand," Rogge told Wilson of the AP (September 3, 2013), "we have to make sure we contain the size, on the other hand we have to help the organizing cities by lowering the demands and the service levels." Wilson reported that Rogge had "instituted a cap of 10,500 athletes and 28 sports for the summer games. The cost of hosting the games has gained urgency at a time of global economic uncertainty, with cities spending tens of billions of dollars on construction projects."

"From surgery I have got a much-needed sense of humility, of the uncertainty of life, of the frailty of every ambition."

Writing on the eve of the London Games in 2012, Jacquelin Magnay provided a glimpse of Rogge's manifold concerns and achievements as he approached the last Games of his tenure, noting that "He has already determined which new sports to add to the schedule for the Winter Olympics in Sochi, Russia, in 2014 (including women's ski jumping and the luge relay). He has delivered his verdict on a new code of conduct for athletes' entourages—their coaches, trainers, support personnel—especially in relation to doping, fixing and illegal betting. He has approved work on a new global advertising campaign and worked on procedures to reduce the number of core Olympic sports from 26 in London to 25 at the Rio Games in 2016. He has signed off on guidelines that will determine how millions of dollars will be distributed between the international sports federations, from swimming to track and field. All of these decisions will have significant ramifications for world sport."

According to the BBC, as IOC president Rogge "earned praise for his zero tolerance approach to doping (doubling the number of tests at the Games to 5,000). According to Stephen Wilson, Rogge "implemented rigorous pre-games and out-of-competition checks, retested samples from previous games to catch cheaters retroactively and championed the biological passport for monitoring an athlete's blood profile." Rogge also "set up a system to monitor betting patterns during the Olympics, suspended or forced out members implicated in ethics violations, spoke out against the rise in youth obesity, and created the Youth Games (an event for athletes aged 15–18, which debuted in the summer of 2010 in Singapore) "On Rogge's watch," Jacquelin Magnay noted, "the IOC has established links with Interpol and money-laundering agencies, and has set up an anti-corruption monitoring company. Within sport, he has sought to strengthen the judging and refereeing rules. … [Rogge] forced international federations to readjust rules in skating, boxing, gymnastics, fencing, taekwondo and wrestling to make them more objective."

Rogge also ensured the financial security of the Games for the foreseeable future. Wilson noted for the Associated Press (September 3, 2013) that the "IOC's coffers also strengthened under Rogge's tenure, with revenues from top-tier global sponsors going from $663 million in 2001–04 to nearly $1 billion for the four-year cycle through London. Television rights deals raised billions, including a record $4.38 billion deal with NBC through 2020. The IOC's financial reserves, designed to allow the organization to continue operating for four years in the event of an Olympics being canceled, have risen from $100 million to $900 million over the past 10 years." "Perhaps Rogge's most significant financial achievement," Wilson explained, "was the signing of a long-term revenue-sharing deal with the USOC [U.S. Olympic Committee] in 2012. Tensions had festered for years over a previous deal going back to 1996 that many Olympic officials felt gave the U.S. too big a share." Rogge, who cultivated, in Wilson's words, a "democratic, collegial and management-oriented approach" to IOC executive decision making, declared in his understated fashion that the IOC and USOC had "found a very good agreement that respected both sides."

Rogge left office in September 2013. Thomas Bach, of Germany, succeeded him, becoming the ninth president of the IOC; Rogge is now honorary president. In assessing Rogge's overall contribution to the Olympic movement, David Bond of the BBC remarked that whatever his administrative and managerial achievements, Rogge would be judged on the quality of the Games while he headed the IOC: "Few will doubt," concluded Bond, "that under Rogge, there have been some of the most memorable Games in history. From Beijing's awesome display of force to London's friendly Games, the power of the Olympic brand has grown and grown."

Rogge was named a count of the Belgian nobility by King Albert II in 2002. In 2010 and 2011 *Forbes Magazine* listed him as one of the most powerful people in the world. In the latter year he was also invested as an Officer of the Legion d'honneur by French President Nicolas Sarkozy. Rogge is fluent in French, Dutch, English, German, and Spanish. He is married to Anne Bovijin. They have two adult children, Caroline and Philippe. Philippe served as delegation leader of the Belgian Olympic Committee for the 2008 Summer Olympics.

Further Reading:

Associated Press Jun. 24, 2001, Sep. 3, 2013

BBC Sport Aug. 24, 2008, Sep. 9, 2013

Boston Globe pD13 Jan. 14, 1999

Chicago Tribune Sports p4 Jan. 24, 1999

Christian Science Monitor p1 Jul. 17, 2001, with photo

(London) *Daily Telegraph* p7 Aug. 28, 2001, Nov. 11, 2001, Jul. 15, 2011

ESPN Web site; *Europe* p41+ Nov. 2001

(London) *Guardian* Nov. 10, 2001, Aug. 12, 2012

(London) *Independent* Sport p25 Nov. 25, 2000

Los Angeles Times pD8 Oct. 8, 2001, pD1 Dec. 9, 2001

New York Times pD4 July 17, 2001, with photo, Aug. 9, 2001, pD5 Feb. 16, 2002, with photo, pD4 Feb. 7, 2003, with photo, Apr. 11, 2008, Sep. 9, 2013

Olympic Movement Web site

(London) *Times* Oct. 11, 2000, pS7 Jul. 17, 2001

Washington Times pA1 Feb. 25, 2002

Books:

Barney, Robert K., Stephen R. Wenn, and Scott G. Martyn, *Selling the Five Rings: The International Olympic Committee and the Rise of Olympic Commercialism* (Salt Lake City: University of Utah Press, 2002)

Schiller, Daniela

Israeli cognitive neuroscientist, researcher, educator

Born: 1972, Rishon LeZion, Israel

According to the Israeli-born cognitive neuroscientist Daniela Schiller, "These are really interesting times in science, because in the last ten years there has been a change in the way we see memory." One of the most significant aspects of that change stems from the discovery that unlike, say, a diamond necklace, which remains the same every time it is retrieved from and then replaced in a safe-deposit box, a memory is not set in stone after its formation in the brain, in a process called consolidation. Rather, it evolves: every time the memory is retrieved to become a conscious thought, it returns to its storage place in a chemically altered form—that is, it is updated or reconsolidated, with molecular changes at the cellular level. If the memory is associated with fear, the conscious feeling of fear that the memory induces changes as well each time it is recalled; often, that feeling becomes stronger. For her doctoral dissertation, earned at Tel Aviv University, in Israel, Schiller studied memory formation and retrieval in mice.

Since 2004, when she arrived at New York University (NYU) as a postdoctoral student to conduct research under the neuroscientists Joseph LeDoux and Elizabeth Phelps, Schiller has studied the same phenomena in humans. "That's exactly where the science is now," she told *Current Biography* (the source of the quotations from Schiller that follow unless otherwise stated): "starting to translate everything to the human brain and the clinical population"—that is, people with psychological problems. In an article published in the journal *Nature* in January 2010, Schiller reported that in an experiment with humans that did not include the use of drugs, she and her team at NYU had determined that in applying therapeutic techniques to eliminate fear associated with painful memories, the timing of those techniques appears to be crucial. According to an NYU press release ("NYU Researchers Develop Non-Invasive Technique to Rewrite Fear Memories," December 9, 2009), Schiller explained that her team's research "suggests that during the lifetime of a memory there are windows of opportunity where it becomes susceptible to be permanently changed. By understanding the dynamics of memory we might, in the long run, open new avenues of treatment for disorders that involve abnormal emotional memories." In particular, Schiller's work may lead to more effective ways to help the many people who suffer from post-traumatic stress disorder (PTSD) as a result of having experienced such frightening events as earthquakes and other natural disasters, armed conflicts, rape, torture, terrorist attacks, and plane or car crashes. According to Stephen S. Hall, writing in *Technology Review* (June 17, 2013), her hypothesis—that one can alter the emotional impact of a memory by adding new information to it or recalling it in a different context, "challenges 100 years of neuroscience and overturns cultural touchstones from Marcel Proust to best-selling memoirs. It changes how we think about the performance of memory and identity, and it suggests radical nonpharmacological approaches to treating pathologies like PTSD, other fear-based anxiety disorders, and even addictive behaviors." For her highly innovative work and its potential benefits to humanity, Schiller earned a regional Blavatnik Award for Young Scientists from the New York Academy of Sciences in 2010. Also that year the Mount Sinai Medical Center in New York City recruited Schiller to set up a research program in cognitive and affective neuroscience within its Department of Psychiatry. With a staff of eight, she is currently the director of the Schiller Laboratory of Affective Neuroscience and assistant professor of psychiatry and of neuroscience at Icahn School of Medicine at Mount Sinai.

Education and Early Career

The youngest of four children of Zigmund Schiller and his wife, Daniela Schiller was born on October 26, 1972, in Rishon LeZion, Israel, near Tel Aviv. Her mother, a nurse, worked at night. In an instance of her childhood anxieties, Schiller remembers calling out for her mother on many nights even when she knew her mother was not at home. Her father was a "very reserved" man, as she described him, and he steadfastly refused to talk about his experiences as a Holocaust survivor. But in Israel schoolchildren begin learning about the Holocaust from a young age, "and what I heard in school was very horrifying," Schiller said. On Holocaust Remembrance Day, an annual event in Israel, documentaries about the Holocaust air on TV, and when a siren sounds at 10:00 a.m., all activities in the country halt for two minutes, to honor the estimated six million Jews and millions of others killed by German Nazis during World War II. Early on Schiller absorbed the lesson that "everything that happens to you is nothing compared to the Holocaust," and "that's how you judge things." Among those "things" were a childhood skateboard accident, to which she forced herself to respond without tears, and the beatings she occasionally suffered at the hands of neighborhood children who thought she looked German.

In Israel, with a few exceptions, military service is required after high school for all non-Arab Israeli men (who must serve three years) and women (who must serve two years). Schiller wanted to serve in a combat unit, but in 1991, when she joined the army, such assignments were virtually nonexistent for women. The recommendation of a teacher who had seen her in a high school play led to her recruitment as a producer by the army's entertainment and education division. She produced shows written, directed, and performed for active-duty soldiers by members of the Israeli army and reservists. After she completed her military service, in 1993, she became a producer of concerts and lectures on science, history, and art for the general public. She also became the drummer for a band, called the Rebellion Movement, which played "original Hebrew rock influenced by American folk-rock," in her words.

Concurrently, Schiller attended Tel Aviv University. She earned a B.A. degree in psychology and philosophy in 1996 and a Ph.D. degree in cognitive neuroscience in 2004; in the interim she taught courses in psychology at the Open University (2000), Tel Aviv University (2001–03), and Derby College (2004). Schiller also taught a music course in the Music Academy at Lewinsky College (2000–01). Her dissertation concerned a facet of emotional learning in schizophrenics: "the ability to acquire emotional responses to previously ignored stimuli, which is impaired in patients suffering from chronic schizophrenia," as she describes it at her Phelps Lab of New York University Web page. The failure to react to stimuli is called persistent latent inhibition. Working in the laboratory of Ina Weiner, who studies the use of antipsychotic drugs in treating schizophrenia at Tel Aviv University, Schiller developed a model for studying persistent latent inhibition in mice. (Injecting certain viruses in pregnant mice has been found to produce schizophrenia-like behavior in their offspring during what is equivalent to adolescence in humans.) Schiller then examined the neural circuitry associated with schizophrenia in the rodents' brains and investigated the benefits, if any, of antipsychotic drugs given to the mice. An article (co-authored with Ina Weiner) about her research appeared in the journal *Neural Plasticity* in 2002, and abstracts of another paper (coauthored with Weiner and Lee Zuckerman) were published in the journals *European Neuropsychopharmacology* and *Biological Psychiatry* in 2003.

Later Career

In experiments regarding memory formation and retrieval in rats or mice, scientists observe the animals' behavior, measure their physiological responses (for example, changes in blood pressure and quantities of hormones circulating in the blood), and observe changes in brain scans. In Joseph LeDoux's experiments involving conditioned learning, rats would soon ignore a repeated, nonthreatening sound; they would freeze and arch their backs and their hearts would beat faster when their feet were subjected to mild electric shocks accompanied by the same sound. After a sufficient number of repetitions of those two stimuli, the sound and the shock, they would freeze, and their heartbeats accelerate, upon hearing the sound alone, without the shock. LeDoux discovered that only one part of the brain—the amygdala—was necessary for such fear conditioning. Furthermore, every time the sound triggered the retrieval of the rats' "fear" memory, reconsolidation of that memory took place: particular neurons in the amygdala underwent molecular changes, including the synthesis of new proteins. These changes could be detected after the memory went back into storage.

"Memory is best preserved in the form of a story that collects, distills, and fixes both the physical and emotional details of an event."

According to Stephen S. Hall, the "table had been set for Schiller's work on memory modification in 2000, when Karim Nader, a postdoc in LeDoux's lab, suggested an experiment testing the effect of a drug on the formation of fear memories in rats." In an extension of LeDoux's work, Nader established that injecting a drug that blocked protein synthesis into the amygdala soon after a fear memory had been retrieved by the rats prevented the animals from recalling the fear memory again later. If the drug was administered after an interval, the "original memory remained intact. This was a big biochemical clue that at least some forms of memories essentially had to be neurally rewritten every time they were recalled."

Researchers can observe behavioral responses to stimuli in humans, too, and they can measure people's physiological responses and scan their brains. In addition, while with nonhuman animals "you don't have access to what they actually know," in Schiller's words, scientists can ask people to describe their memories and their feelings (although such descriptions can never be considered complete, since no person can know precisely what another person is thinking or feeling). But everyday memory formation and retrieval is far more complicated in humans than it is in mice or other animals, not least because of the role of language in those phenomena and the far more complex cultural and social environments in which people form their memories. "It's not at all clear that you can translate all the information acquired in animals to humans, especially to traumatic memories, because we don't have a laboratory model for traumatic memories; [they are] just too intense, too complex to create," Schiller has said.

Schiller came to NYU as a postdoctoral researcher in 2004. Encouraged by the psychologist Elizabeth Phelps, Schiller initially intended to extend Nader's work to humans using beta-blocker antianxiety drugs (the drug used by Nader was too toxic for use on human subjects), but while she waited for approval to proceed, she devised the groundbreaking three-day experiment later reported in *Nature,* with the aid of LeDoux and Phelps. Since memory research is still in its infancy, experiments involving humans rely on a simple, clearcut stimulus-response setup. Schiller's subjects, 65 men and women, faced a computer screen on which a blue square and yellow square would flash repeatedly, but not at the same time. Sometimes the flashing yellow square would be accompanied by a mild electric shock administered to the subjects' wrists. The shock caused the subjects to sweat (a classic fear response), which in turn reduced their skin's resistance to the conduction of electricity—a phenomenon known as galvanic skin response. (Galvanic skin response is the basis of lie-detector tests.) The next day Schiller divided the subjects into three groups. The people in each group experienced fear when the yellow squares flashed on the screen, though no shocks were administered. Then, between ten minutes and six hours later, the first group received therapy known as "extinction training": the yellow squares were again flashed repeatedly without any shocks. The second group underwent extinction training more than six hours later. The third group (the control) received no extinction training. On the third day the subjects in the first group had no fear response when they saw the flashing yellow squares, but those in the second and control groups responded with increased sweating. Those results indicated that within six hours of the retrieval of a memory of a fearful experience, that memory can be replaced by a new one (through extinction training) that does not induce fear. When conducted after six hours, extinction training leads to the formation of a second, newly consolidated memory, and both the first and the second memories return to the brain's storage cells. When Schiller retested 19 of her subjects a year later, those from the first group, for whom extinction training had erased their fear, reacted with little fear (as measured by their galvanic skin response) to the combination of flashing yellow squares and shocks, while people in the other two groups responded as fearfully as they had a year earlier. "The aim is not to erase the memory altogether; we just want to block the emotional aspect of it," Schiller said.

According to the December 9, 2009, NYU press release, Elizabeth Phelps said, "Previous attempts to disrupt fear memories have relied on pharmacological interventions"—that is, drugs. "Our results suggest such invasive techniques may not be necessary." Avoiding the use of drugs would avoid the side effects, ranging from mild to potentially life-threatening, that are associated with virtually every medication (although some individuals may not experience any). Moreover, the testing of drugs for use in humans is invariably a years-long, enormously expensive process that must start with extensive testing in nonhuman animals. Thus, "using a more natural intervention that captures the adaptive purpose of reconsolidation," in Phelps's words, would be both far less expensive and safer.

Currently Schiller is using magnetic resonance imaging (MRI) to determine the neurological links between memory and fear. "That's the next big question," she said. "In animals, we know that in particular the amygdala is an area that is critical for the formation of such associations. If you target this particular region during reconsolidation, you can permanently block emotional memories in animals. In humans I'm working on the same thing with MRI scanners—scan the brain while [people] form these memories and they reactivate them, while they are exposed to a new learning, and how it's incorporated—and how they express the memory later." In his profile of Schiller and her work in *Technology Review*, Stephen S. Hall wrote that the "potential cultural impact and personal implications of reconsolidation are even more staggering. To put it in an extreme way, if we are all rewriting our memories every time we recall an event, the memory exists not as a file in our brain but only as the most recent rewrite of a scenario. Every memoir is fabricated, and the past is nothing more than our last retelling of it. Archival memory data is mixed with whatever new information helps shape the way we think—and feel—about it." Hall then quoted Schiller: "'My conclusion is that memory is what you are now. Not in pictures, not in recordings. Your memory is who you are now. ... Memory is best preserved in the form of a story that collects, distills, and fixes both the physical and emotional details of an event.'" At her Web page for the Schiller Laboratory of Affective Neuroscience, Schiller further explains her team's focus: "Our research—how emotions are formed in the human brain—is situated within the critical link between animal models and the clinical population. Our research strategy, therefore, typically relies on fundamental findings in animals. We aim to collect, through collaborative projects, parallel findings in animals and humans and examine cross species similarities."

Schiller, whose recreational interests include skydiving, said, "I think I did my own independent investigation of fear in my personal life because the aim was always to overcome fear, so I was very attuned to what I feel, how to overcome it, what I feel after. . . . Fear is like a barrier and I was annoyed. I think it's the general relationship people have with their emotions. . . . Emotions can take over. They steer you in a certain way, they color the way you think, what you do, what you're willing to do, what you avoid, so they have a lot of power. I'm interested in that power because I think it's unjustified."

Schiller's work has been published in numerous scholarly journals, including the *Journal for Neuroscience, Trends in Cognitive Science, Learning and Memory,* and the *Journal for Psychiatric Research.* She has contributed work to a number of books, such as *The Human Amygdala* (2009), *The Neuroscience of Emotional Learning* (2009), *Emotional Reaction and Action: From Threat Processing to Goal-Directed Behavior* (2009), *Memory Reconsolidation* (2013), and *Behavioral Neurobiology of Depression and Its Treatment* (2013). She is a neuroscience advisory board member for the Lifeboat Foundation and a scientist advisory board member for the National High School Journal of Science. Schiller has been invited to speak on psychology and neuroscience in the United States (Baylor College of Medicine, 2007; Rutgers University, 2007; Princeton University, 2008; Cornell University, 2008; Caltech, 2008; MIT, 2009, University of Illinois, 2009; Yale University, 2010) and internationally (Cambridge University, 2006; University College London, 2009; Freie University [Berlin], 2009; Tel Aviv University, 2010).

Schiller lives in New York City. She is the drummer for the Amygdaloids, a band whose songwriter, lead vocalist, and rhythm guitarist is Joseph LeDoux. Its other current members are Tyler Volk (lead guitarist), an NYU professor of biology and environmental studies, and Amanda Thorpe, a singer-songwriter who studied psychology at University College London, neuropsychology at Padova (Padua) University, and music therapy at NYU. Songs on the band's debut recording, *Heavy Mental* (2007), bear such titles as "Mind Body Problem" and "An Emotional Brain." The country singer Roseanne Cash and the autism expert Simon Baron Cohen contributed to their second album, *Theory of My Mind* (2010), whose 13 tracks include "Mind Over Matter," "Brainstorm," "How Free Is Your Will," "Mists of Memory," and "Fearing." The band performed at NYU's graduation ceremony at Madison Square Garden, in New York City, in May 2007 and at the Kennedy Center, in Washington, D.C., in 2008. Schiller has also participated in storytelling events and contests arranged by an organization called the Moth. "You think that either you're an artist or that you're a scientist, but it's actually the same," Schiller said. "You heavily rely on your own creativity and your own ideas. ... Science, I think more than we realize, relies upon hunch and intuition. It is very methodical, analytical, and logical—but your ideas and the way you think about things is very similar to the creative process. You have insights and unique associations—different feelings that give you a new perspective—like art."

Further Reading:

Amygdaloids Web site
Discovery Dec. 28, 2009
Israel21c Dec. 10, 2009, Nov. 28, 2010
(London) *Guardian* Dec. 9, 2009
National Institutes of Health Dec. 9, 2009

New York Academy of Sciences Oct. 21, 2010

New York Times Mar. 6, 2007, Dec. 10, 2009, Feb. 7, 2010

Scientific American Mar. 23, 2010, Jun. 28, 2010, Jul. 20, 2010

Technology Review Jun. 17, 2013

Sears, William

American pediatrician, writer, educator

Born: 1939, Alton, Illinois, United States

Sears, Martha

American nurse, writer, breastfeeding consultant

Born: 1945, St. Louis, Missouri, United States

The pediatrician William Sears and his wife, Martha Sears, a registered nurse and breastfeeding specialist, are the foremost proponents in the United States of a philosophy and approach to child rearing known as attachment parenting. The Searses maintain that through specific practices that, they believe, satisfy a child's physical and emotional needs more successfully than other methods, parents will form closer, more loving bonds with their children than would otherwise be possible; by so doing, they will help children develop self-esteem and the capacity for intimacy and compassion, which in turn will enable the children to form "secure, empathic, peaceful, and enduring relationships," as the Web site of Attachment Parenting International put it. (William Sears, who coined the term "attachment parenting," is a member of Attachment Parenting International's advisory board.)

William and Martha Sears have co-written numerous books, among them *The Baby Book: Everything You Need to Know about Your Baby—From Birth to Age Two* (1993), *The Discipline Book: Everything You Need to Know to Have a Better-Behaved Child—From Birth to Age Ten* (1995), *The Breastfeeding Book: Everything You Need to Know about Nursing Your Child from Birth through Weaning* (2000), *The Attachment Parenting Book* (2001), *The Fussy Baby Book: Parenting Your High-Need Child from Birth to Five* (2005), *The Good Behavior Book: To Have a Better-Behaved Child from Birth to Age Ten* (2005), *The N.D.D. Book: How Nutrition Deficit Disorder Affects Your Child's Learning, Behavior, and Health* (2009), and *The Portable Pediatrician: Everything You Need to Know about Your Child's Health* (2011). As sole author, William Sears has written *Nighttime Parenting—How to Get Your Baby and Child to Sleep* (1985), *Keys to Becoming a Father* (1999), *Becoming a Father: How to Nurture and Enjoy Your Family* (2003), and other books. He has co-authored additional titles with his wife and others, such as *Eat Healthy, Feel Great* (2002), *The Successful Child: What Parents Can Do to Help Kids Turn Out Well* (2002), *Dr. Sears' LEAN Kids: A Total Health Program for Children Ages 6–11* (2003), *The Baby Sleep Book: The Complete Guide to a Good Night's Rest for the Whole Family* (2009), *The Healthy Pregnancy Book: Month by Month, Everything You Need to Know from America's Baby Expert* (2013). Besides maintaining a pediatric family practice with his wife and two of his sons, James and Robert, William Sears is an Associate Clinical Professor of Pediatrics at the School of Medicine of the University of California at Irvine. He is now semiretired but still practices at the clinic two afternoons a week.

Education and Early Career

William Sears was born on December 9, 1939, in Alton, Illinois. He was raised as a Roman Catholic and briefly considered becoming a priest. (He and his wife, who also was raised as a Catholic, later attended an evangelical Baptist church for many years but more recently have again become practicing Catholics.) Sears received a B.S. degree from St. Louis University, in Missouri, in 1962 and earned an M.D. from the university's school of medicine four years later. He then completed an internship at the Children's Hospital Medical Center of Harvard Medical School, in Boston, Massachusetts. From 1967 until 1969, he worked for the U.S. Public Health Service at the National Institutes of Health in Bethesda, Maryland. Sears then spent three years in Canada, as a pediatric resident at the University of Toronto's Hospital for Sick Children, one of the largest children's hospitals in the world. While there he also received training in neonatology and cardiology. In 1972 he earned pediatric certification from Canada's Royal College of Physicians.

Martha Sears was born Martha Vivian McMenamy on January 24, 1945, in St. Louis, Missouri. She received her license as a registered nurse (R.N.) from the DePaul School of Nursing in St. Louis, in 1965, and then trained for a year on a postgraduate fellowship at St. Louis University. While working on a ward at the university hospital, she met her husband-to-be, at the bedside of a patient; the two married in 1966 and had their first child, James, about a year later. Martha Sears later trained at the International Childbirth Education Association, in 1975, and in 1983 she received certification as a breastfeeding consultant from the Lactation Institute of Los Angeles, one of the largest such facilities in the country. Her advice to nursing mothers and mothers-to-be draws upon her many years of experience in breastfeeding. (She and her husband have seven biological children, all of whom she breastfed; their eighth child was adopted.) She directs the Breastfeeding Center in San Clemente, California, and is a leader in La Leche League International, an organization dedicated to promoting breastfeeding and assisting women who breastfeed. Martha Sears speaks at many national parenting conferences and is noted for advice on how to handle the common problems modern mothers face. She connects with both working mothers and stay-at-home mothers because she was both at different times in her life. At the Web site of the Sears family practice, she refers to herself as a "professional mother."

Later Career

Attachment parenting, the approach to child-rearing that the Searses advocate, aims to foster intimacy between parent and child and help the child to feel that he or she is loved. Not a rigid system, it involves developing a closeness that will increase the parents' ability to intuit their child's specific needs grows. Toward that goal some parents use what is known as a "baby sling," a carrying device, worn over the shoulder, that allows the infant to be physically close to his or her mother or father at all times. Some parents choose to sleep with their child in what they refer to as the "family bed." Sears has recommended that parents who wish to try this sleeping arrangement purchase a king-size bed. "The sleeping arrangement whereby all three of you (mother, father, and baby) sleep best is the right one for your individual family," he wrote in *Nighttime Parenting—How to Get Your Baby and Child to Sleep* (1985). "Your baby trusts that you are open and receptive to the cues that he is giving you about where he needs to sleep. You are also trusting yourself to respond to your baby's needs for a certain sleeping arrangement even though this may not be in accordance with the norms of your neighborhood." He also wrote, "If sleeping with your baby feels right to you and is working, then it is okay. As with any feature of a parenting style, if it is not working and does not feel right, then drop it."

According to Sears, attachment parenting leads both parents and children to feel more secure, which ultimately helps children to become more independent than they might otherwise. "Parents who practice the attachment style of parenting know their child well," Sears wrote in *Nighttime Parenting*. "They are observant of their infant's cues, respond to them intuitively, and are confident that their responses are appropriate. They have realistic expectations of their child's behavior at various stages of development, and they know how to convey expected behavior to their child. Their children are a source of joy. The feeling that the attachment style of parenting gives you and your child can be summed up in one word, harmony." The Searses have warned against "calendar parenting," that is, expecting—unrealistically—that all children will develop at the same pace and thus should, for example, be weaned or should sleep through the night by a certain age.

"The feeling that the attachment style of parenting gives you and your child can be summed up in one word, 'harmony.'"

Attachment-parenting proponents hold that mothers who adopt this approach produce more prolactin than other mothers; in *Nighttime Parenting*, Sears wrote that this hormone "may enhance a woman's ability to mother as well as create a feeling of calmness and well-being during trying times." He explained, "In experiments where this hormone is injected into male birds, they act like mothers. … Science is finally catching up to what intuitive mothers have known all along: Good things happen when mothers and babies spend more time with each other." William and Martha Sears contend that fussy children, whom they prefer to label "high need" children, are most in need of this style of parenting.

William Sears believes that attachment parenting leads both parents and children to feel more secure, which ultimately helps children to become more independent than they would otherwise be. In an article for *Babytalk* (September 2000), he described studies conducted by doctors at Johns Hopkins University in the 1970s that showed that children who were raised this way "were able to crawl away from their mothers, play by themselves, and return to them less anxiously than infants who were less attached" and demonstrated that children who are raised to depend entirely on their parents in the earliest stages of development find it easier to make the transition to independence as they grow. Critics of attachment parenting, however, have charged that the method results in uncontrollable behavior in children and ineffectuality in parents.

As a pediatrician with more than 35 years of experience, William Sears has noted that breastfed children are often healthier than children who have been fed formula or other forms of milk. "Mothers who breastfeed are more connected to their infants," he wrote for the Web site breastfeeding.com. "Breastfeeding is an exercise in baby reading. Because breastfeeding is such a social interaction, a mother gets to know her infant intimately, which sets her up to be a more effective disciplinarian." The Searses have often pointed to the more than 11 scientific studies that showed that breastfed babies grow to become healthier, smarter adults, in part because breast milk contains docosahexaenoic acid (DHA), a fatty acid that plays a crucial role in the development of an infant's brain (and is also necessary for the proper functioning of an adult's brain). William Sears has also noted that breastfed infants are generally less anxious than formula-fed babies. "I look upon breastfeeding as one of the best long-term investments that a parent can make," he wrote for breastfeeding.com.

William and Martha Sears's articles appeared regularly in the magazines *Babytalk, Parenting,* and *Prevention.* (*Babytalk* and *Parenting* are no longer published, having been acquired and closed in May 2013 by Meredith Corporation, owner of the competing *American Baby* and *Parents* magazine; *Parenting*'s Web site remains active.) William Sears has been a guest on more than 100 television talk or news shows, among them *Dr. Phil, The Doctors, 20/20, Good Morning America, The Oprah Winfrey Show,* and *Dateline.* The couple share their child-rearing expertise on their two Web sites, askdrsears.com and www.drsearswellnessinstitute.org. William Sears also serves as a medical and parenting consultant for parenting.com; he filled the same role for *Babytalk* magazine until it ceased publication. As parenting.com's pediatric expert, Sears notes at the Web site of the All American Speakers Bureau, he would like parents to "think of me as their live-in pediatrician, easily accessible online for the most common problems they face. This new avenue for information is always current and I'm excited to give parents the most up-to-date, groundbreaking news."

Sears is the developer of the "Original Baby Sling," an infant carrier that received the 1989 Infant Product of the Year Award from the National Independent Nursery Furniture Retailers Association (NINFRA). He is also a consultant for Arm's Reach, which manufactures cribs that allow babies and parents to have their own sleeping space yet still remain close enough to touch. In addition, he serves as a medical adviser to Martek Biosciences Corp., which makes nutritional products for pregnant and nursing women.

William Sears was diagnosed with Stage 3 colon cancer in 1997. According to Kate Pickert, writing in a widely discussed *Time* magazine cover story (May 21, 2012) about attachment parenting, he "is in remission after surgery, radiation and chemotherapy, but ever since, he's been obsessed with his health. … Sears says he takes no prescription drugs and subsists on a daily diet that revolves around a smoothie packed with fruit, vegetables and supplements. He exercises at least two hours a day." Writing in the *Owensboro* (Kentucky) *Messenger-Inquirer* (April 29, 2013), Angela Oliver recounted her discussion with William Sears about an initiative he founded called LEAN—Lifestyle, Exercise, Attitude, Nutrition, a "nationwide program to encourage better eating habits, more physical activity, and positive emotional energy." He developed the program by practicing it himself. The program, he holds, is effective for both adults and children but is especially valuable for the latter. In 2003 Sears coauthored a book for children on the program (with Peter Sears and Sean Foy) entitled *Dr. Sears' LEAN Kids: A Total Health Program for Children Ages 6–11.* In the book Sears wrote that the program originated in his "passion to teach healthy habits to kids, ages 6 to 12, when their way of living is most open to being shaped—early in middle childhood."

After writing more than 30 books on childcare over the years, William and Martha Sears turned to a new topic of interest: healthy aging. In *Prime-Time Health: A Scientifically Proven Plan for Feeling Young and Living Longer* (2010), they provide an interesting perspective on aging. In an article posted at Oprah Winfrey's Web site, Williams Sears wrote: "Aging, in a nutshell, means 'rust,' too much sticky stuff accumulates in the body, and the body's garbage disposal system weakens so it can't get rid of the sticky stuff." The authors' ten-step health plan, Sears explained, "simply keeps the rust and sticky stuff out of your body and strengthens your garbage disposal—or immune system."

James and Robert Sears, the Searses' eldest sons, are now partners in the Sears family pediatric practice in San Clemente, California. James, known as Dr. Jim, is a co-host on the *Dr. Phil* spinoff series *The Doctors,* and Robert, called Dr. Bob, is the author of the best-selling *The Vaccine Book: Making the Right Decision for Your Child* (2007; a significantly expanded second edition was published in 2011). James Sears has coauthored several books with his father, including *The Premature Baby Book* (2004) and *The Healthiest Kid in the Neighborhood* (2006). The Searses' third son, Peter, practices family medicine in Nashville, Tennessee.

A fourth son, Matthew, is in medical school. The Searses' other children are Hayden, Erin, Stephen (who has Down syndrome), and Lauren. William and Martha Sears told *Current Biography* that their children make up "the cast of characters in the Sears Family Drama who provide much of the material for our books."

William Sears is a member of the Orange County Pediatric Society and a fellow of the American Academy of Pediatrics and the Royal College of Pediatricians.

Further Reading:

All American Speakers Bureau Web site

Ask Doctor Sears Web site

Attachment Parenting International Web site

Contemporary Authors Vol. 160 (1998)

Doctor Sears Wellness Institute Web site

Oprah Web site

Owensboro (Ky.) *Messenger-Inquirer,* Apr. 29, 2013

parenting.com Web site

Time magazine May 10, 2012, May 21, 2012.

Selected Books:

By William and Martha Sears:

The Baby Book: Everything You Need to Know about Your Baby—From Birth to Age Two, 1993 *The Birth Book: Everything You Need to Know to Have a Safe and Satisfying Birth,* 1994

25 Things Every New Mother Should Know, 1995

The Discipline Book: Everything You Need to Know to Have a Better-Behaved Child—From Birth to Age Ten, 1995

Parenting the Fussy Baby and High Need Child, 1996

The Complete Book of Christian Parenting and Childcare: A Medical & Moral Guide to Raising Happy, Healthy Children, 1997

The Family Nutrition Book: Everything You Need to Know about Feeding Your Children—From Birth through Adolescence, 1999

The Breastfeeding Book: Everything You Need to Know about Nursing Your Child from Birth through Weaning, 2000

The Attachment Parenting Book, 2001

The Fussy Baby Book: Parenting Your High-Need Child from Birth to Five, 2005

The Good Behaviour Book: How to Have a Better-Behaved Child from Birth to Age Ten, 2005

The N.D.D. Book: How Nutrition Deficit Disorder Affects Your Child's Learning, Behavior, and Health, and What You Can Do about It—Without Drugs, 2009

Prime-Time Health: A Scientifically Proven Plan for Feeling Young and Living Longer, 2010

The Portable Pediatrician: Everything You Need to Know about Your Child's Health, 2011.

By William Sears:

Nighttime Parenting: How to Get Your Baby and Child to Sleep, 1985

Keys to Becoming a Father, 1999

Becoming a Father: How to Nurture and Enjoy Your Family, 2003

Siemionow, Maria

Polish-born reconstructive and transplantation surgeon, researcher, educator

Born: 1950, Poznań, Poland

In December 2008 Maria Siemionow led a medical team of 50 to carry out what one of the doctors involved called the "most complex surgical procedure ever performed"—a face transplant. The operation included removing a recently deceased donor's face—skin, eyelids, blood vessels, nerves, and muscles—and attaching it to a disfigured patient. The intricate process is potentially life-threatening; the patient's immune system might reject the new tissue, among other possible complications. Before Siemionow and her team performed the operation, at the Cleveland Clinic, in Ohio, only three partial face transplants had been carried out in the world, but none had been as complicated, controversial, or extensive. (In the procedure led by Siemionow, 80 percent of the patient's face was replaced). Siemionow's expressed goal in performing the face transplant was to further the cause of restoring a sense of normality to people whose lives have been marred by severe disfigurement. Lawrence K. Altman, writing in the *New York Times* (December 17, 2008) noted that the woman's surgeons had concluded that they "were left with no conventional treatment options to restore her facial function.' Our patient was called names and was humiliated,' Dr. Siemionow said. 'Children ran away.' She added, 'You need a face to face the world.'"

Siemionow has been affiliated with the Cleveland Clinic since 1995; she is currently the clinic's Director of Plastic Surgery Research and Head of Microsurgical Training in its Department of Microsurgery, where she specializes in hand surgery, microsurgery, peripheral-nerve surgery, transplantation, and microcirculation. According to the clinic's Web site, Siemionow was the "first U.S. physician to have received Institutional Review Board (IRB) approval for facial transplantation surgery." In her position at the Cleveland Clinic, she has "trained over 100 international fellows in the field of microsurgery and transplantation research." Siemionow is also "leading the way in developing new technology for minimal immunosuppression in transplantation, and enhancement of nerve regeneration."

Education and Early Career

The daughter of Bronisław and Zofia Kusza, the surgeon was born Maria Kusza on May 3, 1950, in Poznań, Poland, located between the Polish capital, Warsaw, and the German capital, Berlin. She attended college and university in her hometown, graduating in 1974 from the Poznań Medical Academy. She served her residency at hospitals in Poznań and Finland.

During her residency in Finland, Siemionow had an experience that changed her life: she was asked to assist in an operation on a man who had accidentally cut off his hand with a circular saw. During the 15-hour operation, as Siemionow helped reattach the bone, vessels, tendons, and nerves of the hand to the arm, she saw the hand turn from white to pink, which indicated that blood was flowing into it again. "That you could restore to people a part of themselves that had been lost, and actually see it become vital again, was miraculous to me," Siemionow told Michael Mason of the *New York Times* (July 26, 2005). "I have never forgotten that day."

In 1978 Siemionow became the assistant clinical instructor at the Institute for Orthopaedics and Rehabilitation Medicine, in Poznań. Three years later she became a senior assistant lecturer at the institute, where she specialized in hand surgery. In 1985 Siemionow received a Ph.D. degree in microsurgery from the Poznań Medical Academy. She then went to the United States with a hand-surgery fellowship at the Christine Kleinert Institute for Hand and Microsurgery, in Louisville, Kentucky. "I got off the plane in Louisville at the end of June 1985," Siemionow wrote in her memoir, *Transplanting a Face: Notes on a Life in Medicine* (2007). "After hours of breathing the stale air-conditioning of planes and airports, I walked outside under the open sky of Bluegrass Country and felt as if I were diving into an aquarium left too long in the sun. I was prepared to learn medicine. I was prepared to spend the next several years of my life in America. I was prepared to meet new colleagues and make new friends. I was not prepared for a Kentucky summer. I was also unprepared for the pace of American life." Siemionow returned to Poland after completing the fellowship. The last position she held in her native country before immigrating to the United States, in 1995, was in the Department of Hand and Microsurgery at the Institute for Orthopaedics and Rehabilitation Medicine. After a brief stint as a professor and research director at the University of Utah, in Salt Lake City, also in 1995, Siemionow moved on to the Cleveland Clinic.

Later Career

In her book Siemionow pointed to the unusual opportunity she has to conduct research and practice medicine at the same time: "The great majority of practicing physicians have little opportunity to pursue research. They're simply too busy. They also lack the funding and facilities to conduct proper investigations. Laboratories and equipment are expensive." Most importantly, she wrote, research "taught me not only to always ask questions but to ask them in a way that suggests a path to an answer." The practical search for answers has defined the surgeon's research for over three decades. In 2004 she began to conduct research on animals in hopes of proving it possible to transplant hands, limbs, and faces without patients' having a permanent dependency on drugs that are meant to help the immune system adjust to the flesh, veins, nerves, skin, and tendons of new body parts. When the health reporter Harlan Spector, writing for the Cleveland *Plain Dealer* (October 31, 2004), visited Siemionow's animal-research lab at the Cleveland Clinic in the fall of 2004, he observed "white rats with brown faces and scalps. One with a half-brown, half-white face; another with a brown limb," which constituted "evidence of successful transplants of body parts. Using sutures one-third the thickness of human hair, Siemionow and the researchers who train under her stitch arteries under microscope[s], in experiments that one day could lead to routine human transplants of limbs, hands and faces." Siemionow "is essentially and uniquely a research worker," Graham Lister, one of Siemionow's mentors at the University of Louisville and the University of Utah, told Spector. "She's a workaholic," Lister added. "She's better now. But she used to be a bit uncomfortable if she wasn't doing three things at once."

Worldwide media reports about Siemionow's most ambitious—and controversial—undertaking began to emerge after late 2004. Siemionow and her team began planning what, as Michael Mason of the *New York Times* put it, "may be the most shocking medical procedure to occur in decades." A face transplant would involve removing the facial skin, eyelids, blood vessels, nerves, and muscles from a recently deceased donor and connecting them to the skinless face of a patient who had a severe disfigurement. While there are no precise statistics as to how many people have facial disfigurements caused by disease, burns, trauma, accidents, or birth defects, medical experts maintain that the number is significant. Many people suffering from severe facial disfigurement become overwhelmingly self-conscious and sometimes receive harsh looks and comments when they are in public. Some feel so self-conscious, depressed, and defeated that they very rarely—if ever—leave their homes. Facial disfigurement also hampers communication. Even after standard reconstructive face surgery (with skin taken from the victim's own back, buttocks, or thighs), facial expressions such as slight smiles, raised eyebrows, narrowed eyelids, and dozens of others are either impossible to detect or barely discernible; and because body language is such an important element of communication, victims of facial disfigurement are at a further disadvantage. Human faces, Siemionow wrote in her book, "are essential to our communication with the world. It has been estimated that verbal communication conveys only 35 percent of the meaning we're expressing. Our looks, gestures, and body language carry 65 percent of the information received by the person at the other end of the conversation." For those reasons Siemionow worked passionately and diligently to make possible a successful face transplant that in time would look and feel relatively natural.

The world's first partial face transplant was performed in France in 2005 on a woman who lost her cheeks, nose, lips, and chin when she was attacked by her dog. (The operation, albeit controversial, was a success.) Because the operation being proposed by Siemionow was more complicated and risky than any other face transplant that had ever been attempted, she faced some opposition. Some objections were medical: the body's immune system can react violently to a transplanted organ, such as a kidney, and even more intensely to transplanted skin. That led to an ethical objection: is it right to perform an operation that will certainly endanger the health or life of a patient if it is not essential to saving that life? Siemionow and many doctors, nurses, ethicists, philosophers, and psychologists have argued that while a patient with severe facial deformities does not need a face transplant to preserve his or her life, such a patient needs the operation in order to have a quality of life others take for granted.

In December 2008 Siemionow and her team performed a 23-hour operation on a woman whose face had been disfigured by a shotgun blast that left her with only upper eyelids, one eye, forehead, lower lip, and chin and countless bits of shattered bone in her flesh. Lawrence K. Altman, writing in the *New York Times* (December 17, 2008) described the surgery: "The highly experimental procedure, performed within the last two weeks, was the world's fourth partial face transplant, the country's first, and the most extensive and complicated such operation to date." Siemionow, speaking at a press conference a few days after the operation, said that the woman—who had undergone more than two dozen earlier, smaller surgeries involving skin grafts and other procedures to repair the damage to her face—had often been taunted and humiliated as a result of her injury. The patient did not end up resembling the donor of the facial tissue, because bone structure greatly determines one's appearance; nor did she look as she previously had. Rather, her features became something of a hybrid of two faces, the patient's and the donor's. In February 2009, about two months after the operation, the patient was released from the hospital. "She accepted her new face," Siemionow was quoted as saying in the *Los Angeles Times* (February 7, 2009), meaning that the patient's immune system did not reject the new skin, nerves, muscle tissue, and blood vessels. In fact, by February the patient could eat pizza, drink coffee, smell perfume, and purse her lips. In a prepared statement, the woman's siblings thanked the donor, the hospital, and the surgical team led by Siemionow: "We never thought for a moment that our sister would ever have a chance at a normal life again."

For the rest of her life, however, the patient will have to take drugs that suppress her immune system, which, although necessary to prevent the body's rejection of the new tissue, increases risk of infection and cancer. In her memoir Siemionow frankly discusses the postoperative demands on the patient: "At present, all composite-tissue allografts—transplants that involve differing tissues—require a lifelong commitment to a strict regimen of healthy living and immunosuppressive drugs. In this regard the patient is perhaps more responsible for the success of the procedure than are all the medical specialists involved." In May 2009 the patient—revealed to be Connie Culp—appeared at a press conference; later she was interviewed on *Good Morning America* and *ABC World News with Diane Sawyer.* The dosages of the immunosuppression drugs that she was taking had been greatly reduced by then. In July 2010, after the nerves and muscles of her new face developed sufficiently, she underwent the last of her facial surgeries. In May 2013 Elizabeth Landau of CNN reported that Siemionow had "been seeing Culp on a monthly basis since the transplant" and had "described Culp as 'fully integrated back in her community.'" Furthermore, Landau wrote, "Researchers have determined that Culp's brain accepts the new face, based on activity in key brain areas."

"You need a face to face the world."

To some, face transplant surgery remains a controversial subject. In the September 2008 *Annals of Plastic Surgery* article "Face as an Organ," Siemionow and coauthor Erhan Sonmez write that the benefits of face transplants outweigh the risks: "Although transplantation of solid organs is essential for a patient's physical survival [facial transplantation] is essential both for physical and social survival. Optimal social survival is what makes physical life worth living. … It would be degrading to those signing the consent form to have the faces of their loved ones considered as merely skin."

Beginning in February 2009 Siemionow and her colleagues at the Cleveland Clinic cared for Charla Nash, a Connecticut woman whose face and hands had been severely damaged when her friend's pet chimpanzee attacked her. In May 2011, after undergoing other remedial surgeries over approximately two years, Nash received a face transplant at Boston's Brigham and Women's Hospital; Dr. Daniel Alam, currently head of the Section of Facial Aesthetic and Reconstructive Surgery in the Head and Neck Institute at Cleveland Clinic, participated in the transplant surgery.

Siemionow presented her research related to transplantation, nerve regeneration, and prevention of ischemia reperfusion injury in reconstructive surgery to the public in numerous media appearances, including on NPR's *All Things Considered, The Today Show,* CNN, *Oprah,* and *NBC Nightly News.* She is a member of the scientific advisory boards of SANUWAVE Health, Inc., and Tolera Therapeutics, Inc.

Siemionow is president of the American Society for Reconstructive Transplantation and project leader of the composite tissue allograft program under the Armed Forces Institute of Regenerative Medicine Rutgers–Cleveland Clinic Consortium. She is a past president of the International Hand and Composite Tissue Allotransplantation Society and past president and a current council member for the American Society for Peripheral Nerve. She received an honorary academic appointment in 2008 as Professor of Surgery at the Karol Marcinkowski University of Medical Sciences in Poznań, Poland. In April 2009 she received, from the President of Poland, the Polish Order of Merit, the Commander's Cross Polonia Restituta Award "in recognition of her outstanding accomplishments." Siemionow is the holder of eight patents in the field of transplantation tolerance and peripheral nerve research.

Siemionow serves on the editorial boards of eight professional society journals and as ad hoc reviewed for six journals. She has won numerous awards for her research and publications. She received the Folkert Belzer Award in Transplantation in 2001 and the James Barrett Brown Award for the best publication in a plastic-surgery journal in 2004 and 2007. In 2010 she was selected by the Plastic Surgery Educational Foundation (PSEF) to receive the 2010 PSEF Outstanding Achievement in Clinical Research Award. She has more than 300 scientific publications, including contributions to numerous edited volumes, including *Innovations in Plastic and Aesthetic Surgery* (2007), *Hand Transplantation* (2007), *Transplantation of Composite Tissue Allografts* (2008), and *Essays on Peripheral Nerve Repair and Regeneration, Volume 87* (2009). In addition to the works named above, she is also the author of *Tissue Surgery* (2005) and *Face to Face: My Quest to Perform the First Full Face Transplant* (2009; a reworking with an epilogue of *Transplanting a Face*). She edited *The Know-How of Face Transplantation* (2011) and, with Marita Eisenmann-Klein, *Plastic and Reconstructive Surgery* (2010) as well as special journal issues, including *Composite Tissue Allograft Transplantation* for *Seminars in Plastic Surgery* (vol. 21, no. 4, November 2007).

Siemionow is a member of the American Society of Plastic Surgeons, the American Association of Plastic Surgeons, the American Association for Hand Surgery, the American Society for Reconstructive Microsurgery, the International Hand and Composite Tissue Allograft Society, the Plastic Surgery Research Council, the World Society for Reconstructive Microsurgery, Ohio Valley Society of Plastic Surgeons, International Hand and Composite Tissue Allograft Society, and the Transplantation Society.

Siemionow and her husband, Wlodzimierz Siemionow, a doctor and biomedical engineering consultant, were married in 1975. They have a son, Krzysztof; Kris B. Siemionow is Chief of Spine Surgery and Assistant Professor of Orthopaedics and Neurosurgery at the University of Illinois in Chicago.

Further Reading:

Associated Press May 6, 2009

Cleveland Clinic Web site

CNN May 3, 2013

Lancet Jul. 18, 2009

Los Angeles Times pA14 Feb. 7, 2009

New York Times Jul. 26, 2005, Dec. 1, 2005, Dec. 6, 2005, pA18 Dec. 17, 2008, May 6, 2009 (Cleveland) *Plain Dealer* Oct. 31, 2004, Dec. 16, 2008, Dec. 18, 2008, May 5, 2009

Slate Dec.18, 2008

USA Today pA1 May 25, 2006

Selected Books:

As author:

Tissue Surgery, 2005, *Transplanting a Face: Notes on a Life in Medicine,* 2007, reworked edition with an epilogue *Face to Face: My Quest to Perform the First Full Face Transplant,* 2009

As editor:

Siemionow, Maria, and Marita Eisenmann-Klein, eds., *Plastic and Reconstructive Surgery,* 2010

Siemionow, Maria, ed., *The Know-How of Face Transplantation,* 2011

Thomas, William H.

American geriatrician, writer

Born: 1959, Tioga County, New York, United States

"I never wanted the words 'nursing home doctor' attached to my name in any way," William H. Thomas told Lou Waters on CNN's *Early Prime* (October 7, 1996). That sentiment notwithstanding, Thomas has become one of the most innovative nursing-home doctors in the world. With the two related programs that he has set up—the Eden Alternative and the Green House Project—he has established an approach to nursing-home care that recognizes that—as the 1986 report of the Committee on Nursing Home Regulation of the Institute of Medicine put it—"quality of life [is] as important as quality of care." Nell Porter Brown, writing in Harvard Magazine (November-December 2008), noted that Thomas "has spent his career pushing for seismic cultural and economic changes in long-term care and public policy toward aging, which has meant challenging the $122-billion nursing-home industry. In some ways the timing for such reforms could not be better. Many nursing homes built in the 1960s and 1970s in response to Medicare and Medicaid legislation now need major renovations just as aging baby boomers begin to create rising demand for geriatric care." According to Chuck Salter, writing in *Fast Company* (February 2002), Thomas sees the nursing home industry as obsolescent, with even the best facilities ultimately failing their residents: "Ultimately, Eden Alternative is a repair for a broken industry. The replacement, says Thomas, is his Green House Project." Thomas has written several books to explain and promote his philosophy and strategies, among them *The Eden Alternative: Nature, Hope, and Nursing Homes* (1994), *Life Worth Living: How Someone You Love Can Still Enjoy Life in a Nursing Home: The Eden Alternative in Action* (1996), *Learning from Hannah: Secrets for a Life Worth Living* (1999), *What Are Old People For? How Elders Will Save the World* (2004), *In the Arms of Elders: A Parable of Wise Leadership and Community Building* (2006) and *Second Wind: Navigating the Passage to a Slower, Deeper and More Connected Life* (2014).

Thomas is helping to usher in what will likely be the last revolution of the baby boomers (generally defined as people born between 1946 and 1964). That group, Thomas believes, will insist that his innovations become standard. "The boomers have this rebellious streak in them, and at least some forward-thinking part of the boomer generation is going to say, 'Wait a minute, what is this? I'm not going to be afraid.' They're going to wake up and start telling everybody else that old age is cool," Thomas has said, as quoted by Jane Glenn Haas in the *Orange County* (California) *Register* (November 11, 2004). According to Thomas, the baby boomers will then create what he has dubbed "eldertopia," a society in which the elderly are not segregated, all generations interact, and the oldest people are recognized as the most valuable members of the populace.

In 2008 the *Wall Street Journal* named Thomas one of the "12 most influential Americans shaping aging in the twenty-first century," and *U.S. News and World Report* described him as a revolutionary: "With his startling common-sense ideas and his ability to persuade others to take a risk, this creative and wildly exuberant 46-year-old country doctor has become something of a culture changer—reimagining how Americans will approach aging in the twenty-first century. And with 35 million Americans over 65—a number that will double by 2030—that takes a big imagination indeed."

Education and Early Career

William H. Thomas was born on October 13, 1959. He was raised in Nichols, a rural community on the Southern Tier in upstate New York. After completing high school, he entered the State University of New York (SUNY) at Cortland, where he studied biology to prepare himself for admission to medical school. While in college he became interested in politics; he was elected president of the student association and ran unsuccessfully for mayor of Cortland. He graduated from SUNY Cortland summa cum laude in 1982. He then entered Harvard Medical School, in Cambridge, Massachusetts, from which he earned an M.D. degree in 1986. That year he began a three-year residency in family medicine at the University of Rochester. After he completed his residency, he secured a job as an emergency-room doctor, concurrently planning to establish a rural family practice. (Some sources, including *Fast Company*, assert that he intended to make his career in emergency-room medicine.) In the early 1990s he was persuaded to take a job as the medical director of Chase Memorial Nursing Home, in New Berlin, New York, an 80-bed facility at which he served as the only in-house physician. "For the first time in my career," Thomas told Bruce Taylor Seeman of the *Miami* (Florida) *Herald* (December 26, 1996), "I was searching for the answer to the question: What does it mean to take care of another person?" He took to his new responsibilities with enthusiasm, recalling years later that he thought he had one of the best jobs on earth.

One day, Thomas told a conference audience in Australia, as Margaret Wenham reported for the Queensland, Australia, *Courier Mail* (December 9, 2000), "I was called to see a woman who had a rash on her arm. She reached up and took hold of my hand, pulled me over the bed and said: 'I'm so lonely.' In that moment all of my bravado, all my good cheer and professionalism escaped me. She was lonely. She was dying of loneliness." The episode transformed Thomas's perspective, making him understand that the people living in the nursing home were not simply patients who required physical care but also men and women who depended on the nursing-home staff to provide an emotionally satisfying world for them. He concluded that in that light, Chase Memorial, despite its reputation as one of the best nursing homes in the United States, was a distressing failure. Those whom he had been hired to care for were suffering from acute loneliness, boredom, and feelings of helplessness—what Thomas has called the three plagues of the nursing-home environment. The roots of those plagues, he later wrote in his book *The Eden Alternative,* "cannot be traced neatly back to an imbalance of the metabolism or psyche. These three problems receive such little attention because they do not fit well with the medical model of care." That epiphany led to his conception of the Eden Alternative. The name refers to the garden in the Bible's Book of Genesis; it has since become a registered trademark of Thomas's organization, which was founded in 1991 and has the same name.

Later Career

The "Edenizing" of Chase Memorial began in 1991 with the assistance of a $200,000 grant from the federal and New York State governments. As a first step in the process, Thomas had pets, plants, and children brought into the facility. Introducing living things into a nursing home was not a new idea, but Thomas did so in a significantly different way. Rather than having children and animals at the nursing home during regimented therapeutic activities, he integrated them into the daily lives of the residents. Dogs and cats were allowed to roam freely throughout the facility, and residents who wanted birds were allowed to care for them in their rooms. The presence of children, too, became usual at Chase, as the home established programs with local kindergartens so that the same children visited the home Monday through Friday. Residents could thus build relationships with individual children. Similarly, plants were placed not only in the lobby, as in other nursing homes, but throughout the home, and some residents welcomed the opportunity to take care of them. Thomas also introduced his charges to the pleasures of vegetable gardening and the rewards of eating what one has grown.

The Edenizing process, however, is not only a matter of introducing animals, children, and plants into the nursing-home environment; it also requires changing the atmosphere so that the facility seems less like a hospital and more like an actual home. The Eden Alternative concept, wrote Salter, "involves major organizational and cultural change, because the facility has to think differently about care, priorities, and old habits." Salter recounted the experience of Kathleen Perra, the director of nursing at St. Luke's Home in New Hartford, New York, where Thomas was medical director: "Every day last summer, we had school-age day care here. There were kids screaming down the hall, cats jumping on tables. It was bedlam, but it was great. You want those unpredictable things happening for the residents. Of course, health-care workers favor predictability. We work around schedules. I'd say the biggest change with the Eden program is for the staff."

At Chase, instituting those changes was not easy. Thomas had not anticipated some of the problems that arose, and his staff resisted taking on some new responsibilities, such as cleaning up after dogs. "We stumbled and fell at times," he told Laura Bruck for *Nursing Homes* (January 1997), "but we kept pushing. In the end, resistance became tolerance and, finally, acceptance as the vision began to materialize." Within three years of its start, Thomas's experiment had proved to be a success. Not only had the lives and emotional well-being of the home's residents improved, but Chase's expenses had dropped, as demonstrated by a study conducted by the New York State Health Department. According to the *Orange County* (California) *Register* (October 12, 1998), there was "a 50 percent decrease in infections, a 71 percent drop in daily drug costs per resident and a 26 percent decrease in nurse's aide turnover"—the last-named problem a common one in nursing homes and one that raises costs because of the need to train new staff. The decline in expenses surpassed start-up costs at other homes where the program was adopted (often as much as $20,000) and the costs of caring for the animals and other elements of the program (approximately $21,000 per year). Chase's program was so successful that New York State introduced it to three other institutions, and Thomas established a nonprofit organization for the purpose of teaching workers at other nursing homes how to Edenize their facilities. Nell Porter Brown explained Thomas's "Eden Golden Rule: As management does unto the staff, so shall the staff do unto the Elders. 'We teach the people who own and operate these facilities how to provide staff with the same vital experiences that they want the staff to offer to the elders: dignity, respect, affection.'"

Drawing upon his experiences at Chase, Thomas formulated ten basic Eden Alternative principles. Two principles concern the easy access of residents to plants, animals, and children. The other eight focus on the attitudes of nursing-home administrators and staff. They must recognize that loneliness, boredom, and helplessness are the primary causes of suffering among nursing-home residents; be willing to abandon the hierarchical model of authority found in most institutions by giving those working directly with residents more decision-making powers and giving residents opportunities for making choices as well; make it possible for residents to help maintain their surroundings; and minimize, to the extent possible, the use of prescription drugs and dependence on programmed activities, so as to encourage spontaneity.

As his name gained recognition within the nursing-home industry, Thomas began to introduce his ideas to a wider audience through nationwide lectures and books. His goal had become, as he told Bruce Taylor Seeman, "to change every last nursing home in America. We are going to look back on the old nursing home with dismay." Still, in some places Thomas's ideas were not welcomed. One administrator, he told an audience in North Carolina, said that his facility had gotten a dog but the staff could not care for the animal. "I'm thinking," Thomas told Ann Doss Helms for the *Charlotte* (North Carolina) *Observer* (March 27, 1997), "he wants to charge me $35,000 a year to take care of my mother, and they can't take care of a dog?" As he has often pointed out, the "top-down" model of authority in nursing homes is not consistent with the Eden Alternative, yet making the necessary changes requires strong leadership. By the end of 1996, more than a hundred nursing homes nationwide had adopted the Eden Alternative, and Thomas's organization had abandoned its nonprofit status. Thomas had published his first book, *The Eden Alternative: Nature, Hope, and Nursing Homes,* in 1994. He expanded and revised some of his ideas in his second book, *Life Worth Living: How Someone You Love Can Still Enjoy Life in a Nursing Home: The Eden Alternative in Action* (1996), which contains a chapter on how the Eden Alternative can be adapted for use in private homes. Ten years later *U.S. News and World Report* (June 11, 2006) cited "300 Eden Home conversions in America and an additional 200 overseas." As of 2013, according to its Web site, the Eden Alternative had "trained over 25,000 Eden Associates."

In 1997 the America's Award Foundation, established by the influential minister and writer Norman Vincent Peale, presented to Thomas its eponymous award, sometimes called the "Nobel Prize for Goodness," which "honors unsung heroes who personify the American character and spirit," according to various sources. By the end of 1998, the first Canadian nursing home to adopt his program was preparing to open. Thomas was optimistic about the prospects for his ideas in Canada, telling Monte Stewart of the *Calgary* (Alberta, Canada) *Herald* (October 27, 1998), "It's probably going to be more successful in Canada than the U.S." He added, as paraphrased by Stewart, "Canadian society is more community-minded while U.S. elder care is more profit-oriented." The year 1999 saw the publication of Thomas's book *Learning from Hannah: Secrets for a Life Worth Living*, a fictionalized account of the creation of the Eden Alternative in which he and his wife are shipwrecked on an island; during their yearlong stay, they absorb the lessons of a society whose oldest members (among them a woman named Hannah) are valued for their wisdom and experience. After Thomas and his wife return home, they develop the Eden Alternative. To promote the book Thomas embarked on his "Eden across America Tour," during which, in addition to book-signing events and lectures, he presented a two-act, one-man show based on *Learning from Hannah*. According to Chuck Salter in *Fast Company* (February 2002), the show was an excellent medium for Thomas, whom he described as "alternately funny, exuberant, and sincere, offering glimpses of a natural theatricality." In 1999 Thomas traveled to Australia to spread his message there.

According to Kelly Greene, writing in the *Wall Street Journal* (February 16, 2008, on his Eden across America book tour, Thomas realized that "America's nursing homes are getting older faster than we are." In 2000 he announced his idea for a radical alternative to the Edenization of large nursing homes: the Green House Project, through which ordinary houses would become homes to elderly people in need of nursing care. Each house would have ten residents and round-the-clock staff. "The time has come to reinvent the long-term care environment in America for the 21st century," Thomas told the U.S. Newswire (September 25, 2000). "We believe that the Green House can become a high quality, safe, cost-effective alternative to institutionalization for the frail and disabled." "I want to create an environment where Eden-like ideas can flourish more readily than in a 200-bed nursing facility," Thomas explained to Julia Malone for the Cox News Service (September 26, 2000). "My heart breaks when I see how many people try hard to make it work and are knocked down by an institutional structure that is more powerful than they are." In the *Chicago Tribune* (July 24, 2005), Jane Adler reported that "Thomas has a map of the United States in his office with three pins showing the locations of existing Green Houses. He hopes his map will someday have 16,000 pins in it, representing the new Green Houses that have replaced all the nation's old nursing homes."

Moving as many as 150 nursing-home residents, some with serious illnesses, into 10 or 12 separate houses while still following state regulations was an arduous task, and initially the Green House Project was met with skepticism from senior-services companies. Through diligent efforts at persuasion, however, and the evidence provided by the positive results from his earliest Green Houses, Thomas's organization gained momentum. The first Green Houses were constructed in 2003 in Tupelo, Mississippi.

"We teach the people who own and operate these facilities how to provide staff with the same vital experiences that they want the staff to offer to the elders: dignity, respect, affection."

In 2006 the Green House Project received a $10 million grant from the Robert Wood Johnson Foundation, to be used to replace more than 100 nursing homes (at least one in each of the 50 states) with clusters of small, comfortable homes. In Baltimore and New York City, apartment-style, vertical Green Houses will be built, so as to offer prospective residents the option of living in an urban area, according to Caroline Hsu in *U.S. News & World Report* (June 19, 2006). In a blog post at the A Place for Mom Web site (October 8, 2012), Dana Larsen wrote, "There are "already more than 100 Green House Project homes in 32 states, with more than 100 more in the works." Larsen explains the differences between the Eden Alternative and the Green House project while noting that their ultimate aim—quoting Tiffany Wise of A Place for Mom, "to provide seniors the opportunity to be cared for in a non-institutionalized environment"—while distinguishing both from the traditional nursing home model. The Green House project is different from traditional senior housing, she writes, "in that it provides residents with intimacy [clusters of smaller homes with six- to ten residents]; autonomy [seniors have their own private room and bathroom]; warmth [the living situation encourages social activity and provides comfort]; smart technology [computers, pagers, and ceiling lifts]; and green living [plants, garden areas, and outdoor access]." Nell Porter Brown notes Thomas's conclusion that "Operationally, the Green Houses cost the same to run on a daily basis as a nursing home." She quotes Thomas as saying, "This should not be that much of a surprise, since the nursing home was never a paragon of efficiency."

In 2004 Thomas published his fourth book, *What Are Old People For? How Elders Will Save the World*, in which he argued that people in the United States must "end the American tendency of equating being old with being sick. Seeing old age solely in terms of disease and disability and condoning ageism damage all of society, especially the elderly. Instead, old age should be seen as a natural, developmental stage of life, rather than a difficult decline," as Korky Vann wrote for the *Orlando Sentinel* (November 1, 2004). To begin effecting that change in attitude, Thomas attempted to re-create people's understanding of the so-called ages of man. Instead of Shakespeare's seven ages, Erik Erikson's eight, or Sigmund Freud's five, Thomas focused on three: childhood, adulthood, and what he called "elderhood." Childhood, he explained, is a time of being, when humans simply experience the world and use their imaginations. Adulthood is a time of doing; in American society, as G. Allen Power wrote for the Rochester, New York, *Democrat and Chronicle* (April 2, 2004), "We value people for what they do, not who they are." During elderhood, humans once again seem to "be" rather than "do." In Thomas's view, however, the elderly do not simply re-enter a state of being and experience a second childhood. Rather, they become our greatest teachers: in his words, according to Power, "Elders … teach us how to make a community. When we come together to meet their needs, we learn how to live as human beings. They instruct us in the art of caring."

Thomas has been named one of America's Best Leaders by the John F. Kennedy School of Government, and he is a "thought leader" for the American Association of Retired Persons's (AARP's) Life Reimagined Institute. He has received the Heinz Award for the Human Condition (2006), the Molly Mettler Award for leadership in Health Promotion (2002), and a three-year fellowship from Ashoka (2002–2005) "for his social entrepreneurship work with the Eden Alternative." In 2009 he received the Picker Award for Excellence in the Advancement of Patient-Centered Care, in the field of long-term care; according to the award announcement, he was "honored for his outstanding achievements in envisioning and implementing a new paradigm for long-term care that focuses on nurturing and sustaining a meaningful life for the aging."

Thomas is a professor at the Erickson School of Aging Studies at the University of Maryland Baltimore County and co-founder, with Kavan Peterson, of the blog ChangingAging, a "multiblog platform [for] challenging conventional views on aging." Thomas and his wife, Judith Meyers-Thomas (whom he hired in 1992 as the Eden Alternative program director; they married soon afterward) and their five children live on a 258-acre working farm powered by solar- and wind energy in Sherburne, a rural community in upstate New York. Thomas is developing a multigenerational and international "intentional community" project called Eldershire, which he launched in Sherburne in 2006. He writes daily and schedules 35 to 40 speaking engagements a year. His most recent novel is *Tribes of Eden* (2012), which he describes at his ChangingAging Web site as a "postapocalyptic thriller that explores the value of community in a world that is increasingly defined by and dependent on digital technology." Thomas's *Second Wind: Navigating the Passage to a Slower, Deeper and More Connected Life* (2014) is a "reconsideration of the mythology that surrounds America's Post War Generation."

Further Reading:

Asheville (North Carolina) *Citizen-Times* pA7 Apr. 28, 1999

ChangingAging Web site

Chicago Tribune pC4 Jul. 24, 2005

Detroit Free Press pA1 Oct. 17, 1997

Eden Alternative Web site; *Fast Company* p78+ Feb. 2002, Mar. 2005

Green House Project Web site

Harvard Magazine Nov.–Dec. 2008

Orange County (California) *Register* Nov. 11, 2004

Orlando (Florida) *Sentinel* pE2 Nov. 1, 2004

A Place for Mom Web site Oct. 8, 2012

U.S. News and World Report Jun. 11, 2006

Ventura County (California) *Star* pE1 Oct. 28, 2001

Wall Street Journal Feb. 16, 2008

Books:

Weiner, Audrey, and Judah L. Ronch, eds., *Culture Change in Long-Term Care* (New York: Haworth Social Work Practice Press, 2003) [Includes Thomas, William H., "Evolution of Eden," in Section 2: "Models of Culture Change in Long-Term Care"]

Weiner, Audrey, and Judah L. Ronch, eds., *Models and Pathways for Person-Centered Elder Care* (Baltimore: Health Professions Press, 2014) [Includes Thomas, Bill, "Culture Change beyond the Nursing Home"]

Selected Books:

The Eden Alternative: Nature, Hope, and Nursing Homes, 1994

Life Worth Living: How Someone You Love Can Still Enjoy Life in a Nursing Home: The Eden Alternative in Action, 1996

Learning from Hannah: Secrets for a Life Worth Living, 1999

What Are Old People For? How Elders Will Save the World, 2004

In the Arms of Elders: A Parable of Wise Leadership and Community Building, 2006

Tribes of Eden, 2012

Second Wind: Navigating the Passage to a Slower, Deeper and More Connected Life, 2014

Trehan, Naresh

Indian cardiothoracic surgeon, researcher, educator

Born: 1946, Karachi, British India

The pioneering cardiothoracic surgeon Dr. Naresh Trehan is often described as India's most prominent heart doctor. He has operated on many of the country's political, civic, and business leaders. He is also one of the world's foremost practitioners of robotic surgery. Trehan was executive director and chief cardiothoracic and vascular surgeon at one of the most advanced heart care facilities in Asia, the Escorts Heart Institute and Research Center (EHIRC), in New Delhi, from 1988 to 2007. His pioneering facility often outpaced some hospitals in the United States, many of which hesitate to perform technically demanding "beating heart" surgery. (Traditionally, the heart is stopped during surgery; circulation is maintained by artificial means. Beating heart surgery reduces trauma to the patient but is more difficult to perform.) In addition to his duties as executive director of EHIRC, Trehan often performed a dozen or more surgeries per day, also teaching, doing research, and traveling the world to present scientific papers and chair sessions at conferences in the United States, the United Kingdom, Israel, Japan, China, and elsewhere in the Far East. In 2007 he left Escorts—by then owned by Fortis Healthcare—and, after an interval with Apollo Hospitals, became majority owner, CEO, executive director, and chief cardiac surgeon of Medanta Medicity, an "integrated healthcare facility [that] includes a hospital, a research centre and a medical and nursing school," according to Sudhir Chowdhary of the *Financial Express* (July 2010). Medanta, Chowdhary continued, "has collaborated with Siemens Healthcare to introduce advanced imaging and IT solutions in India. These include SOMATOM Definition Flash CT scanner, Artis Zeego cathlab, ACUSON SC2000 ultrasound system and Biograph mCT, a PET.CT scanner." Trehan's ambition is to create a healthcare institution "specifically on the lines of a Mayo, Cleveland, Harvard, and Johns Hopkins in its basics," he told Chowdhary. "Medanta intends to go beyond what any conventional medical institute has attempted. … At Medanta, technology and innovation will be the key drivers for providing high-end services and at the same time keeping patient cost low."

Education and Early Career

Naresh Trehan was born on August 12, 1946, in Karachi, in what was then British India but today is Pakistan. Both of his parents were successful doctors: his father, a Punjabi, was an ENT surgeon, and his mother, a Sindhi, was a gynecologist. Soon after Trehan's birth, the British partitioned the Indian subcontinent into two countries: the Islamic state of Pakistan and the secular (although Hindu-dominated) state of India. Amidst the widespread rioting and social upheaval that ensued, Trehan's family relocated to New Delhi, the capital of India, where the family lived for a time as refugees before finding a three-room apartment that doubled as a medical clinic: one room for surgery, one for gynecology, and one in which the family—which also included Naresh Trehan's sister, Neena—lived. In New Delhi, Trehan's parents often treated the impoverished and destitute—an experience that had a significant impact on the future surgeon. He "saw the gratitude of people so poor they offered his parents a cooked chicken or handmade shoes in place of cash," Amy Waldman wrote for the *New York Times* (May 18, 2003).

Trehan was highly competitive from a young age. He was an avid cricketer and field hockey player, and he demonstrated a keen interest in how things work. For a time he entertained the idea of becoming a pilot, but his father opposed that plan, and he later settled on a career as a heart surgeon. Trehan earned a bachelor of medicine and bachelor of surgery (MBBS) degree from King George's Medical College in Lucknow, India, before traveling to the United States, where he studied cardiology under Dr. Frank Spencer at New York University (NYU) Medical Center in New York City.

Beginning in 1971, after completing his American board certification as a cardiothoracic surgeon, Trehan worked for three years as a clinical instructor and teaching assistant at NYU Medical Center. Trehan told Anubha Sawhney of the *Times of India* (May 5, 2002), "Only if one is 150 per cent better than the Americans can one neutralise discrimination. And I had to be just that. When I began work at the [Bellevue] Hospital, there were 32 residents. Each year, half were asked to leave till just two doctors remained to become heart surgeons. I made the cut." In 1979 Trehan began serving as an attending cardiothoracic surgeon at NYU Medical Center, the New York Infirmary-Beekman Downtown Hospital, and St. Vincent's Hospital. In 1981 he was named an assistant professor of surgery at NYU Medical Center. It was at NYU that Trehan performed pioneering work in coronary bypass surgery, a difficult procedure that involves diverting blood-flow from the heart around blocked arteries. He performed more than three thousand coronary artery operations while at NYU. Trehan has also worked as chief of thoracic and cardiovascular surgery at New York's Veterans Administration Hospital and as attending cardiothoracic surgeon and consultant at New York's Bellevue Hospital.

Later Career

By the mid-1980s, Trehan's career was flourishing, and his annual income was about $1.5 million. Despite his success he often considered returning to India with his family. Yet he knew of no suitably advanced hospitals there—a circumstance that disturbed him. As many as 10 percent of Trehan's patients in New York were middle- and upper-class Indians who had flown to America to receive the advanced care they were unable to find at home. Driven, he told Amy Waldman, by "a certain amount of arrogance—a kind of national pride," Trehan resolved to build in India his own hospital, a world-class cardiothoracic-care facility on par with the best the West had to offer. He believed that wealthy Indians, given the choice, would prefer to undergo advanced cardiac procedures in their home country, foregoing the difficulty and expense of international travel. Their fees could then be used to subsidize care for India's less fortunate. Trehan also wanted to pass on the advanced techniques he had learned in the United States to his fellow Indians. "It's a passion for me to come back and train others," he told Earleen Fisher of the Associated Press, as published in the *Los Angeles Times* (October 16, 1988).

In 1988, with the financial backing of H. P. Nanda, a wealthy industrialist, Trehan founded Escorts Heart Institute and Research Center in New Delhi. The center was far more sophisticated than typical Indian hospitals. While flies are a persistent problem in other Indian health facilities, Trehan told Fisher that his hospital would be "100 percent fly-proof." Powerful fans were installed at the entrances, barring the pests from the immaculate lobby, where security is tight and personnel are much more highly trained than at other Indian hospitals.

In spite of careful preparation and the assistance of a dozen other Indian surgeons who also had left lucrative American practices behind to join the EHIRC team, Trehan worried that the facility wouldn't be able to handle the demanding workload right away and requested help from his old mentor at NYU, Dr. Frank Spencer. Spencer and NYU offered to send 20 surgeons to India for two months to help EHIRC get established. At the last moment, however, Trehan changed his mind. As he told Amy Waldman, he recalls thinking: "If we bring these guys … our whole lives we—and they—will be saying the Indians couldn't do it themselves." Trehan asked the American surgeons not to come and opened the institute without American assistance.

One of Trehan's principal goals in establishing EHIRC was to help provide healthcare not only to middle- and upper-class patients but also to at least some of India's impoverished masses. "The government does not have the resources to service the needs of this sector appropriately, and therefore we should step in and do our bit," he said, according to a reporter for *Business India* (May 27, 2002). Ten percent of the hospital's income went toward free and subsidized care for those who couldn't afford the standard rates, which were already a fraction of those charged in the United States for the same procedures. The hospital also subsidized care for government employees, military personnel, and retirees. In addition, Escorts Community Outreach Programme, a division of the hospital, provided a variety of services for India's poor, from public awareness programs to a free heart check-up camp that traveled across India, making eight- to ten stops per month. Advanced mobile echocardiogram vans also traveled the country, providing heart examinations for more than a hundred thousand villagers a year. When he first returned to India in 1988, Trehan discovered that Western influences on lifestyle and diet were making Indians more susceptible to heart disease. "For many decades we were living with the myth that heart disease was a disease of corrupt, money-minded Western societies," Trehan told Amy Waldman, adding that by 2020, half of all deaths in India were expected to be from cardiac illnesses. Trehan expressed that hope that early screening and prevention by his outreach programs and mobile vans would contribute to the fight against this new epidemic. In 2000, in partnership with the American corporation General Electric (GE), EHIRC introduced the Mobile Cathlab, a state-of-the-art ambulance equipped to host procedures ranging from a thorough cardiac exam to angioplasty. Trehan explained the benefits of the Mobile Cathlab: "People living in small towns and villages don't have to travel to big cities like Delhi, Mumbai, Calcutta and Chennai for cardiac treatment. The Cathlab ambulance can now come to them. … Our dream is to have a Cathlab in all the 425 districts so that we can cover the entire country."

In addition to his work in making advanced medicine available to ordinary Indians, Trehan is considered one of the pioneers of robot-assisted heart surgery. The first surgical robot Trehan acquired for EHIRC was an Aesop 3000, which consisted of a voice-activated camera mounted on a robotically manipulated endoscope, providing the surgeon with an extra pair of eyes inside the patient's chest during conventional operations. "It makes it possible for me to visualize the surgical field without having to open the chest [enough] to get my head in there," he told Victoria Button for the Melbourne *Age* (May 10, 2000). Trehan performed India's first robot-assisted surgery with the Aesop 3000 in November 1998. In 2002 EHIRC acquired a new, more sophisticated robot: Da Vinci, originally developed by the National Aeronautics and Space Administration (NASA) to operate remotely on astronauts in orbit. (NASA later abandoned the Da Vinci project, which was then taken over by a private company.) When EHIRC obtained its model of the $1.5 million machine, Da Vinci had only recently been approved for surgical use in the United States. EHIRC's state-of-the-art facilities made India only the second country in Asia—after Japan—where robotic surgery was performed.

The Da Vinci robot made it possible for Trehan to perform surgery from a distance. Using joysticks similar to those used for computer games, he could manipulate the Da Vinci's arms inside the patient, using a video feed from a robotic camera to see his way around. The Da Vinci—used for relatively noninvasive surgical procedures—provides a host of advantages for a heart surgeon. Traditional coronary bypass operations involve opening the patient's chest with a saw, stopping the heart, and directing blood flow to a heart-lung machine before the procedure itself can be performed. Using the Da Vinci robot, Trehan could bypass the same artery with three incisions, each less than an inch across. Camera-guided robotic arms snake their way inside the patient's body, and broad movements of the joystick budge the robotic hands only millimeters, allowing for unprecedented accuracy—even if the surgeon's hands tremble or slip. And, because the heart remains beating throughout the operation, there is less risk of infections forming in pooled blood. Patient recovery time is reduced from a month or more to mere days, and the experience is far less traumatic to the patient. Speaking with Waldman, Trehan likened robotic surgery to "going to the moon."

Trehan frequently worked 16 hours each day running EHIRC, performing surgeries, training others, and researching the very latest medical techniques. In his capacity as head of the National Healthcare Committee of the Confederation of Indian Industry, Trehan proposed in October 2003 that every industrial business in India "adopt" approximately 30 square miles of the surrounding area, providing affordable primary healthcare to anyone in their environs. Such a plan would "give a big boost to healthcare in the country," he explained, as quoted by a writer for the *Times of India* (October 5, 2003).

"Excellence is a never-ending journey, while mediocrity is omnipresent."

Fortis Healthcare acquired EHIRC in 2005, in a development bitterly opposed by Trehan (and legally contested by Rajan Nanda's brother, Anil Nanda). In May 2007, as reported in the *Economic Times* (May 19, 2007), Fortis management, citing a conflict of interest regarding Trehan's development of Medanta, removed Trehan from his position as EHIRC's executive director. Fortis Hospitals managing director Shivinder Mohan Singh "reiterated that the cardiologist had been asked to give up his responsibilities as a doctor and administrator at the hospital." Both parties sought legal redress. Trehan, however, continued to hold a 10 percent stake in EHIRC. A week after Trehan's removal, as reported at OneIndia (May 26, 2007), an out-of-court settlement was announced that reinstated Trehan as EHIRC's executive director. Within days, however, Trehan resigned from EHIRC and joined the Apollo Hospitals, a Fortis competitor, leading an exodus of his entire medical team from EHIRC and selling his stake in the company. Trehan was senior cardiovascular and thoracic surgeon at Apollo Hospitals in New Delhi until 2009.

Medanta Medicity open on a limited basis in November 2009 and became fully operational in the first half of 2010. According to Trehan's Web site, the Medicity is a "multi-super-specialty hospital located in New Delhi. The hospital is built on 45 acres of land, is equipped with 1,500 beds and 45 operation theatres, and makes available services for 20 areas of expertise. Medanta wants to provide medical healthcare, research opportunities, and education services that are experienced in Cleveland and Harvard/Mayo Clinics. … All this, while giving affordable treatments. … The Medicity, which is a dream project of Dr. Trehan, is one of its kind in the world that has integrated the traditional and modern forms of medicine." As Sudhir Chowdhary wrote for the *Financial Express* (July 19, 2010), "Patients from developed markets such as the US and European countries … started trickling in, lured by the affordability factor. Treatment for diverse therapeutic areas such as cardiac, cancer, kidney transplants, diabetes, and plastic surgery is being made available at one-tenth the cost of what is offered in the West." Chowdhary notes that Medanta was partnering with Duke University on a clinical research facility, with Medanta funding the creation and operation of the facility on the Medanta campus (close to the Indira Gandhi International Airport in the Delhi Capital District) and Duke providing scientific, clinical research and operational expertise. "Indian systems of medicine such as Ayurveda will also be integrated with Western medicine to offer mind-body solutions for chronic conditions," Trehan says.

Trehan has published more than 500 medical research papers to date. With philanthropists Reeta Khattar and Pam Kapoor, he founded the Insaniyat Trust (*Insaniyat* means "humanity" in Hindi), a humanitarian aid organization based in New Delhi. Past president of the International Society for Minimally Invasive Cardiac Surgery, he is an honorary fellow of the Royal Australasian College of Surgeons and an honorary visiting professor at Bangladesh Medical College and LPS Institute of Cardiology in Kampur.

Over the years Trehan has received numerous awards and honors for his work. In April 1991 he was appointed personal surgeon to the president of India, the country's largely ceremonial figurehead. Three years later, in March 1994, Trehan was named an honorary consultant to Cromwell Hospital in London. Also in 1994, he was honored by the National Council on Medical Affairs of the Association of Indians in America for his "outstanding qualities and achievements in the field of medicine and surgery," according to John Perry of the *News-India Times* (September 30, 1994). In 2002 Trehan was honored by IBM and the India Times Web site as a man who "dared to think and work differently," according to the *Economic Times* (August 24, 2002). "Excellence is a never-ending journey, while mediocrity is omnipresent," Trehan declared, after being presented with this award. "It is important to add current knowledge to experience for striving towards perfection." Trehan has also received two of India's highest civic distinctions, the Padma Sree and the Padma Bhushan. Other awards Trehan has been given include the Shiromani Award (1992); the Sushruta Award, from the Association of Indians in America (1994); the Lok Seva Award (1995); the Rotary Ratna Award (1996); the Indira Gandhi Millennium Award, from the All India Feroze Gandhi Memorial Society (2000); the Rashtriya Ratan Award (2001); the American Medical Association's Physician Recognition Award, from the CME Alliance (2001); the Lifetime Achievement Award, from the International Society of Cardiovascular Ultrasound (2002); and the Lal Bahadur Shastri Institute's National Award, presented by the president of India (2005). He holds honorary doctorates from Banaras Hindu University, Chhatrapati Shahu Ji Maharaj University, and King George's Medical University.

Naresh Trehan lives in New Delhi, India, with his wife, Madhu, an award-winning journalist, and their two children, Shyel and Shonan. With her father, V. V. Purie, and her brother Aroon Purie, Madhu Trehan started *India Today,* one of the country's leading news magazines. Naresh and Madhu Trehan have been married since 1969. To relax, Naresh Trehan practices yoga.

Further Reading:

(Melbourne) *Age* p3 May 10, 2000

Economic Times Aug. 24, 2002, Sep. 29, 2005 Oct. 23, 2005, May 19, 2006

Financial Express

Hindustan Times Nov. 18, 2009

India Today p75 Nov. 9, 1998, p55 Dec. 23, 2002

Los Angeles Times p2 Oct. 16, 1988, with photo

News-India Times p39 Sep. 30, 1994, with photo

New York Times p3 May 18, 2003, with photo, Apr. 7, 2005, with photo, Dec. 2, 2005

One India May 26, 2007

(India) *Statesman* Nov. 11, 2000

Vasella, Daniel

Swiss pharmaceutical executive, physician, consultant

Born: 1953, Fribourg, Switzerland

The pharmaceutical industry, known as "pharma" to industry insiders, is big business. In the United States alone, consumers spend $200 billion a year on prescription drugs. In the early 2000s the Swiss firm Novartis, under the leadership of its chief executive officer, Daniel Vasella, emerged as the most innovative and fastest-growing company in the field, thanks largely to Vasella's dedication to research and development (R&D). "He changed the whole R&D model at Novartis to much more of an entrepreneurial focus," Gerald J. McDougal of PricewaterhouseCoopers, an accounting firm, told Fran Hawthorne for *Chief Executive* (July 1, 2004). "They are incredibly innovative."

Once the chief resident at the University of Bern's hospital, Vasella developed an interest in medicine—and compassion for the ailing—while watching his teenaged sister succumb to cancer. "He epitomizes a kind of leadership that puts equal emphasis on the social value created by the product and its economic value," Rosabeth Kanter, a consultant and professor at Harvard Business School, told Unmesh Kher for *Time* (April 26, 2004). "We want to discover drugs that change people's lives and change the way medicine is being practiced," Vasella told Patrick Clinton for *Pharmaceutical Executive* (November 2004). "I think the combination of being engaged for the patient and being competitive with your peers is a very good one."

In January 2010 Vasella decided to step down as CEO of Novartis, and in January 2013 the company announced that in February 2013, Vasella would be retiring as chairman of the board of directors. Vasella was named an honorary chairman.

Education and Early Career

Daniel L. Vasella was born in Fribourg, Switzerland, on August 15, 1953. His formative years were plagued by death and disease: he contracted tuberculosis and meningitis at age eight and was confined to an Alpine sanatorium for a year; his 18-year-old sister Ursula died from cancer when he was ten; and three years later his father, Oskar, died during a routine surgical procedure. While the kindness of one particular doctor at the sanatorium made an impression on Vasella, it was really his sister's death that inspired him to become a doctor. "Her tragic illness and death had a lasting effect on me," he once wrote, according to Tom Wright of the *International Herald Tribune* (July 16, 2005). "More than any other event, it would inspire me in later life to help others as much as I could."

Vasella earned his medical degree from the University of Bern Medical School in 1979 (some sources state 1980). He then served as a resident at several hospitals and lived for a short time in Zürich, where he earned his certification as a chemist. In 1984 Vasella returned to Bern and accepted a job as an attending physician at the university's hospital, working his way up to chief resident. "I enjoyed myself at the hospital, and I particularly enjoyed the contact with patients," he told Wayne Koberstein of *Pharmaceutical Executive* (November 1995). "So, I never thought of quitting medicine." In his early 30s, however, he suffered a mental breakdown and began re-evaluating his career. "Around age 32 to 33, the question obviously comes up, what do you want to do with the rest of your life?" he told Koberstein. "Do you pursue the same pathway always? Or are there areas you would like to learn about and understand more? I was willing to take a chance."

Later Career

Vasella left the hospital in 1988 and moved to the United States, where he had accepted a marketing job, pitching drugs to general practitioners in New Jersey for the American branch of the Swedish drug company Sandoz Pharma. His wife's uncle, Mark Moret, was the CEO of Sandoz at the time; he had discouraged Vasella from switching careers, but Vasella excelled in his new position. According to Rik Kirkland, who interviewed Vasella for the global management consulting firm McKinsey and Company, the "switch from medicine to business … gave him the opportunity to do work that could benefit [in Vasella's words] 'not one or a hundred but thousands' of people." Vasella was soon promoted to product manager. Recognizing that Sandoz was slow getting its products to market, giving competitors an advantage, he thought that the company should adopt a more aggressive, American-style business model. He got the opportunity to try a new approach while overseeing the production of a pancreatic cancer drug. Traditionally researchers, production chemists, and marketers worked separately from each other, but Vasella had them collaborate to find alternative uses for the drug; they discovered it could also treat the side effects of other types of cancer.

In 1992, after the sales of the pancreatic cancer drug skyrocketed, Vasella returned to Switzerland to apply his new method to all of Sandoz's drug development at the company headquarters, in Basel. He worked as the assistant vice president in the chief operating officer's office. A year later he was promoted to the head of corporate marketing, and in 1994 he took charge of worldwide development and became a member of the board. Ten months later Vasella was appointed chief operating officer and then, in May 1995, CEO. His swift rise through the ranks led to rumors of nepotism, but his adept management quickly appeased the critics.

Sandoz merged with rival Ciba-Geigy in 1996 to form Novartis—a name suggested by Vasella and drawn from the Latin phrase "novae artis," meaning "new skills." Vasella was named CEO and head of the Group Executive Committee. (He became the chairman of the board in April 1999.) As the leader of this newly formed company—then the seventh-largest in the pharmaceutical industry—he was faced with a daunting task. The hierarchical leadership at Sandoz discouraged initiative among its employees, and Ciba-Geigy's structure discouraged strong decision making among its managers. Vasella reorganized the company, laying off 12,500 workers and 15 of the top 21 managers. For the remaining employees he introduced performance-linked compensation and encouraged open debate about the company's direction. "Showing weakness among good people builds trust," he told Jorn Madslien for the *BBC News* (January 19, 2005). "Transparency is an outstanding mechanism to keep you on the right track." Although Vasella also fortified the marketing budget, sales increased only slightly the first few years. In 1997 Novartis introduced Diovan, a highly profitable drug for hypertension, but the patents on two of the company's most successful drugs, Sandimmune (for organ transplants) and Voltaren (for arthritis), were about to expire, which would allow generic drug makers to reproduce their formerly proprietary formulas. In response Vasella invested heavily in R&D, increasing research spending 46 percent from 1996 to 2000.

Shortly after the merger that created Novartis was completed, Vasella traveled around the world to meet the researchers at the company's many labs. At one stop on his tour, a lab technician told him that a particularly promising drug compound for the treatment of chronic myeloid leukemia (CML)—a form of leukemia in which too many white blood cells are made in the bone marrow, crippling the immune system—had been languishing in the lab. Critics of the pharmaceutical industry often complain that companies neglect rarer diseases, focusing instead on so-called "blockbuster" drugs that treat more common ailments and promise higher profit margins. When Vasella decided to invest in this CML drug, later named Gleevec, most of his colleagues thought it was foolhardy to pursue a treatment for such a narrow market; only about 10,000 people in the United States and Europe are diagnosed with CML each year. "I told people not to worry about excess supplies of [Gleevec] that might never be sold. ... We want to get this drug available to patients quickly and to do that you simply can't stick to bureaucratic rules," Vasella told Stephen D. Moore of the *Wall Street Journal* (June 6, 2000).

Vasella recognized something unique in Gleevec; while most cancer treatments kill healthy cells along with cancerous ones, this drug attacked only the cancer-causing agent. In April 1999 he saw the result of a Phase I trial and was astounded: the white blood cell count was reduced to normal levels in all of the trial's 31 patients. As word of the successful trials spread on the Internet, Novartis was inundated with e-mails from interested patients. Vasella, who personally answered many of the queries, accelerated manufacturing; when staffers learned that this was a potentially life-saving drug, some worked around the clock. Novartis filed a new drug application with the U.S. Food and Drug Administration (FDA) only 32 months after the first test on humans, and the FDA approved its use in May 2001, after a record-breaking two-and-a-half-month review. Shortly thereafter researchers announced that Gleevec was also effective in treating an advanced form of intestinal cancer, gastrointestinal stromal tumor (GIST). The FDA approved the drug for the treatment of GIST in February 2002.

What was initially predicted to be a $100 million drug—a trifling figure in the pharmaceutical industry—turned into a blockbuster; in 2004 global sales of Gleevec reached $1.6 billion. Patrick Clinton, editor-in-chief of *Pharmaceutical Executive* (November 2004), wrote that the process by which Gleevec made it to market "was a model of speed and efficiency, but something more as well ... the Gleevec story had an almost science-fiction feel. This in a real sense was how many people believe the drug companies are supposed to operate—and will. It was as if Novartis got to live for a while in pharma's future." Vasella co-wrote an account of Gleevec's development with Robert Slater. Their book, *Magic Cancer Bullet: How a Tiny Orange Pill Is Rewriting Medical History*, was not especially well received when published in 2003. "Although the story's components—devoted scientists, risk-taking executives, and activist patients—lend themselves to a gripping insider narrative," a reviewer wrote for *Publishers Weekly* (March 24, 2003), "the book lacks the details and depth of feeling needed to make the story come alive. ... Gleevec may indeed represent a new direction for cancer research, but the excitement that fact should generate is not captured here."

Most companies prefer to invest in the acquisition of other companies that hold valuable patents, because research is a riskier investment; it is rare for research to produce a treatment that makes it to market. Vasella appeared to have mixed views on the matter. His primary focus was on R&D, and he called large mergers within the pharmaceutical industry disruptive. Yet he also argued that consolidation increases overall productivity and, by extension, benefits to patients. In May 2001 Novartis purchased a 20 percent stake in its Basel-based competitor Roche. At the time Vasella said that he considered the purchase a long-term investment and was not interested in merging with Roche, a deal that would create the third-largest company in the industry (some sources reported that it would be the second largest). After failed attempts to collaborate with Roche, however, Vasella later acknowledged that he was interested in pursuing a merger, and Novartis announced in January 2003 that it had increased its stake in Roche's voting shares from 21.3 percent to 32.7 percent. The Oeri and Hoffmann families, who owned a controlling stake in the company, opposed any merger, and Vasella said he would respect their wishes, But in January 2004 Novartis increased its share again, to 33.3 percent. Industry analysts interpreted the move as an attempt to place more pressure on Roche to merge. "Under Swiss rules," noted Fiona Fleck in the *New York Times* (January 23, 2004) "passing that threshold would effectively mean beginning a formal takeover bid." Ultimately Vasella kept Novartis's stake in Roche as an investment, taking the view that selling it "would be very short-term thinking," according to Caroline Copley, writing for Reuters (May 16, 2013). Over time "the rise in Roche's valuation," she observed, "has put the group out of reach of Novartis as a takeover target, but the holding has proved a rewarding investment."

Later that year the French drug company Aventis was the subject of a hostile takeover bid from another French firm, Sanofi-Synthélabo. Aventis invited Novartis to offer a bid as well, preferring to merge with the Swiss company; it had superior distribution to doctors in the United States—the world's most lucrative drug market—and better results from its research labs compared with Sanofi-Synthélabo. In addition, Switzerland enjoys a lower corporate tax rate than France (18 percent and 34 percent, respectively). While Vasella showed some interest in Aventis, French nationalists were outraged at even the suggestion that a Swiss company might purchase a French firm. After French finance minister Nicolas Sarkozy personally called the board of Aventis, the company relented, agreeing to Sanofi-Synthélabo's offer. "I don't think government should be intervening so directly," Vasella told Heather Tomlinson of the London *Guardian* (July 31, 2004), "but obviously the French have a very different understanding of the government's role."

On the opposite end of the political spectrum stands the United States, which is considered the cash cow of the pharmaceutical industry. Unlike most other industrialized nations, the U.S. government does not does not impose price controls on the cost of prescription drugs. Though analysts warned that there is downward pressure on prices in the United States, with drug companies slashing prices in pursuit of bigger market shares, Vasella tripled Novartis's sales force in United States, to 6,200. Furthermore, in 2002 Vasella moved Novartis's research and development headquarters from Switzerland to Cambridge, Massachusetts, to capitalize on the abundance of medical researchers at the surrounding universities. He personally recruited Harvard Medical School professor Mark Fishman, known for his gene-discovery work with zebra fish, to head the lab.

Novartis reported record profits and sales for 2004; sales rose 9 percent, to $28.25 billion, and net profits rose 15 percent, to $5.77 billion. "If we are growing dynamically today," he told Clinton, "it has to do with the fact that we were able to introduce a series of innovative products and have relatively little generic erosion ahead of us. I think the commitment has to stay on innovation."

In 2004 Novartis spent $3.5 billion, or 18.8 percent of its sales, on research; the industry standard was 13- to 16 percent. Vasella set no upper limit on his company's research budget and took a personal interest in the development process, frequently visiting labs and interviewing candidates even for low-level positions. As a result of Vasella's emphasis on innovation, in 2004 Novartis had 64 drugs in the medium- or late stage of development. That year Novartis acquired Idenix Pharmaceuticals, an antiviral-treatment developer in Cambridge, Massachusetts, and Sabex, a Canada-based company that manufactures generic drugs, making Novartis the fastest-growing and fifth-largest pharmaceutical company in the world. The following February the company acquired Hexal, a German company that produced generic drugs, and Eon Labs, Hexal's U.S. affiliate; Novartis thereby became the world's second largest producer of generic drugs. In an interview published in the *New York Times* (August 13, 2005), Tom Wright asked Vasella how he would respond to critics who were "skeptical" of Novartis's move into generics. "With patented medicines," Vasella replied, "after a certain life span and patent expiry, there is a cliff and the fall is long and deep. Unless you have a strong pipeline, you are in big, big trouble as generics penetrate the market. So, indirectly generics force companies to innovate."

Although an opponent of government price controls, Vasella acknowledged that a market-driven approach to healthcare does not work as well for the third-world countries that cannot afford the pharmaceuticals they need to treat endemic diseases such as malaria and AIDS. "The problem with our industry is the products are so desirable, are so needed, by so many people, and so many people can't afford them, that it creates a tension," he told Heather Tomlinson of the *Guardian* (July 31, 2004). "We as an industry have clearly made mistakes." Vasella told Tomlinson that he thought the industry made a public-relations blunder when more than 30 pharmaceutical firms sued Nelson Mandela in 2001 for breaking international patent laws while trying to provide South Africans with affordable AIDS drugs. Still, Vasella emphasized the importance of profitability in creating incentives for innovation. "You cannot count on a company to engage out of personal commitment and acceptance of a role within society that goes beyond making a profit," he told Lowry Miller of *Newsweek* (February 21, 2005). "Profit is absolutely essential. More vital, maybe, is intellectual property. If you destroy it, you destroy the basis for rewarding innovation."

"People want you to lead. And if you lead, you will also hurt. You will satisfy sometimes. ... That's all part of your job. You have to have the backbone and the integrity to be straight with people."

Vasella oversaw the establishment of several charitable entities at Novartis. For example, the Novartis Foundation for Sustainable Development provides free treatment for leprosy patients. In July 2004 the company established the Novartis Institute for Tropical Diseases (NITD) to research new drugs to be sold at cost to people in developing countries. According to its Web site, NITD "is a small-molecule drug discovery research institute that focuses on finding new medicines against infectious diseases," particularly malaria, tuberculosis, and dengue fever. In the United States Novartis offers Gleevec on a sliding scale for poor Americans and also offers discounts of up to 40 percent on all its drugs to the estimated 11 million elderly Americans who are without prescription coverage.

In 2004 Vasella was the only pharmaceutical executive on *Time* magazine's list of the world's 100 most influential people, and the readers of the *Financial Times* voted him the most influential business leader in Europe in the past 25 years. That same year Vasella was named the Pharmaceutical Executive of the Year at the Pharmaceutical Achievement Awards, and he received the Cancer Research Institute's Oliver R. Grace Award for Distinguished Service in Advancing Cancer Research. In 2007 he was awarded the University of Marburg's Karl Winnacker Prize. The Global Institute for Leadership Development (GILD) bestowed its Walter Bennis Award for Excellence in Leadership on Vasella in 2010.

Shortly the creation of Novartis, Vasella embarked on an exceedingly ambitious plan to develop an imposing new corporate campus for the company. Writing for the *New York Times* (December 23, 2009), architectural critic Nicolai Ouroussoff, who called Novartis " one of the most innovative and ferociously aggressive drug makers in the world," provided an analysis of the project, which was then approximately half completed and featured the work of internationally renowned architects, including Vittorio Lampugnani—with whom Vasella designed the project—Frank Gehry, Rafael Moneo, Alvaro Siza, Adolf Krischanitz, and the team of Kazuyo Sejima and Ryue Nishizawa. The aim, Ouroussoff wrote, was to transform a "grim" collection of "aging office buildings and mostly boarded-up chemical factories into one of the most ambitious undertakings in a decade." Vasella "saw the design as a way to reorganize the entire social fabric of his company and foster better communication between those who develop and market his drugs." The project, in Ouroussoff's view, reflected a "desire for extreme order; anything that might detract from the overall purpose has been carefully filtered out. … And at Novartis that feeling is further reinforced by a degree of isolation that is unusual even for a corporate campus: there are no poor or homeless people walking the streets, no children, no parents with strollers — no outsiders of any kind. 'We have had many attacks, like many other companies, especially by animal-rights extremists,'" Mr. Vasella explained to Ouroussoff. 'They burned down a vacation lodge I own. They attacked the graves of my mother and of my sister. So inside we want to feel completely free of controls'. … The result is an exclusive and somewhat cool aesthetic oasis."

In the introduction to his interview with Daniel Vasella for McKinsey and Company, Rik Kirkland stated that, "As CEO, Vasella built Novartis into one of the world's largest drug companies by sales. He shifted research away from making incremental advances in older medicines for common maladies to focusing instead on drugs for rare, critical diseases whose biological origins could be understood and treated. He pushed Novartis to invest in new areas of health care, such as generics, and led efforts to expand the company's presence in China. He also spearheaded Novartis's $52 billion acquisition of U.S. eye-care company Alcon. That purchase, completed in 2010, positioned Novartis as a global leader in one of the health care industry's fastest-growing segments." In conducting the interview, Kirkland took a particular interest in Vasella's views on leadership. "Your job," Vasella told Kirkland, "is to recognize the right goal and path forward and then to align and persuade people to do the things you believe will be relevant for the long-term success of the company. People want you to lead. And if you lead, you will also hurt. You will satisfy sometimes. You will celebrate and you will blame. That's all part of your job. You have to have the backbone and the integrity to be straight with people."

Vasella has been a member of the European Institute for Business Administration, International Business Leaders Advisory Council for the Mayor of Shanghai, International Institute of Management Development, International Board of Governors of the Peres Center for Peace, and Global Leaders for Tomorrow Group of the World Economic Forum. He is also a member of the Global Health Program Advisory Panel of the Bill & Melinda Gates Foundation and a foreign honorary member of the American Academy of Arts and Sciences as well as a member of the board of trustees of the Carnegie Endowment for International Peace. He serves on the board of directors of PepsiCo Inc. (New York), Alcon Inc. (Switzerland), Genetic Therapy Inc., KBL Healthcare Ventures, American Express Company, Harvard Business School, Credit Suisse Group, and SyStemix, Inc. He is a member of the Chairman's Council of DaimlerChrysler AG (Germany). In 2002 Vasella was awarded an honorary doctorate by the University of Basel. He has also been honored with Brazil's Order of the Southern Cross and the French Legion of Honor.

One of the best-paid executives in Europe, Vasella purchased a luxurious home on Zugersee Lake and regularly came under fire for his salary, which was among the highest for a Swiss executive. Executive pay was a controversial political issue in Switzerland at the time Vasella left Novartis. His proposed exit package, which (owing to a restrictive non-compete component) was valued at some $78 million over six years, drew outrage—especially because, as Julia Werdigier wrote in the *New York Times* (February 18, 2013), the package was announced shortly before a Swiss referendum on imposing limits on executive compensation. Werdigier reported that the president of Switzerland's Christian Democratic People's Party and the Swiss federal justice minister were among those who strongly criticized Vasella's package; the latter called it an "enormous blow for the social cohesion of our country." Werdigier noted that Vasella "said he understood that many in Switzerland found the amount of the compensation 'unreasonably high, despite the fact I had announced my intention to make the net amount available for philanthropic activities.'" Peter Stamm wrote in a follow-up story on the Op-Ed page of the *New York Times* (November 22, 2013) that when, in March 2013, the "Swiss electorate voted by a two-thirds majority to ban bonuses and golden handshakes and force companies to consult shareholders on executives' remuneration, … many observers agreed that Daniel Vasella … played a decisive role in the plebiscite's success." Vasella, Stamm said, "renounced his $78 million deal and, declaring himself upset by so much personal criticism, retired to quiet seclusion. In the United States."

Vasella and his wife, Anne-Laurence, have one daughter and two grown sons. He avoids social events whenever possible, preferring the company of his family. He enjoys outdoor sports, such as skiing and scuba diving, and he drives a motorcycle. He also collects rare books and Asian sculpture. "You obviously have to enjoy business, have a successful company and make money," he told Jorn Madslien for *BBC News* (January 19, 2005), "but it cannot be the end goal."

Asked how he succeeded so well at leading Novartis, Vasella told an interviewer for *Leaders* magazine (November–December 2013): "When you get into a position like this, you owe the success to predecessors initially. After that, you work to ensure you hand it over to the next leader in better shape than when you got it. … The choice of people is crucial and the way you drive performance matters. This has to do with capturing the hearts of people so you need a real purpose that touches people's own beliefs. You also have to believe it while you're in charge. You have to have an aspiration concerning where you want to go. People rally around positive aspirations. You need to set very clear boundaries. … To share some of what I have learned with others has been motivating for me. I don't believe in giving recipes but in challenging, exploring, and helping people come to their own conclusions."

Further Reading:

Businessweek Jan. 23, 2013

Chief Executive p30+ Jul. 1, 2004

Financial Times Aug. 25, 2013

(London) *Guardian* p28+ Jul. 31, 2004

Leaders Vol. 36, no. 4 (Nov.–Dec. 2013), with photo

McKinsey and Company Web site Sep. 2012 with photo

Novartis Web site

Novartis Institutes for BioMedical Research Web site

New York Times Jan. 23, 2004, Aug. 13, 2005, Feb. 12, 2006, Dec. 23, 2009, Feb. 18, 2013, with photo, Feb. 19, 2013, pA23 Nov. 23, 2013

Pharmaceutical Executive p54+ Nov. 2004

Reuters May 16, 2013

(London) *Telegraph* Aug. 5, 2009

Wall Street Journal Jan. 24, 2013, Feb. 18, 2013, Feb. 20, 2013, Feb. 22, 2013, Jul. 17, 2013.

Selected Books:

Vasella, Daniel, with Robert Slater, *Magic Cancer Bullet: How a Tiny Orange Pill Is Rewriting Medical History,* 2003

Wood, Fiona

British-born Australian plastic surgeon, burn care specialist

---

Born: 1958, Yorkshire, United Kingdom

Fiona Wood is arguably the most prominent female medical professional in all of Australia. Then the only female plastic surgeon in the state of Western Australia, she came to widespread public attention when 28 survivors of the October 12, 2002, terrorist bombings in Bali, Indonesia, were airlifted to the burn unit she headed at Royal Perth Hospital. Through the use of her own patented medical technology, a "spray-on" skin called CellSpray, she and her staff saved the lives of 25 individuals who had sustained severe burns in that incident. Named Australian of the Year by Prime Minister John Howard in 2005, Wood was also deemed Most Trusted Australian in four consecutive polls (2005, 2006, 2007, and 2008) conducted by the Australian edition of *Reader's Digest.* Despite such honors, she told Mark Chipperfield of the London *Sunday Telegraph* (October 20, 2002), "Every time I walk away from an operation, I'm thinking: 'I've got to do better tomorrow.'" Julietta Jameson of the Web site Australia Unlimited commented, quoting Wood (December 13, 2011), "She shuns the hero tag. 'I am the team leader as a result of my education and training, not a hero. I would say the heroes are those who survive.'"

Education and Early Career

Fiona Wood was born in Pontefract, Yorkshire, in February 1958. She was raised by her parents, Geoff and Elsie Wood, in the small village of Ackworth, in West Yorkshire. Her father had lofty ambitions for Wood and her three siblings. "He was a coal miner from a very young age and he didn't like it at·all. He was very keen that we should be given the opportunity to get up in the morning and enjoy what we did," she told Catherine Madden for the Western Australia Science Network Web site. Fiona Wood was an avid athlete as a child and thought for a time that she might become an Olympic sprinter. (It eventually became obvious, however, that because of her diminutive stature, she was at a great disadvantage when competing against runners with longer legs.) "Sport was a big focus for [my father] because that was an opportunity," Wood explained to Madden, "but education rapidly overtook that because opportunities in sport are one in a million. But he knew that if we worked and studied hard, the opportunities for us were that much broader."

From an early age, Wood was interested in mathematics and science. She told Madden, "I was hungry to learn. I was actually a right royal pain the neck—always asking 'Why? Why?' And I wasn't necessarily in an environment that was conducive to learning. The public schools in mining villages weren't forward-thinking. I felt distinctly that I was the odd one out. I tried very hard to fit in but I couldn't." Her parents sent her instead, at age 13, to the Ackworth School, a local boarding- and day school that had been founded by the Quakers in 1779. Elsie worked at Ackworth, so Wood was able to attend the exclusive school without paying tuition. While there she served as head girl, a role similar to that of a student-body president in a U.S. school.

Wood's mother had repeatedly stressed to her that a career in medicine would allow her to always retain her independence and earn a good living. One of her older brothers was already in medical school, and he encouraged her as well. After graduating from the Ackworth School, in 1975, Wood entered St. Thomas's Hospital Medical School, in London. In addition to her hectic class schedule, she worked a series of part-time jobs; despite this heavy load, she found it a heady period. "It was a fantastic time. To be in London in the '70s was exciting [from] many different points of view," she said in an interview with ABC Radio Australia (March 5, 2007). "But one of the things that was really interesting to me was medicine at the time. I was sort of sucked in straight away. My first day [is] really [as] clear to me today as it was then in 1975. I walked in and we had an introductory lecture, and then we were given white coats and we were taken to the anatomy demonstration area [and] people who had left their bodies to science [or] medicine were there so that we could understand the science and art of anatomy." She continued, "And then we started working on the forearm and I was blown away by how exquisite we all are on the inside. Now it is just phenomenal how everything fit together and how it all makes sense and how the hand moved, and I came out after that first morning and I was hooked. I was going to be a surgeon. And I remember the guys going 'oh, girls don't do that' and eventually … my standard retort [became] 'well, I'm really good at needlework, so be careful.'" Some of her professors also harbored chauvinistic attitudes. When she graduated, in 1981, she was surprised to find that one professor of surgery had recommended that she not be hired by a major hospital because of her gender. "He'd said that I shouldn't be a surgeon, because I was a woman," she told the ABC Radio reporter. "And I didn't know that he'd written it down until I went for my first [job] interview. And fortunately for me, [a] person who really didn't like him was doing the interviews and I wasn't cognizant of all this at the time, but he sort of pushed his chair back onto two legs and laughed really loud and said 'Oh so the professor says you should never do surgery. We should never give you a job.' And his chair landed on four legs and he goes, 'There you go girl, ha ha. Give it a go.' And I kind of remember coming out scratching my head thinking, 'well, yeah, that was a bit strange,' but I'd gotten my first step on the ladder and having got there, I wasn't going to lose my grip."

In the early 1980s Wood met and married Tobey Keirath, a fellow surgeon who was a native of Western Australia, and she agreed to one day move back to his home state. They had two children in England, and then, in 1987, they moved to Perth, the capital of Western Australia. Wood told a reporter for the *Perth Sunday Times* (January 30, 2005), "I feel very much Australian, although I'm still a Yorkshire lass. There's a similarity in the humour and comradeship. I don't ever recall being homesick—maybe I've been too busy." Wood completed her plastic surgery training in Perth and began working at Royal Perth Hospital. Concurrently, she gave birth to four more children. Wood told a writer for the *Yorkshire Post* (February 7, 2005), "Having your first child is the biggest life change. You really can't prepare for that; going from one to six isn't such a problem." She quipped to Kerry O'Brien of the Australian Broadcasting Corporation (January 26, 2005), "It's very interesting to me that I've been at work and … people will do as I ask, and I come home and I've asked for a week for a bag to be taken upstairs and it's still there, you know. It's a great leveller."

Later Career

In 1992 a schoolteacher arrived at Royal Perth Hospital, which was considered the area's premier trauma center, with gasoline burns on 90 percent of his body. Wood had recently been made head of the hospital's burn unit. "It was a big, difficult time, personally and professionally," she told Madden. "You've worked and you've trained and all of a sudden you're the boss, you make the decisions and that's where the buck stops. I rang a couple of people overseas to help me and they said, 'You've done everything we would do. There's nothing else to offer.'" Wood decided to perform grafts using relatively new technology involving cultured skin grown in a lab, which had to be sent from a facility in Melbourne. The schoolteacher ultimately survived. "I felt if I never did anything again, saving that life was worth it," she told Madden. The incident inspired Wood to begin intensive research on better ways of creating replacement skin for burn victims. She told a reporter for the *Canberra Times* (February 11, 2006), "Burns care is highly complex. There are lots of pieces to the jigsaw, one of which is the wound care. … You're vulnerable until you've achieved skin cover. It's a race between sealing the body and the challenges of waves of infection that can compromise things. … [A badly burnt person is] no longer sealed, the fluid shifts in your body, essentially you are leaking."

In 1993, thanks to money earned during an annual telethon, Wood, along with the scientist Marie Stoner, established a skin-culture laboratory at Princess Margaret Hospital, in Perth. (The lab also serviced Royal Perth Hospital.) Initially they used a patient's cells to grow skin in sheets, but they found that the sheets were fragile and blistered easily. By about 1995, however, Wood had created an innovative method in which the cultured skin cells were sprayed directly onto the patient's wounds using an aerosol device. Other methods of growing cultured skin generally required 14- to 21 days to produce the needed amount. In contrast, Wood's technology took only 5 days. Additionally, because the cells in the spray were taken from the patients themselves, tissue rejection and scarring were less likely to occur.

By 1999 the hospital could no longer fund the skin-culture unit's research, so Wood and Stoner started the McComb Foundation, a nonprofit organization—named in honor of Harold McComb FRACS, an "internationally respected surgeon in the field of Plastic and Reconstructive Surgery and a key mentor to Fiona Wood," according to the foundation Web site—that conducts clinical and scientific research into wound healing, tissue repair, and regeneration. With the help of an investor, they also launched a commercial arm, Clinical Cell Culture, in order to market their aerosol product, which they named CellSpray. The product did not initially undergo the federally required scientific review that would enable Clinical Cell Culture to sell it throughout Australia, but Wood was permitted to use it at Royal Perth Hospital through a special agreement with local health authorities. (It is now available commercially in many countries, as are CellSpray XP, an even faster-acting product, and ReCell, an innovative medical device that enables harvested cells to be delivered onto a wound surface immediately.)

On October 12, 2002, terrorists linked to Al-Qaeda bombed two nightclubs in southern Bali, an Indonesian island that attracts many international tourists, including large numbers of Australians. (A bomb was also set off at the U.S. consulate in the Balinese capital of Denpasar, but only minor damages occurred there.) The nightclub bombings killed more than two hundred people, almost half of them Australians, and injured approximately two hundred more. The local Balinese hospital could not treat the large number of victims and did not have a severe-burn unit. About 60 survivors were flown to Royal Darwin Hospital. (Darwin is the capital of the region known as the Australian Territory, part of a vast area called the Northern Territory.) The staff at Royal Darwin Hospital provided as much immediate pain relief as possible to the patients, who were then dispatched to various hospitals around Australia for more advanced treatment. Because of its sophisticated burn unit, Royal Perth Hospital received 28 of the survivors, who arrived with a wide range of severe burns. Some patients had more than 90 percent of their bodies affected.

Wood worked six consecutive 18-hour days performing surgery on the patients, often using CellSpray. Despite such stress, Wood displayed a positive demeanor. A colleague told Chipperfield, "She is the most remarkable woman. I've never seen her shout or lose her temper in [the operating room]. She's nice to everyone and always cracking jokes." A team of about 60 medical professionals worked with her, and ultimately they saved 25 of the burn victims.

In the months following the Bali bombings, Wood was frequently interviewed for Australian television and newspapers, and many Australians hailed her as a heroine. Her techniques met with some criticism, however. Peter Haertsch, the head of the burn unit at Concord Repatriation General Hospital, in Sydney, for example, treated 12 survivors of the Bali bombings and claimed that Royal Perth Hospital had taken in more patients than it could handle rather than redirecting those patients to hospitals with more room. He told a reporter for the *Canberra Times* (October 8, 2003), "The burns unit in Perth was completely, hopelessly overwhelmed, to the extent that they had collapsing staff members, people who quit their job because they couldn't deal with it anymore. I can relate to the fact that people would think, 'I'm a very good burns surgeon, I have a very good burns unit, I can do it all,' and slip into that hero role." Wood refuted Haertsch's claim, telling the reporter, "We were the closest burns unit to Bali and as such we were prepared and ready to take all the patients. … We had 12 surgeons working in [operating rooms], we had 20 nurses scrubbed up, we had the manpower to do it."

"My personal passion now is really understanding the brain's response to injury and how we can use that to drive injury repair."

Despite the occasional criticism, Wood's handling of the Bali disaster brought international acclaim to Royal Perth Hospital and its staff. In 2004 the Western Australian regional committee of the National Australia Day Council (NADC)—a federally funded network of committees and organizations designed to raise Australian patriotism and pride—chose Wood as its Western Australian of the Year. The following year Wood beat out several state winners for the title of Australian of the Year.

In 2007, Julietta Jameson noted at Australia Unlimited, a plane crash in Yogyakarta, Indonesia, "saw Wood rising to disaster's call again. She was part of the emergency team that treated survivors with burns injuries in Indonesia, then later oversaw their medi-vac to Australia and recovery" at the Royal Perth Hospital.

The tenth anniversary of the Bali bombing elicited numerous commemorative events and commentary. A year later, in a retrospective article for the *Australian* (September 21, 2013), Richard Guilliatt noted that Wood became emotional when talking about the patients who didn't survive. "It doesn't get any easier," she told Guilliatt. The "total devastation" of the injuries shocked her, she said: "It wasn't just burn injury … there was blast injury as well, and the shockwaves damaged the tissues, and then there was the shrapnel. So they were very complicated injuries." "For us [the surgeons]," she continued, "it's not just about the surgery, it's the dressings, the recovery, the going back to surgery. Burns is a long haul—you batten down and you keep going day after day. It's not a linear progression, it's more of a rollercoaster ride." According to Guilliatt, "Wood herself is now so admired—Australian of the Year in 2005, and consistently voted one of our most trusted figures—that the [McComb Foundation] was renamed after her last year." Guilliatt reported that Wood "is now devoting half her time to research, thanks to a three-year funding grant from Royal Perth Hospital. Her focus will be looking at the brain's response to trauma—why burns to one area of skin can trigger nerve changes to undamaged skin, and whether that mechanism can be marshalled to help patients "think themselves well." Woods commented that, "It's kind of high-risk research, and if you asked me whether I know it's going to work, no, I don't. But if we understand this, can we use that information to drive different healing patterns? That's what I want to try and contribute." Wood told Sue Dunlevy of the *Australian* (August 20, 2011), "My personal passion now is really understanding the brain's response to injury and how we can use that to drive injury repair."

At present Wood is the director of the Western Australian Burns Service and a consultant in plastic surgery for the Royal Perth Hospital and the Princess Margaret Hospital, in Perth, and cofounder and director of Avita Medical Limited (formerly Clinical Cell Culture, or C3). She is Winthrop Professor in the School of Paediatrics and Child Health at the University of Western Australia. Over a number of years, she has been involved in a variety of education and disaster-response planning efforts. Wood is past president of the Australian and New Zealand Burns Association and a past board member of the International Society for Tissue Engineering. She is frequently invited as a guest speaker to major burn, wound, and plastic surgery conferences worldwide.

Wood has been given a number of awards for her work. She was named a member of the Order of Australia in 2003 and also received the Australian Medical Association's Contribution to Medicine award in that year. Other honors accorded to Wood include the Paul Stewart Rotary International Award (2002), the Johnny Walker "Keep on Walking" Award (2003), the Australian Medical Association's Contribution to Medicine Award (2003), the Dr. Michael Chin Humanitarian Award (2004), and the Life Education Australia Gold Harold Award (2008). Along with Marie Stoner, Wood won the 2005 Clunies Ross Award for contributions to medical science in Australia. Wood also holds honorary doctorates from the University of Western Australia (2004) and the University of Leeds (2007).

Wood lives with her husband and children, who are now young adults, in Perth. According to her profile at the McComb Foundation Web site, she "likes to stay active and maintain a level of fitness. As her running days were over because her knees wore out, and she never got into swimming, she got into cycling. … She likes to ride as many mornings as she can before work—either behind her kids or with a group. Wood enjoys the physical challenge of riding and one day hopes to ride across Australia." She wakes at 5 a.m. each day to exercise and to drive her offspring to various early-morning sports activities and school. She goes to bed at midnight, contenting herself with just five hours of sleep a night.

Wood told Kerry O'Brien of the Australian Broadcasting Corporation that many of her patients "are amongst the most inspirational people I've met, because you go to hell and back when you have a significant burn like that. I suppose, like Winston Churchill said, 'If you're going through hell, it's a smart thing to keep going,' and it is."

Further Reading:

ABC Radio Australia Mar. 5, 2007

Australia Unlimited Dec. 13, 2011

Australian Aug. 20, 2011, with photo, Oct. 7, 2012, with photo, Sep. 21, 2013, with photo

Australia Academy of Science Web site, with photo

Avita Medical Limited Web site

Canberra Times pA17 Oct. 8, 2003, pA4 Feb. 11, 2006

(London) *Daily Mail* p42 Jul. 13, 2004

Fiona Wood Foundation Web site

McComb Foundation Web site

(London*) Sunday Telegraph* p5 Oct. 20, 2002

(Perth) *Sunday Times* Nov. 3, 2002, Feb. 16, 2003, Jan. 30, 2005

(London) *Times* Jan. 27, 2005

University of Western Australia Web site

Western Australia Science Network Web site

Yorkshire Post Feb. 7, 2005

Zerhouni, Elias

Algerian-born American radiologist, researcher, educator, administrator

---

Born: 1951, Nedroma, Algeria

"There is a tendency for people to go down a well-worn path and see the obvious," Bruce J. Hillman, then chairman of the Department of Radiology at the University of Virginia School of Medicine, told Sheryl Gay Stolberg of the *New York Times* (March 27, 2002). "Elias somehow has this capacity to see something different and often very creative." Hillman was speaking of Elias Zerhouni, who directed the National Institutes of Health (NIH)—a division of the U.S. Department of Health and Human Services—from May 2002 until October 2008. Zerhouni, a native of Algeria, is a radiologist by training and a world-recognized expert in magnetic resonance imaging (MRI), a technique for obtaining high-quality images of the body's interior. He has also worn the hats of researcher, inventor, educator, entrepreneur, administrator, and fund-raiser since he completed his residency at the Johns Hopkins University School of Medicine, in 1978. He spent nearly 20 of the next two-dozen years at Johns Hopkins, serving there as executive vice dean, chairman of the Department of Radiology, and professor of both Radiology and Biomedical Engineering. As principal investigator or co-investigator, he worked on several research projects at Hopkins that were supported by NIH grants. He also worked as a consultant for the National Cancer Institute, the World Health Organization, and, for the three years, the White House. "Zerhouni might be better characterized as a 'research administrator,'" Bruce Hillman told Ceci Connolly of the *Washington Post* (March 27, 2002), describing Zerhouni as a "consensus builder" who, Connolly continued, "knows how to create a profitable research organization where other scientists can thrive."

In a letter to the Johns Hopkins community (March 26, 2002) announcing Zerhouni's NIH appointment, Edward D. Miller, the dean of the medical school, described him as a "visionary leader who understands how science can improve health" and who had "demonstrated that he knows how to build bridges, develop a consensus and marshal financial and human resources to achieve that vision." Miller also took note of Zerhouni's "incredible administrative ability and keen, logical, analytical mind," and he wrote that Zerhouni is "sensitive to the needs of others and has the highest of ethical standards." Miller told Ceci Connolly that Zerhouni "knows as much about finance as he knows about research. He knows about faculty issues and strategic plans for clinical practice. He is very results-oriented." In his letter of resignation from Johns Hopkins for *Johns Hopkins Medicine* (May 17, 2002), dated three days before he assumed the leadership of the NIH, Zerhouni stated, "I wouldn't have left Johns Hopkins for any other job."

The NIH is in charge of government-supported biomedical research. As the nation's largest single source of funding for such research, the NIH plays a significant role in guiding its direction for the entire United States. Accordingly, as head of the NIH, Zerhouni was in a unique position to help steer the national agenda in research on stem cells, cancer, AIDS, heart disease, minority health issues, drug and alcohol abuse, aging, and infectious, immunologic, and allergic diseases, among many other specialties. Nancy Taylor, the president of SurgiVision (later called MRI Interventions Inc.), a company that Zerhouni co-founded, told Ron Kampeas of the Associated Press (March 26, 2002), "He's one of these rare people who can actually predict and envision the future of our health care system and what it's lacking." On announcing Zerhouni's appointment to the NIH, President George W. Bush, quoting one of Zerhouni's former colleagues, described him as a "quadruple threat: a doctor who excels at teaching, researching, patient care and management."

After six months at his new post, in a column for *U.S. Medicine* (January 2003), Zerhouni wrote, "If we are to improve the health of our citizens and gain control of the healthcare burden, NIH must meet the challenge of developing prevention and treatment strategies that are orders of magnitude better than those of today. … With seemingly endless scientific opportunities, strong public support for biomedical research, and a five-year doubling of the NIH budget planned for completion next year, perhaps the biggest challenge facing NIH is investing research resources wisely. … With help from experts within and outside NIH, we are developing a short-list of the most compelling … initiatives that NIH should pursue over the next 3 to 5 years." Collectively, those initiatives became the NIH Roadmap for Medical Research, a far-reaching strategy aimed at transforming the NIH into a fast-moving, innovative organization having as its primary goal the clinical care of patients. "There has been a scientific revolution in the last few years," Zerhouni explained, as quoted in *Health & Medicine Week* (October 27, 2003). "The opportunities for discoveries have never been greater, but the complexity of biology remains a daunting challenge. With this new strategy for medical research, [the] NIH is uniquely positioned to spark the changes that must be made to transform scientific knowledge into tangible benefits for people."

Zerhouni stepped down from his NIH position in October 2008. Assessing his tenure at NIH, the editors of the *Lancet* (October 4, 2008) observed that Zerhouni had "created mechanisms for the NIH's 27 institutes and centres to do more cross-cutting work on common interests such as obesity and neuroscience. He encouraged more out-of-the box research with the NIH pioneer and new innovator awards. He stood up to the President on stem-cell research and has convinced Congress to increase funds for the NIH. Perhaps one of his greatest achievements is the launch of the Clinical and Translational Science Awards in 2006, which have strengthened clinical and translational science in the USA. … Zerhouni has been an effective advocate for science. But many at the NIH feel that he has not been the same for scientists. Top researchers have left the agency as a result."

Zerhouni returned to Johns Hopkins, where he currently is a professor of Radiology and Biomedical Engineering and senior adviser for the Johns Hopkins University School of Medicine. In 2010 Zerhouni formed the Zerhouni Group LLC, a global science- and health consulting firm.

On reflecting on the career path that led him to the NIH post, Zerhouni told Denise Grady of the *New York Times* (July 15, 2003), "I think America treated me well, and I think you have to be grateful and have a sense of duty … Some people ask me, 'What did you think about this? You're an immigrant, you're not born here, you've come through the ranks at Hopkins and then you're picked at NIH.' I say, 'Look, it says more about America than it says about me."

Education and Early Career

One of eight children, Elias Adam Zerhouni was born on April 1, 1951, in Nedroma, Algeria, while the country was a colony of France; his father was a math and physics professor. After his second birthday, he and his family settled in Algiers, the capital. For more than seven years of his childhood, beginning when he was three, a war for independence raged in Algeria. By the time the war ended and Algeria gained its independence, in 1962, at least 350,000 people had died as a result of the fighting between the supporters of the Algerian National Liberation Front and other pro-independence factions, on one side, and French and Algerian soldiers and other opponents of independence, on the other.

Zerhouni graduated from the Lycée Emir Abdelkader (a college named for a nineteenth-century Muslim religious and military leader) with both a French and an Algerian bachelor's degree, in 1968. He then entered the University of Algiers School of Medicine, where he earned an M.D. degree in 1975. After he completed medical school, Zerhouni came to the United States—with his wife, Nadia Azza; only a few hundred dollars in his wallet; and almost no command of English—to study at the Johns Hopkins University School of Medicine, in Baltimore. According to a biographical sketch on the medical school's Web site, he chose to specialize in radiology after one of his uncles, a prominent radiologist, showed him some of the first CAT-scan images ever made of the brain. (*CAT* and *CT* are acronyms for "computed tomography," "computer-assisted tomography," and "computerized axial tomography," all of which are names of a technique that produces images of internal sections of the body.)

In 1978 Zerhouni completed a residency in diagnostic radiology at Johns Hopkins; he performed so well that during his last year, he was the chief radiology resident. Also in 1978 he joined the medical school's faculty as an instructor. Zerhouni's research on computed tomography over the next few years led to the development of a new technique called CT densitometry, which enables doctors to determine whether abnormal masses on the lungs are benign or malignant. (Densitometry is also used for other purposes, such as measuring bone densities and thereby determining the strength of the bone.) In 1981, however, Zerhouni left Johns Hopkins to assume the position of vice chairman of the Department of Radiology and assistant professor at Eastern Virginia Medical School, in Norfolk. Through his research there, he broadened both the availability of CT densitometry (by inventing modifications that enabled all scanners to carry out the lung-mass tests) and its usefulness (by developing high-resolution CT scanning of the lungs).

Later Career

In 1985 Zerhouni returned to Johns Hopkins, reportedly drawn by the offer of the dual position of co-director of the Computed Tomography unit and of the newly established Division of Magnetic Resonance Imaging. He took a leave of absence from Hopkins to direct his own start-up company, Advanced Medical Imaging Institute, in Norfolk, Virginia, from mid-1991 to mid-1992. In 1992 Hopkins promoted him from associate professor to full professor. He became chairman of the Department of Radiology in 1996. For three years, beginning in 1996, he also held the posts of executive vice dean, Vice Dean for Clinical Affairs, and president of the school's Clinical Practice Association. In 1999–2000 he was Vice Dean for Research, and from 2000 to 2002, executive vice dean. Concurrently, during the late 1980s Zerhouni and his Hopkins research colleagues developed a magnetic-resonance-imaging technique known as myocardial tagging; by "marking" particular parts of the myocardium (the middle layer of the muscle wall of the heart) with an injected radioactive substance, radiologists can track the myocardium's motion precisely with every cardiac cycle, the sequence of events that take place with each heartbeat. That procedure—the first that used magnetic resonance imaging to show the heart in motion—enables cardiologists to assess the function of the myocardium in, for example, someone who has had a heart attack. In August 1996 Zerhouni oversaw the formation of a corporation called Johns Hopkins Imaging (JHI); its radiologists offered state-of-the-art diagnostic services at two sites to people in the Baltimore area. During the next year, JHI merged with three other private concerns to form American Radiology Services Inc., in an unusual partnership with Johns Hopkins. (American Radiology Services Inc. began operations in February 1997 and was bought out by an investment firm in 2003.) Persuading private radiologists to join a single practice "required extraordinary negotiating skills," Morton F. Goldberg, the director of Hopkins's Wilmer Eye Institute, told Sheryl Gay

Stolberg. "Even if it is outside of his own field, I find [Zerhouni] can cut to the chase and offer very wise opinions." In 1998, with a half-dozen other Johns Hopkins doctors, Zerhouni co-founded SurgiVision, a private company that seeks to improve MRI technology.

During his tenure as the medical school's executive vice dean, Zerhouni turned both the clinical and research divisions of the school into thriving, business-driven organizations. He also restructured the school's clinical-practice association and reorganized Hopkins's academic structure. Working with Baltimore city officials, Zerhouni also played a major role in the early planning stages of a 22-acre biotechnology research park and urban revitalization project near Johns Hopkins Hospital, an enterprise that, it was anticipated, would generate eight thousand new jobs on the city's east side. Among Zerhouni's most important accomplishments at Hopkins was the establishment of its Institute for Cell Engineering, formed with the aid of an anonymously donated $58.5 million gift that Zerhouni helped to secure. Scientists at the institute work on ways to modify human cells to render them useful in the treatment of diseases. Their research draws on discoveries in a new field called proteomics, which focuses on the approximately 200,000 proteins that have been identified in human cells and the far smaller number of genes—about 33,000—that are coded to produce proteins. Institute scientists also make use of stem cell research.

When President George W. Bush nominated Zerhouni to direct the NIH, in March 2002, the position had been vacant for more than two years. (The previous director, Harold Varmus, had left at the end of 1999 to become president of Memorial Sloan-Kettering Cancer Center, in New York City.) Being considered for the nomination came as a complete surprise to Zerhouni, who recalled for Carol Ezzell of *Scientific American* (August 11, 2003; September 2003 print issue), "To be honest with you, when I was called I thought it was a mistake. I said, 'Are you sure you want to talk to me?'" Nevertheless, Zerhouni's resume already included some work for the federal government. As a White House consultant (1985–88), he advised the medical team treating President Ronald Reagan in 1985, when polyps were found in Reagan's colon. In 1998 Zerhouni became a member of the board of scientific advisers of the National Cancer Institute. As a researcher, he was personally familiar with the process of requesting and monitoring NIH grants.

Bush's selection of Zerhouni was met with some surprise because of Zerhouni's association with the Institute for Cell Engineering. Stem cell research had become highly controversial. Unlike most human cells, each of which remains a particular type of cell during its entire like span, stem cells begin "blank," so to speak, and can develop into any of many different types of cells, in a process called differentiation. Theoretically, a stem cell can be coaxed to develop into, say, an esophageal cell, which could reproduce to form tissue that could repair parts of a diseased esophagus; or it might become a pancreatic cell, with the potential to reproduce and form a whole new organ—an outcome that might save people with pancreatic cancer. Stem cells can be "harvested" from both adult men and women and from human embryos, but those from adults are far harder to work with than embryonic stem cells. Present in bone marrow, an adult's stem cells must be "de-differentiated" to make them "blank." The creation of test-tube embryos as stem-cell suppliers and the "killing" of embryos for stem-cell research is condemned by opponents of abortion. The bitter controversy between supporters and opponents of stem-cell research led President Bush to rule, in August 2001, that federal funds—meaning NIH grants—for stem cell research would be restricted to studies using cells from only one source: existing colonies of stem cells. Earlier that year, in a Johns Hopkins University *Gazette Online* article (February 5, 2001) announcing the launch of the Institute for Cell Engineering, Zerhouni referred indirectly to stem cells when he declared that cells have "enormous untapped potential to treat currently incurable diseases." Zerhouni, described in the release as a "driving force in the institute's creation," was quoted as saying that the use of cells as therapeutic agents was a revolutionary concept with "enormous untapped potential to treat currently incurable diseases." Not to investigate this potential, he added, would be unthinkable. "We as an institution cannot deny to our patients the investigation of the potential of these therapies for them. ... I just thought this was a theme of research that Hopkins could not not do. We wanted this field to progress as unimpeded as possible because it may have a huge potential for all mankind."

After the announcement of his nomination to head the NIH, Zerhouni repeatedly declined to comment on the stem cell issue, thus triggering charges that he had been appointed for political rather than merit-based reasons. He also declined to disclose his stance on cloning human embryos in order to harvest their stem cells for later use. While the White House insisted that candidates for the position had been reviewed based on their credentials rather than their opinions, Ari Fleischer, the White House press secretary at that time, was quoted in the *Los Angeles Times* (March 27, 2002) as saying, "You should expect people who are going to be in these positions to support the ideas that the president has, otherwise they might not be comfortable serving in an administration."

In Zerhouni's first press conference after becoming the fifteenth NIH director, a reporter asked him whether he agreed with President Bush's call for legislation that would criminalize all human cloning. Zerhouni replied, as quoted in the *Boston Globe* (July 3, 2002), "To me, the science is so early that what we need to do is develop the scientific field, get more people into doing the research that needs to be done. At this point, I don't think we are anywhere near clinical implementation. Let's step back for a second." Earlier, at his confirmation hearing before the Senate Health, Education, Labor, and Pensions Committee, Zerhouni had said that scientists could "do a lot" with the few stem cell colonies approved for use. Nevertheless, according to Gardiner Harris, writing in the *New York Times* (September 2008), "in 2004 and 2005, Dr. Zerhouni told Congress that the president's policy was hindering scientific progress." Remarkably, in Harris's view, "he maintained the support of the White House despite this public disagreement."

On September 30, 2003, Zerhouni made public the NIH Roadmap for Medical Research. Reflecting the ideas of 300 biomedical experts from both inside and outside the agency, the plan listed 28 initiatives, grouped under three themes: new pathways to discovery, research teams of the future, and re-engineering the entire field of clinical research. New projects include setting up a national network for clinical trials using identical protocols for data, a "molecular library" of 500,000 synthetic small molecules, and inter-disciplinary, collaborative research centers. "Through these new initiatives, we hope to remove some of the biggest roadblocks that are keeping research findings from reaching the public as swiftly as possible," Zerhouni said, according to *Health & Medicine Week* (October 27, 2003). "These efforts cover a broad spectrum of points between the lab and the clinic—from basic biological research, such as determining protein structure, to the front lines of clinical research, such as improving the training of the physicians and nurses who run clinical trials."

As the first head of the NIH after the September 11, 2001, terrorist attacks, Zerhouni oversaw a big increase in research directed toward countering bioterrorism, the "use of pathogenic microbes or their toxins to harm people or cause widespread fear for political or ideological purposes," as he put it in *U.S. Medicine*. With $1.6 billion in additional funding allocated by Congress for that purpose, the NIH supported expanded investigations of particular microbes, including those that cause anthrax, plague, and botulism, and of existing antigens as well as attempts to find new vaccines. On another front, the NIH intensified its focus on research into the causes and treatment of diabetes, which, as Zerhouni wrote at the time, was the "sixth leading cause of death in the United States."

During his tenure at NIH, Zerhouni led an effort to promote global health and global research. Speaking to *MedlinePlus* Magazine (Spring 2008), he said, "Diseases know no borders anymore. SARS (severe acute respiratory syndrome) spread through the world in a matter of days. The dangers of fast-moving infectious diseases require us to have a global vision. Without a worldwide network of well trained, qualified scientific collaborators, we won't have the radar to protect the American public from emerging and re-emerging infections, like pandemic flu." Zerhouni's accomplishments at the NIH also included the establishment of a research program into the problem of widespread obesity. He also made efforts to reduce healthcare disparities. He created the NIH Blueprint for Neuroscience Research, a cooperative effort among 16 NIH institutes, centers, and offices that support neuroscience research. He also led major efforts to revise aspects of the NIH peer review system and implement access to publications arising from NIH funded research. In April 2006 Zerhouni told a Congressional subcommittee, "We can now clearly envision an era when the treatment paradigm of medicine will increasingly become more predictive, personalized and preemptive. We will strike disease before it strikes us with the hope of greatly reducing overall costs to society."

"We can now clearly envision an era when the treatment paradigm of medicine will increasingly become more predictive, personalized and preemptive."

As the Bush administration prepared to leave office, Zerhouni timed his departure to the run-up to the November 2008 presidential election, hoping to make the NIH a priority for both major political parties. When Zerhouni announced that he would step down, Gardiner Harris of the *New York Times* examined his impact on the NIH over his six-year tenure, saying that Zerhouni "shook up the agency when he barred scientists from consulting for drugmakers, ... pushed scientists to focus more on patient care and less on basic research, and ... forced the agency's independent institutes to cooperate on common projects." Nevertheless, Harris noted, Zerhouni "also faced a stagnant budget that ... curtailed research around the country and demoralized scientists."

Five years after leaving the NIH, at a June 21, 2013, meeting of the NIH's Scientific Management Review Board, Zerhouni discussed his views about how to value NIH research economically in an era of flat federal research budgets. "The notion of value changes over time ... the most important criteria is whether dollars are assigned in a way that satisfies societal expectations. The product of NIH should be knowledge, not products. How do we achieve reduction in the burden of disease and reduction in the burden of health care costs? How do we transform knowledge into societal benefit? In a country where chronic diseases account for 80 percent of health care costs, federal investment needs to be tied to the societal needs of the day. Patients measure, better than anybody, the value of research. The NIH should devote 60 percent of its budget to generate new knowledge."

Zerhouni was re-appointed a professor of Radiology and of Biomedical Engineering at John Hopkins commencing on January 1, 2009. Since 2011 he has been a member of the Executive Committee and the Global Leadership Team at Sanofi-Aventis (a global pharmaceutical and vaccines company) as well as its president of Global Research & Development, covering medicines and vaccines. He is Emeritus Public Trustee at Mayo Clinic Health Systems and serves on the board of directors of the Danaher Corporation, Lasker Foundation, Mayo Clinic, Research America, King Abdullah University of Sciences and Technology, and Actelion Pharmaceuticals, a Swiss biotechnology company. Zerhouni also serves as a member of the advisory council at the National Institute on Alcohol Abuse and Alcoholism (NIAAA). He is a member of the National Academy of Science's Institute of Medicine and the French Academy of Medicine and since 2009 has served as a senior fellow at the Bill and Melinda Gates Foundation.

Zerhouni has published more than two hundred articles in professional publications, and he is chief scientific advisor to the American Association for the Advancement of Science's journal *Science Translational Medicine*. Singly or with others, he holds eight patents for medical devices or techniques. In all Zerhouni also founded or co-founded five start-up companies: Computerized Imaging Reference Systems (CIRS), 1982; the Advanced Medical Imaging Institute (AMII), 1989; Biopsys Corporation, 1993, which became public before being acquired by Johnson & Johnson, effective 1997; American Radiology Services, 1997, which was bought out in 2003; and SurgiVision Inc., 1998, which was renamed MRI Interventions Inc. in 2011.

Among other honors, Zerhouni has received two gold medals from the American Roentgen Ray Society for scientific exhibits (1985 and 1987); two Paul Lauterbur awards for MRI research (1989 and 1993); the Fleischner Society Medal (1997); a Frank T. McClure Fellowship (1990–92); and the Rising to the Extraordinary Award from the Islamic Center of Long Island (2003). In 2008 he was named a chevalier of the French Legion of Honor, and he was elected to the French Academy of Medicine in 2010. Johns Hopkins University awarded him an honorary doctorate in 2010.

Zerhouni's wife, Nadia Azza, is a pediatrician. They met as teenagers, when both were members of the Algerian national swimming team, and they attended medical school together. The couple have three children—Will, Yasmin, and Adam—and live in Maryland. Zerhouni is fluent in English, French, and Arabic. He plays the lute and piano and enjoys opera, tennis, boating, and scuba diving. He became a naturalized citizen of the United States in 1990.

Further Reading:

Associated Press Mar. 26, 2002

Chronicle of Higher Education p19+ Apr. 5, 2002, pA24 Oct. 10, 2003

Health Affairs Vol. 25 no. 3 (May 2006): w94+

Health & Medicine Week p332 Oct. 27, 2003

Johns Hopkins *Gazette Online* Vol. 30, no. 20 (Feb. 5, 2001)

Johns Hopkins Medicine May 17, 2002

Lancet Vol. 359, no. 9318 (May 11, 2002): p1629, Vol. 362, no. 9381 (Aug. 2, 2003): p381+, Vol. 362, no. 9393 (Oct. 23, 2003): p1382+, Vol. 372, no. 9645 (Oct. 4, 2008): p1194

Lancet Neurology Vol. 3, no. 11 (Nov. 2004): p633

Los Angeles Times Mar. 27, 2002

MedlinePlus Spring 2008

National Institutes of Health (NIH) Web site

NIH Blueprint for Neuroscience Research Web site

New York Times Mar. 27, 2002, Jul. 15, 2003, with photo, Sep. 24, 2008, with photo

Sanofi-Aventis Web site

Scientific American p42+ Sep. 2003, with photo

Washington Post pA01 Mar. 6, 2002, pA19+ Mar. 27, 2002

Appendixes

Historical Biographies

Aristídes Agramonte

Cuban-born American physician and scientist

Agramonte's specialization in tropical medicine research as a pathologist and bacteriologist led to his appointment to the four-member Yellow Fever Commission. He confirmed that mosquitoes were the transmitting agents for the devastating disease yellow fever.

Areas of Achievement: Medicine, science, technology

Born: June 3, 1868; Puerto Príncipe (now Camagüey), Cuba

Died: August 17, 1931; New Orleans, Louisiana

Early Life

Aristídes Agramonte y Simoni (ah-grah-MOHN-tay ee see-MOHN-ee) emigrated to the United States from Cuba in 1870 at three years of age, with his mother, Matilde Argilagos Simoni. His father, General Eduardo Agramonte Piña, was killed in the first Cuban war for independence. In addition to serving in the military, Agramonte's father was a prominent physician. Aristídes Agramonte earned his bachelor's degree at New York University in 1886 and subsequently attended medical school at Columbia University. He graduated with honors from Columbia's College of Physicians and Surgeons in 1892.

Life's Work

On graduation from medical school, Agramonte remained in New York City, where he pursued research in pathology and bacteriology at Bellevue Hospital and was hired as an assistant bacteriologist in the health department. In 1898 Agramonte was named acting assistant surgeon of the U.S. Army Medical Corps. The United States recently had taken control of Cuba, which had been liberated from Spain in the Spanish-American War. In July 1898 U.S. Army Surgeon General George Sternberg deployed Agramonte to Santiago de Cuba in southeastern Cuba to study a yellow fever outbreak in the U.S. Army. Agramonte was thought to be immune to the disease because of his exposure to yellow fever as a child in Cuba. Italian bacteriologist Giuseppe Sanarelli, working in Montevideo, Uruguay, had claimed to have established that the bacteria *Bacillus icteroides* caused yellow fever transmission. Subsequently researchers were unable to confirm his results. In Cuba Agramonte performed autopsies on infected individuals in an attempt to verify that this bacterium was linked to yellow fever. As a result of this research, Agramonte disputed

Sanarelli's thesis, having found no evidence that *Bacillus icteroides* was the causative agent for yellow fever. In December 1898 Sternberg again enlisted Agramonte to study the epidemiology of yellow fever, working this time with bacteriologists from the U.S. Marine Hospital Service (later the U.S. Public Health Service). His conclusion was the same.

Having remained in Cuba as laboratory director of the U.S. military hospital, Agramonte was appointed in May 1900 as a pathologist on the Army's Yellow Fever Commission, led by Walter Reed and also including two other researchers, James Carroll and Jesse Lazear. Reed and Carroll had also studied Sanarelli's claims, in 1899, and had likewise discounted them. In 1881 Dr. Carlos Juan Finlay, a Cuban physician, had first proposed that the *Aedes Aegypti* mosquito was the vector of yellow fever, but he had been unable to prove it. He offered Lazear his mosquito egg samples. As was fairly common practice at the time, Carroll and Lazear experimented on themselves after hatching and incubating Finlay's samples. Agramonte, immune from his childhood exposure, could not contribute in this way. In August 1900 Carroll allowed Lazear to place an infected mosquito on his arm; by the end of the month he contracted yellow fever and nearly died. Another volunteer, Private William Dean, also developed the disease, and from these instances of infection Lazear surmised that an incubation period of ten days was necessary for transmission of yellow fever. In September Lazear himself became infected, although the precise circumstances the led to his contracting the disease are unknown. He himself claimed shortly before dying of the disease on September 25, 1900, that he had been accidentally bitten while attending patients. Remarkably, given average death rates from the disease of 20 percent to 40 percent, Lazear's proved to be the only death directly resulting from the experiments. In all, 18 Americans (2 civilians, 15 enlisted men, and one officer) and 15 Spanish immigrants to Cuba voluntarily participated in the commission's experiments, which continued after Lazear's death, for six months overall. The experiments confirmed that the *Aedes Aegypti* mosquito transmitted yellow fever. This discovery led to control over the spread of the disease and dramatically reduced disease prevalence within one year—as well as reducing the incidence of malaria, also known to be a mosquito-borne disease.

Agramonte and his colleagues received a Congressional Gold Medal in 1929 for this work. Although there was considerable pressure for Agramonte (with Reed and Carroll, the surviving commission members) to be honored with a Nobel Prize in Medicine for this discovery, it never came to fruition. Years later, in 1951, Dr. Max Theiler won the prestigious award for his development in 1937 of a yellow fever vaccine.

In addition to yellow fever, Agramonte studied other tropical diseases, such as the plague, dengue, malaria, and typhoid fever. He became a professor of experimental pathology and bacteriology at the University of Havana, Cuba, in 1901. In 1901 Agramonte was elected an honorary member of the American Society of Tropical Medicine, where he served as the society's second vice president. Agramonte's memoir *Yellow Fever; The Inside History of a Great Medical Discovery* was published in Havana in 1915. He also published *Lessons of Experimental Pathology* (1922), *Compendium of Bacteriology; Bacteriological Technique* (1924), *Looking Back on Cuban Sanitary Progress* (1930), and some 150 scientific articles and monographs, mostly of them on tropical medicine. Agramonte was granted honorary degrees by Columbia University (1914), the University of San Marcos, Lima, Peru (1925), and the University of Tulane (1929). In 1930 Agramonte was made an honorary fellow of the American Public Health Association. In 1931 he was elected president of the Pan-American Medical Congress. Shortly before his death, he returned to the United States to serve as professor of tropical medicine at the Louisiana State University Medical School in New Orleans.

Agramonte died on August 17, 1931, at the age of 63, from cardiac complications. He was the last surviving member of the Yellow Fever Commission. In 1940 Camp Lazear, the former site of the commission's mosquito experiments, was made a park, in honor of the men who worked on the commission and all volunteers from that time. A bronze medallion of Agramonte rests there in his honor.

Significance

As a result of the Yellow Fever Commission's research, a vaccine for yellow fever was created; the World Health Organization has promoted its use in routine childhood vaccination programs since 1988. Some have suggested that the eradication of yellow fever in Cuba was the first great accomplishment in the field of public health. The elimination of yellow fever also is credited with facilitating progress in other important development projects; it was a precipitating event in allowing the creation of the Panama Canal.

Because they exposed themselves and other volunteers to the disease and to hazardous conditions, the research of Agramonte and the entire Yellow Fever Commission now is considered inhumane, albeit selfless. Nevertheless, in addition to the inestimable importance of the commission's work medically, the procedures of the commission broke new ground in controlled clinical trials and in the ethics of clinical research, especially with regard to informed consent. Because no animals were known to be susceptible to yellow fever, research on humans was necessary to pursue the commission's work. Sanarelli had conducted his experiments on immigrant hospital patients without their knowledge, a procedure that attracted significant criticism. Reed was determined not to engage in such unethical practices. He devised a written informed consent form, available in Spanish and in English, clearly spelling out the risks of the commission's experiments and specifying compensation. These forms had to be signed by both the volunteer and the researcher.

The Aristídes Agramonte Yellow Fever Collection is housed at the library of the Louisiana State University Health Sciences Center, New Orleans, Louisiana. His collection of books and pamphlets formed a considerable portion of the holdings of the original medical school's library.

Janet Ober Berman

José Celso Barbosa

Puerto Rican-born physician and politician

Throughout his life José Celso Barbosa worked in the area of public medicine but also dedicated himself to political reform. At first, under Spanish rule, an active member of the Autonomist Party, Barbosa founded the Republican Party of Puerto Rico, which advocated acceptance of American rule and eventual American statehood.

Areas of Achievement: Medicine, politics, government

Born: July 27, 1857; Bayamón, Puerto Rico

Died: September 21, 1921; San Juan, Puerto Rico

Early Life

Born in Bayamón, Puerto Rico, to Hermógenes Barbosa Tirado and Carmela Alcalá, José Celso Barbosa (SEHL-soh bahr-BOH-sah) was raised mostly by his maternal aunt, Lucía Alcalá. He first attended the local school of Olegario Núñez and then the public elementary school of Gabriel Ferrer Hernández, both in Bayamón. Barbosa then became the first person of mixed race—his ancestry was African, American, and European—to be enrolled in the prestigious Jesuit minor seminary, which was located in San Juan. He excelled as a student and was awarded his diploma in 1875.

Being from a poor family, Barbosa then tutored younger students, such as the children of José Escolástico Berríos, the owner of the San Antonio Sugar Mill, in order to earn enough money to go to the United States to attend college. At that time, Puerto Rico did not yet have a university. In 1876 he went to New York City to study English, which he learned fairly well in one year's time, and to pursue studies in either law or engineering. He briefly enrolled in the School of Engineering at Fort Edwards, New York, but he soon contracted pneumonia. At the urging of his physician, Barbosa instead investigated the possibility of a career in medicine. In 1877 he began his studies in general medicine and surgery at the University of Michigan, Ann Arbor, having previously been rejected by the College of Physicians and Surgeons (which became Columbia University Medical School) because of his race. Barbosa completed these studies in 1880 and received his M.D.; he was the valedictorian of his class. In 1917 the University of Michigan conferred on him an honorary Master's degree.

After taking several months to tour a number of American clinics and hospitals, Barbosa returned to Puerto Rico in October 1880. There he encountered difficulties in establishing his medical practice, because the Spanish government would not accept a degree from an American institution. Moreover, the medical elite in Puerto Rico did not welcome a doctor of poor backgraound and mixed race. At the request of the American consulate, however, Spanish officials relented and accepted Barbosa's medical degree as valid. He began to practice medicine in San Juan just as a smallpox epidemic broke out.

Life's Work

Barbosa quickly earned a reputation as an excellent physician, distinguishing himself through his use of innovative techniques in treating the smallpox. He was named a staff physician at the Society for Mutual Aid, which put him in contact with poor and often desperately ill patients, whom he treated with respect, kindness, and competence. Barbosa advocated for an early version of a health insurance system, urging employers to pay small ongoing fees into a fund to cover the future healthcare needs of their employees. In 1882 he joined the Liberal Reformist Party—Puerto Rico's first political party, formed in November 1870—beginning a lifelong involvement in politics.

Barbosa married Belén Sánchez Jiménez in 1886; the couple was to have 12 children. Barbosa was elected a member of the Liberal Reformist Committee. His increasing interest in the civil affairs of the island led Barbosa to participate in the organizational meeting of the Autonomist Party of Puerto Rico, led by Román Baldorioty de Castro, in Ponce in 1887. The party advocated both home government for Puerto Rico and representation in the Spanish parliament. In 1890 Barbosa was appointed professor of natural history at the Institute of Higher Learning, which was organized under the auspices of the Puerto Rican Athenaeum. At the institute he offered courses in zoology, botany, and mineralogy. Two years later, he was named professor of anatomy and physiology and taught classes in various aspects of anatomy and obstetrics. Meanwhile, the first Puerto Rican *cooperativa* ("cooperative"), a credit union named El Ahorro Colectivo ("The Thrift Collective") was founded by Barbosa in 1893. Seeking greater political liberty for Puerto Rico, Barbosa founded the Orthodox (or "Pure") Autonomist Party in 1897 and served as its undersecretary for public instruction.

With the arrival of American rule after the Spanish-American War of 1898, Barbosa was energized to work for a new and more stable system of government and a higher standard of living for all of Puerto Rico's citizens. He actively supported closer cooperation with American attempts to modernize the island's health and educational systems and encouraged his fellow Puerto Ricans to embrace the ideals of democracy.

On July 4, 1899, Barbosa founded the Republican Party of Puerto Rico, which was dedicated to strengthening the island's ties to the United States and to obtaining acceptance of Puerto Rico as a state. Recognizing the need for linguistic and cultural integration, Barbosa founded Puerto Rico's first bilingual newspaper, *El tiempo ("Time"),* in 1907, and he wrote a regular column for it. In 1900 President William McKinley had appointed him a member of the executive cabinet of Governor Charles H. Allen, a position Barbosa would hold until 1917. During this time, he worked for U.S. citizenship for Puerto Ricans, and on March 2, 1917, President Woodrow Wilson signed the Jones-Shafroth Act, making Puerto Rico a U.S. territory. Puerto Ricans were granted statutory citizenship, that is, citizenship was granted by an act of Congress. The act also created a bill of rights for the territory; organized its government in executive, legislative and judicial branches; and declared English to be Puerto Rico's official language. Barbosa deepened his governmental commitments by serving as a member of the senate of Puerto Rico from 1917 until his death in 1921. His legislative accomplishments included the incorporation of trial by jury and habeas corpus into Puerto Rico's criminal justice system. Barbosa succumbed to cancer in San Juan at the age of sixty-four.

Significance

Barbosa was not only a powerful supporter of a strong public health system but a dedicated professor who brought advanced scientific learning and medical techniques to Puerto Rico from the United States. Today he is most remembered as the father of the Puerto Rican statehood movement and as the founder of the Republican Party of Puerto Rico, which worked for American statehood for the island. Puerto Rico's political status always has been the central issue in the search for Puerto Rican identity; Barbosa's was one of the most important voices in that debate, under both Spanish and American rule. His birthday is commemorated in Puerto Rico as an official holiday.

Mark T. DeStephano

Martha Bernal

American psychologist and educator

Bernal was the first woman of Mexican heritage to receive a doctorate in clinical psychology from an American university. She became a leading researcher on methods of correcting behavioral problems in children and an expert in the training of psychologists on minority and multicultural issues.

Areas of Achievement: Psychology, social issues, education

Born: April 13, 1931; San Antonio, Texas, United States

Died: September 28, 2001; Black Canyon City, Arizona, United States

Early Life

Martha Elda Bernal (behr-NAHL) was born in San Antonio, Texas, and was raised in El Paso by her parents, Alicia and Enrique de Bernal, who emigrated from Mexico in the 1920s, during the Mexican Revolution. Bernal's parents instilled in her traditional Mexican values, including an emphasis on the importance of family. The family spoke Spanish at home. When Bernal, as yet unable to speak English, enrolled in elementary school, she began learning about discrimination toward Mexican culture. She experienced difficulties growing up in a bicultural community from this young age because interaction among children of different races was discouraged.

Bernal graduated from El Paso High School and desired more formal education—a choice that was not typical for Mexican American women, who generally were encouraged to marry and raise families after high school graduation. Although resistant, her parents eventually agreed to Bernal's wishes and financially supported her while she attended Texas Western College, now known as the University of Texas at El Paso.

After graduating from college with a bachelor's degree in psychology, Bernal, wishing to continue her education, spent an unsatisfying year at Louisiana State University and then went on to earn a master of arts degree from Syracuse University in New York (1957). She worked for two years before entering Indiana University's graduate psychology program. In 1962 she obtained her doctoral degree in clinical psychology. As a woman, Bernal was not allowed to participate in research projects with her psychology professors and often considered dropping out because of this gender discrimination. Persevering, however, Bernal became the first Mexican American woman to earn a doctorate in clinical psychology.

Life's Work

After graduating Bernal searched unsuccessfully for an academic job; institutions wanted to hire only male psychologists. Instead she completed a two-year postdoctoral fellowship in human psychophysiology through the U.S. Public Health Service, at the University of California at Los Angeles (UCLA). With this added academic qualification, Bernal eventually obtained her first academic position, as assistant professor at the University of Arizona at Tucson. Consulting at a mental health center in Tucson, she focused on marriage counseling of minority couples when mental illness was diagnosed in the wife, developing a behavioral approach that proved successful.

In 1965 Bernal returned to UCLA's Neuropsychiatric Institute to begin her scientific research. That year she was awarded a grant by the National Institute of Mental Health (NIMH) to study learning theory and classical conditioning in children with behavior problems, most notably autism. Her research concentrated on altering the parents' behavior by teaching them skills and lessons to help change their children's behavior. Bernal believed that children with autism did not have an innate cause for their disorder but rather had learned their behaviors. For this work, Bernal was granted several National Research Service Awards from the NIMH, and she is cited as one of the first psychologists to study this subject in an empirical manner.

In 1971 Bernal, now nationally recognized as an expert in behavioral modification, relocated to the University of Denver with a substantial grant to continue her work. There, in addition to her professional research, Bernal became more involved in minority issues regarding race- and gender discrimination after attending an influential conference, Increasing the Educational Opportunities for Chicanos in Psychology, organized by Alfredo Castanda and Manuel Ramirez at the University of California at Riverside in spring 1973. Bernal identified a sabbatical year in 1979 as making a sharp change in her work. She had long been interested in addressing the needs of Hispanic children; having completed her outcome study on her previous work, she turned to studying the Mexican American experience. According to her brief memoir, published in *Models of Achievement: Reflections of Eminent Women in Psychology* (volume 2, 1988), she read extensively on this subject in the fields of sociology, political science, history and psychology. What she learned moved her to re-evaluate the efficacy and validity of her previous studies and refocus her scientific research in order to make it more applicable to minority issues. She acted as an advocate for minorities and professionally sought the help of the American Psychological Association to bring attention to minority issues in the profession. In 1979, the NIMH gave Bernal another National Research Science grant to educate psychologists about multicultural issues.

Bernal's initial findings regarding diversity in the psychology field were not encouraging. Training programs lacked appropriately sensitive multicultural lectures and curricula, had few or no minority students enrolled, and did not employ minority professors. She completed a second postdoctoral fellowship through the Ford Foundation, in the course of which she studied ways to eliminate these disparities. In 1986 Bernal moved to Arizona State University, where she was to perform much of her groundbreaking work on how identities are established in Mexican American children and families. She created a method of measuring ethnic identity called the Ethnic Identity Questionnaire. Bernal used this tool to interview Mexican- and Mexican American children and families. The research brought to light common themes, including how Mexican identity is influenced and formed and how American society can better appreciate Mexican culture. She published these findings, along with the findings of other studies, in a book entitled *Ethnic Identity: Formation and Transmission among Hispanics and Other Minorities* (1993), which she edited with George P. Knight. She also published her work in several peer-reviewed scientific journals. Bernal frequently lectured about her research in order to raise multicultural awareness. For three years, she also coordinated an annual Ethnic Identity Symposium to address these issues. The research has been hailed as pioneering because of the creative new interview approaches she used in an attempt to understand how ethnicity is created and transmitted from influences such as parents, families, other adults, and peers.

Over her career Bernal raised awareness of multicultural issues by speaking at many professional conferences. She spoke at the Vail Conference on Training in Psychology in 1972 and the Lake Arrowhead National Conference of Hispanic Psychologists in 1979. She was influential in drafting the bylaws of the Board of Ethnic Minority Affairs (1979) and helped establish the National Hispanic Psychological Association

(1979; now known as the National Latina/o Psychological Association), of which she became the second president. Bernal was appointed to the Commission on Ethnic Minority Recruitment, Retention and Training (1994) and served on the board for the Advancement of Psychology in the Public Interest (1996–1998). She was also a member of the Committee on Gay, Lesbian and Bisexual Affairs.

Among the noteworthy awards that Bernal received are the Distinguished Life Achievement Award from Division 45 of the Society for the Psychological Study of Ethnic Minority Issues (1979), the Hispanic Research Center Lifetime Award (1979), the Pioneer Senior Women of Color Honor (1999), the Carolyn Attneave Diversity Award for lifelong contributions to ethnic minorities psychology (1999), and the Award for Distinguished Contributions to the Public Interest from the American Psychological Association (2001).

After three occurrences of cancer over two decades, Bernal died of lung cancer at 70 years of age. The Martha E. Bernal Memorial Award at Arizona State University was established in her honor.

Significance

Bernal overcame cultural- and gender discrimination in her youth and throughout her career. She convinced not only her family but also her colleagues that Mexican women could become productive and successful in the professional and academic worlds. Although Bernal's early career path was not focused on ethnicity or minority issues, she realized the importance of these issues and spent more than 20 years advocating that they be incorporated into the field of psychology. Bernal's groundbreaking research on minority populations serves as a basis for the now-common multicultural studies classes in undergraduate and graduate psychology and counseling programs.

Janet Ober Berman

David Cardús

Spanish-born physician and scientist

Trained in cardiology, Cardús combined his medical expertise with knowledge of computers and mathematics in order to advance the field of sports medicine by studying the effects of physical exercise on the body. He was one of the physicians who monitored astronauts in the first U.S. space mission.

Areas of Achievement: Medicine, science, technology

Born: August 6, 1922; Barcelona, Spain

Died: June 2, 2003; Houston, Texas, United States

Early Life

David Cardús y Pascual (kahr-DUHS ee pahs-KUHL) was born to Jaume and Ferranda Pascual Cardús in Barcelona on August 6, 1922. His mother died when he was only 11 years old. Cardús went to secondary school at the Institut-Escola de la Generalitat de Catalunya in Barcelona in 1938. Because of the Spanish Civil War, he had to travel back and forth from Spain to France in order to complete his higher education. He earned both B.A. and B.S. degrees from the University of Montpellier in France in 1942.

Cardús returned to Spain to serve in the army for four years and then to attend medical school at the University of Barcelona, receiving his medical degree in 1949. He completed his internship through the University of Barcelona's Hospital Clinico and performed his respiratory disease residency at the Barcelona Sanatorio del Puig d'Olena. Following this training, Cardús received funding from the French government for a two-year cardiology fellowship in Paris. At the end of the fellowship, Cardús once again returned to Spain, where in 1956 he earned a postgraduate cardiology degree at the University of Barcelona's School of Cardiology. He received a second fellowship at the Royal Infirmary at the University of Manchester, England.

Life's Work

Cardús moved to the United States after completion of his fellowships. From 1957 until 1960, he was a research associate at the Lovelace Foundation, an organization based in Albuquerque, New Mexico, that assessed astronauts' physical preparedness for flight. Cardús began working with the National Aeronautics and Space Administration (NASA) in 1958. Through both NASA and Lovelace, Cardús helped select the first astronauts for the space program by providing medical evaluations. He additionally assisted in the health monitoring of the first seven astronauts in space during Project Mercury.

After leaving the Lovelace Foundation, Cardús accepted a teaching position at Baylor College of Medicine's Institute for Rehabilitation and Research in Houston, Texas. He began as a lecturer for the Physiology and Rehabilitation Departments and eventually became professor of physical medicine and rehabilitation, remaining at the college from 1960 until 1999. Cardús also was appointed head of the Department of Biomathematics, a field that applies mathematical principles to the understanding of biological functions, and he ran the exercise and cardiopulmonary laboratories. While at Baylor College, his research focused on advances in computer technology and mathematical programs in physical rehabilitation. He recorded respiratory data through digitalized computer programs rather than through hand calculations.

Cardús earned a doctorate in mathematics for life scientists from the University of Michigan at Ann Arbor in 1966. He lectured at Rice University in Houston, Texas, through the Department of Statistics and Mathematical Science and as an adjunct professor of physiology there from 1970 to1988. Cardús also served as a planning consultant for the U.S. Public Health Service, and in this position he helped to design and construct health facilities.

In the 1990s Cardús was involved in a joint effort with NASA and the Texas Medical Center at Baylor College, in which his team developed a spinning centrifuge to simulate gravity. Although the spinning centrifuge was originally created to test the effects of space on an astronaut's muscles, such as the heart, Cardús used this invention to study other patient populations, such as those with spinal cord or cardiovascular injuries. He found that this centrifuge improved the sitting and standing tolerance of these patients.

Cardús's awards and honors include a gold medal from the U.S. International Congress of Physical Medicine and Rehabilitation (1972), the Elizabeth and Sidney Licht Award for Excellence in Scientific Writing (1981), the Narcis Monturiol Medal for scientific and technical merit (1984), and an honorary doctorate from the University of Barcelona (1993). He published numerous peer-reviewed scientific journal articles, edited the book *Rehabilitation in Ischemic Heart Disease* (1983), and wrote the introduction to *A Hispanic Look at the Bicentennial* (1976). Cardús was an active member of professional and cultural societies in both the United States and Spain, serving as vice chair of the Gordon Conference on Biomathematics (1970), president of the International Society for Gravitational Physiology (1993), president of Spanish Professionals in America, and chairman of the board of the Institute of Hispanic Culture. In 1970, he founded the American Institute for Catalan Studies (1979).

Cardús married Francesca Ribas in 1951; the couple had four children. Francesca Ribas Cardús held a Ph.D. in pharmacy from the University of Barcelona and was associated with the Baylor College of Medicine from 1972 until 2000. She died in 2013. David Cardús became an American citizen in 1969. He died of a stroke on June 2, 2003, at age 80, and his ashes were scattered in the Mediterranean Sea after an official Catalonian ceremony.

Significance

Cardús had the foresight to integrate computer technology and mathematical programs into medical care decades before the field of telemedicine gained popularity. His groundbreaking work with NASA laid the foundation for an understanding of the physical effects of space on the human body. Although he became an American citizen, Cardús continued to advocate for the Catalonian community both from a cultural and educational perspective. Through the American Institute for Catalan Studies, he promoted the careers of several Catalan musicians and artists, including composer Joaquin Rodrigo and famed tenor José Carreras. Cardús's research was based in the United States, but he was involved with the Spanish community by using computer technology to collect and share data for experiments between Spain and America.

Janet Ober Berman

Margaret Chung

Chinese-born physician

Margaret Chung was the first American-born Chinese woman physician in the United States. She was also responsible for organizing and inspiring members of the U.S. Armed Forces in the fight against the occupying Japanese troops in China during World War II.

Areas of Achievement: Medicine, politics

Born: October 2, 1889; Santa Barbara, California, United States

Died: January 5, 1959; San Francisco, California, United States

---

Early Life

Margaret Chung was born on October 2, 1889, in Santa Barbara, California. Her mother, Ah Yane, had emigrated from China in 1874 at a young age. At age 11, Ah Yane was arrested in a San Francisco brothel, removed from her guardians' care, and transferred to the Chinese Presbyterian Mission Home. Margaret's father, Chung Wong, arrived in California in 1875 as a teenager, eventually establishing himself as a merchant of imported Chinese goods. Ah Yane and Chung Wong likely met through their work with Presbyterian missionaries and, in November of 1888, the couple married and relocated to Santa Barbara. Less than a year later, their first child, Margaret, was born.

Racial discrimination made life difficult for the Chung family, and Chung Wong's retail business eventually failed, forcing him to file for bankruptcy and to take on manual jobs as a fruit vendor, ranch foreman, and truck driver. When Margaret was about ten years old, her father became bedridden owing to rheumatism and her mother became increasingly weakened from tuberculosis. As the eldest of 11 children, Margaret assumed most of the responsibility for caring for her parents and siblings and took a job at a restaurant to supplement her father's income. Through her determination and hard work, she earned enough money from scholarships and odd jobs to put herself through college and medical school.

Life's Work

In 1916 Margaret Chung graduated from the University of Southern California's College of Physicians and Surgeons, where she had been the only female student. She completed her residency at Kankakee State Hospital in Illinois, specializing in surgery, psychiatry, and criminology. Following her father's death in 1917, Chung returned to Southern California and began work as a staff surgeon at the Santa Fe Railroad Hospital, eventually establishing a small practice in Los Angeles.

In 1922 Chung moved to San Francisco and established a private practice there, slowing expanding it as she gained the respect of the local community. She nevertheless maintained her practice in Los Angeles, making frequent trips by plane between the two cities and eventually attracting a large clientele of Hollywood celebrities. In 1925 Chung became one of the founding physicians of Chinese Hospital in San Francisco's Chinatown, which was one of the first modern medical clinics in the neighborhood. Through her practice, Chung established many important connections and loyal friendships and was known to host dinners for her clients at her home.

In 1931 Chung was responsible for conducting the medical examinations of seven young aviators in the U.S. Navy reserve. She quickly took the men under her wing and began hosting them and their friends at her home, where the servicemen mingled with Hollywood celebrities such as Ronald Reagan, John Wayne, Tallulah Bankhead, Tennessee Williams, and Helen Hayes. As more such servicemen established ties with Chung, they began calling her Mom Chung. Because Chung was unmarried, the group began referring to themselves as her "fair-haired bastards." By 1941 Mom Chung had "adopted" more than a thousand "sons" in the Army and Navy.

Through her many connections, Chung recruited the first two hundred American aviators of the Flying Tigers, the volunteer group of American aviators who flew combat missions for China against the Japanese. Retired US Army Air Corps Captain Claire Chennault had been hired in 1937 by Nationalist Chinese leader Chiang Kai-shek to establish an air force to fight the invading Japanese as well as the Chinese Communist forces waging civil war. In spring 1941 Chennault returned to the United States to build a Chinese air force with recruited pilots, mechanics, and logistical support from the U.S. military. President Franklin D. Roosevelt issued an unpublished executive order in April 1941 authorizing reserve officers and enlisted men to resign from the military if they agreed to join Chennault's American Volunteer Group (AVG). Margaret Chung lobbied actively for American support for China. The Flying Tigers defended Chinese cities against aerial attacks.

After the Japanese attack on Pearl Harbor in Honolulu, Hawaii, on December 7, 1941, Chung helped to organize and ship emergency supplies to the naval base. She was recognized for her efforts by President Harry S. Truman. Throughout World War II, Chung provided encouragement and support to her "sons" stationed overseas through personal letters and gifts. She also made a number of radio broadcasts and speeches promoting the war effort. Chung was also instrumental in lobbying for the creation of the Naval Women's Reserve (known at the time as WAVES) in 1942. The comic book series *Real Heroes,* which presented biographies of wartime role models for young people, included an autobiographical story ("Mom Chung and Her 509 Fair-Haired Sons starring Dr. Margaret Chung," published in issue #9, February-March, 1943. In 1945 Chung was presented the People's Medal by the Chinese government for her tireless efforts to support China throughout the war.

Chung was not permitted to join the WAVES, owing to her age and her race. Another possible obstacle was her suspected sexual orientation; she had close romantic friendships (described by her biographer, Judy Tzu-Chun Wu, as "homoerotic") with Enid Gidlow, an openly lesbian poet, and with singer and comedian Sophie Tucker (whom Chung met after the end of Tucker's third marriage). Chung and Tucker remained close until the end of Chung's life. Chung, however, never embraced an openly lesbian identity.

Chung died in San Francisco on January 5, 1959, after a long battle with ovarian cancer. Among her papers, gathered in the Margaret Chung Collection in the Ethnic Studies Library at the University of California, is an unpublished autobiography.

Significance

Though Margaret Chung is best remembered for her efforts to support the Allied forces during World War II, she pioneered across both racial- and gender lines and challenged widespread prejudicial attitudes regarding the abilities both of women and of Asian Americans. Through her personal, professional, and political efforts, Chung not only bridged the gap between disparate communities but also worked tirelessly for the greater good. She is remembered for her patriotism and for her tireless efforts to support her community and her country.

Mary Woodbury

Wilson Greatbatch

American biomedical engineer, inventor, businessman

Wilson Greatbatch was a biomedical engineer who in 1958 developed the first reliable pacemaker small enough to be implanted into a human chest. The company he founded in 1970 to bring his invention to market, now named Greatbatch Inc., is a leading supplier of pacemakers and other medical devices.

Areas of Achievement: Biomedical engineering, business

Born: September 6, 1919; Buffalo, New York, United States

Died: September 27, 2011; Williamsville, New York, United States

Early Life

Named in honor of President Woodrow Wilson, Wilson Greatbatch was born in Buffalo, New York, on September 6, 1919. His father, Warren Greatbatch, was a construction contractor who had immigrated from England; his mother, Charlotte Recktenwalt Greatbatch, was a secretary. The family moved from Buffalo's West Side to West Seneca, a Buffalo suburb, when Wilson Greatbatch was three years old. He attended Winchester Elementary public grade school and graduated from West Seneca High School in 1937. Greatbatch worked as a radioman for the U.S. Navy, either in the reserves or on active duty, from 1938 until the end of World War II. He had qualified for his amateur radio license at age 16, and his license entitled him to a Navy ranking of noncommissioned officer and third-class radioman. While in the reserves, he studied to become an industrial arts teacher. In 1940, once the United States was drawn into World War II, he went on active duty. He repaired electronics on a destroyer tender, the USS Melville; served as radioman on convoys to Iceland; and crewed aboard an aircraft carrier, the USS Monterrey, in the Pacific, flying combat missions as a radioman and gunner on dive bombers and torpedo bombers. He studied radar, set up a radio school at Annapolis (although unconnected with the Naval Institute), and flew on the first radar patrols along the Texas coastline against German subs. In six months of combat, a third of Greatbatch's squadron crew perished, and the violence of the war led him to embrace religion. He was discharged from the Navy in 1946.

On January 1, 1945, Greatbatch had married his childhood sweetheart, Eleanor Wright, a home economics teacher. After the war he worked briefly as a telephone repairman before entering Cornell University on the GI bill. To supplement his income—by the time he graduated, he and Eleanor were the parents of three children—he ran the university's radio transmitter, built the electronics for the university's radio telescope, and worked at the Cornell Psychology Department's animal-behavior farm, attaching instruments to monitor blood pressure, heart rate, and brain waves to about a hundred sheep and goats. While working at the farm, in about 1951, Greatbatch became acquainted with two visiting surgeons and first learned of heart block, a disease that occurs when electrical impulses from the heart's upper chambers (atria) fail to reach the heart's lower chambers, or ventricles, causing irregular heartbeats that can result in shortness of breath, loss of consciousness, and even death. He immediately concluded that electrical technology ought be able to help heart-block patients, but he did not think that the available electronic tools were adequate.

Greatbatch graduated from Cornell University with a B.E.E. in electrical engineering in 1950 and was an associate engineer with the Cornell Aeronautical Laboratory in Buffalo in 1952–1953. In the latter year he became an assistant professor of electrical engineering at the University of Buffalo and worked with the university's Chronic Disease Research Institution, investigating the analysis of high-frequency heart sound components. After receiving his master's degree in electrical engineering at SUNY Buffalo in 1957, he became a division manager at Taber Instrument Corporation in nearby North Tonawonda, N.Y., working on amplifiers and technology later used with primates on the early U.S. space missions.

Life's Work

The discovery that led Greatbatch to develop the pacemaker was the result of a fortunate accident. In 1956, while still an assistant professor, he was working at the Chronic Disease Research Institute with a doctor who was recording the sound of a heartbeat. Greatbatch was using silicon transistors to make an oscillator to record the sound. He later explained that the oscillator required a 10,000-ohm resistor at the transistor base, but he misread the color coding on a resistor in his parts box and pulled out a 1-megaohm resistor instead. When he installed it, the circuit it produced emitted intermittent electrical pulses instead of oscillating ones, in a distinctive pattern that he recognized at once as replicating the rhythm of the human heart. Recalling his conversations with the visiting researchers at the Cornell animal behavior laboratory about the electrical activity of the heart, he decided that it might be possible to build an implantable pacemaker device, and he set about developing one.

The discovery took years to perfect. Greatbatch approached Taber about supporting his work, but finding that insurance for the venture could not be obtained, the company declined because of the substantial risks involved. Greatbatch decided to quit his job to work on the pacemaker at his home workshop in Clarence, New York, supporting his family with $2,000 in savings and a large home vegetable garden. In two years, with his wife assisting by administering shock tests to the device to test its reliability, he had managed to miniaturize a pacemaker down to two cubic inches. Greatbatch presented his prototype device to Dr. William Chardack, chief of surgery at Buffalo's Veterans Administration Hospital. The two became collaborators, along with Dr. Andrew Gage, whom Greatbatch had known since grammar school in West Seneca. (Greatbatch, Chardack, and Gage would become known as the "bow-tie team.") Three weeks later, on May 7, 1958, Chardack and Gage demonstrated that Greatbatch's device could take control of a dog's heartbeat. That first implant lasted only four hours, chiefly because body fluids penetrated the pacemaker. Switching tactics, they began to cast the unit in a solid block of epoxy. Within a year, they had devices that could last four months. Dr. Chardack was active in engineering the electrodes, which he patented.

Meanwhile Greatbatch quickly discovered that other researchers in the United States and Sweden were getting close to perfecting a practical implantable pacemaker for humans. In 1957 Earl Bakken, the founder of Medtronic Inc., had built a battery-powered external pacemaker that could be worn on a belt; this, however, had wires going right through the skin, posing a serious risk of infection. In October 1958 Dr. Rune Elmqvist of Sweden implanted a pacemaker in a 43-year-old patient. It failed after three hours. A second device lasted six weeks. Three years elapsed before a reliable unit was developed. (The patient, however, went on to have nearly 30 pacemakers implanted over the course of his life; he died in 2001 at age 86.) Elmqvist's initial stainless steel pacemaker leads to the heart proved inadequate, and he used nickel cadmium batteries that needed to be recharged each week. He, too, used an epoxy resin casing and silicon transistors.

Over the first two years, 1958 through 1960, Greatbatch, Chardack, and Gage conducted experiments with animals. Greatbatch built 50 handmade pacemakers, 40 of which were implanted in animals. By 1960 the team thought the pacemaker was ready for a human patient. Beginning on April 15, 1960, Greatbatch's device was implanted in 10 human patients, including two children, all of whom had at the time less than a 50 percent chance of surviving for a year. The first patient, a 77-year-old-man, lived 18 months; another member of the initial group lived for 30 years. Greatbatch credited Dr. Chardack with securing swift and widespread clinical acceptance of the device, notably through a paper published in *Surgery* in 1960. In 1961, without the resources to launch a major medical device company and unwilling to become enmeshed in running a business, Greatbatch licensed his device to Bakken's Medtronic. Greatbatch patented the implantable pacemaker in 1962. When Medtronic could not pay its licensing fee the first year, Greatbatch accepted Medtronic stock and a seat on the board of directors in lieu of payment, and consequently he retained quality control of all the implantable units made by Medtronic until 1970.

Greatbatch remained dissatisfied with the zinc-mercury batteries used in his pacemaker, which needed to be changed surgically every two years. He told Earl Bakken that to get a better pacemaker, Medtronic was going to have to make its own batteries. Bakken was unwilling to take on this task, and in 1970 Greatbatch—already chafing over design changes proposed by Medtronics's engineers—amicably canceled his contract with Medtronic and sold all his patents to the company. He promptly founded Wilson Greatbatch Ltd. to manufacture, market, and license the lithium iodide battery. The lithium iodide battery had been invented in 1968 by researchers in Baltimore but had considerable technical shortcomings; by 1972 Greatbatch had re-engineered it so that it could power an implanted pacemaker for a decade or more. Wilson Greatbatch Ltd. became an internationally successful power-component supplier for the medical equipment industry and eventually expanded into related businesses, including power for artificial hearts and implantable defibrillators. Greatbatch never relinquished his interest in improving his pacemaker. In 2001 he replaced the pacemaker's metal wires (which had prevented patients with pacemakers from undergoing MRIs) with glass fiber. His lithium iodide batteries were used by NASA to power equipment for space-shuttle missions.

Greatbatch's interests were not confined to the implantable pacemaker. In 1963, with Herbert Mennen, he formed Mennen-Greatbatch Electronics Inc. to manufacture medical monitoring equipment such as that he had first developed for the early primate space shots. Greatbatch remained with Mennen-Greatbatch until 1970. (Now Mennen Medical, the company develops and markets cardiac catheterization and electrophysiology systems as well as patient monitoring and clinical data information systems.) In 1985 Greatbatch launched Greatbatch Gen-Aid Ltd. to provide genetic assistance to the medical and agricultural professions. In his later years, Greatbatch became interested in the AIDS human immunodeficiency virus, and with John C. Sanford of Cornell University, he succeeded in inhibiting viral replication in cats similar to the replication of the AIDS virus in humans. In 1999 Greatbatch created Greatbatch Enterprises Inc. to pursue work on alternative fuels—biofuels and nuclear power generation through nuclear fusion of helium-3 ions.

Greatbatch was awarded the National Medal of Technology in 1990, and in 1992 he was profiled in six-part documentary series, *The Entrepreneurs: An American Adventure.* In 1996 he received the Lemelson-M.I.T. Lifetime Achievement award, administered by the Massachusetts Institute of Technology. The National Academy of Engineering chose Greatbatch and Earl Bakken as the first recipients, in February 2001, of its Fritz J. and Dolores H. Russ Prize, an engineering award created as a complement to the Nobel Prizes (there is no Nobel Prize for engineering). Greatbatch was awarded honorary Sc.D. degrees, from the State University of New York at Buffalo, Clarkson University, and Roberts Wesleyan College. In addition to

English, Greatbatch spoke French and German, which was an important asset in his international marketing and sales activities. Greatbatch's memoir, *The Making of the Pacemaker,* was published in 2000. He also published more than a hundred papers on pacemakers and power-source topics.

Eleanor and Wilson Greatbatch had five children. Greatbatch became wealthy through his work but put most of his money back into research or donated it to charities and educational institutions. He regularly spoke to schoolchildren about science and invention. The East Hill Foundation was established in 1986 to administer the Greatbatch family's philanthropic activities. Wilson Greatbatch suffered a heart attack in November 2001, which curtailed some of his public activities but not his scientific endeavors. Eleanor Greatbatch died in January 2011. Greatbatch died at his home in Williamsville, New York, on September 27, 2011.

Significance

Wilson Greatbatch's inventions are credited with largely shaping modern cardiology. In an interview with Frederik Nebeker for the Institute of Electrical and Electronics Engineers's Global History Network (IEEEGHN), Greatbatch observed that if he had not come up with the implantable pacemaker, someone else would have. Greatbatch, however, brought to the task perseverance, an insatiable curiosity, and a strong commitment to refining and improving his invention. According to an obituary in the *New York Times,* he held more than 325 patents (the majority of them international patents) on a variety of inventions, among them a long-life lithium battery used in a wide range of medical implants and tools used in AIDS research.

Greatbatch proved to be a canny businessman as well as a biomedical engineer with a knack for perceiving practical applications for his work. His decision to delegate manufacture of his device to Medtronic is considered to have launched the modern medical device industry, as Seymour Furman wrote in the foreword to Greatbatch's memoir. Wilson Greatbatch Technologies Inc. became a publicly traded company in 2000, just three years after it was founded. It reorganized as Greatbatch Inc. in 2005 and, according to its Web site, currently develops and manufactures critical medical device technologies for the cardiac, neuromodulation, vascular and orthopaedic markets as well as batteries for applications in the portable medical, energy, military, and other markets. By late 2013 the company held more than a thousand patents.

The Editors

Philip Jaisohn

Korean-born activist, journalist, and physician

Philip Jaisohn, the first Korean to become a naturalized U.S. citizen, played an important role in the Korean independence movement. Traveling between the United States and Japanese-occupied Korea, Jaisohn founded and led independence organizations and promoted political unity of the Korean people.

Areas of Achievement: Political activism, journalism, medicine

Born: January 7, 1864; Bosung, Korea (now South Korea)

Died: January 5, 1951; Norristown, Pennsylvania, United States

Early Life

Philip Jaisohn (JAY-suhn), also known by his birth name—Sŏ Chaep'il (anglicized as Jae-pil Seo or Jae-pil Suh)—was born in January 1864 in Bosung, Jeollanam-do, Korea, which later became part of South Korea. As a member of the elite *yangban* class, he received education in Korean and Chinese classics. When he was seven, Sŏ Chaep'il moved to Seoul to study with his uncle, who was himself without a son and therefore adopted Sŏ Chaep'il in order to continue the uncle's family line. In 1882 Sŏ became the youngest person ever to pass the civil-service examination and was appointed minister of defense. Sŏ associated with reformists, and, following the advice of reform leader Kim Okkyun, he went to Japan for higher education. Among the first Korean students to be sent abroad to study, he attended the Youth Military Academy in Tokyo in 1883–1884. Becoming fluent in Japanese, he returned to Korea after completing his eight-month training. His criticisms in reports to the king of Korea's outmoded military earned him the enmity of the conservative political faction then dominant at the palace.

In 1884 Sŏ became involved in the Kapsin Coup (Gapsin or Gap-Shin; in Korean, *kapsin chŏngbyŏn,* the "political disturbance of the year kapsin [1884]"). The coup leaders hoped to abolish the privileges of the *yangban* class and open Korea's borders to international relations and trade in order to modernize the country and help it rise to the challenges posed by encroaching Western powers. On December 4, 1884, with Kim, Pak Yŏnghyo, Hong Yŏngsik, and Sŏ Kwangbŏm—and supported by Japanese officials in Seoul—Sŏ Chaep'il participated in a bloody coup, seizing a royal palace. The revolutionary attempt lasted only three days; it was put down by soldiers from the Chinese garrison in Seoul after a clandestine appeal by Queen Min. Sŏ Chaep'il was forced into exile in Japan and later in the United States. His wife and infant son had died in the aftermath of the coup. Once in the United States, he anglicized his name, to Philip Jaisohn. He attended Harry Hillman Academy in Wilkes-Barre, Pennsylvania, and studied medicine at George Washington University, then known as Columbian University, in Washington, D.C. He supported himself by working as a cataloguer and translator at the Smithsonian Society. In 1890 Jaisohn became the first Korean to naturalize and become an American citizen. Jaisohn graduated from Columbian University in 1892, the first Korean to complete a medical degree at a Western university. In 1895 he patented a thermometer case. Jaisohn married Muriel Armstrong, whose father was the U.S. postmaster general and a relative of President James Buchanan, in 1893; the couple was to have two daughters.

Life's Work

With political instability and turmoil increasing in Korea, Jaisohn returned to his homeland in December 1895 to support the country's development. In April 1896, with the financial support of the Korean government, Jaisohn began the publication of the *Independent* (*Tongnip sinmun,* or *Doknip shinmun*), which was Korea's first modern newspaper and the first to use the Korean alphabet rather than Chinese characters. In the same year, he became one of the founding members of the Independence Club, along with Syngman Rhee and Sang-je Li. The club promoted Western ideas, science, and education for Koreans, and it is considered Korea's first modern political party. He also lectured on democracy and politics, and in 1897 he designed and built the Independence Gate (Tongnimmun, now romanized Dongnimmun), in Seoul, replacing a gate commemorating Korean-Chinese diplomatic relations.

Jaisohn again went into exile in the United States in 1898 when conservatives and foreign influences accused him of plotting to overthrow the Korean government. Back in the United States, he worked at the Wistar Institute of the University of Pennsylvania. Jaisohn continued working on his newspaper, the *Independent*, and established himself as a printer and stationer. He became co-owner of Deemer and Jaisohn Co., a Wilkes-Barre, Pennsylvania, stationers' business, and later of Philip Jaisohn Co., a printing shop in Philadelphia. Japan had annexed Korea in 1910; when he learned of the Korean independence movement of March 1919, Jaisohn brought the cause to the attention of the world through a joint publication endeavor with Philadelphia's *Evening Ledger.* He supported the independence movement financially; founded the Korean Information Bureau; published the *Korean Review,* a monthly journal; and in April 1919, in Philadelphia, led the First Korean Congress.

Jaisohn was one of the leading figures in organizing the League of Friends of Korea, which brought together intellectuals and politicians with pro-Korean attitudes throughout the United States and Europe. Although Jaisohn had not been able to return to Korea for several decades, he maintained close ties to reformists and independence activists in Korea and China and continued to advocate for Korean independence from Japan. In 1925 he participated in a pan-Pacific conference in Honolulu, Hawaii, as a Korean delegate, and he vehemently criticized the Japanese occupation of Korea. His activities eventually forced him into bankruptcy, in 1925, but he took courses at the University of Pennsylvania to qualify to resume medical practice, and he worked successfully as a physician and microbiologist through the 1920s and 1930s.

When World War II broke out, Jaisohn served the U.S. Army as a physical examination officer and received recognition from the U.S. government for his contributions. After World War II, at which point Korea was divided into North Korea and South Korea, Jaisohn traveled to South Korea at the invitation of John R. Hodge, a U.S. Army general, to serve chief advisor to the U.S. military government. Jaisohn, however, had become estranged from Syngman Rhee, the president of the newly independent Republic of Korea (South Korea), regarding Rhee as having become autocratic. Jaisohn returned to Pennsylvania, where he died in January 1951 at age 87. He was buried in the West Laurel Hill cemetery in Philadelphia. In April 1994 his ashes were returned to South Korea and re-buried in the national cemetery in Seoul.

In addition to his role as an activist and journalist, Jaisohn (as befitted his *yangban* education) maintained his interest in literature. He copyrighted one of the first works of Korean American fiction, *Hansu's Journey: A Korean Story*, which was published in Philadelphia's *Korean Review* in 1922. *My Days in Korea,* a collection of his writings in English, was published by Yonsei University Press in 1999.

Significance

Jaisohn devoted his life to Korean independence and the unification of the Korean peninsula. Based chiefly in the United States, he struggled to achieve his goals by publishing newspapers, participating in international political activities, and raising funds for independence activists. His contributions to the Korean independence movement have been acknowledged through the establishment of memorials and monuments both in the United States and in South Korea. The Philip Jaisohn Memorial Foundation was established in Philadelphia in 1975. In 2008 a statue of Jaisohn was unveiled in Washington, D.C., and in the same year, the Seo Jae-Pil Memorial Park opened in his hometown in South Korea. Another portrait statue commemorating Jaisohn stands close to the Independence Gate in Seoul.

Ji-Hye Shin

Wilhelm Conrad Röntgen

German physicist

Wilhelm Conrad Röntgen made important contributions to several areas of physics but is best known for his revolutionary discovery of X-rays and his investigations of their properties.

Areas of Achievement: Atomic and molecular physics, science, technology

Born: March 27, 1845; Lennep, Prussia (now Remscheid, Germany)

Died: February 10, 1923; Munich, Germany

Early Life

Wilhelm Conrad Röntgen was the only child of Friedrich Conrad Röntgen, a German textile manufacturer and merchant, and Charlotte Constanza Frowein, who came from a Dutch merchant family. When he was three, his family moved to Apeldoorn, his mother's hometown in Holland. There he attended primary public school and later became a student at Kostschool, a private boarding school. In 1862 Röntgen went to Utrecht, where he entered a secondary technical school. He was later expelled for refusing to inform on a fellow student who had drawn an unflattering caricature of a teacher. Although he attended some classes at the University of Utrecht, Röntgen was unable to become a formal student because he lacked a secondary-school diploma. He resolved his academic problems by passing the difficult entrance examination of the recently established Federal Institute of Technology (or Polytechnic) in Zürich, Switzerland.

In November 1865 Röntgen began his education as a mechanical engineer. Over the next three years, he studied various technical courses but found his greatest fulfillment in a physics course taught by Rudolf Clausius, a distinguished scientist who helped found modern thermodynamics. Röntgen eventually passed his final examinations with excellent grades and received his diploma on August 6, 1869.

Röntgen remained in Zürich after graduation to work in the laboratory of August Kundt, a Polytechnic physics professor who had befriended him. Röntgen studied different gases to see if they all expanded uniformly with increases in temperature, as predicted by Gay-Lussac's law, and discovered that some had expanded to greater volumes than the law predicted. Less than a year later, he submitted his dissertation, "Studies on Gases," to the University of Zürich, which granted him a doctorate on June 22, 1869. While working in Zürich, Röntgen met his future wife, Anna Bertha Ludwig. In 1871, when Kundt accepted a position at the University of Würzburg, Röntgen accompanied him as his assistant, and the following year he married Bertha.

Life's Work

Röntgen's lack of a secondary-school diploma again hindered his academic advancement at Würzburg, so he and his wife subsequently moved, with Kundt, to the Kaiser Wilhelm University in Strasbourg. Based on the success of his scientific investigations with Kundt, he received an offer of a full professorship from the Agricultural Academy in Hohenheim, Württemberg, in 1875. He was unhappy, however, with that institution's experimental facilities, and he returned to Strasbourg a year and a half later as an assistant professor in theoretical physics.

Röntgen wrote a series of papers on the properties of gases that exhibited his growing skills as an experimental physicist, and in 1879, he was offered the chair of physics at the University of Giessen. During the ensuing nine years, he did important work on crystals, their generation of electricity when subjected to heat (pyroelectricity), and their generation of electricity when subjected to mechanical stress (piezoelectricity). His greatest discovery, however, was his confirmation of a prediction made by Scottish physicist James Clerk Maxwell that a magnetic field would be generated within dielectrics such as glass plates when they were moved back and forth between two electrically charged plates. Dutch physicist Hendrik Antoon Lorentz named this effect, which Röntgen detected with a sensitive device, the "roentgen current." Röntgen later considered this discovery as an important step in his work on X-rays.

Recognition of Röntgen's accomplishments in physics brought him offers from other universities. In 1888 he turned down the chair of physics at the University of Utrecht but accepted the University of Würzburg's proposal that he occupy Kundt's former position. During his first six years at Würzburg, he published 17 papers on such topics as the properties of solids and liquids. His fame as a physicist and respect for his political sagacity led to his election in 1894 to the rectorship of the university. One year later, however, he left his position as rector and took up a new field of scientific research.

German physicists Heinrich Hertz and Philipp Lenard had discovered that a cathode-ray tube could have an external electrical effect within a few centimeters of the tube's outer wall. (A cathode-ray tube—also known as a Crookes tube, after its inventor, English physicist William Crookes—is a glass tube with two electrodes lodged within—a cathode, which receives a negative charge of electricity, and an anode, which receives the positive charge. In Röntgen's time, the cathode was not heated, as in later practice.) By passing a large current at high voltage through the tube, they could produce many observable interesting electrical effects. In other words, they could produce rays that caused the air to become ionized. These effects differed depending on whether the tube was evacuated or filled with different gases.

Röntgen had become interested in exploring these rays, and he designed an experiment to verify and extend Hertz's and Lenard's observations. On November 8, 1895, to further analyze the external effects of the electrical discharge, he completely darkened his room with window curtains and began work with a very heavy, empty cathode-ray tube that he had covered with thick cardboard to make it completely light-tight and further protected with an external layer of tin foil. He applied a very high voltage generated by an induction coil to the tube. No light leaked through, and Röntgen was about to proceed with his planned experiment when, by chance, he noticed a glimmer of light coming from the barium platinocyanide screen with which the experiment was to have been performed. This fluorescent screen was on his workbench, about a meter from the glass tube. He performed the experiment repeatedly, each time moving the screen farther and farther from the tube. Even at a distance of two meters, the screen glowed.

This puzzled him, because cathode rays had an effective range of only a few centimeters. He therefore suspected that he might have come upon a previously unknown kind of radiation, which he termed "X-rays." Röntgen realized that some sort of ray was being emitted from the tube, and he began to investigate its nature. He set the screen up at different angles to the tube and directed the invisible beam through paper, wood, and sheets of aluminum, copper, silver, gold, and platinum of varying thicknesses. He found that the rays penetrated all the materials he used with the exception of a sheet of lead. Intrigued by the blocking power of the lead, he tried again, holding a small disk of lead between his finger and thumb. When the apparatus was energized, he was astonished to find the outline of his fingers and even more startled to observe that he could see the outline of his finger bones. Over the following weeks, he experimented to ensure that his observations were not in error. Through these experiments, he discovered that X-rays travel in straight lines, are unaffected by magnets or electrically charged plates, and can ionize gases. Unlike light rays, X-rays can neither be reflected from a mirror nor refracted in a prism. Like light rays, they can blacken photographic plates, which Röntgen used to record the first X-ray images, including one famously revealing the bones of his wife's hand.

Röntgen communicated his discovery to the scientific community by letter and by the publication, on December 28, 1895, of his famous paper "On a New Kind of Ray: A Preliminary Communication." Both scientists and the public were fascinated by the mysterious rays that could even reveal the skeletons inside living humans. Physicians in Europe and America quickly put them to medical use in diagnosing broken bones and foreign objects in human bodies. Röntgen knew that his rays had commercial potential, but out of altruism, he refused to patent his discovery.

Kaiser Wilhelm II of Germany was the first dignitary to honor Röntgen with an award, on January 14, 1896. The kaiser's award was following by many others, culminating in Röntgen's reception of the first Nobel Prize in Physics, in 1901. By that time, he had accepted a distinguished position as professor of experimental physics and head of the physical institute at the University of Munich, where he would remain for the next 20 years. During that period, he witnessed the use of X-rays by physicians to treat skin diseases and cancer and by physicists to study atomic arrangements in crystals. His own work centered on crystals, their electrical conductivity, and the influence of radiation on them. Röntgen also faced claims that other scientists had observed the effects of X-rays before him. Yet although Lenard may have observed fluorescence near a Crookes tube, he never investigated this observation in the way Röntgen later did.

Although Röntgen received many honors on the occasion of his seventieth birthday in 1915, the privations brought on by World War I had a negative influence on his scientific work. His wife died in 1919 after a long illness. Furthermore, he, like most Germans, was affected by postwar political turmoil, ruinous inflation, and food shortages. His own health began to fail, and other physicists took over his work. Röntgen died in Munich on February 10, 1923, from intestinal cancer.

Significance

The medical applications of X-rays were quickly recognized, but the impact of X-rays on physics and chemistry proved to be even more momentous. For example, Henry Becquerel's investigation of X-rays led directly to his discovery of radioactivity. In 1912 Max von Laue suggested that X-rays may be diffracted by crystals, and scientists soon discovered that diffracted rays allowed them to determine the three-dimensional structures of many crystals. English physicist Henry Moseley discovered characteristic X-rays emitted by each of the chemical elements, leading to a deeper understanding of the periodic table. So significant were these and other discoveries that some scholars called Röntgen's discovery of X-rays the event that initiated a second scientific revolution, because it ushered in the modern physics of the twentieth century, just as the discoveries of Galileo Galilei, Johannes Kepler, and Isaac Newton had forged the new science of the seventeenth century.

With the passage of time, the practical uses of X-rays multiplied. So many medical applications were developed that an entirely new medical specialty, radiology, was created, and new technologies such as computerized axial tomography (CAT) rely on high-resolution X-ray pictures to study the human brain. In industry, engineers use X-rays to study stresses in various materials and the strengths of welds, while computer technicians use them to etch integrated circuits. Scholarship has benefitted as well; archaeologists use

X-rays to study mummies and other ancient artifacts without harming the objects, and astronomers study the X-rays emanating from different parts of the universe to better understand stars, pulsars, and black holes. Significant applications that continue to be discovered more than a century after Röntgen first found and characterized these powerful rays.

Robert J. Paradowski

Yellapragada SubbaRow

Indian-born physician and scientist

Yellapragada SubbaRow was a biochemist regarded as eminent in the field because of his numerous laboratory discoveries. He is best known for describing the function of adenosine triphosphate in muscle contractions and for having synthesized numerous novel chemotherapeutic agents, vitamins, and antibiotics.

Areas of Achievement: Medicine, science, technology

Born: January 12, 1895; Bhimavaram, Madras Presidency, British India

Died: August 9, 1948; Pearl River, New York, United States

Early Life

Yellapragada SubbaRow (SOO-bah-ROW; also anglicized as Subbarow, Subbarao, or SubbaRao) was born on January 12, 1895, in Bhimavaram in the Madras Presidency (or province) of British India. (The area where the city is located is now called the Coastal Andhra region of Andhra Pradesh state, India.) He was the fourth of seven children of Jagganadham SubbaRow, a revenue inspector, and his wife, Venkamma SubbaRow. Yellapragada SubbaRow initially lacked an interest in schooling. In 1908 he ran away to Benares (Varanasi) to seek his fortune but was soon retrieved. Later, however, he credited his mother with instilling in him an understanding of the value of an education and a career.

Jagganadham SubbaRow died in 1913 from tropical sprue, a chronic intestinal disease, leaving the family in poverty. Later Yellapragada's two brothers also died of the disease, in July and August 1921. The loss of his family members would motivate SubbaRow to pursue a career in medical research.

After switching secondary schools several times, SubbaRow enrolled at Hindu High School in Triplicane, Madras (now Chennai). He graduated after taking the final examination three times. SubbaRow subsequently attended the Madras Presidency College, where he originally pursued a major in religion, with the intention of entering a Hindu monastic order. His mother and his spiritual teachers eventually convinced him to concentrate on mathematics, physics, and chemistry in order to study medicine, and he entered Madras Medical College in 1915. At college SubbaRow supported the movement for Indian independence from the British Empire. Because his professors were British, they denied SubbaRow a full medical degree (M.B.B.S.), awarding him a certificate (L.M.S.) instead. Therefore he could not gain entry into the Madras State Medical Service.

It was SubbaRow's hope to immigrate to the United States for further studies in tropical medicine at Harvard University. He was denied admission on his first attempt, in 1921, and became an anatomy and physiology lecturer at Madras Ayurvedic College. Here he hoped to perform scientific research that would standardize the practice of using Indian herbs in medical care, but the college environment did not permit such research. SubbaRow then applied to join the Madras Medical Service, but he was again rejected.

On his second attempt, in 1923, SubbaRow gained admission to Harvard Medical School, but he did not receive any financial aid. Nevertheless both his father-in-law and the head of the Department of Tropical Medicine, Dr.

Richard Strong, contributed money toward SubbaRow's education. He left for Cambridge, Massachusetts, by way of London, arriving in Massachusetts in October 1923. To earn money to pay his tuition and support himself, he took a job as an evening janitor at the Peter Bent Brigham Hospital in Boston. He earned a diploma in tropical medicine in 1924 and entered the Harvard medical School Ph.D. program in biochemistry. His work on determination of inorganic and organic phosphorus was published in the *Journal of Biological Chemistry* in 1925, under the name of his Harvard mentor, Dr. Cyrus Fiske, as primary author.

Life's Work

SubbaRow made significant discoveries from the outset of his Harvard career. In 1927 he and Fiske developed a new test, called the Fiske-SubbaRow method, to detect phosphorus levels in blood and urine. As a result they were able to determine that the molecules phosphocreatine and adenosine triphosphate (ATP) provided the energy responsible for a muscle contraction. Initially this discovery was not well received in the scientific community; a Nobel Prize had been awarded in 1922 to scientists (Archibald Hill and Otto Meyerhof) who identified a different reason for muscle contractions. SubbaRow and Fiske were eventually proved correct, and their discovery earned SubbaRow a Ph.D. in biochemistry from Harvard in 1930. The Fiske-SubbaRow method continues to be used by scientists today. SubbaRow, however, was unable to capitalize on his groundbreaking work at Harvard. He was deemed to be little more than Fiske's laboratory technician, a misapprehension actually encouraged by SubbaRow, apparently to advance Fiske's career. SubbaRow became a teaching fellow and subsequently, in the late 1930s, an instructor and then an associate, but he never attained a position as a full faculty member. Subsequently he left Harvard.

In 1940 SubbaRow accepted a position at a pharmaceutical company, Lederle Laboratories, in Pearl River, New York. His work had caught the attention of William Bell, the president of American Cyanamid, Lederle's parent company, and SubbaRow had been working for Lederle on weekends. At Lederle he was finally acknowledged as a leader in his field and was appointed director of research and development. When SubbaRow relocated to Lederle Laboratories, he was contacted by Dr. Sidney Farber, whose research focused on the treatment of childhood leukemia. Farber was researching folic acid's connection to cancer, and the two men consequently became collaborators. At first, both thought that the treatment for leukemia lay in modifying the vitamin, but they eventually realized that the actual answer was an analogue, or a vitamin with the opposite properties of folic acid. While SubbaRow synthesized new potential drugs, Farber tested these on healthy and affected rats in the laboratory. They eventually discovered that aminopterin destroyed leukemia cells, as well as some healthy cells. The duo tested a derivative of aminopterin, called methotrexate, in children with acute lymphoblastic leukemia (ALL). The initial 1946 treatment was so successful that it began the modern era of chemotherapy with drugs that targeted specific cancers.

SubbaRow and his team continued to make new discoveries, including the isolation and synthesis of the vitamins folic acid and B12. (Folic acid was later shown to cure sprue.) SubbaRow and his team also created the antibiotics gramicidin, aureomycin, hetrazan, and aminopterin. Aureomycin became the first oral tetracycline antibiotic to combat a broad spectrum of infections. Hetrazan cured filariasis, an infectious parasitic tropical disease that causes elephantitis and can be fatal. It was used during World War II to treat soldiers who contracted malaria and filariasis while fighting in the Pacific region and is still recommended by the World Health Organization for the treatment of filariasis. SubbaRow's work extended to early cancer treatment as well. When he and his colleagues created aminopterin, they noted that the medication stopped cancer cell growth. SubbaRow also helped develop other chemotherapeutic agents to treat leukemia.

Awards and honors for SubbaRow include the Bharat Ratna, India's highest civilian honor. The one-hundredth anniversary of his birth was widely celebrated in India in 1995, and a series of memorial lectures exists in his name.

SubbaRow was married in May 1919 to Seshagiri Murthy, a child bride from a well-to-do family. After four years of marriage, SubbaRow left India for the United States, vowing to return to his wife in India three years later. A son was born to him and his wife in April 1924, after his departure for the United States, but the child died the following December of erysipelas, a strep infection. SubbaRow corresponded with his wife (in Telugu) and his father-in-law (in English) until the 1930s. In the late 1920s he had made an inconclusive effort to bring Seshagiri to the United States. Aware that he could not pursue his work in India, he never returned, and he did not see his wife again after choosing to devote his life to his career. He did, however, repay the debt he owed to his father-in-law, sometime in 1946–1947.

SubbaRow, a heavy smoker, died of a heart attack on August 9, 1948, at the age of 53. Although he had lived in the United States for 25 years, SubbaRow never became an American citizen. When the ban preventing most Asians from becoming U.S. citizens was lifted after World War II, SubbaRow did not file the necessary paperwork and therefore remained an Indian citizen.

Significance

Early in his career, SubbaRow met with resistance to almost all of his educational and career aspirations. He nevertheless persevered and eventually made numerous enduring contributions to the medical field. SubbaRow initially proposed using folic acid to treat anemia; this vitamin is now known to prevent significant birth defects in pregnancy, and since 1988 the U.S. government has mandated that food be fortified with it. Methotrexate, a derivative of aminopterin, is now used for treating ectopic pregnancies and childhood leukemia and other cancers. The antibiotics SubbaRow discovered continue to be some of the most-prescribed medications in the world.

SubbaRow's biographer, S. P. K. Gupta, obtained SubbaRow's personal papers from his wife's family. Together with SubbaRow's Harvard papers, papers from his years at Lederle, audio files, interview transcripts, and other materials, these are held by the Nehru Memorial Museum and Library in New Delhi.

Janet Ober Berman

Henry Wellcome

British pharmaceutical company executive

Wellcome used his entrepreneurial abilities to revolutionize the drug industry. He and his partner, Silas Burroughs, established one of the leading pharmaceutical companies of the nineteenth- and twentieth century.

Areas of Achievement: Pharmaceuticals, business

Born: August 21, 1853; Almond, Wisconsin, United States

Died: July 25, 1936; London, United Kingdom

Early Life

Henry Solomon Wellcome (WEHL-kuhm) was born in rural Wisconsin on August 21, 1853, the son of a Quaker mother, Mary Curtis, and Solomon Wellcome, a farmer. When Solomon Wellcome's potato crop failed in 1861, the family moved to Garden City, Minnesota, a trip of several weeks by covered wagon. Like most poor boys of that era, Wellcome left school in his early teens and went to work in his uncle's drugstore. His tasks included compounding medicines; he also formulated his own compounds, including a lemon juice-based mixture that he attempted to peddle as "invisible ink." This job engendered an interest in medicine that Wellcome retained all of his life. He also was ingrained with deep religious feelings and a strong work ethic. Several of Wellcome's family members were evangelicals who believed in temperance, a belief to which he strictly adhered.

The small town in which the Wellcomes lived was very much a frontier settlement, and clashes with local Native American tribes were not uncommon. In 1862 Garden City was attacked by the Sioux, and as a result, several of the tribe's chiefs were hanged. Although most of the citizens were rabidly anti-Indian, the young Wellcome apparently harbored sympathy for the Native Americans' plight. This feeling was to manifest itself later, when he devoted a portion of his fortune to Indian causes. When he was 17, Wellcome moved to Rochester, Minnesota, where William W. Mayo, a physician and family friend who would found the Mayo Clinic with his two sons, helped Wellcome obtain a position in a drugstore.

Mayo encouraged Wellcome to attend college in Chicago. When the college was destroyed in the great Chicago Fire of 1871, Wellcome relocated to Philadelphia, where he was apprenticed to a pharmacist and attended a college of pharmacy. He specialized in the marketing and production of drugs, and while there he met Silas Burroughs, who was to become important in his later business ventures. By age 21, Wellcome was working out of New York City as a traveling salesman for a major pharmaceutical company. Within two years he had obtained a position with the prestigious pharmaceutical firm of McKesson & Robbins.

As a rising star within the company, Wellcome was sent to South America to find herbs and medicinal plants that could be used to manufacture new drugs. In particular, his company desired a steady source of the tree bark used to make the antimalaria drug quinine. Wellcome's exposure to the Indian culture in South America apparently reawakened his empathy for native peoples. He began recording his experiences in a popular series of papers that were published in pharmaceutical journals. He was still in his twenties when he became reacquainted with Burroughs, who was then working for the Wyeth drug company. Their meeting ultimately led to the establishment of a hugely successful pharmaceutical firm, Burroughs Wellcome & Company.

Life's Work

By the time Burroughs Wellcome was founded, the American pharmaceutical industry had progressed beyond grinding drug components in a mortar and pestle to the manufacture of pills by machine. American drug companies envisioned great business opportunities in Europe and other areas of the world, where medicine was still primarily dispensed in powdered or liquid form. McKesson & Robbins awarded Wellcome the exclusive right to sell its products overseas—including in Africa, Asia, and Australia—and Wellcome and Burroughs set up a London office in 1880. A few years later, because of heavy tariffs, the two partners decided to stop importing medications from the United States and to manufacture their own drugs in England instead. They set up a factory, and by the time he reached age 30, Wellcome was already a rich man.

The partners purchased a larger factory in England and had new machinery designed that produced pills at a rate of six hundred per minute. Wellcome used the brand name Tabloid, a combination of tablet and alkaloid, and registered it as a trademark for the company's product line of compressed medicines, a strategy that proved wildly successful. Burroughs Wellcome fought and won several court cases that enabled the firm to retain the name Tabloid as its own proprietary trademark. Burroughs initiated successful marketing techniques that gained the company acceptance among physicians and medical institutions; before this time, relations between the medical profession and drug manufacturers had been adversarial. On the death of Burroughs in 1895, Wellcome assumed full control of the company and oversaw the opening of branches in Australia, New York City, Canada, China, and South Africa. In order to retain employees' loyalty, Burroughs Wellcome established an eight-hour workday and offered workers paid tuition for attending night classes. In the 1890s Wellcome bought an English estate where his workers could enjoy company-sponsored outings, and the company also provided facilities for employees to participate in various sporting events and hobbies. Whether his beneficence sprang from altruism or from profit motives, the company did gain a more contented workforce.

Wellcome did not marry until 1901, when he was 48 years of age. His wife was a prominent doctor's daughter, Gwendoline Barnardo, known as Syrie, who was 26 years his junior. They had one son, born in 1903, named Henry Mounteney Wellcome, who appeared to be a disappointment to both of them. When their son was still very young, he was temporarily raised by foster parents. The Wellcomes' marriage proved to be an unhappy one, and in 1910 they separated, eventually divorcing in 1916 after a sensational trial. Syrie had begun an affair with the author W. Somerset Maugham, whom Wellcome named as co-respondent in his divorce suit. Wellcome won custody of his son and apparently established an amicable relationship with him. After the divorce Syrie and Maugham married; they were divorced ten years later, after which Syrie launched a very successful career as an interior designer.

In 1910 Wellcome became a British subject, having lived in the country for some 30 years. In 1924 he combined all of his business interests into a holding company called the Wellcome Foundation. He was honored with a knighthood in the early 1930s, thus becoming Sir Henry Wellcome, and was also made an honorary fellow of the Royal College of Surgeons of England. The company he cofounded, Burroughs Wellcome & Company, was one of the firms that eventually merged to form the pharmaceutical giant GlaxoSmithKline.

As an adjunct to his business activities, Wellcome was a passionate collector of items related to medicine. In order to house his collection, he established the Wellcome Historical Medical Museum in London in 1913, with his artifacts forming the core of its collection. By the end of World War I, the collection was his primary interest; in size it far exceeded the holdings in this area of Europe's major museums. The Wellcome Foundation estimates that no more than a tenth of Wellcome's collection was exhibited during his lifetime. In 1932 the collection, along with two Wellcome laboratories and a medical library were moved into a new building on Euston Road. At the time of Wellcome's death, in London, on July 25, 1936, the Wellcome Collection contained more than one million items, but when the company's Holborn headquarters was destroyed in the Blitz, the company moved to the Euston Road site, ending plans to give over much of the building to a museum. Wellcome's ambitious plans for the collection were never realized, and gradually about half of its holdings were dispersed. A majority of the nonmedical items were removed from the collection over the years. In 1968 the collection and library were merged into the Wellcome Institute for the History of Medicine, and by 1972 it had been decided to make the institution's focus postgraduate medical research. Again the artifact collection was stranded, and in 1976 it was acquired by the national Science Museum in London. Some of the previously dispersed items remain on display in other museums. Wellcome also had a great interest in archaeology and participated in many digs in Africa; at one time he planned to expand his collection into a Museum of Man.

Significance

Henry Wellcome's business acumen helped to bring the pharmaceutical industry into the modern era, particularly outside the United States, with technological advances in the production of medicines. His large fortune was used to establish a prominent biomedical charity, the Wellcome Trust, that has significantly aided medical research in numerous fields. Established at Wellcome's death in 1936, the trust received the bulk of his assets. Its initial stated purpose was to promote and support research aimed at improving the health of human beings and animals. Eventually the trust grew to become one of the world's largest private biomedical charities.

In order to separate itself from the industry, in 1986 the trust began divesting itself of stock in the Wellcome pharmaceutical company, and this divestiture was completed in 1995 with the sale of all remaining stock to the Wellcome company's former competitor Glaxo when the two firms merged to become GlaxoWellcome. (The name Wellcome was later dropped in the formation of GlaxoSmithKline.) The Wellcome Trust is the largest nongovernmental source of funds for biomedical research in the United Kingdom. In 2012–13 its endowment was about £13.1 billion, and it spends about £600 million each year on its programs. Part of its mission is the funding of research programs in the medical humanities and biomedical fields, and it also supports activities that promote public engagement with science. Among its programs are those involved with technology transfer, the treatment of malaria, the sequencing of the human genome, the establishment of the United Kingdom Biobank, medical techniques for saving premature babies, cognitive therapy for bulimia, brain imaging and psychological disorders, and skin cancer research.

One of the Wellcome Trust's major initiatives, funded by a total grant of £150 million, is a 50:50 partnership with Merck & Co., a pharmaceutical firm, to create a nonprofit research center in India. The center seeks to facilitate the development of new vaccines for use in developing countries. This is the first time that a pharmaceutical company and a medical charity have formed such a partnership for this purpose. The trust is also engaged in a partnership with the U.S. National Institutes of Health; this partnership supports a four-year training program for Ph.D. candidates in international collaborative biomedical research at campuses in the United Kingdom, Ireland, and the United States (in Maryland).

The Wellcome Trust also supports research at universities and other academic facilities in both the United Kingdom and abroad. It financed the construction of the Wellcome wing of the Science Museum in London and the establishment of a national network of Science Learning Centres. The trust sponsors a publications program and funds the Wellcome Book Prize, an annual award of £30,000—one of the richest literary awards in the world—to a book about some aspect of health, illness. or medicine. In addition, the trust makes its published research available online without cost. The Wellcome Trust Case Control Consortium, comprising 50 research groups, was created in 2005 to help in the understanding of human genome sequencing and to identify genes associated with diseases and serious medical conditions, including glaucoma, multiple sclerosis, ulcerative colitis, and Parkinson's disease.

Roy Liebman

Bibliography

Agatston, Arthur

Belkin, Lisa. "The School Lunch Test." *New York Times Magazine*, August 20, 2006.

Daniels, Soriya. "Straight Talk from the South Beach Diet Doctor." *Cleveland Jewish News,* February 13, 2004.

Diaz, Johnny. "The Accidental Diet Guru." *Boston Globe*, September 22, 2003.

Goodnough, Abby. "New Doctor, New Diet, Still No Cookies." *New York Times,* October 7, 2003.

Hollar, Danielle, Michelle Lombardo, Gabriella Lopez-Mitnik, Theodore L. Hollar, Marie Almon, Arthur S. Agatston, and Sarah E. Messiah. "Effective Multi-level, Multi-sector, School-based Obesity Prevention Programming Improves Weight, Blood Pressure, and Academic Performance, Especially among Low-Income, Minority Children." *Journal of Health Care for the Poor and Underserved* 21, no. 2 (May 2010 Supplement): 93–108.

Leonhardt, David. "What's a Pound of Prevention Really Worth?" *New York Times,* January 24, 2007.

Tanasychuk, John. "Man behind the Diet." (Fort Lauderdale, Florida) *Sun-Sentinel,* April 11, 2004.

Witchel, Alex. "Doctor Wants 'South Beach' to Mean Hearts, Not Bikinis." *New York Times,* April 14, 2004.

Agramonte, Aristídes

"Aristídes Agramonte." Canadian Medical Association Journal 25, no. 4 (October 1931): 460.

"Biography of Aristídes Agramonte." Military Medicine 166, no. 9 Supplement (September 2001): 23.

Claude Moore Health Sciences Library, University of Virginia. Historical Exhibits [online]. "Yellow Fever and the Reed Commission." http://exhibits.hsl.virginia.edu/yellowfever/mosquitoes/. [Consulted February 3, 2014.]

Crosby, Molly Caldwell. *The American Plague: The Untold Story of Yellow Fever, the Epidemic that Shaped Our History.* New York: Berkley Books, 2006.

Endy, T. P., S. J. Thomas, and J. V. Lawler. "History of U.S. Military Contributions to the Study of Viral Hemorrhagic Fevers. *Military Medicine,* 170, no. 4 Supplement (April 2005): 77–91.

John P. Ische Library at the Louisiana State University Health Sciences Center [online]. "Aristides Agramonte Yellow Fever Collection." http://louisdl.louislibraries.org/cdm/about/collection/LSUBK01. [Consulted February 3, 2014.]

Lederer, Susan E. "Walter Reed and the Yellow Fever Experiments," in *The Oxford Textbook of Clinical Research Ethics,* ed. by Ezekiel J. Emanuel et al. New York: Oxford University Press, 2008.

Petri, William A. "America in the World: 100 Years of Tropical Medicine and Hygiene." American Journal of Tropical Medicine and Hygiene 71, no. 1 (2004): 2–16.

Pierce, J.R., "'In the Interest of Humanity and the Cause of Science': The Yellow Fever Volunteers." *Military Medicine* 168, no.11 (November 2003): 857–63.

Reed, Walter, et al. "The Etiology of Yellow Fever: A Preliminary Note." Public Health Papers and Reports 26 (1900): 37–53.

Antinori, Severino

Abbott, Alison. Trepidation Greets Plan for Cloning Humans. *Nature* 410, no. 6826 (March 2005): 293.

Adams, Tim. "The Clone Arranger." *Observer,* December 2, 2001.

Carroll, Rory, Michael Ellison, and Helena Smith, "Dr Miracle and the Showman—The Pair Plotting a 'Revolution'" *Guardian,* August 8, 2001.

Crewdson, John, "Gynecologist Claims Impending Births of Five Cloned Human Babies." *Chicago Tribune,* June 23, 2002.

Harss, Marina. "Italy: Human Cloning." *New York Times,* August 7, 2001.

Johnson, Jo. "Italy's Unpopular Pioneer: Severino Antinori." *Financial Times,* August 11, 2001.

Mallon, Margaret. "Prepare for the First Human Clone." *The Herald* (Scotland), August 8, 2001.

Pistoi, Sergio. "Father of the Impossible Children: Ignoring Nearly Universal Opprobrium, Severino Antinori Presses Ahead with Plans to Clone a Human Being." *Scientific American* April 2002.

Stolberg, Sheryl Gay. "Despite Warnings, Three Vow to Go Ahead on Human Cloning." *New York Times,* August 8, 2001.

Ayala, Francisco J.

Davies, Caroline. "Pro-Religion Scientist Wins £1m Templeton Prize." *Guardian,* May 5, 2010.

Dean, Cornelia. "Francisco J. Ayala: Roving Defender of Evolution, and of Room for God."
New York Times, April 29, 2008.

Gale, Elaine. "God Welcome in Biologist's Lab: Ex-Priest's Unique Perspective Bridges Gap between Science, Religion." *Los Angeles Times,* September 4, 1999.

Heffern, Rich. "Biologist, Former Dominican, Wins Templeton Prize." *National Catholic Reporter,* April 16, 2010.

Lehrman, Sally. "The Christian Man's Evolution." *Scientific American* 299, no. 5 (November 2008): 100.

Saslow, Rachel. "Genetics Researcher Francisco Ayala Discusses His Life, His Work and Creationism." *Washington Post,* April 26, 2010.

Slack, Gordy. "A Good Life." *UC Irvine Today.* UCI Communications, August 29, 2002.

Vernon, Mark. "Francisco Ayala Wins Templeton 2010." *Guardian,* March 25, 2010.

Bang, Abhay; Bang, Rani

Bavadam, Lyla. "Irreversible Violation of the Right to Live." *Frontline* [a publication of the *Hindu*] 22, no. 19 (September 10–23, 2005).

Day, Elizabeth. "Dr Abhay Bang: The Revolutionary Paediatrician." *Observer,* March 19, 2011.

D'Silva, Jeetha. "Giving a New Meaning to Public Service." *Mint* (October 3, 2007).

Goswami, Rahul. "Putting Women First: Women and Health in a Rural Community" [book review]. *Reproductive Health Matters* 19, no.37 (May 2011): 154.

Perry, Alex. "The Listeners: Abhay and Rani Bang." *Time,* October 31, 2005.

Rosenberg, Tina. "Villages without Doctors." *New York Times,* February 14, 2011.

Subramanian, Anusha. "Baby Formula." *Business Today,* August 19, 2012.

Barbosa, José Celso

Ayala, César J., and Rafael Bernabé. *Puerto Rico in the American Century: A History since 1898.* Chapel Hill: University of North Carolina Press, 2009.

Cabán, Pedro A. *Constructing a Colonial People: Puerto Rico and the United States, 1898–1932.* Boulder, Colorado: Westview Press, 1999.

Malavet, Pedro A. *America's Colony: The Political and Cultural Conflict between the United States and Puerto Rico.* New York: New York University Press, 2004.

Bernal, Martha

García, Jorge G., and María C. Zea, eds. Psychological Interventions and Research with Latino Populations. Boston: Allyn and Bacon, 1997.

Vasquez, Melba J. T. "The Life and Death of a Multicultural Feminist Pioneer: Martha Bernal (1931–2001)." *The Feminist Psychologist Newsletter* 30, no. 1 (Winter 2003).

Vasquez, M. J. T. "Complexities of the Latina Experience: A Tribute to Martha Bernal." American Psychologist, 57 (2002): 880–888.

Villarruel, Francisco, et al., eds. *Handbook of U.S. Latino Psychology: Developmental and Community-Based Perspectives* (Thousand Oaks, California: SAGE, 2009).

Blanks, Billy

Autuori, Jenna. "Meet the Trainer: Tae Bo Creator Billy Blanks." *Fitness,* January 30, 2012.

Collins, Scott. "Tae-Bo Infomercial Kicks Up Success—and Legal Disputes." *Los Angeles Times,* March 3, 1999.

Conroy, Tom. "The Prince of Tae Bo." *Us* 256 (May 1999): 47.

Gardetta, Dave. "Elvis Has Just Entered the Building." *Los Angeles Times,* August 15, 1999.

Green, Penelope. "Mirror, Mirror: Punching and Kicking All the Way to the Bank." *New York Times,* March 21, 1999.

Harden, Blaine. "Igniting a Fervor for Fitness in Japan: American Becomes Household Name." *Washington Post,* September 29, 2007.

Kyles, Kyra. "Five Things about: The Blanks." *Jet* 122, no.2 (January 28, 2013): 29.

Labi, Nadya. "Tae-Bo or Not Tae-Bo?" *Time,* March 14, 1999.

Cardús, David

Guerrero, Richard. "A Man of Science." *Catalonia Today* (November 2003): 21–24.

Wendler, Rhonda. "Out of This World Research Seeks to Improve Health on Earth." *Texas Medical Center News* 23, no. 19 (October 2001).

Margaret Chan

Abraham, Thomas. "There Is No 'False Pandemic'" New York Times, January 29, 2010.

Altman, Lawrence K. "Her Job: Helping Save the World from Bird Flu." New York Times, August 9, 2005.

Benitez, Mary Ann. "Propelled to Fame by Two Bugs." South China Morning Post, August 22, 2003.

Bulletin of the World Health Organization. "Pandemic Flu—Communicating the Risks; The Bulletin Interview with Dr Margaret Chan." Vol. 84, no. 1 (January 2006). http://www.who.int/bulletin/volumes/84/1/interview0106/en/. [Consulted February 4, 2014.]

"China's Chan Assumes Helm of WHO with Bird Flu in Focus." Agence France Presse, January 3, 2007.

Council on Foreign Relations. "The World Health Organization (WHO) in a Shifting Global Governance Landscape, November 16, 2010." Presider: Yanzhong Huang; speakers, Jack Chow and Jennifer Ruger. Washington, D.C.: Federal News Service, 2010.

Editorial. Lancet 368, no. 9549 (Nov. 18–24, 2006): 1743.

Fidler, David P., "The Challenges of Global Health Governance; Working Paper." Council on Foreign Relations, May 2010.

Foreman, William. "Hong Kong's Margaret Chan Says Will Serve World, Not Just China, If Named WHO Director. Associated Press, August 2, 2006.

Harris, Gardiner, and Lawrence K. Altman. "Managing a Flu Threat with Seasoned Urgency." New York Times, May 9, 2009.

LeFanu, James. "Doctor's Diary: Swine Flu Scientists Were Too Close to Big Pharma." Telegraph, November 17, 2013.

McNeil, Donald G. Jr., and Denise Grady. "To Flu Experts, 'Pandemic' Label Confirms the Obvious." New York Times, June 12, 2009.

Moore, Malcolm. "Profile: Dr Margaret Chan, Leading the World's Response to Swine Flu." Telegraph, May 1, 2009.

Shuchman, Miriam. "Improving Global Health—Margaret Chan at the WHO." New England Journal of Medicine 356, no.7 (February 15, 2007): 653.

Zarocostas, John. "WHO Chief Urges Member States to Step Up Efforts for Flu Pandemic." British Medical Journal 334, no.7584 (January 13, 2007): 61.

Margaret Chung

Miller, Johnny. "Margaret Chung, a One-Woman USO in WWII." *SFGate*, January 4, 2009.

Wu, Judy Tzu-Chun. *Doctor Mom Chung of the Fair-Haired Bastards: The Life of a Wartime Celebrity.* Berkeley: University of California Press, 2005.

Wu, Judy Tzu-Chun. "'The Ministering Angel of Chinatown': Missionary Uplift, Modern Medicine, and Asian American Women's Strategies of Liminality," in *Asian/Pacific Islander American Women: A Historical Anthology,* ed. Shirley Hune and Gail M. Nomura. New York: New York University Press, 2003.

Wu, Judy Tzu-Chun. "Was Mom Chung a 'Sister Lesbian'?" *Journal of Women's History* 13, no. 1 (Spring 2001): 58–82.

Susan Desmond-Hellmann

Asimov, Nanette. "UCSF Seeks to Ease Ties with UC." *San Francisco Chronicle*, January 20, 2012.

Berenson, Alex. "Cancer Drugs Offer Hope, but at a Huge Expense." *New York Times,* July 12, 2005.

Bole, Kristen. "Tech, Health, Policy, Finance Leaders Launch Precision Medicine Initiatives." University of California San Francisco Web site, May 1, 2013. http://www.ucsf.edu/news/2013/04/105556/tech-health-policy-finance-leaders-launch-precision-medicine-initiatives. [Consulted February 6, 2014.]

Breitstein, Joanna. "HBA [Healthcare Businesswomen's Association] Woman of the Year: Susan Desmond-Hellmann." *Pharmaceutical Executive,* April 1, 2006.

Dolan, Kerry. "UCSF Chancellor Susan Desmond-Hellmann on How Healthcare Is Changing." *Forbes*, April 30, 2012.

"From Uganda to San Francisco, the President of Product Development at Genentech describes her 'chaotic' career." *Nature Reviews: Drug Discovery* 4, no. 7 (July 2005): 532.

Guthrie, Julian. "Cancer Warrior Takes the Helm of UCSF." *San Francisco Chronicle,* April 11, 2010.

Johnson, Carolyn. "UCSF Chancellor Honored by Commonwealth Club." KGO-TV San Francisco, April 5, 2012.

Grady, Denise. "An Innovator Shapes an Empire." *New York Times,* October 10, 2011

Ivory, Danielle. "Chancellor at University of California to Become Chief at Gates Foundation." New York Times, December 17, 2013.

Mullard, Asher. "An Audience with Susan Desmond-Hellmann." *Nature Reviews: Drug Discovery* 10, no. 3 (March 2011): 170.

Greatbatch, Wilson

Adam, John. "Innovative Lives: Making Hearts Beat." Smithsonian Institution Web site, February 5, 1999. invention.smithsonian.org/centerpieces/ilives/lecture09.html. [Consulted February 6, 2014.]

Bigelow, W. G . *Cold Hearts: The Story of Hypothermia and the Pacemaker in Heart Surgery*. Toronto: McClelland and Stewart, 1984. [Excerpt by Bernard S. Goldman published as "The Pacemaker Story: A Cold Heart Spinoff," *Pacing and Clinical Electrophysiology* 10, no. 1 (January 1987): 142–150.]

Drucker, Peter. *Management Cases,* rev. ed., ed. by Joseph Maciariello. New York: HarperBusiness 2008. ["Case Number 40: The Chardack-Greatbatch Implantable Pacemaker."]

Jeffrey, Kirk. *Machines in Our Hearts: The Cardiac Pacemaker, the Implantable Defibrillator, and American Health Care.* Baltimore: Johns Hopkins University Press, 2001.

Lee, W. David, et al., From X-Rays to DNA: How Engineering Drives Biology. Cambridge, MA: MIT Press, 2014.

Nebeker, Frederik. "Oral-History: Wilson Greatbatch." Interview #396 for the IEEE [Institute of Electrical and Electronics Engineers] History Center, 4 April 2000 [online]. http://www.ieeeghn.org/wiki/index.php/Oral-History:Wilson_Greatbatch. [Consulted February 6, 2014.]

Greenfield, Susan

Anton, Ted. *Bold Science: Seven Scientists Who Are Changing Our World.* New York: W. H. Freeman, 2000.

"Are We Becoming Cyborgs? Global Agenda; Conversation." Moderated by Serge Schmemann; participants, Susan Greenfield, Evgeny Morozov, Maria Popova. *New York Times,* November 30, 2012.

Bingham, Roger. "The Baroness, Consciousness, and the Twitterverse; A Conversation with Susan Greenfield." The Science Network Science Studio, May 22, 2009 [online]. http://thesciencenetwork.org/programs/the-science-studio/a-conversation-with-susan-greenfield. [Video; run time 48 minutes. Full transcript provided. Consulted February 6, 2014.]

Bohannon, John. "Profile: Susan Greenfield, The Baroness and the Brain." *Science* 310, no. 5750 (November 11, 2005): 962–963.

Elmhirst, Sophie. "The NS Interview: Sophie Elmhirst Talks to the Neuroscientist Susan Greenfield. New Statesman no. 4970 (October 8, 2009): 24–25.

"Susan Greenfield: The End of an Institution?" *Economist* no. 8665 (January 14, 2010): 79–80.

Youde, Kate, "Greenfield Exits Royal Institution, Claiming Sex Discrimination." *Independent,* January 10, 2010.

Heymann, David L.

Altman, Lawrence K. "A Specialist in Fighting New Diseases Is Chosen to Wipe Out an Old One." New York Times, August 12, 2003.

Drexler, Madeleine. "Interview with David L. Heymann, MD." Biosecurity and Bioterrorism: Biodefense Strategy, Practice, and Science 1, no. 4 (December 2003): 233–237.

Garrett, Laurie, The Coming Plague: Newly Emerging Diseases in a World Out of Balance (New York: Farrar, Straus and Giroux, 1994).

"Health Woes Grow in a Shrinking World." JAMA 279, no. 8 (Feb. 25, 1998).

McNeil, Donald G, Jr., and Celia W. Dugger. "To Conquer, or Control? Disease Strategy Debated." New York Times, March 20, 2006.

Soares, Christine. "A Strategy of Containment." Scientific American 290 (March 2004): 48ff.

Philip Jaisohn

Lankov, Andrei. "Seo Jae-Pil: Pioneering Reformer, Independence Fighter.*" Korea Times,* December 28, 2011.

Liem, Channing. *Philip Jaisohn: The First Korean American—A Forgotten Hero.* Seoul: Kyujang, 2001.

Oh, Se-ŭng. *Dr. Philip Jaisohn's Reform Movement, 1896–1898: A Critical Appraisal of the Independence Club.* Washington, DC: University Press of America, 1995.

Oh, Seiwoong. "*Hansu's Journey* by Philip Jaisohn: The First Fiction in English from Korean America." *Amerasia Journal* 29, no. 3 (2003–04): 43–55.

Parreñas, Rhacel, and Lok Siu. *Asian Diasporas: New Formations, New Conceptions.* Stanford: Stanford University Press, 2007.

Yŏng-ho Ch'oe, "The Kapsin Coup of 1884: A Reassessment." *Korean Studies* 6 (1982):

105–124.

Jalal, Massouda

Campbell, Duncan. "We Will Have Our Say." *Guardian,* July 15, 2004.

Clark, Kate. "Profile: Massouda Jalal." BBC News, June 12, 2002.

Gall, Carlotta. "Afghan Women in Political Spotlight." *New York Times,* June 26, 2002.

Halloran, Richard. "For Afghan Woman, Candidacy Is Victory." *Honolulu Advertiser,* September 19, 2004.

Hobson, Victoria, and Constance Borde. "Women of Afghanistan: Mobilizing in the Land of the Burka." *New York Times,* December 18, 2003.

Kolhatkar, Sonali. "Afghan Women Continue to Fend for Themselves." *Foreign Policy in Focus,* March 2004.

"Massouda Jalal Sets Precedent for Afghan Women." Agence France Presse, January 26, 2004.

Skaine, Rosemarie, *Women of Afghanistan in the Post-Taliban Era* (Jefferson, NC: McFarland, 2008).

"Spanish PM Aznar & Afghan women's equality advocate win UN Watch human rights awards." *UN Watch,* May 31, 2010.

Viqar, Said Habib, and Ghulam Sayeed Najami. "Massouda Jalal: Physician Talks Up Her Neutrality." *Institute for War and Peace Reporting,* October 7, 2004.

Kaleeba, Noerine

Abraham, Curtis. "Angel of Africa." *New Scientist,* March 8, 2003.

"Interview: Noerine Kaleeba." The Age of AIDS. Frontline Web site. Interview conducted May 5, 2005. http://www.pbs.org/wgbh/pages/frontline/aids/interviews/kaleeba.html. [Consulted February 6, 2014.]

Namaganda, Agnes K. "Noerine Kaleeba: An Iconic Leader in Our Midst. *Daily Monitor* [Kampala], March 24, 2012.

Fresh Air from WHYY. "Ugandan AIDS Activist Noerine Kaleeba." National Public Radio Web site. Program for April 22, 2002. http://www.npr.org/templates/story/story.php?storyId=1142001. [Consulted February 6, 2014.]

Scheier, Rachel, and Nicole Itano. "AIDS at 25; How a Country Fought Back." *Newsday,* June 12, 2006.

Kuipers, André

Chow, Denise. "Space Station Astronauts Return to Earth aboard Soyuz Capsule." SPACE.com Web site. July 1, 2012. http://www.space.com/16377-space-station-astronauts-land-soyuz-capsule.html. [Consulted February 6, 2014.]

Hall, Rex D., David J. Shayler, and Bert Vis. *Russia's Cosmonauts: Inside the Yuri Gagarin Training Center* (Berlin: Praxis Publishing, 2005).

Kelly, John, and Chris Kridler. "Station Crew Set for Soyuz Launch." *Florida Today,* April 18, 2004.

Kremer, Ken, ed. "Incredible Dragon Approach and Berthing—Image Gallery from Andre Kuipers aboard ISS." May 27, 2012. http://www.universetoday.com/95460/incredible-dragon-approach-and-berthing-image-gallery-from-andre-kuipers-aboard-iss/. [Consulted February 6, 2014.]

NASA. "Preflight Interview: André Kuipers." November 1, 2011. [online] http://www.nasa.gov/mission_pages/station/expeditions/expedition30/kuipers_interview.html. [Consulted February 6, 2014.]

Llinás, Rodolfo

Bingham, Roger. "Enter the 'I of the Vortex' with Neuroscientist Rodolfo Llinás " The Science Network Science Studio, April 17, 2007 [online.] http://thesciencenetwork.org/programs/the-science-studio/enter-the-i-of-the-vortex. [Video; run time 1 hour, 12 minutes. Full transcript provided. Consulted February 6, 2014.]

Blakeslee, Sandra. "In a Host of Ailments, Seeing a Brain Out of Rhythm." *New York Times,* December 1, 2008.

Blakeslee, Sandra. "New Way of Looking at Diseases of the Brain." *New York Times,* November 2, 2008.

Blakeslee, Sandra. "Theory on Brain's Rhythms Offers Some New Hopes." *New York Times,* October 26, 1999.

Hilts, Philip J. "Listening to the Conversation of Neurons." *New York Times,* May 27, 1997.Horgan, John. *The Undiscovered Mind; How the Human Brain Defies Replication, Medication, and Explanation.* New York: Free Press, 1999.

Margulis, Lynn, and Eduardo Punset, eds. *Mind, Life, and Universe: Conversations with Great Scientists of Our Time.* White River Junction, VT: Chelsea Green Pub., 2007.

Naam, Ramez. *More Than Human; Embracing the Promise of Biological Enhancement.* New York: Broadway Books, 2005.

Squire, Larry R., *The History of Neuroscience in Autobiography,* vol. 5 (Burlington, MA: Elsevier Academic Press, 2006).

Maung, Cynthia

Bock, Paula. "A Journey of the Heart," Special Project [online]. *Seattle Times,* September 28, 1997. http://seattletimes.com/special/burma/index.html. [Consulted February 6, 2014.]

Bradley, Sharon. "Peace Prize Winner Fights for Survival of Her Health Clinic." *Sydney Morning Herald,* August 17, 2013.

Fuller, Thomas. "Across the River: Two Divergent Paths in Southeast Asia." *New York Times,* October 25, 2007.

Kluger, Jeffrey, and Bryan Walsh. "Medic in Exile; Cynthia Maung." *Time,* October 31, 2005.

Kyaw Kha. "'There is No Room for Discrimination in Health Care.'" *Irrawaddy News Magazine,* November 9, 2013.

Nan Thoo Lei. "Dr. Cynthia Maung: People in Burma Still Oppressed." *Karen News,* December 10, 2012.

Saw Eh Htee. "Clinic's Workload Doubles as Funding Shrinks" *Karen News,* July 19, 2012.

Villarino, Eliza. "Dr. Cynthia Maung: How Foreign Donors Can Help Bring Peace to Burma." Devex Web site, 29 August 2013. https://www.devex.com/en/news/dr-cynthia-maung-how-foreign-donors-can-help-bring-peace-to-burma/81707. [Consulted February 6, 2014.]

Wai Moe. "Dr Cynthia Meets with Aung Min." *Irrawaddy News Magazine,* June 26, 2012.

Olopade, Olufunmilayo

Adegun, Aanu. "Dr. Olufunmilayo Olopade, Nigeria's Gift to the Medical World." *Daily Newswatch,* September 19, 2013.

Allers, Kimberly L. "True Genius: Why Does Breast Cancer Hit Black Women So Hard?" *Essence* 36, no.9 (January 2006): 90.

Bennett, Joy T. "Dr. Olufunmilayo I. Olopade: Unlocking the Mysteries of Breast Cancer." *Ebony* 62, no.12 (October 2007): 146.

Children's Hospital Boston. "New Clue to Racial Disparity in Breast Cancer Survival Rates." Science Daily, February 22, 2007. http//:www.sciencedaily.com/releases/2007/02/070221101400.htm. [Consulted February 6, 2014.]

Couzin, Jennifer. "Probing the Roots of Race and Cancer." *Science* 315, no.5812 (February 2, 2007): 592.

Grady, Denise. "Wielding Genomes in the Fight against Cancer." *New York Times,* June 3, 2011.

Grady, Denise. "Racial Component Is Found in Lethal Breast Cancer." *New York Times,* June 7, 2006.

Grady, Denise. "Young Black Women Prone to Deadly Cancer." *New York Times,* June 6, 2006.

Hevrdejs, Judy. "A Lifelong Commitment." *Chicago Tribune,* October 04, 2009.

Klein, Sarah A., "U of C Oncologist Traces Overseas Links to Medical Mystery." *Crain's Chicago Business* 23, no. 49 (November 27, 2000): 15.

Scudellari, Megan. "Cancer Knows No Borders." *Scientist,* August 1, 2013.

Sweet, Lynn. "Another Chicagoan, Olufunmilayo Falusi Olopade, Gets Obama White House Post." *Chicago Sun-Times,* February 25, 2011. [Includes White House press release.]

Omichinski, Linda

Douglas, Ann. "Success: Lives Changed, Not Pounds Lost." *Radiance,* Spring 1998.

Ball, Geoff D.C., et al. "Weight Relapsers, Maintainers, and Controls: Metabolic and Behavioural Differences." *Applied Physiology, Nutrition, and Metabolism* 24, no.6 (December 1999) 548.

Andersen-Parrado, Patricia. "Common Sense Approaches to Weight and Health." *Better Nutrition* 60, no. 3 (March 1998): 26.

Schuster, Karolyn. "The Dark Side of Nutrition." *Food Management* 34, no.6 (June 1999): 35.

Pitanguy, Ivo

Edmonds, Alexander. *Pretty Modern: Beauty, Sex and Plastic Surgery in Brazil.* Durham, NC: Duke University Press, 2010.

Edmonds, Alexander, "Surgery as Therapy." *New York Times,* August 14, 2011.

Faiola, Anthony. "Plastic Surgeon to Rich and Poor; Doctor Made Rio International Hub of Nip and Tuck." *Washington Post,* November 10, 1997.

Gil-Montero, Martha. "Ivo Pitanguy: Master of Artful Surgery." *Americas* (English Edition) 43, no. 2, March–April 1991): 24.

Gilman, Sander L, *Making the Body Beautiful.* Princeton: Princeton University Press, 1999.

Ginsburg, Ina "Plastic Makes Perfect: Ivo Pitanguy." *Interview* 17, no.9 (September 1987): 86ff.

Goering, Laurie. "Jet-Setting Celebs and the Disfigured Poor of Rio Agree That Plastic Surger Ivo Pitanguy Is a Cut Above." *Chicago Tribune,* May 23, 1995.

Hoge, Warren. "Doctor Vanity—The Jet Set's Man in Rio." *New York Times,* June 8, 1980.

Lapper, Richard, and Amy Stillman. "Boom and Busts." *Financial Times,* February 22, 2013.

Reginato, James. "Dr. Ivo." *W,* July 2008.

Rogge, Jacques

Abrahamson, Alan. "Belgian Wins Olympic Presidency." *Los Angeles Times,* July 17, 2001.

Abrahamson, Alan. "Rogge Is Granted Veto Power." *Los Angeles Times,* September 21, 2001.

Barney, Robert K., Stephen R. Wenn, and Scott G. Martyn, *Selling the Five Rings: The International Olympic Committee and the Rise of Olympic Commercialism.* Salt Lake City: University of Utah Press, 2002.

Clarey, Christopher. "Q&A; Jacques Rogge: Olympics Chief Aims to Cure Sport's 'Diseases.'" *New York Times,* August 9, 2001.

Coe, Sebastian. "Rogge's Scalpel Poised." *Telegraph,* 11 November 2001.

Gibson, Owen. "London 2012 Olympics Were 'Absolutely Fabulous', Says IOC Chief." *Guardian,* August 12, 2012.

Holt, Oliver. "Rogge Promises to Restore Popular Touch." *Times* (London), July 17, 2001.

Holt, Oliver. "Rogge Sails over Final Hurdle to Become President of IOC." *Times* (London), July 17, 2001.

Longman, Jére. "Experienced Helmsman: Jacques Rogge." *New York Times,* July 17, 2001.

Magnay, Jacquelin. "Interview: Jacques Rogge, IOC President." *Telegraph,* July 15, 2011.

Masback, Craig A. "Olympics; Rogge Can Make His Term as President of I.O.C. Count." *New York Times,* July 22, 2001.

Vecsey, George. "Steady Hand Steers I.O.C.'s Sometimes Rocky Course." *New York Times,* February 7, 2003.

Weir, Fred. "His Vision: Down-to-Earth Olympics." *Christian Science Monitor,* July 17, 2001.

White, Jim. "He's Got the Whole World in his Hands." *Guardian,* November 10, 2001.

Wilson, Stephen. "Jacques Rogge in Final Days as IOC President." Associated Press, September 3, 2013.

Röntgen, Wilhelm

Baigrie, Brian S. "Shadow Pictures." *Scientific Revolutions: Primary Texts in the History of Science.* Upper Saddle River: Pearson, 2004. [Includes an English translation of Röntgen's "On a New Type of Rays" preceded by a helpful historical introduction.]

Nitski, W. Robert. *The Life of Wilhelm Conrad Röntgen, Discoverer of the X-Ray.* Tucson: University of Arizona Press, 1971. [Includes English translations of Röntgen's three most famous papers.]

Thomsen, Volker. "Atomic Perspectives: Wilhelm Conrad Röntgen and the Discovery of X-Rays." *Spectroscopy* 23.7 (2008): 30–34.

Schiller, Daniela

Adler, Jerry. "Erasing Painful Memories." *Scientific American* 306, 56–61 (April 17, 2012) Published online: 17 April 2012.

Bingham, Roger. "Daniela Schiller, Mount Sinai School of Medicine." The Science Network Science Studio, March 31, 2011 [online.] http://thesciencenetwork.org/programs/the-science-studio/daniela-schiller. [Video; run time 30 minutes. Consulted February 7, 2014.]

Hall, Stephen S. "Repairing Bad Memories." *Technology Review* 116, no.4 (July-August 2013): 48.

Jahme, Carole. "Who Wouldn't Want to Take the Sting Out of Painful Memories?" *Guardian,* July 12, 2011.

Kloosterman, Karin. "Rewiring Responses to Painful Memories." Israel21c, December 10, 2009.

Lametti, Daniel. "How to Erase Fear—In Humans." *Scientific American,* March 23, 2010.

Reynolds, Gretchen. "Overcoming Fear." *New York Times Magazine,* February 7, 2010.

Sample, Ian. "Ancient Brain Circuits Light Up So We Can Judge People on First Impressions." *Guardian,* March 8, 2009.

Sears, William; Sears, Martha

Browning, Dominique. "Why Breast-Feeding Isn't the Bugaboo." *Time,* May 10, 2012.

Dell'Antonia, KJ. "Never Mom Enough." *New York Times,* May 10, 2012.

Eberlein, Tamara. "Attachment Parenting." *American Baby* 58, no.7 (July 1996): 26ff.

Giarrusso, Theresa Walsh. "Attachment Parenting 20 Years Later." *Atlanta Journal-Constitution,* May 10, 2012.

Groskop, Viv. "Cruel to be kind: the rise of detachment parenting." *Times* (London), May 11 2013.

Kluger, Jeffrey. "The Science behind Dr. Sears: Does It Stand Up?" *Time,* May 10, 2012.

Livingston, Kathryn E. "Are You Touching Your Child Enough?" *Redbook* 179, no. 6 (October 1992): 190ff.

Moyer, Melinda Wenner. "Cry, Baby, Cry." Slate, July 17, 2013.

Pickert, Kate. "Attachment Parenting: Dr. Sears and the Origins of a Movement." *Time,* May 10, 2012 [online]. http://content.time.com/time/video/player/0,32068,1630929351001_2114407,00.html#ixzz2sff0vACq. [Consulted February 7, 2-14.]

Pickert, Kate. "The Man Who Remade Motherhood." *Time,* May 21, 2012.

Raphael, Amy. "Do Try This at Home." *Financial Times,* March 25, 2006.

Siemionow, Maria

Altman, Lawrence K. "Cleveland Surgeons Perform First Major Face Transplant in U.S." *New York Times,* December 17, 2008.

Altman, Lawrence K. "First U.S. Face Transplant Described." *New York Times,* December 17, 2008.

Altman, Lawrence K. "The Ultimate Gift: 50 Years of Organ Transplants." *New York Times,* December 21, 2004.

Blackburn, Bradley, and Lana Zak. "Face Transplant Patient Connie Culp Undergoes Final Procedure, Learns to Smile Again." ABC News [online], August 26, 2010.

Freeman, Michael, and Pauline Abou Jaoudé. "Justifying Surgery's Last Taboo: The Ethics of Face Transplants." *Journal of Medical Ethics* 33 (2007): 76–81.

"Lead Surgeon Who Performed Face Transplant Prepped for Years." *USA Today,* December 17, 2008.

Mason, Michael, and Lawrence K. Altman. "Ethical Concerns on Face Transplant Grow." *New York Times,* December 6, 2005.

Okie, Susan, "Brave new face." *New England Journal of Medicine* 354, no.9 (March 2, 2006): 889ff.

"Recipient of Face Transplant Shares Her Story and Results." Associated Press, May 6 2009.

Rubin, Rita. "Doctors Detail First U.S. Face Transplant." *USA Today,* December 17, 2008.

Yi Chenggang and Shuzhong Guo. "Facial Transplantation: Lessons So Far." *Lancet* 374, no. 9685 (July 18, 2009): 177–178.

Zeltner, Brie. "Cleveland Clinic Face Transplant Patient Connie Culp Hopes Her Story Teaches People Not to Judge." *Plain Dealer,* May 5, 2009.

SubbaRow, Yellapragada

Bhargava, Pushpa Mitra. "Dr. Yellapragada SubbaRow (1895–1948): He Transformed Science; Changed Lives." *Indian Academy of Clinical Medicine Journal* 2, no.1–2 (January–June, 2001): 96–100.

Gupta, S. P. K., and E. L. Milford. *In Quest of Panacea—Successes and Failures of Yallapragada SubbaRow.* New Delhi: Evelyn Publishers, 1987.

Nagendrappa, Gopalpur. "Yellapragada SubbaRow; The Man of Miracle Drugs." *Resonance, A Journal of Science Education* 17, no. 6 (June 2012): 538–557. http://www.ias.ac.in/resonance/Volumes/17/06/0538-0557.pdf. [Consulted February 10, 2014.]

Nathan, David G. The Cancer Treatment Revolution: How Smart Drugs and Other New Therapies Are Renewing Our Hope and Changing the Face of Medicine. Hoboken, NJ: Wiley, 2007.

Simoni, Robert, Robert Hill, and Martha Vaughan. "The Determination of Phosphorus and the Discovery of Phosphocreatine and ATP: The Work of Fiske and SubbaRow." Journal of Biological Chemistry 277, no. 32 (August, 2002): e1–e2.

Thomas, William H.

Brown, Nell Porter. "At Home with Old Age; Reimagining Nursing Homes." *Harvard Magazine* November–December 2008.

Greene, Kelly, "Twelve People Who Are Changing Your Retirement." *Wall Street Journal,* February 16, 2008.

Hsu, Caroline. "The Greening of Aging; William Thomas; Physician, Farmer." *U.S. News and World Report,* June 11, 2006.

Salter, Chuck. "[Not] the Same Old Story." *Fast Company,* February 2002.

Salter, Chuck. "Healthy Alternative; A Report from the Past." *Fast Company,* March 2005.

Trehan, Naresh

Button, Victoria. "Robots Lend a Helping Hand with Surgery." *Age* (Melbourne), May 10, 2000.

Chowdhary, Sudhir. "Magic of Medanta." *Financial Express,* July 19, 2010.

"Four Days after Recall, Trehan Quits Escorts for Apollo." *Times of India,* May 31, 2007.

Sharma, Sanchita. "City Gets Another Mega Hospital." *Hindustan Times,* November 18, 2009.

Sawhney, Anubha. "Naresh Trehan... Straight from the Heart." *Times of India,* May 5, 2002.

"Top Indian Heart Doctor Leaves Longtime Home." *International Business Times,* June 4, 2007.

Waldman, Amy. "Indian Heart Surgeon Took Talents Home." *New York Times,* May 18, 2003.

Vasella, Daniel

Copley, Caroline. "DealTalk—Novartis' Vasella Exit Opens Door to Roche Stake Sale." Reuters, May 16, 2013.

Edwards, Richard. "Animal Rights Militants Target Novartis Pharmaceutical Boss Daniel Vasella." *Telegraph,* August 5, 2009.

Fleck, Fiona, "A Healthy Novartis Increases Stake in a Rival." *New York Times,* January 23, 2004.

Holstein, William J. "Diplomat without Portfolio in Davos." *New York Times,* February 12, 2006.

Jack, Andrew. "Reticent Daniel Vasella Remains Proud of Legacy and Record at Novartis." *Financial Times,* August 25, 2013.

Kirkland, Rik. "Leading in the 21st Century: An Interview with Daniel Vasella." McKinsey and Company [online], September 2012.

Ouroussoff, Nicolai. "Many Hands, One Vision." *New York Times,* December 23, 2009.

Tomlinson, Heather. "Interview: Daniel Vasella, Chief Executive of Novartis; Smooth Talker, Thorny Issues." *Guardian,* July 30, 2004.

"Vasella's Vision." *Leaders* 36, no. 4 (November–December 2013).

Werdigier, Julia. "Critics of Executive Pay Put Pressure on Novartis." *New York Times,* February 18, 2013.

Werdigier, Julia. "Novartis Scraps Non-Compete Payment to Departing Chairman." *New York Times,* February 19, 2013.

Wright, Tom. "Saturday Interview: With Daniel L. Vasella; The Pharmaceutical Horizon Beckons." *New York Times,* August 13, 2005.

Wellcome, Henry

Addison, Frank. *The Wellcome Excavations in the Sudan*, 3 vols. London: Oxford University Press, 1949–1951.

Arnold, Ken, and Danielle Olsen, eds. *Medicine Man: The Forgotten Museum of Henry Wellcome*. London: British Museum Press, 2003.

Hall, Rupert A. *Physic and Philanthropy: A History of the Wellcome Trust, 1936–1986*. Cambridge, England: Cambridge University Press, 1986.

James, Robert Rhodes. *Henry Wellcome*. London: Hodder and Stoughton, 1994.

James, Robert Rhodes. "Sir Henry Solomon Wellcome, 1853–1936." In *Oxford Dictionary of National Biography: From the Earliest Times to the Year 2000*, ed. H. C. G. Matthew and Brian Harrison. New York: Oxford University Press, 2004.

Larson, Frances. *An Infinity of Things: How Sir Henry Wellcome Collected the World*. Oxford, England: Oxford University Press, 2009.

Walton, John, et al., eds. *The Oxford Companion to Medicine*. Oxford, England: Oxford University Press, 1986.

Wood, Fiona

Chipperfield, Mark. "Yorkshire Surgeon Leads Fight to Save Victims." *Sunday Telegraph,* October 20, 2002.

Dunlevy, Sue. "The Healing Power of Imagination." *Australian,* August 20, 2011.

Guilliatt, Richard. "2002: Fiona Wood, Bali Burns Surgeon." *Australian,* September 21, 2013.

Henderson, Michelle. "Burns Specialist Prof Fiona Wood Says Her Team's Response to the Bali Bombings Is a Source of Pride." *Australian,* October 7, 2012.

Jameson, Julietta. "Pushing Boundaries." Australia Unlimited [online], December 13, 2011. http://www.australiaunlimited.com/science/pushing-boundaries#sthash.EA0TX0zb.dpuf. [Consulted February 10, 2014.]

Laurie, Victoria. "Skin Deep, Mountain High." *Weekend Australian Magazine,* June 21–22, 2003.

Leser, David. "Thank God for Fiona: One Day with the Australian of the Year."

Australian Women's Weekly, November 2005, p.54-58.

Maynard, Roger. "Strewth! Aussie of the Year Is a Pommy Sheila." *Times* (London), January 27 2005.

Zerhouni, Elias

Connolly, Ceci, "Bush Names Hopkins Administrator to Head NIH; Some Researchers Concerned That Choice May Be Driven by Nominee's Stance on Cloning, Stem Cell Research." *Washington Post,* March 27, 2002.

Connolly, Ceci, and Dana Milbank. "Bush Selects a Top Official At Johns Hopkins to Head NIH."

Washington Post, March 6, 2002.

Culliton, Barbara J. "Extracting Knowledge from Science: A Conversation with Elias Zerhouni."

Health Affairs 25, no. 3 (May 2006): w94–w103.

"Editorial: Leadership and the NIH." *Lancet* 359, no. 9318 (May 11, 2002): 1629.

"Editorial: NIH in the Spotlight over Conflicts of Interest." *Lancet Neurology* 3, no. 11 (November 2004): 633.

Ezzell, Carol. "A Biomedical Politician." *Scientific American* 289 (September 2003).

"Former NIH Director Elias Zerhouni Rejoins Johns Hopkins Medicine as Senior Advisor." Johns Hopkins Medicine Press Release [online], April 20, 2009. http://www.hopkinsmedicine.org/news/media/releases/Former_Nih_Director_Elias_Zerhouni_Rejoins_Johns_Hopkins_Medicine_as_Senior_Advisor, [Consulted February 10, 2014.]

Grady, Denise. "A Conversation with Elias Zerhouni; Learning the Science of Leading." *New York Times,* July 15, 2003.

Harris, Gardiner. "A Businessman-Scientist Shakes Up the Health Institutes." *New York Times,* August 30, 2005

Harris, Gardiner. "Federal Health Official to Step Down." *New York Times,* September 24, 2008.

"Institute for Cell Engineering Is Launched." Johns Hopkins Gazette Online 30, no. 20 (February 5, 2001)http://www.jhu.edu/~gazette/2001/feb0501/. [Consulted February 10, 2014.]

Kaiser, Jocelyn. "Money, Mission, Management Top Zerhouni's Agenda." *Science,* April 5, 2002.

Kaiser, Jocelyn. "Zerhouni's Parting Message: Make Room for Young Scientists." *Science,* November 7, 2008.

Larkin, Marilynn. "Can Zerhouni Create a Bold, Risk-Taking NIH?" *Lancet* 362, no. 9393 (October 25, 2003): 1382–1383.

Marshall, Eliot. "Zerhouni Pledges Review of NIH Consulting in Wake of Allegations." *Science,* December 19, 2003.

McLellan, Faith. "NIH Director Reviews First Year on the Job." *Lancet* 362, no. 9381 (August 2, 2003): 381–382.

Stolberg, Sheryl Gay. "Man in the News; From Algeria to a Dream—Elias Adam Zerhouni*." New York Times,* March 27, 2002.

Wadman, Meredith. "NIH Director Resigns." *Nature* [online], September 24, 2008. http://www.nature.com/news/2008/080924/full/news.2008.1131.html. [Consulted February 10, 2014.]

Selected Works

Agatston, Arthur

Agatston, Arthur. *The South Beach Diet: The Delicious, Doctor-Designed, Foolproof Plan for Fast and Healthy Weight Loss.* Emmaus, PA: Rodale, 2003.

Agatston, Arthur. *The South Beach Diet Cookbook: More Than 200 Delicious Recipes That Fit the Nation's Top Diet.* Emmaus, PA: Rodale, 2004.

Agatston, Arthur. *The South Beach Diet Good Fats/Good Carbs Guide: The Complete and Easy Reference for All Your Favorite Foods.* Emmaus, PA: Rodale, 2004.

Agatston, Arthur. *The South Beach Diet Heart Program: The 4-Step Plan That Can Save Your Life.* Emmaus, PA: Rodale, 2007.

Agatston, Arthur. *The South Beach Diet Super Quick Cookbook.* Emmaus, PA: Rodale, 2010.

Agatston, Arthur. *The South Beach Diet Taste of Summer Cookbook.* New York: Rodale, 2007.

Agatston, Arthur. *The South Beach Diet Wake-Up Call: Why America is Getting Fatter and Sicker* Emmaus, PA: Rodale, 2012.

Agatston, Arthur, and Joseph Signorile. *The South Beach Diet: Super Charged.* New York: Rodale, 2008.

Agatston, Arthur, and Natalie Geary. *The South Beach Diet Gluten Solution Cookbook: 175 Delicious, Slimming, Gluten-Free Recipes* Emmaus, PA: Rodale, 2013.

Agramonte, Aristídes

Agramonte, Aristídes. *The Campaign against Yellow Fever.* Berlin? : International Congress of Hygiene and Demography?, 1907?

Agramonte, Aristídes. *Yellow Fever; The Inside History of a Great Medical Discovery.* Havana: Times of Cuba Press, 1915.

Agramonte, Aristídes, Philip S. Hench, and Mary Kahler Hench. *Looking Back on Cuban Sanitary Progress.* Austin, TX: np, 1930.

Walter Reed, James Carroll, and Aristídes Agramonte. *The Etiology of Yellow Fever; An Additional Note.* Havana: Departamento de Sanidad, 1902. [Sanitary department Havana, Cuba, Series 3].

Ayala, Francisco

Ayala, Francisco J. *Am I a Monkey? Six Big Questions about Evolution.* Baltimore: Johns Hopkins University Press, 2010.

Ayala, Francisco J. *Darwin and Intelligent Design.* Minneapolis: Fortress Press, 2006.

Ayala, Francisco J. *Darwin's Gift to Science and Religion.* Washington, DC: Joseph Henry Press, 2007.

Ayala, Francisco J. *Evolution* London: Quercus, 2012.

Ayala, Francisco, ed. *Molecular Evolution.* Sunderland, MA: Sinauer Associates, 1976.

Ayala, Francisco J. *Population and Evolutionary Genetics: A Primer.* Menlo Park, CA: Benjamin/Cummings Pub., 1982.

Ayala, Francisco J., and Camilo J. Cela-Conde. *Human Evolution: Trails from the Past.* New York: Oxford University Press, 2007.

Ayala, Francisco J., and James W. Valentine. *Evolving: The Theory and Processes of Organic Evolution.* Menlo Park, CA: Benjamin/Cummings Pub.,1979.

Ayala, Francisco J., and John C. Avise, eds. *Essential Readings in Evolutionary Biology.* Baltimore: Johns Hopkins University Press, 2014.

Ayala, Francisco J., and John A. Kiger Jr. *Modern Genetics* (1980; second edition, Menlo Park, CA: Benjamin/Cummings Pub.,1984.

Ayala, Francisco J., and Robert Arp, eds. *Contemporary Debates in Philosophy of Biology.* Malden, MA: Wiley-Blackwell, 2010.

Dobzhansky, Theodosius, and Francisco J. Ayala, eds. *Studies in the Philosophy of Biology.* London, Macmillan, 1974.

Russell, Robert John, Francisco J. Ayala, and William R. Stoeger, eds. *Evolutionary Molecular Biology: Scientific Perspectives on Divine Actions.* Vatican City: Vatican Observatory/Berkeley, CA: Center for Theology and the Natural Sciences, 1999.

Bang, Abhay
Bang, Rani

Bang, Abhay. "Dr. Abhay Bang: Research with the People." *Forbes India,* June 4, 2010. http://forbesindia.com/article/ideas-to-change-the-world/dr-abhay-bang-research-with-the-people/13742/1#ixzz2peXX2QEX. [Consulted February 10, 2014.]

Bang, Abhay, and Alvin J. Patel, eds. *Health Care, Which Way to Go?; Examination of Issues and Alternatives.* Pune: Medico Friend Circle, 1981.

Bang, Abhay, Rani Bang, Sanjay B. Baitule, M. Hanimi Reddy, and Makesh D. Deshmukh. "Effect of Home-Based Neonatal Care and Management of Sepsis on Neonatal Mortality: Field Trial in Rural India." *Lancet* 354, no. 9194 (December 4, 1999): 1955–1961.

Bang, Rani, with Sunanda Khogade and Rupa Chinai. *Putting Women First: Women and Health in a Rural Community.* Kolkata: Stree-Samya Publications, 2010.

Bernal, Martha

Bernal, Martha E. "Behavioral Feedback in the Modification of Brat Behaviors." *Journal of Nervous and Mental Disease* 148, no. 4 (April 1969): 375–385.

Bernal, Martha E. "Ethnic Minority Mental Health Training: Trends and Issues." In F. C. Serafica, et al., eds. *Mental Health of Ethnic Minorities.* New York: Praeger, 1990.

Bernal, Martha E., "Martha E. Bernal," in O'Connell, Agnes N., and Nancy F. Russo, eds. *Models of Achievement: Reflections of Eminent Women in Psychology,* vol. 2. Hillsdale, NJ: Lawrence Erlbaum, 1988.

Bernal, Martha E., and F. G. Castro. "Are Clinical Psychologists Prepared for Service and Research with Ethnic Minorities? Report of a Decade of Progress." *American Psychologist* 49, no. 9 (1994): 797-805.

Bernal, Martha E., and George P. Knight. *Ethnic Identity: Formation and Transmission among Hispanics and Other Minorities.* Albany: State University of New York Press, 1993.

Bernal, Martha E., and J. L. Chin. "Recommendations from the Working Group on Curriculum Development." In H. F. Myers, et al., eds. *Ethnic Minority Perspectives on Clinical Training and Services in Psychology.* Washington, DC: American Psychological Association, 1991.

Bernal Martha E., et al., eds. *Mexican American Identity.* Mountain View, Calif.: Floricanto Press, 2005.

Knight, G. P., and Martha E. Bernal, eds. *Ethnic Identity: Formation and Transmission among Hispanics and Other Minorities.* New York, NY: State University of New York Press, 1993.

Ocampo, K. A., G. P. Knight, and Martha E. Bernal. "The Development of Cognitive Abilities and Social Identities in Children: The Case of Ethnic Identity." *International Journal of Behavioral Development* 21, no. 3 (1997): 479–500.

Blanks, Billy

Blanks, Billy *The Tae-Bo Way.* New York: Bantam Books, 1999.

Cardús, David

Cardús, David, and Lawrence Newton. "Development of a Computer Technique for the On-Line Processing of Respiratory Variables." *Computers in Biology and Medicine* 1, no. 2 (December, 1970): 125–131.

Cardús, David, ed. *A Hispanic Look at the Bicentennial.* Houston: Institute of Hispanic Culture of Houston, 1978.

Chan, Margaret

Chan, Margaret. "Margaret Chan: Now Is the Time for WHO to Achieve Results."
Lancet 369, no. 9565 (March 17, 2007): 899.

Chan, Margaret, "Pandemic Flu—Communicating the Risks." World Health Organization, January 2006.

Chan, Margaret. "A Turning Point in the History of Humanity's Oldest Diseases."
PLoS Neglected Tropical Diseases 1, no. 1(2007): e65.

Chan, Margaret. "WHO—Accountability of Dr Margaret Chan during Her First Term as WHO Director-General." [Online.] Geneva: WHO, June 2012. http://www.who.int/entity/dg/Report_card_cover_28_06.pdf. [Consulted February 10, 2014.]

Greatbatch, Wilson

Greatbatch, Wilson. *The Making of the Pacemaker.* Amherst, NY: Prometheus Books, 2000.

Jaisohn, Philip

Jaisohn, Philip. *My Days in Korea and Other Essays, ed.* by Sun-Pyo Hong. Seoul: Yonsei University Press, 1999.

Greenfield, Susan

Blakemore, Colin, and Susan Greenfield. *Mindwaves: Thoughts on Intelligence, Identity, and Consciousness.* New York: B. Blackwell, 1987.

Greenfield, Susan. *Brain Story: Unlocking Our Inner World of Emotions, Memories, Ideas, and Desires.* New York: Dorling Kindersley, 2001.

Greenfield, Susan. "Down with the Masters in Lab Coats." *New Statesman,* August 13, 2010.

Greenfield, Susan. *The Human Brain: A Guided Tour.* New York: Basic Books, 1997.

Greenfield, Susan. *The Human Mind Explained: An Owner's Guide to the Mysteries of the Mind.* New York: Henry Holt, 1996.

Greenfield, Susan. ID: *The Quest for Identity in the 21ˢᵗ Century.* London: Sceptre, 2008.

Greenfield, Susan. *Journey to the Centers of the Mind: Toward a Science of Consciousness.* New York: W. H. Freeman, 1995.

Greenfield, Susan. *Private Life of the Brain.* London: Allen Lane/Penguin, 2000.

Greenfield, Susan. *Tomorrow's People: How 21ˢᵗ-Century Technology Is Changing the Way We Think and Feel.* London: Allen Lane, 2003.

Greenfield, Susan. *2121: A Tale from the Next Century.* London: Head of Zeus, 2013.

Greenfield, Susan. "What Makes Us Human: Sin, Status and Symbols." *New Statesman,* July 4, 2013.

Heymann, David L.

Heymann, David L. "How SARS Was Contained." *New York Times,* March 14, 2013.

Heymann, David L., ed. *Control of Communicable Diseases Manual,* 19th ed. Washington, DC: American Public Health Association, 2008.

Heymann, David L., Thomson Prentice, Lina Tucker Reinders, et al. *The World Health Report 2007: A Safer Future; Global Public Health Security in the 21st Century.* Geneva: World Health Organization, 2007.

Jalal, Massouda

Ferriera, Anne, and Massouda Jalal. "Chantilly to White-Wash the Taliban?" Discussion Point [online], January 14, 2013.

Jalal, Massouda. "Afghanistan: An All-Time Struggle for Women." Open Democracy Web site, October 14, 2013. http://www.opendemocracy.net/author/massouda-jalal. [Consulted February 10, 2014.]

Jalal, Massouda. "Afghanistan: Fundamentalism, Education, and the Minds of the People." Open Democracy Web site, July 14, 2013. http://www.opendemocracy.net/author/massouda-jalal. [Consulted February 10, 2014.]

Jalal, Massouda. "CSW [Commission on the Status of Women]: Voices from Afghanistan." Open Democracy Web site, March 7, 2013. http://www.opendemocracy.net/author/massouda-jalal. [Consulted February 10, 2014.]

Jalal, Massouda. "Karzai: A Legacy of Failure on Afghan Women's Rights?" Open Democracy Web site, August 19, 2013. http://www.opendemocracy.net/author/massouda-jalal. [Consulted February 10, 2014.]

Jalal, Massouda. "There Are No Moderate Taliban." *Wall Street Journal,* December 2, 2011.

Jalal, Massouda, Malalai Joya, Fawzia Koofi, and Azita Rafat. "Voices of Parliamentarians: Four Women MPs Share Their Thoughts." In Heath, Jennifer, and Ashraf Zahed, eds. *Land of the Unconquerable: The Lives of Contemporary Afghan Women.* Berkeley: University of California Press, 2011.

Kaleeba, Noerine

Kaleeba, Noerine. "Address by Noerine Kaleeba, UNAIDS Programme Development Advisor, Division for Africa, to the World Health Assembly, May 2001." Geneva: UN AIDS, 2001. [UN AIDS series.]

Kaleeba, Noerine. *TASO Uganda: The Inside Story: Participatory Evaluation of HIV.* Kampala: TASO/Geneva: WHO, 1995.

Kaleeba, Noerine. *We Miss You All: AIDS in the Family,* 2d ed. Harare: SAFAIDS, 2002.

Kaleeba, Noerine, et al. *Open Secret: People Facing Up to HIV and AIDS in Uganda.* London: ActionAid, 2000.

Sharpe, Ursula, and Noerine Kaleeba. *Witness to Faith: AIDS and Development in Africa.* London: CAFOD, 1993. [Pope Paul VI Memorial Lecture, 7 (1993).]

Llinás, Rodolfo

Llinás, Rodolfo. *I of the Vortex: From Neurons to Self.* Cambridge, MA: MIT Press, 2001.

Llinás, Rodolfo. *The Squid Giant Synapse: A Model for Chemical Transmission.* New York: Oxford University Press, 1999.

Llinás, Rodolfo, ed. *The Biology of the Brain: From Neurons to Networks; Readings from* Scientific American *Magazine.* New York: W. H. Freeman, 1989.

Llinás, Rodolfo, ed. *Neurobiology of Cerebellar Evolution and Development: Proceedings of the First International Symposium of the Institute for Biomedical Research.* Chicago: American Medical Society, 1969.

Llinás, Rodolfo, ed. *The Workings of the Brain: Development, Memory, and Perception; Readings from* Scientific American *Magazine.* New York: W. H. Freeman, 1990.

Llinás, Rodolfo, and Constantino Sotelo, eds. *The Cerebellum Revisited.* New York: Springer-Verlag, 1992.

Llinás, Rodolfo, and Patricia S. Churchland, eds. *The Mind-Brain Continuum: Sensory Processes.* Cambridge, MA: MIT Press, 1996.

Steriade, Mircea, Edward Jones, and Rodolfo Llinás. *Thalamic Oscillations and Signaling.* New York: Wiley, 1990.

Von Euler, Curt, Ingvar Lundberg, and Rodolfo Llinás. *Basic Mechanisms in Cognition and Language.* New York: Elsevier, 1998

Olopade, Olufunmilayo

Fackenthal, James D., and Olufunmilayo I. Olopade. "Breast Cancer Risk Associated with BRCA1 and BRCA2 in Diverse Populations." *Nature Reviews Cancer* 7 (December 2007) 937–948.

Gulden, Cassandra, Tovah Moss, Olufunmilayo I. Olopade, and Sonia Kupfer. "Racial Differences in a High-Risk Colorectal Cancer Referral Population: A Single-Center Experience." *Hereditary Cancer in Clinical Practice* 9, Supplement 1 (March 10, 2011): 15.

Olopade, Olufunmilayo I. "Approach to Cancer Management in a Tertiary Centre: The Example of Breast Cancer." *Archives of Ibadan Medicine* 1, no. 2 (2000): Oncology; 29–33,

Olopade, Olufunmilayo I. "Genetics in Clinical Cancer Care—The Future Is Now." *New England Journal of Medicine* 335, no. 19 (November 7, 1996): 1455f.

Olopade, Olufunmilayo I. "Genetics of Breast Cancer in Blacks." Ft. Belvoir Defense Technical Information Center, September 2002.

Polite, Blase N. and Olufunmilayo I. Olopade. "Breast Cancer and Race: A Rising Tide Does Not Lift All Boats Equally." *Perspectives in Biology and Medicine* 48, no. 1 Supplement (Winter 2005): 166–175.

Williams, Christopher Kwesi O., Olufunmilayo I. Olopade, and Carla I. Falkson, eds. *Breast Cancer in Women of African Descent* (Dordrecht: Springer, 2006).

Omichinski, Linda

Omichinski, Linda. *Nondiet Weight Management: A Lifestyle Approach to Health & Fitness.* Ashland, OR: Nutrition Dimension, 2004.

Omichinski, Linda. *Staying Off the Diet Rollercoaster.* Washington, DC: AdviceZone, 2000.

Omichinski, Linda. *You Count, Calories Don't.* Winnipeg: Tamos Books, 1992.

Omichinski, Linda, and Heather Wiebe Hildebrand, "No Counting Allowed." *Shape* 16, no. 5 (January 1997): 80.

Omichinski, Linda, and Heather Wiebe Hildebrand. *Tailoring Your Tastes.* Winnipeg, Tamos Books, 1997.

Ivo Pitanguy

Pitanguy, Ivo. *Aesthetic Plastic Surgery of Head and Body.* New York: Springer-Verlag, 1981.

Pitanguy, Ivo. "Evaluation of Body Contouring Surgery Today: A 30-Year Perspective."

Plastic and Reconstructive Surgery 105, no. 4 (April 2000): 1499–1514.

Pitanguy, Ivo. "Facial Cosmetic Surgery: A 30-Year Perspective." *Plastic and Reconstructive Surgery* 105, no. 4 (April 2000): 1517–1526.

Pitanguy, Ivo. "Repair of the Bilateral Cleft Lip: A Personal Approach." *Head & Neck Surgery* 1, no. 3 (January/February 1979): 223–234.

Pitanguy, Ivo. "Surgical Treatment of Breast Hypertrophy." *British Journal of Plastic Surgery* 20 (1967): 78–85.

Pitanguy, Ivo, et al. "Relative Implant Volume and Sensibility Alterations after Breast Augmentation." *Aesthetic Plastic Surgery* 31 no. 3 (2007): 238–243.

Pitanguy, Ivo, et al. "Repeated Expansion in Burn Sequela." *Burns* 28, no. 5 (2002): 494–499.

Pitanguy, Ivo, Natale Ferreira Gontijo de Amorim, and Henrique N. Radwanski, "Contour Surgery in the Patient with Great Weight Loss." *Aesthetic Plastic Surgery* 24, no. 6 (2000): 406.

Pitanguy, Ivo, Francisco Salgado, Henrique N. Radwanski, and Sheila C Bushkin. "The Surgical Importance of the Dermocartilaginous Ligament of the Nose." *Plastic and Reconstructive Surgery* 95, no. 5 (1995): 790.

Röntgen, Wilhelm

Baigrie, Brian S. "Shadow Pictures." *Scientific Revolutions: Primary Texts in the History of Science.* Upper Saddle River: Pearson, 2004. [Contains an English translation of Röntgen's *Eine neue Art von Strahlen.*]

Glasser, Otto. Dr. W. C. Röntgen, 2d ed. Springfield, IL: Thomas [1958]. [Includes Glasser's translation of Röntgen's *Eine neue Art von Strahlen.*]

Nitski, W. Robert. *The Life of Wilhelm Conrad Röntgen, Discoverer of the X-Ray.* Tucson: U of Arizona P, 1971. [Includes English translations of Röntgen's three most famous papers.]

Röntgen, Wilhelm. *Röntgen Rays; Memoirs.* Ed. and tr. by George Frederick Barker. New York: Harper & Brothers, 1899.

Röntgen, Wilhelm. *X-Rays and the Electric Conductivity of Gases*; Comprising Papers by W. C. Röntgen (1895, 1896). Edinburgh: Published for the Alembic Club by E. & S. Livingstone, 1958.

Schiller, Daniela

LeDoux, Joseph, and Daniela Schiller. "The Human Amygdala: Insights from Other Animals." In *The Human Amygdala,* ed. by Paul J. Whalen and Elizabeth A. Phelps. New York: Guilford Press, 2009.

Phelps, Elizabeth A., and Daniella Schiller. "Reconsolidation in Humans." In *Memory Reconsolidation,* ed. by Cristina M. Alberini (New York: Academic Press, 2013).

Schiller, Daniella. "The Abnormal Neural Circuitry Underlying Persistent Latent Inhibition as a Model of Negative Symptoms in Schizophrenia." Ph.D. diss., University of Tel Aviv, 2004. [2004].

Schiller, Daniela. "Affective Neuroscience: Tracing the Trace of Fear." *Current Biology* 21, no.18 (September 27, 2011): R695–R696.

Schiller, Daniela, and Joshua Johansen. "Prelimbic Prefrontal Neurons Drive Fear Expression: A Clue for Extinction-Reconsolidation Interactions*." Journal of Neuroscience* 29, no. 43 (2009): 13432.

Schiller, Daniela, Ifat Levy, Yael Niv, Joseph E Ledoux, and Elizabeth A. Phelps. "From Fear to Safety and Back: Reversal of Fear in the Human Brain." *Journal of Neuroscience* 28, no. 45 (2008): 11517.

Schiller, Daniela, Marie-H Monfils, Candace M. Raio, David C Johnson, Joseph E. LeDoux, and Elizabeth A. Phelps. "Preventing the Return of Fear in Humans Using Reconsolidation Update Mechanisms." *Nature* 17, no. 7277 (January 7, 2010).

Sears, William
Sears, Martha

Sears, William. *Becoming a Father: How to Nurture and Enjoy Your Family.* Franklin Park, IL: La Leche League International, 1986.

Sears, William, *The N.D.D. Book: How Nutrition Deficit Disorder Affects Your Child's Learning, Behavior, and Health, and What You Can Do about It—Without Drugs.* New York: Little, Brown, 2009.

Sears, William. *Nighttime Parenting: How to Get Your Baby and Child to Sleep.* Blackburn, Victoria: Collins Dove, 1985.

Sears, William, and Martha Sears. *The Attachment Parenting Book.* Boston: Little, Brown, 2001.

Sears, William, and Martha Sears. *The Birth Book: Everything You Need to Know to Have a Safe and Satisfying Birth.* Boston: Little, Brown, 1994.

Sears, William, and Martha Sears. *The Breastfeeding Book: Everything You Need to Know about Nursing Your Child from Birth through Weaning.* Boston: Little, Brown, 2000.

Sears, William, and Martha Sears. *The Discipline Book: Everything You Need to Know to Have a Better-Behaved Child—From Birth to Age Ten.* Boston: Little, Brown, 1995.

Sears, William, and Martha Sears. *The Family Nutrition Book: Everything You Need to Know about Feeding Your Children—From Birth through Adolescence.* Boston: Little, Brown 1999.

Sears, William, and Martha Sears. *The Fussy Baby Book: Parenting Your High-Need Child from Birth to Five.* London: Thorsons, 2005.

Sears, William, and Martha Sears. *The Good Behaviour Book: How to Have a Better-Behaved Child from Birth to Age Ten.* London: Thorsons, 2005.

Sears, William, and Martha Sears. *Parenting the Fussy Baby and High-Need Child—From Birth through Age Five.* Boston: Little, Brown, 1996.

Sears, William, and Martha Sears. *The Pregnancy Book: A Month-by-Month Guide.* Boston: Little, Brown, 1997.

Sears, William, and Martha Sears. *Prime-Time Health: A Scientifically Proven Plan for Feeling Young and Living Longer.* New York: Little, Brown, 2010.

Sears, William, and Martha Sears. *25 Things Every New Mother Should Know.* Boston: Harvard Commons Press, 1995.

Sears, William, Martha Sears, Robert Sears, and James M. Sears. *The Baby Book: Everything You Need to Know about Your Baby—From Birth to Age Two,* 3d ed. New York: Little, Brown, 1993.

Sears, William, Martha Sears, Robert Sears, James Sears, and Peter Sears. *The Portable Pediatrician: Everything You Need to Know about Your Child's Health.* New York: Little, Brown, 2011.

Siemionow, Maria

Siemionow, Maria Z. "Composite Tissue Allograft Transplantation and Nonhuman Primates." *Transplantation* 83, no. 2 (2007): 242.

Siemionow, Maria Z. *Tissue Surgery.* London: Springer, 2005.

Siemionow, Maria Z. *Transplanting a Face: Notes on a Life in Medicine.* Cleveland: Cleveland Clinic Press, 2007. [Reworked edition with an epilogue: *Face to Face: My Quest to Perform the First Full Face Transplant.* New York: Kaplan, 2009.]

Siemionow, Maria Z., ed. *The Know-How of Face Transplantation.* London: Springer, 2011.

Siemionow, Maria Z., and Aleksandra Klimczak. "Advances in the Development of Experimental Composite Tissue Transplantation Models." *Transplant International* 23, no. 1 (January 2010): 2–13.

Siemionow, Maria Z., and Erhan Sonmez. "Face as an Organ." *Annals of Plastic Surgery* 61, no. 3 (2008): 345.

Siemionow, Maria Z., and Marita Eisenmann-Klein, eds. *Plastic and Reconstructive Surgery.* London: Springer, 2010.

Siemionow, Maria, et al. "Near-Total Human Face Transplantation for a Severely Disfigured Patient in the USA." *Lancet* 374, no. 9685 (July 18, 2009): 203–209.

Thomas, William H.

Thomas, Bill [William H.]. "Culture Change beyond the Nursing Home." In Weiner, Audrey, and Judah L. Ronch, eds., *Models and Pathways for Person-Centered Elder Care* (Baltimore: Health Professions Press, 2014).

Thomas, William H. *The Eden Alternative: Nature, Hope, and Nursing Homes.* Sherburne, NY: The Eden Alternative, 1994.

Thomas, William H. "Evolution of Eden." In Weiner, Audrey, and Judah L. Ronch, eds. *Culture Change in Long-Term Care.* New York: Haworth Social Work Practice Press, 2003.

Thomas, William H. *In the Arms of Elders: A Parable of Wise Leadership and Community Building.* Acton, MA: Vanderwyk and Burnham, 2006.

Thomas, William H. *Learning from Hannah: Secrets for a Life Worth Living.* Acton, MA: Vanderwyk and Burnham, 1999.

Thomas, William H. *Life Worth Living: How Someone You Love Can Still Enjoy Life in a Nursing Home: The Eden Alternative in Action.* Acton, MA: Vanderwyk and Burnham, 1996.

Thomas, William H. *Second Wind: Navigating the Passage to a Slower, Deeper and More Connected Life.* New York: Simon & Schuster, 2014.

Thomas, William H. *Tribes of Eden.* Ithaca, NY: Sana Publications, 2012.

Thomas, William H. *What Are Old People For? How Elders Will Save the World.* Acton, MA: Vanderwyk and Burnham, 2004.

Trehan, Naresh

Meharwal, Zile Singh, Anil Mishra, and Naresh Trehan. "Safety and Efficacy of One Stage Off-Pump Coronary Artery Operation and Carotid Endarterectomy*."* *Annals of Thoracic Surgery* 73, no. 3 (2002): 793–797.

Trehan, Naresh. "Techniques and Results in Minimally Invasive Cardiac Surgery and Robotic Surgery in India." *Indian Journal of Thoracic and Cardiovascular Surgery* 20, no. S1 (January 2004): 71–78.

Trehan, Naresh, and Rajneesh Malhotra. "Innovations in Cardiac Surgery." *Apollo Medicine* 4, no. 3 (September 2007): 164–169.

Vasella, Daniel

"Daniel Vasella,Chairman and Chief Executive of Novartis AG." In *Boss Talk: Top CEOs Share the Ideas That Drive the World's Most Successful Companies,* ed. by the Editors of the *Wall Street Journal.* New York: Random House, 2002.

Vasella, Daniel. "Novartis' Role in 21st Century Drug Development." *Nature Biotechnology* 15, no. 6 (June 1997): 485–485.

Vasella, Daniel, and Kathy Bloomgarden. "For Patient Relations, Novartis' Handling of Gleevec Sets the Standard; CEO Daniel Vasella Tells the Inside Story." *Pharmaceutical Executive* 23, no. 4 (2003): 14.

Daniel Vasella, Daniel, et al.," Soft Governance." Geneva: Fondation pour Genève, 2007. [Booklet.]

Vasella, Daniel, with Robert Slater, *Magic Cancer Bullet: How a Tiny Orange Pill Is Rewriting Medical History.* New York: HarperBusiness, 2003.

Zerhouni, Elias

Naidich David P., Elias A Zerhouni, and Stanley S. Siegelman. *Computed Tomography and Magnetic Resonance of the Thorax.* New York: Raven Press, 1991.

Zerhouni, Elias. *Cardiovascular System.* Frederick, MD: Aspen, 1990.

Zerhouni, Elias. *CT and MRI of the Thorax.* New York: Churchill Livingstone, 1990.

Zerhouni, Elias. " Elias Zerhouni." *Nature Biotechnology* 29, no. 3 (March 2011): 188.

Zerhouni, Elias. "Elias Zerhouni, Head of the National Institutes of Health, Talks about the Road That Took Him from Being a Medical Graduate in his Native Algeria to the Leadership of One of the US's Most Influential Agencies." *New Scientist,* no. 2429 (January 10, 2004): 46–48.

Zerhouni, Elias. "NIH Director Calls for Easing Administration's Stem-Cell Restrictions." *Chronicle of Higher Education* 53, no. 30 (March 30, 2007): A26.

Profession Index

Activist

Jaisohn, Philip

Administrator

Zerhouni, Elias

AIDS Activist

Kaleeba, Noerine

Astronaut

Kuipers, André

Athlete

Rogge, Jacques

Biomedical Engineer

Greatbatch, Wilson

Biotech Executive

Desmond-Hellmann, Susan

Breastfeeding Consultant

Sears, Martha

Broadcaster

Greenfield, Susan

Burn Care Specialist

Wood, Fiona

Businessman

Greatbatch, Wilson

Cardiologist

Agatston, Arthur

Cardiothoratic Surgeon

Trehan, Naresh

Cognitive Neuroscientist

Schiller, Daniela

Community Health Physician

Bang, Abhay

Bang, Rani Chari

Consultant

Vasella, Daniel

Dietician

Omichinski, Linda

Educator

Bernal, Martha

Heymann, David L.

Kaleeba, Noerine

Llinás, Rodolfo

Schiller, Daniela

Sears, William

Siemionow, Maria

Trehan, Naresh

Zerhouni, Elias

Epidemiologist

Heymann, David L.

Evolutionary Biologist

Ayala, Francisco